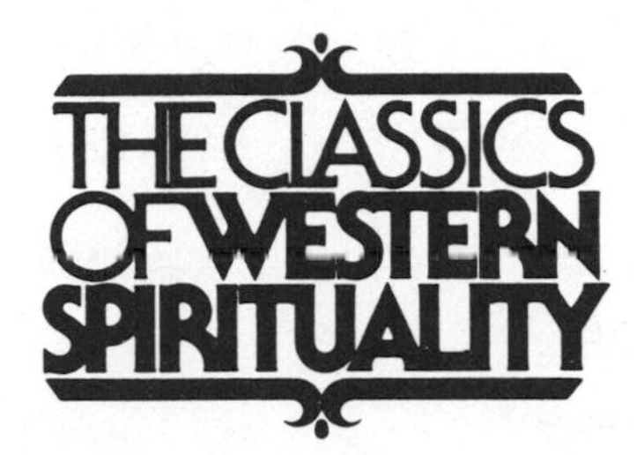
THE CLASSICS
OF WESTERN
SPIRITUALITY

Other volumes in this series

Julian of Norwich • SHOWINGS

Jacob Boehme • THE WAY TO CHRIST

Nahman of Bratslav • THE TALES

Gregory of Nyssa • THE LIFE OF MOSES

Bonaventure • THE SOUL'S JOURNEY INTO GOD, THE TREE OF LIFE, and THE LIFE OF ST. FRANCIS

William Law • A SERIOUS CALL TO A DEVOUT AND HOLY LIFE, and THE SPIRIT OF LOVE

Abraham Isaac Kook • THE LIGHTS OF PENITENCE, LIGHTS OF HOLINESS, THE MORAL PRINCIPLES, ESSAYS, and POEMS

Ibn 'Ata' Illah • THE BOOK OF WISDOM *and* Kwaja Abdullah Ansari • INTIMATE CONVERSATIONS

Johann Arndt • TRUE CHRISTIANITY

Richard of St. Victor • THE TWELVE PATRIARCHS, THE MYSTICAL ARK, BOOK THREE OF THE TRINITY

Origen • AN EXHORTATION TO MARTYRDOM, PRAYER AND SELECTED WORKS

Catherine of Genoa • PURGATION AND PURGATORY, THE SPIRITUAL DIALOGUE

Native North American Spirituality of the Eastern Woodlands • SACRED MYTHS, DREAMS, VISIONS, SPEECHES, HEALING FORMULAS, RITUALS AND CEREMONIALS

Teresa of Avila • THE INTERIOR CASTLE

Apocalyptic Spirituality • TREATISES AND LETTERS OF LACTANTIUS, ADSO OF MONTIER-EN-DER, JOACHIM OF FIORE, THE FRANCISCAN SPIRITUALS, SAVONAROLA

Athanasius • THE LIFE OF ANTONY, A LETTER TO MARCELLINUS

Catherine of Siena • THE DIALOGUE

Sharafuddin Maneri • THE HUNDRED LETTERS

Martin Luther • THEOLOGIA GERMANICA

Native Mesoamerican Spirituality • ANCIENT MYTHS, DISCOURSES, STORIES, DOCTRINES, HYMNS, POEMS FROM THE AZTEC, YUCATEC, QUICHE-MAYA AND OTHER SACRED TRADITIONS

Symeon the New Theologian • THE DISCOURSES

TRANSLATION AND INTRODUCTION
BY
MOTHER COLUMBA HART, O.S.B.

PREFACE
BY
PAUL MOMMAERS

PAULIST PRESS
NEW YORK • RAMSEY • TORONTO

Cover art:
The artist, MOTHER PLACID DEMPSEY, O.S.B., is a nun of the Abbey of Regina Laudis, Bethlehem, Connecticut. Coming from a family of many accomplished artists, she began her artistic training at an early age, receiving lessons from her sister Eleanor, a professional in the field. She graduated from Marymount College, Tarrytown, New York, with honors in art. After entering the monastery she was encouraged to continue studying privately with many distinguished artists, including Louisa Jenkins and Tomie de Paola. A sculptor, painter and graphic designer, she has exhibited her works in Europe as well as in the United States. Regarding the cover and illustrations for this volume she says: "The force and vitality of Hadewijch and her writings became tangible to me through the illuminated manuscripts of her time as these burst forth with the spiritual energy of the early Gothic period. The challenge for me was to express in a contemporary way this interior world of dynamic perception swirling in the relentless movement of elongated lines twisting, almost dancing off the page, yet everywhere held by the large provocative eyes of Christ persons, centering each lively scene with the penetrating gaze of their profound stillness."

Design: Barbini, Pesce & Noble, Inc.

Library of Congress
Catalog Card Number: 80-84500

ISBN: 0-8091-0311-7 (cloth)
0-8091-2297-9 (paper)

Published by Paulist Press
545 Island Road, Ramsey, N.J. 07446

Printed and bound in the
United States of America

CONTENTS

The Editor of this Volume

MOTHER COLUMBA HART graduated from Smith College in 1924 *summa cum laude,* having studied under Eleanor S. Duckett and Howard R. Patch. She remained for the MA degree in English with emphasis on Anglo-Saxon and continued graduate work at Radcliffe and Harvard in romance philology, Middle English, and Latin paleography under John L. Lowes, John S. Tatlock, and Charles H. Haskins. Through her uncle, Professor Albert Bushnell Hart, she met Etienne Gilson, whose public lectures she attended. Her earliest article, *The Pearl,* appeared in *Modern Language Notes* in 1927. After European travel she studied French intensively while living in Paris for two years, and later translated *Ouvrons la Bible* by Roger Poelman (*How to Read the Bible,* New York: Kenedy, 1953, and London: Longmans, 1955). Her first original book, *Mary of the Magnificat,* had come out in 1942 (Sheed and Ward). The work of translating from the Latin *The Exercises of Saint Gertrude* (Newman, 1956) brought to her attention the dearth of information about Gertrude's life and suggested research on thirteenth-century women, especially the Flemish mystics. Thus she discovered Hadewijch, some of whose letters she presented in *The American Benedictine Review* (1962). Her translation from the Latin of William of Saint Thierry's *Exposition on the Song of Songs* was begun at this time and appeared in Cistercian Fathers Series (1970). In 1972 she contributed to *The American Benedictine Review* another article on medieval women, "Consecratio Virginum: Thirteenth-Century Witnesses." Her study on the Holy Spirit, *Spirit of Grace,* published in 1946 (St. Anthony Guild Press), and in Italian translation in 1947 (Milan: Società Editrice "Vita e Pensiero") has now been republished (Daughters of St. Paul, 1979). At present she is translating a volume of Saint Hildegard for The Classics of Western Spirituality. She has been a nun of Regina Laudis Abbey in Bethlehem, Connecticut, since 1949.

Author of the Preface

PAUL MOMMAERS (born in 1935 in Antwerp) first studied Greek and Latin philology, philosophy and theology in Belgium, France and Scotland. He received his direct schooling in the study of mystical texts at the Sorbonne, where he worked under the direction of Jean Orcibal, and he earned his degree in the Science of Religion (1971) with a thesis on the seventeenth-century mystic Benet of Canfield. In this semantic study of the *Rule of Perfection* (published in the *Revue d'Histoire de la Spiritualité* in 1971–72–73) he pointed out how the first great figure of the French school in fact depended on the Flemish mystical tradition. In 1973 he wrote *Phenomenology of the Union of Love as Presented in the Works of John Ruusbroec* (American edition: *The Land Within*, Chicago 1975). A more general work on the question *What Is Mysticism?* was brought out in 1977, and in 1979 he published *The Visions of Hadewijch*, comprising the edition of the original text, a translation into modern Dutch and a commentary on each of the Visions. He is now a professor at Antwerp University, where he also conducts a research project on Hadewijch and Ruusbroec.

Acknowledgements

My thanks are due first of all to Richard J. Payne, editor in chief of The Classics of Western Spirituality, for his professional guidance and ready help in all the problems of the work on this volume, and especially for his establishment, with the transatlantic assistance of Dr. Louis Dupré, of a collaboration with the scholars of the Ruusbroecgenootschap in Antwerp. I am deeply grateful to Dr. Joseph Andriessen, S.J. for help with a faulty text, and to Dr. Joseph Alaerts, S.J., Dr. Guido De Baere, S.J., and Dr. Paul Mommaers, S.J., for their critiques on the volume. Dr. Mommaers, author of the article on Hadewijch that will appear in the *Verfasserlexikon* edited by Dr. Kurt Ruh, suggested that the latter might allow me to quote from it, and I thank Dr. Ruh for granting this permission. Also I particularly appreciate the help afforded by Dr. Herman Vekeman's critique of the translation of the poems.

At home I am indebted to Dr. Patricia Kuppens and Sr. Helen Rolfson, O.S.F., for their critiques of the Introduction, and to Sr. Helen and Dr. Dupré for valuable suggestions about the translations. I have also to thank Fr. Timothy Fry, O.S.B., editor of *The American Benedictine Review,* for granting permission to use the translation of nine of Hadewijch's *Letters* from my article "Hadewijch of Brabant," published in that journal in 1962.

Since the Hadewijch texts and practically all scholarly books and articles on Hadewijch, being published in Europe, are difficult if not impossible to obtain here, I am much obliged to all who have helped me to obtain materials for the necessary survey of the field of Hadewijch studies. I thank Dom Jean-Baptiste Porion, O.Cart., for the gift of his out-of-print book *Hadewijch d'Anvers: Ecrits mystiques des Béguines.* I am grateful for special kindnesses of the Sterling Memorial Library and the Divinity School Library of Yale University, and the Van Pelt Library of the University of Pennsylvania. For securing articles from foreign periodicals, I thank Mr. Payne, the Ruusbroecgenootschap, Region One Cooperating Library Service of Waterbury, Mrs. Elizabeth M. Chitty, and Miss Elviara Di Bianco.

I am very grateful indeed to Kathryn Cousins for answering questions and for producing the index. Last but far from least I am under obligation to the Lady Abbess and the entire community of Regina Laudis Abbey for granting me the long period of time required for the completion of this volume.

FOREWORD

Once on the Sunday after Pentecost, probably some year in the second decade of the thirteenth century, it happened that Hadewijch felt unable to go to church for Mass. The priest unobtrusively brought her Communion as she lay in bed in her own room. After receiving the Sacrament she was drawn into deep Eucharistic union with Christ and then suddenly found herself as it were in a vast meadow, where an Angel presented himself to be her guide and to explain the symbolism of the trees growing there.

In the center of the meadow they came to a tree that stood with its roots upward and its summit downward. This tree had many branches; those nearest the ground were faith and hope, with which souls begin. The Angel said to her: "You climb this tree from the beginning to the end, all the way to the profound roots of the incomprehensible God!" Hadewijch understood that it was the tree of the knowledge of God—knowledge that begins with faith and ends with love.

Viewed according to the thought patterns of Hadewijch's day, the "climbing" of this tree would have meant gaining a knowledge of the truths that pertain to God, considered according to both the literal sense and the spiritual senses.

The literal sense would be the knowledge of God that, by climbing this tree, one finds in the scriptural manifestation of his attributes and works. The allegorical sense would see in the upside-down tree a symbol of God's infinite Being, which we can know only by a spiritual ascent from faith and hope, which are nearest us, to charity, which is nearest God. The tropological sense would regard climbing the tree as our persevering to perfection because of our knowledge of God's infinite perfection. The anagogical sense would look toward the face-to-face vision of God in heaven, where we shall see him as he is—a vision to be reached only after climbing the tree.

Biographical information about Hadewijch is almost entirely lacking, but we do know that she belonged to the women's movement of her day and country, that of the Beguines, and we know she headed a small contemplative group. She recognized her call to communicate to this circle the understanding of spiritual things—take for example the upside-down tree—granted to her in her mystical life. Her experience and her message, however, remained hidden; she attained to no celebrity status among her contemporaries. The lives of Saint Hildegard (1098–1179) and Saint Lutgard (1183–1246) are known in detail, but no "life" of Hadewijch ever appeared, and her writings, after passing through the hands of John of Ruusbroec (1293–1381) and his disciples, were progressively lost to sight.

The hidden dimension of Hadewijch's life is now open, so that we may share it according to the particular needs of our own day. The present volume contains her complete works: *Letters, Poems in Stanzas, Visions,* and *Poems in Couplets.* For the first few pages we may find her mode of expression difficult. But as we read on we shall soon begin to respond to the thrust of her prose, to her poetic paradox, and to her visionary allegory and anagogy. Thus we shall gradually learn the meaning she sees for our own personal life in the Humanity and Divinity of Christ, in the Trinity and the Unity of God, and in the wonderful interplay—taking place in our individual lives—of Divine Love, our own deepest sufferings, and our power to love and help those around us.

PREFACE

Hadewijch, a Flemish Beguine of the thirteenth century, is undoubtedly the most important exponent of love mysticism and one of the loftiest figures in the Western mystical tradition.

Love mysticism sprang up during the second half of the twelfth century, in the area roughly corresponding to present-day Belgium. It is a preeminently feminine phenomenon, and its essential hallmark, as shown by the term "love" (minne), is that union with God is lived here on earth as a love relationship: God lets himself be experienced as Love (Minne) by the person who goes out to meet him with love (minne). The most striking hallmark of this love mysticism, however—which is also well depicted by the medieval writers of lives (*vitae*) of holy persons and by enlightened historians of religion—is its strongly emotional and ecstatic character. The touch of Love also throws the minds and senses of these persons into commotion, so violent indeed that all sorts of psychosomatic phenomena arise from it. And it seems that the experience of oneness and Love must go hand in hand with a psychological withdrawal from self that usually finds its reaction in visions.

Now obviously Hadewijch fits perfectly into this frame. The keyword of all her literary work is love, and besides poetry (*Poems in Stanzas, Poems in Couplets*) and *Letters*, she has also left her collection of *Visions*. The rushing emotion of love, which grows to a real madness and can be perilous to life, she has summed up repeatedly, and in a particularly arresting manner. The beginning of Vision 7, for instance, reads thus:

> On a certain Pentecost Sunday I had a vision at dawn. Matins were being sung in the church, and I was present. My heart and my veins and all my limbs trembled and quivered

> with eager desire and, as often occurred with me, such madness and fear beset my mind that it seemed to me that if I did not content my Beloved, and my Beloved did not fulfil my desire, dying I must go mad, and going mad I must die. On that day my mind was beset so fearfully and so painfully by desirous love that all my separate limbs threatened to break, and all my separate veins were in travail.

(See also the beginning of Vision 1 and Vision 14.)

Now it is an instructive surprise for a person who reads any work of Hadewijch's that this more or less rambling presentation by her does not touch at all on the essence of what she is in fact imparting. Certainly Hadewijch is affirming that she has lived ecstatic moments and that she knew a being-one without difference. She also says herself that her violent longing was initially directed to the "fruitive being-one" with God, which means that she saw this being-one as a state that afforded man joy: an acquisition and a satisfying possession. She obviously departed from the normal conception with which a person spontaneously enters into a love relationship—with God or with another person: "I expect that I shall feel (and continue to feel) how happily I am united to you." But this ecstatic-fruitive aspect of her mystical experience is simply not the point of that which she imparts in both the *Letters* and the *Visions.* What she principally wants to make clear is that her attraction for the "fruitive being-one" is a sign of non-full-grownness, and that in mysticism what matters is so to grow up that one is enabled to live wholly other aspects of the being-one with God. Hadewijch also does not uphold mysticism as being a liberating ecstasy to demystify. Her question always is where the nonecstatic periods actually form part of the mystical experience; she tries again and again to show that a life stripped of "experiences" can be a truly mystical life. In a word, the genuine, "full-grown" mystical experience, as Hadewijch understands it, is free from the idealizing haze with which this form of knowledge is time and again envisioned. According to her, it is a loving knowledge that is at once much more human and much more refined than everything the label "ecstatic mysticism" leads us to suppose.

Just as surprising as what Hadewijch says about the mystical experience is what she writes about the Reality that makes itself known in that experience. Her descriptions of experiencing the in-being in God belong to the most convincing and daring that mystical literature has to offer. God is such that he allows himself to be possessed in an incredibly intimate manner. But you can seldom find a mystical author who—at the same time—throws such light on God's transcendency as Hadewijch does. This Beloved who gives himself without reserve continues to exceed man: He is the wholly Other. This Beloved who lifts the mystic wholly into himself never takes away her human being; on the contrary, he establishes her more and more deeply in human existence. From out of the divine Other, Hadewijch must be herself—"You must live as man," we read repeatedly in *Visions.* Expressed in explicitly Christian terms: "being-one" with God, according to Hadewijch, always includes the imitation of the Man Jesus.

This is the moment to pause over a few anthropological implications of Hadewijch's mystical experience. It is above all, is it not, her experience of God as unfathomable that determines her conception of what man is. And the most important point here is, beyond any doubt, that this unique creature, in spite of all his definiteness and limitations, is no determined being. He who can become one with a never-to-be-comprehended Beloved is, in his essence, an openness and an unlimited dynamic. In Letter 12 Hadewijch says this as follows:

> But they who stand ready to content Love are also eternal and unfathomable. For their conversation is in heaven, and their souls follow everywhere their Beloved who is unfathomable. But then, although they are loved with an eternal love, they are never seized by the ground of Love, just as they can never seize what they love. (1. 40)

And in Letter 18 our mystic, to the question of what the soul is, answers this:

> If it maintains its worthy state, the soul is a bottomless abyss in which God suffices to himself; and his own self-sufficiency ever finds fruition in this soul to the full, as the soul, for its part, ever does in him. Soul is a way for the passage of God from his depths into his liberty; and God is a way for the passage of the soul into its liberty, that is, into his inmost depths, which cannot be touched except by the soul's abyss. And as long as God does not belong to the soul in his totality, he does not truly satisfy it. (1. 63)

There is then no further cause for wonder that according to Hadewijch a person can touch Love herself only with longing: "And nothing can touch her except desire," we read in Letter 20. Only a faculty that continually goes outside its own reach, so that by way of conquest it will immediately seize yet more, is suited to come in contact with the Reality that surpasses all measure and all comprehension. Especially in *Poems in Stanzas* this theme of the longing that never lets itself be appeased—that possesses in seeking and seeks in possessing—is developed in an arresting manner:

> What is this light burden of Love
> And this sweet-tasting yoke?
> It is the noble load of the spirit
> With which Love touches the loving soul
> And unites it to her with one will
> And with one being, without reversal. (12, st. 3)

In this mystical being-one as Hadewijch experiences it, God lets himself be known not only as inexhaustible and self-sufficient, but also as other, as the wholly Other. And this distinction is never pointed out. It makes a permanent part of the most absolute love relationship. Neither is there any mention of the fact that Love, who nevertheless "devours all works," would ever absorb a man, without remainder, in herself. Even less will the most exalted mystical state consist in a nirvanaish torpor. On the contrary: It is exactly *in* the being-one that Hadewijch learns a demand that relates to her as a human being. Love, who is willing to be possessed unbraked, is at the same time the Other, "who tells her what is still wanting to her." The same woman who can sink in abysmal fruition is immediately placed again in herself: the human being truly dies in God, but not in order, as human being, to come to its end. One who experiences the blessed "feeling that surpasses all things" is sent back into the world with impressionable senses and sharpened spiritual powers—"pure man like myself," says Jesus in *Visions.*

It is worth the trouble to pause over what Hadewijch has to say about the human understanding. Wherein consists the enlightenment of the understanding? Not in the fact that it is upholstered with new principles—such as the truths of the faith—and therefore could judge more justly and orthodoxly. This enlightenment is an insight into her relation with God, which falls to her lot only in the oneness experience, an insight that in a certain sense corresponds with what the still not enlightened understanding held out to her on the subject. In a certain sense, for what the understanding, working naturally, brought to the fore—God is too great for man—in a manner that now excludes in advance the possibility of an actual being-one with God is now taken up by Love herself. The intellectual warning has become an outcry that springs from the being-one. In the union with the Beloved, his incomparable being-Other must now be known. Reason therefore is going to play a part in the highest mystical experience; it throws light on the lasting transcendency of God. Through its intervention the mystic learns to love him in his independence and wholly being-Other.

> Love's soft stillness is unheard of,
> However loud the noise she makes,
> Except by him who has experienced it,
> And whom she has wholly allured to herself,
> And has so stirred with her deep touch
> That he feels himself wholly in Love.
> When she also fills him with the wondrous taste of Love,
> The great noise ceases for a time;
> Alas! Soon awakens Desire, who wakes
> With heavy storm the mind that has turned inward.
> (P. 25, st. 4)

Also in the poems the basic problem is not the absence in itself, but the alternation of presence and absence of the Beloved. That she who knows herself to be experientially united with Love must live in taking and giving, that is the riddle:

> Sometimes indulgent and sometimes harsh,
> Sometimes dark and sometimes bright:
> In liberating consolation, in coercive fear,
> In accepting and in giving,
> Must they who are
> Knight-errants in Love
> Always live here below. (P. 5, st. 7)

And this instability of her experience is not the result of any moral shortcoming. Love's incomprehensible—if you wish, immoral—way of acting is the cause of it. Why then these strange tricks?

> Alas, Love! your wrath or your favor
> We cannot distinguish—
> Your high will and our debt,
> Why you come, or why you fly?
> For you can give, in response to small service,
> Your sweet splendors in great clarity;
> But for small faults this seems withheld,
> And then you give blows and bitter death.
>
> Alas! on dark roads of misery
> Love indeed lets us wander,
> In many an assault, without safety,
> Where she seems to us cruel and hostile;
> And to some she gives, without suffering,
> Her great and multiform joy:
> For us these are truly strange manners,
> But for connoisseurs of Love's free power, they are joy.
> (P. 41, st. 3, 5)

Or further: The great question mark for her to whom Love lets herself be known in the oneness experience as incomparably "sweet" is that the same sweet Love also repels her again:

> What amazes me about sweet Love
> Is that her sweetness conquers all things,
> And yet she subjugates me from within
> And so little knows my heart's distress.
> She has brought me into such woe,
> I feel I am not match for it. . . .
>
> Sweet as Love's nature is,
> Where can she come by the strange hatred
> With which she continually pursues me
> And transpierces the depths of my heart with storm?
> I wander in darkness without clarity,

Without liberating consolation, and in strange fear.
(P. 35, st. 8)

Hadewijch discovers thus in her oneness experience with Love an unacceptable contradiction—no right-thinking man accepts it that a beloved behave in such an unpredictable manner, that there are in the being-one such dark, empty places. Now there is further the question whether she in spite of that has acquired an insight into the phenomenon of the coming and going of Love. And that indeed she has: More than the outpourings of a tortured mind, the poems offer exactly Hadewijch's successful attempt to clarify the contradiction of her experience *in* the being-one. However dark also the land wherein the adventure with Love causes her to lose her way, she wishes nevertheless, relying on her experience, to place a few beacons. She will let it be seen that in the "strange tricks" a meaning is truly hidden, and that there exists a form of experience that is capable of integrating the being absent of the Beloved. On this head we must especially observe two points.

The first is that Hadewijch in this lyrical work directs an uncompromising criticism at her—and our—conception of what experience properly so-called is. In our tasting of the other (so she gives us to understand) there always hides an insidious tasting of ourself: if I am touched by the other, my attention not merely goes out to him but is also deflected—and gradually more and more—to what concerns me, that being grateful at the touch, I begin to tremble. My gaze is likewise retrospect, so that I run the danger of staring blindly at the gifts and losing sight of the Giver. In short, in our experience, *affection* comes into power, and it hinders us from knowing the other as other.

But—and this is the second, more positive point—Hadewijch shows not only under what oppression our knowledge of the other can suffer; she has also something new to impart about the possibilities of our experience. On this head a decisive insight has fallen to her share—a truth that remains forever hidden from many persons. She, the complaining and critical poetess, knows. She belongs to the "brave knights" of whom mention is made in Poem 10, st. 3: "They know what Love teaches with love, And how Love honors the loyal lover with love." She is one of the *old.* They, conquered by Love, have learned to know an unsuspected peace.

> He who conquers Love is vanquished himself:
> So he is served;
> And when she cherishes anyone, she consumes in a new
> chase all he owns.
> So, being old, he learns through the power of Love to
> conquer peace,
> Where he discovers the price of Love in misery. (P. 27, st. 3)

More precisely, then, what knowledge has Hadewijch laid up in her adventurous association with Love? According to the poems, she has come to the finding that in the life of love there is possible a form of experience that is no longer determined by self-feeling. That does not mean at all that at any given moment the inexplicable alternation of giving and taking, coming and going, is removed without more ado. Even less is it true that, as if by magic, misery would no longer cause pain. What according to Hadewijch really does happen is that, thanks to this cruel game, there regularly comes in man a free ability to look at the Other. This looking, or tasting, or whatever you call this new contact, touches the other as other: Love is, apart from what I feel of her. I taste her without there even being a taste to have left over. I gaze now without feeling myself see. If and insofar as it falls to a man's lot to have this consciousness, which is no longer assessed by self-consciousness, the alternation of joy and pain becomes for him insufficient.

The taste of the Other that for such a long time remained limited to moments of consolation now also includes misery. On the level of the experience that was ruled by affection, man can live the alternation in no other way than as an interruption of the being-one. Now the facets of a steady living of oneness are coming and going:

> Consolation and ill-treatment both at once,
> This is the essence of the taste of Love.
> Wise Solomon, were he still living,
> Could not interpret such an enigma.
> We are not fully enlightened on the subject in any sermon.
> The song surpasses every melody! (P. 31, st. 4)

Let us now take a close look at the visions of Hadewijch. As people are probably inclined to interpret the poems as a long complaint of her who loves and is forsaken, there is a risk that the *Visions*, simply on account of the word vision, may be treated a bit compassionately as a collection of texts about ecstasies, uncontrolled religious longing, and incomprehensible phantasms. The *Visions* of Hadewijch should consequently be considered and not, unjustly of course, written off as the down-beat of a mystic who fled from ordinary human existence.

Now it is remarkable about Hadewijch's *Visions*—one need only read them in order to see it clearly—that their principal theme is precisely this: being-man must be taken up in the mystical experience. In every vision but especially, and probably not by chance, in the first and last of the series, this twofold question makes its bid: What does the concrete life of man mean for the mystic who is one with the wholly Other? What share do the periods of darkness and nonexperience have in the mystic's experience? Already in the first lines of Vision 1 Hadewijch trenchantly presents her basic problem:

> And that desire which I had inwardly was to be one with God in fruition. For this I was still too childish and too little grown-up; and I had not as yet sufficiently suffered for it or lived the number of years requisite for such exceptional worthiness.

The demand for full-grownness, which resounds here and in so many other places, does not mean that she must forego her longing for fruitive being-one—that she must prefer only to lead an ordinary Christian life without mystical oneness experience—but that her conception of the being-one and her manner of experience must be enlarged. Hadewijch must learn *in* her living of oneness, alongside fruition, to integrate positive elements that at first sight seem to come to an end in the being-one.

Let us now attempt to specify in what, according to Hadewijch, the full-grown mystical experience consists. In the beginning of the speech of Jesus stands this enigmatic little statement: "And all griefs will taste sweeter to you than all earthly pleasures" (V. 1, 1. 193). Here we must notice the word "taste." A first manner of interpreting it is this—to discover here a more or less perverse propensity for pain. Since normal joys and healthy pleasure are wanting to her, she must make a virtue of necessity. The difficulty with this fashionable interpretation is, however, that in Hadewijch's writing you never come across anything in the genre "I am fortunate if I suffer." On the contrary, apart from the already mentioned fact that Hadewijch in Vision 7, without any puritanical camouflage, describes how union with the God-Man can have sensual repercussions, she never ceases to offer resistance to pain and affliction, even if they come from the Beloved. A second interpretation, which is already more plausible, amounts to this: This paradoxical taste should refer to a "mystical" gift that enables a man to make abstraction from the concrete situation in which he moves. The mystic should raise himself interiorly above what touches the sensibility. It would thus be a matter here of the "higher" fruition, which in a "spiritual" manner compensates for the pain in body and in feeling. Hadewijch seems always to have conceived of the mystical taste in this manner—this you can at least infer from the reproach that she had repeatedly made to Christ: "You have said to me at times that it was easy for me to live as man because I possessed the seven gifts" (V. 1, 1. 325). Hadewijch had evidently thought that the life of Christ on earth was not really painful, because he, above all human affliction, could enjoy the seven gifts. She had imagined to herself a man who was never actually immersed in misery, since he at every moment could raise himself to the glorious and reassuring experience of the "spiritual."

But the mystic is gradually going to imagine the Man otherwise. It is undoubtedly her own spiritual experience and a long-matured insight into the spiritual taste that she imparts to us in a few *mises au point* that relate to Christ's earthly existence. No, she says, there is no mention that Jesus in his life here among us withdrew to the level of sublime spirituality. Not for a single instant did he escape from the desolation of the human condition. But how then could this Man, who lived *exile* perfectly, feel being-one with God?

Feel! To have the experience of the Other in emptiness, now that is exactly what Jesus, according to Hadewijch, was able to do. In loneliness itself he knew a taste that sharpened not only all earthly joy—both that of the senses and that of the spirit—but joy unlimited. He received from his Father the ultimate consolation: "That I was certain of my Father."

In the second part of vision 4 (1. 72) Christ makes clear to Hadewijch that she will attain her "full-growth," by means of four "works." This text is nothing but a succinct description of the manner in which full-grownness in the love relationship comes about in the mystic's consciousness. Hadewijch wishes to show that this person, through the attempt to be conformed to Jesus, changes also psychically; inwardly he outgrows his original measure; he becomes so broad—so like to God—that he is able to experience the Other as other. These works are thus no definite virtues or actions but interior states. They are the most important moments of the broadening of the mystic's consciousness. And now it is again surprising that what we usually call "mystical" or "experience" appears only in the first work, where there is "taste" in love. The remaining works sound anything but mystical; on the contrary, they are in the sign of nonexperience. Once again, however, it will not suffice Hadewijch to let the desolate aspect of her experience of God become known. She attempts again to give the mystical sense—the exact sense for the experience. She plainly tries, for the person who realizes he has gotten nowhere, to enable him to open to what is actually other: He who gives up the hope of his own religious completeness and gets rid of all self-consciousness has a chance of the perfect experience.

The first work is the moment of consolation. The second work consists in undergoing loneliness. By the third work, the mystic is confronted with a demand that surpasses all human measure, namely, the demand to follow Jesus fully.

To recapitulate: According to the *Visions* the apex of the mystical experience of oneness consists not at all in a disappearance of man in God, and still less in a one-sided ecstatic or fruitive experience. On the contrary, through this whole wonderful book runs like a golden thread this knowledge, Hadewijch's highest: The being-one with God demands of man that he is man; the experience must not, exclusively or by preference, aim at the Godhead; it must also—at the same time—be able to *taste* everything that belongs to the concrete, disconcerting, human Humanity. Now let us hear Hadewijch herself speaking, in three passages from Vision 14:

> The Countenance which he there made visible was invisible and inaccessible to the sight for all creatures who never lived human and divine love in one single Being, and who could not grasp or cherish in the undivided taste the one nature. (1. 77)

> For each revelation I had seen partly according to what I was myself, and partly according to what I had been chosen for; but now I saw this and had attained that to which I was chosen: in order that I might taste Man and God in one

> knowledge, what no man could do unless he were as God, and wholly such as he was who is our Love. (1. 155)

> The voice said to me: O strongest of all warrioresses, you have conquered everything and opened the closed totality, which was never opened by creatures who did not know, with painfully won and distressed love, how I am God and Man! (1. 172)

What Hadewijch wishes to make clear in *Visions*, has she not best formulated in the following passage from Letter 6?

> With the Humanity of God you must live here on earth, in the labors and sorrow of exile, while within your soul you love and rejoice with the omnipotent and eternal God in sweet abandonment. For the truth of both the Humanity and the Divinity is in one single fruition. (1.117)

Paul Mommaers S.J.

INTRODUCTION

HADEWIJCH'S WORKS

In the early thirteenth century the religious currents stirring in western Europe showed particular vitality throughout the Low Countries. In this new and strong movement of devotion, which sought a return to the pure spirit of the Gospel, both nuns and secular women took part. A number of women mystics gifted with ecstatic contemplation gained such respect that much information concerning them has been preserved in Latin "lives" written by contemporary authors and based in some cases—as in the lives of Saint Mary of Oignies (1177–1213) and Saint Lutgard of Aywières (1183–1246)—on close personal acquaintance between the writer and the subject of the biography.[1] To this group of mystics Hadewijch belongs, but her life was never written. She and her works were known in the fourteenth century, especially in the houses of the Canons Regular of Windesheim and to the Carthusians of Diest. By the middle of the sixteenth century, however, her name and everything she wrote (partly, perhaps, because no "life" perpetuated her memory) had fallen into oblivion.

The rediscovery of Hadewijch's works happened in Brussels in 1838. Three medieval specialists, J. F. Willems, F. J. Mone, and F. A. Snellaert, let it be known that in the manuscript collection of the Royal Library they had seen two volumes, both of which contained four works (two in prose and two in poetry) composed in Medieval Dutch and copied in a fourteenth-century hand. These manuscripts, which are catalogued in the Royal Library as MS. A (2879–80) and MS. B (2877–78), had originally belonged to the Canons Regular of Rooklooster, of the Congregation of Windesheim. Both originated in Brussels.

A fourteenth-century manuscript of her works, MS. C (a little earlier in date than MS. B), owned originally by the Canons Regular of Bethlehem, near Louvain, had come into the possession of the Bollandists in the seventeenth century. Heribert Rosweyde (1569–1629), the scholar who first conceived the idea of the great series *Acta Sanctorum,* noticed inside the cover of the book the inscription "Beata Hadewigis de Antwerpia." Because of his veneration for the saints he endeavored, in 1622–1623, to identify this Beata, but his efforts proved fruitless.[2] This same volume, having been acquired in 1878 by the library of the University of Ghent, where it is catalogued as 941, was utilized for the first edition of her complete works in two volumes (the poems in 1875 and the prose in 1895) under her name.[3] By the turn of the century it became possible for Josef Van Mierlo (1878–1958) to undertake critical editions, which, starting in 1908, he published, revised, and reissued up to 1952. A fourth manuscript (incomplete), dating from about 1500, is now in the library of the Ruusbroecgenootschap in Antwerp, MS. D (385 II).[4] Its text of the *Poems in Stanzas* was edited for publication by J. Alaerts in 1977.[5]

In the manuscripts, the *Visions* are followed by a supplement known as "the list of the perfect," referring to Vision 13. It gives the names of the saints most revered by Hadewijch, and of nearly eighty living persons known to her in various countries. The names appear to be authentic; a number of them designate persons historically identifiable, and with relation to certain of whom dates can be established that have been used to good advantage in Hadewijch studies. The comments that accompany the listings, however, lack the mature discretion that characterizes all her other writings. The "List" as it has come down to us does not, therefore, enhance her literary standing,[6] and for this reason it is omitted from the present translation.

WHO WAS HADEWIJCH?

Who then exactly was this Hadewijch? Scholars endeavored for years to solve the mystery of her family name, but since for the twelfth and thirteenth centuries 111 pious women named Hadewijch are known of,[7] no answer could be found. Her familiarity with chivalry and courtly love, however, and the refinement of character she invariably displays, permit little doubt that she belonged to the higher class.

The long-discussed problem of her dates is not settled yet. Anyway, she most probably lived in the middle of the thirteenth century.

Hadewijch was not a nun but a Beguine—that is, she was one of the devout women of her day who chose to lead a life of apostolic poverty and contemplation without taking vows as nuns. This movement came into being toward the end of the twelfth century, originating largely among women of noble and patrician familes. Apparently they rejected not only the narrow life of the lady in the castle, but the strict obligations of the nun in the cloister. The Beguines sought not vows or enclosure, but a new way of life to be arranged by themselves, in which to the recitation of the Hours they could add manual work, study, or teaching, according to their desires. As they rapidly increased in numbers, various socio-economic factors influenced the development of their life.

The exact origin of the name *Beguine* has been disputed. In the seventeenth century some writers claimed that the name was intended to honor the seventh-century Saint Begga, sister of Saint Gertrude of Nivelles; others held that it went back to Lambert le Begue (d. 1177), a priest of Liẽge. Alcuin Mens, in his study of the Beguine and Beghard movement in the Low Countries, states his belief that the word is really derived from the name of the grey cloth of their characteristic dress.[8] Jacques de Vitry (c. 1170–1240), the friend and biographer of the eminent early Beguine Mary of Oignies, in one of his extant sermons simply said that this name was used for the religious women of Flanders and Brabant.[9] The first Beguines lived at home individually; but gradually they formed groups, reciting the Hours together, supporting themselves by their common work and submitting to the government of a mistress. Both Beatrice of Nazareth and her Cistercian friend Ida of Nivelles (1197–1231) had lived in Beguine groups before they became nuns.

From the Low Countries and northern France, the Beguine movement spread into Germany, numbering hundreds of adherents. Adversely criticized by clergy and laity alike, it acquired a surer status in 1216 when Jacques de Vitry obtained from Pope Honorius III authorization for the Beguines to live in common and to exhort one another to a good life (*sese invicem mutuis exhortationibus invitare*).[10]

INTRODUCTION

Taking Hadewijch's writings as a whole, we can discover a few clear points toward an autobiographical outline.

She had either founded or joined a Beguine group and had become its mistress; when the Angel addresses her as "Mistress" (Vision 1: P. 185), he may have been using this title. She had under her authority a number of young Beguines whom she believed to be specially called to the mystical state, although they only too often fell short of their calling. Hadwijch's presence in the community as spiritual guide is referred to for instance in Letter 15: P. 51.

In the course of time, however, Hadewijch's authority among the Beguines met with opposition. It is not hard to see why this happened. Some of them found her unremittingly high standards a grievance; at the same time, her ascendancy aroused jealousy. Ill feeling toward the Beguines on the part of outside persons no doubt played a part, and meanwhile a few of the Beguines themselves secretly engaged in undermining her position. This may explain why the Angel in Vision 4: P. 44 greeted her as "Unknown to all your friends and to all your enemies!" Means were devised to send her companions away from her. At length she was threatened with an accusation of teaching quietism, a charge that carried with it the possibility of being turned out of the community to wander the countryside, or even of imprisonment if she were denounced to the Inquisition. She laments the pain of separation from Sara, Emma, Margriet, and the unnamed Beguine who was dearest to her of all, and in Letter 25 she speaks of being one day reunited with them. Van Mierlo thought from this that she was actually planning a reunion in a new community in another place. This happy ending theory is however rejected, and no doubt correctly, by J.-B. Porion, who believes that she referred rather to being with them in heaven.[11]

The general opinion of scholars at present seems to be that Hadewijch actually was evicted from her Beguine community and exiled; that she was made the talk of the town (as Spaapen thinks) and thrown out because of her doctrine that one must live Love.[12] Statements from her letters taken out of context might have been used to formulate a charge of quietism. In the "life" of her contemporary Ida of Nivelles, presumably by Gosuin of Bossut, we read that Ida suffered much from persecutions aroused by slanderous tongues.[13] In Ida's case, the persecution was apparently due to doubt of the genuineness of her ecstasies and fear of her knowledge of the secrets of conscience. She, however, as a Cistercian nun, enjoyed the protection of the rule of enclosure and the strong organization of the order, whereas Hadewijch had no such advantages.

It may perhaps be conjectured, considering how often Hadewijch urged her Beguines to care for the sick,[14] that when she finally became homeless she offered her services to a leprosarium or hospital for the poor, where she could nurse those who suffered and sleep at least part of the night in some corner, with access to the church or chapel always attached to such establishments in her time.

HADEWIJCH'S EDUCATION AND THE SOURCES OF HER SPIRITUALITY

To form some idea of Hadewijch's education, we may turn to the lives of two other women mystics, in order to learn what their education was. Beatrice, already mentioned, was taught at home by her mother to read the Latin Psalter (the medieval primer), and likewise learned from her the rudiments of Latin grammar. Then, after attending a school of liberal arts for over a year, she entered the school maintained in the enclosure of the Cistercian abbey of Florival for intending novices. Here she continued her school course. Her "life" does not define this course, but considering the customs of the time there can be no reasonable doubt that she went on studying the seven liberal arts—that is, the *trivium* (grammar, rhetoric, and dialectic) and the *quadrivium* (arithmetic, geometry—including geography, astronomy, and music).[15] Ida of Gorsleeuw (c. 1203–1260) likewise attended a school of liberal arts and in addition took lessons in calligraphy. At the age of thirteen she entered the school of the Cistercian abbey of La Ramée, where a few years later she took the veil.[16]

We have no direct statement that Hadewijch ever attended a school, but her many allusions to the school of love in *Poems in Stanzas*, and particularly in Stanzaic Poem 14, which speaks of the curriculum and the masters of this school, lead us to suppose that she probably did.[17] Her education, wherever she acquired it, is reflected in her familiarity with the Latin language, the rules of rhetoric, medieval numerology, Ptolemaic astronomy, and the theory of music. She knew the rules of letter writing (the *ars dictaminis*) and of versification. She was also proficient in French, and she introduces a number of French words into her writings.

Among her principal sources, first place belongs to the Scriptures, which color her whole thought. She quotes numerous texts from both Testaments, names scriptural personages, and refers to incidents of the Old Testament as well as to the mysteries of Christ and Mary. On occasion a Scripture text serves as starting point for the development of her thought, most notably in Letter 12 where she uses a text from Obadiah, and in Poem 12, which is a loose commentary on Psalm 44:11–12.

Either in her works or in the "List," Hadewijch names several of the great Church writers—Origen, Hilary of Poitiers, Augustine, Gregory the Great, and Isidore of Seville. Of the great twelfth-century writers, she is indebted in varying degrees to the Victorines–Hugh (1079–1141), Adam (c. 1110–1177), and Richard of Saint Victor (d. 1173); and to the Cistercians—Bernard of Clairvaux (1091–1153), William of Saint Thierry (1085–1148), and Guerric of Igny (c. 1087–1147). The ones most important to us are Richard, from whom Hadewijch borrowed in Letter 10, and William, from whom she borrowed in Letter 18. It is highly probable that she did not know William by name, since in her day and long afterward his works circulated under the name of Bernard of Clairvaux; but William is the closest to her in spirituality. With regard to Thomas Aquinas, we must bear in mind that Hadewijch wrote too early to undergo any influence from him.

As sources for her poetry, the Latin poems of the Church's liturgy must not be passed over, especially the sequences, from which she derived no less than eleven of her metrical patterns for the *Poems in Stanzas.*[18] She is also much indebted to the poetry of courtly love.[19] Scholars in this field conclude that she was well acquainted with this poetry in the vernacular, and that thanks to her lyrical genius she surpassed in virtuosity its most celebrated practitioners. It also seems fairly certain that some of the Latin verses in the *Complaint of Nature* by Alan of Lille (d. 1203) are reflected in Poem 13.[20]

The provenance of a few themes frequent in Hadewijch's works is still to be considered. For a certain Father of the Church of whom we have already spoken, namely for Augustine, Hadewijch felt much more than admiration. She loved Augustine because of his burning love for the Trinity, as she states in Vision 11: P. 49; and we notice that he is the only nonbiblical saint who ever appeared to her in her recorded visions. We are not surprised, therefore, to find in Hadewijch some specific instances of dependence on him.

Scholars have pointed out in Hadewijch's thought a few traits characteristic of Eastern rather than Western theology. In the tradition of the Greek Fathers is found the Trinitarian concept according to which the Father is the Source without source of the divine fecundity, in the sense in which Western theology would say that the Divine Nature is its source.[21] This explains the numerous passages where Hadewijch speaks of the Father, not in the Western but in the Greek sense.

Another theme of Greek origin is prominent in Hadewijch, namely the idea of eternal progress, which runs through all the works of Gregory of Nyssa (335–395).[22]

We must not close this survey of Hadewijch's sources without adding two cases where she borrows from some author a certain thought sequence that she proceeds to develop in a completely independent manner. The first instance is found in Letter 22, which is based on a Latin hymn, "Alpha et Omega, magne Deus." This hymn is classified by Migne both among the works of Hildebert of Lavardin, Archbishop of Tours (d. 1134), and among those of Peter Abelard (d. 1142).[23] The paradoxical ideas expressed in this strophe had seen the light long before in the prose of Isidore of Seville,[24] who is named in the "List."

The second instance occurs in Poem 2, which is based on a legend narrated in 3 Esdras 3:1–5:6. Three Esdras is an apocryphal book composed about 90 B.C. and included by Jerome in the Vulgate. (It was finally deleted from the canon of Scripture by the Council of Trent.) This legend is also recounted by Flavius Josephus (d. A.D. 95) in *The Antiquities of the Jews*, composed A.D. 93; and in the twelfth century it was taken over by Peter Comestor (d. 1180) in his *Scholastic History*.[25] Hadewijch certainly does not depend on the Comestor, who changes the order of the narration; and one would suppose she used the Vulgate, as more accessible than Josephus.

HADEWIJCH'S DOCTRINE OF THE MYSTICAL LIFE

Hadewijch proposes a love mysticism that is both Christological and Trinitarian. The central theme of love had taken possession of her heart and mind very early, with her experience of Divine Love at the age of ten. Her mystical concepts, necessarily expressed in different manners in her works depending on the literary genre she employs, recur constantly. None of her four works, however, gives a systematic treatment of her doctrine, since all of them are made up of numerous separate pieces in which her thought presents itself as circumstances happened to call it forth.

The theme of love appears on practically every page. Hadewijch has several different terms for love. *Karitate* usually refers to love for men, for neighbor. *Lief* means the beloved; she employs the word either for Christ or for the soul (where it refers to the soul, we have translated it, for clarity, as "the loved one"). *Minne,* a word of feminine gender and belonging to the language of courtly love, she uses far oftener than the other two terms.

Van Mierlo and Axters explained Hadewijch's use of *minne* as signifying primarily God, or Christ, or Divine Love.[26] N. De Paepe, however, in his book *Hadewijch, Poems in Stanzas: A study of love [minne] in connection with 12th- and 13th-century mysticism and profane love-lyric* (1967), arrives at the conclusion that

> *Minne* in Hadewijch's *Poems in Stanzas* is not God, Christ, or Divine Love—except in a very limited number of places. . . . *Minne* is an experience, the way in which the soul experiences its relation to God, a dynamic experience of relationship.[27]

For an opinion on De Paepe's views we might cite that of Spaapen, who praises this new approach to the *Poems in Stanzas* as "bringing a marked widening and deepening to the interpretation of Hadewijch," while at the same time he notes certain reservations: "The theological side of the question is almost entirely left out of consideration. One may wonder whether this is admissible."[28]

TRINITARIAN MYSTICISM

The Trinitarian aspect of Hadewijch's mysticism is particularly rich. It goes back to the analogy of the Trinity in the memory, understanding, and love of the human mind, which was originally discovered by Augustine.[29] There can be little doubt, however, that Hadewijch accepts this analogy as it is presented by William of Saint Thierry, for William uses the term *reason* where Augustine has *understanding;* and what is of far greater importance, William gives Augustine's parallel a dynamic character, regarding the triad in the soul as a participation in the Trinitarian life of God. She was surely familiar with the passage in *The nature and dignity of love* in which William says that when God breathed in the face of man on creating him, he placed in the highest part, so to speak, of his mind

> the power of memory, that he might always remember the Creator's power and goodness; immediately and without a moment's delay, memory generated from itself reason; and memory and reason together brought forth will. For memory possesses and contains in itself that to which man should tend; reason knows he must so tend; the will tends; and these three constitute a kind of unity, but three powers; just as in the sublime Trinity there is one substance and Three Persons. As in the Trinity the Father is the begetter, the Son begotten, and the Holy Spirit is from both, so reason is generated from memory, and from memory and reason proceeds will. In order therefore that the rational soul created in man may cleave to God, the Father claims for himself memory; the Son, reason; and the Holy Spirit, proceeding from both Father and Son claims the will, proceeding from both memory and reason.[30]

Hadewijch presents this doctrine in Letter 22: P. 137, where she writes:

> He gave us his Nature in the soul, with three powers whereby to love his Three Persons: with enlightened reason, the Father; with the memory, the wise Son of God; and with the high flaming will, the Holy Spirit.

Discussing the medieval use of the word *memory*, R. Vanneste explains that the passage of Hadewijch just quoted does not mean either that reason is the image of the Father or that memory is the image of the Son. Rather it means that we love the Father with the Son, to whom reason is appropriated; and we love the Son with memory, that is to say, with the Father.[31]

Hadewijch's longest development of the theme of the image is in Poem 4:5–24:

> I pray the Holy Trinity,
> Through its grace and for its goodness,
> As it has honored you with its image . . .

> That you may understand by reason
> What God has accomplished through you . . .
> If you live with reason in truth,
> You enlighten all your labor;
> So your will is pleased to live well . . .
> And then your memory becomes valiant,
> And within it shall reign glory,
> With confidence and fidelity,
> That it may fully contemplate its God.

In Letter 4: P. 1, she states the theme in the negative:[32]

> When reason is obscured, the will grows weak and powerless and feels an aversion for effort, because reason does not enlighten it. Consequently the memory loses its deep notions, and the joyous confidence, and the repeated zealous intentions by which its confidence taught it to endure more easily the misery of waiting for its Beloved.

Hadewijch's doctrine of living the Trinity appears in Letter 1. Her statement of the theme there is not easy to follow; the reason may be that chronologically Letter 1 (as we shall soon explain in discussing the letters) is not the first of the series but one of the last, and therefore a full explanation in Letter 1 was not necessary. She says in Letter 1 that we must first contemplate ourselves in God, and therefore learn to contemplate what God is, namely, the Trinity. She goes on to explain how we live the life of the Trinity; we live the life of the Father, when we allow his irresistible power to work in us; the life of the Holy Spirit, when we allow his holy will to be done in us; and the life of the Son, when we allow ourselves to be enlightened by his radiance and truth.

The full depth of what Hadewijch can tell us about the relations with the Trinity that perfect souls may one day attain begins to dawn on us when she explains living the Trinity and the Unity.[33] This doctrine of hers, although it corresponds in a general manner to a truth known to all the greatest contemplatives—namely, that the soul that has reached perfection must give itself both to the activity of virtues and to the repose of contemplation—is not found in her sources. What is new in her conception is, in the words of Porion, "the mysterious parallel" she finds "between this structure of our spiritual life and the Trinitarian life in the very bosom of the Divine Being." It is indubitably from her that Ruusbroec inherited this theme and used it consistently throughout his works.[34]

This is set forth by Hadewijch particularly in Letters 17 and 30. Both form and content of Letter 17 call for an explanation. She begins in verse with a series of commands and prohibitions arranged to form three mnemonic couplets that refer in order to the Holy Spirit, the Father, and the Son. In each couplet the first verse concerns the outward activity of the Divine Person, in the works attributed to him, while the second verse concerns his unity with the other two Divine Persons. Hadewijch would have us shape our life on this rhythm by turning outward in the activity of the virtues, and turning inward again into union with God. Here she is not merely making a comparison; when she speaks of passing from the aspect of activity (the Divine Persons) to the aspect of repose in love (the Divine Essence, the Unity), she envisages the entrance of our life into the Divine Life. To show that there is no quietistic error in Hadewijch's emphasis on the soul's refraining from the exercise of the virtues while it is called into the Unity, Van Mierlo outlines the general thought:

> While we are engaged in love, we are serving God in the Divine Persons, and we must strive for the different virtues; but when love predominates and establishes us in simplicity, we can only love. The reason is that in this love we practice the virtues far more perfectly; they flow from the fulness and unity of our life, and we no longer need to strive for them separately.[35]

Porion for his part argues that the whole doctrine should be free from question, since Ruusbroec took it over and stated it repeatedly.[36]

Hadewijch is not afraid to say in Letter 17: P. 101 that the commands and prohibitions she has set forth were given her by the Father in a vision that took place on Ascension Day four years earlier.

CHRISTOLOGICAL MYSTICISM

Hadewijch never tires of preaching that we must be conformed to Christ in his Humanity in order to be conformed to him in his Divinity. In this conformity she wants us to find the motivation for the pursuit of the virtues; we must practice all the virtues for the reason that Christ chose to do so during his life on earth. She says in Letter 15: P. 16 that, with regard to Christ, we must consider how

> although he was himself God—how he gave all, and how he lived exclusively for veritable love of the Father and for charity toward men. He worked with wakeful charity, and he gave to Love all his Heart and all his soul and all his strength. (Cf. Luke 10:27)

Or as she states more explicitly in Letter 6: P. 316ff.

> It is man's obligation to practice virtues, . . . solely out of homage to the incomparable sublimity of God, who created our nature to this end. . . . This is the way in which the Son of God took the lead, and of which he himself gave us knowledge. . . . He perfectly accomplished, amid multiplicity, the will of the Father in all things and at all times.

Hadewijch's doctrine of our duty to live Christ seems to be illustrated in a notable way in the passage on the virtue of Peacefulness, one of the bridesmaids in Vision 12: P. 112. With the boldness that we have learned to associate with her deep desire for union with God, Hadewijch here is actually inviting us to "live Christ" in the sense of participating in all his mysteries.

She speaks here of the soul as sharing in the Annunciation—being announced with him; and in the Nativity, being born with him. We shall see that in Vision 13: P. 15 she wants the soul to join him in the flight into Egypt; and here she insists we must grow up with him. She has often before said that the soul must live as man with his Humanity, for instance in Letter 6: P. 249; here she urges living "together with him in all like pains, in poverty, in ignominy, and in compassion for all those with whom justice was angry" and, like him, never receiving alien consolation. At once we recall what she heard Christ say in Vision 1: P. 288: "If you wish to be like me in my Humanity, . . . you will desire to be poor, miserable, and despised by all men."

As a preliminary to entering with Christ into the mysteries of the Passion, the soul must accept being forsaken like him, as Hadewijch learned from him in Vision 1: P. 288 and 364:

> "All persons will fall away from you and forsake you, and no one will be willing to wander about with you in your distress and in your weakness. . . . When I had worked miracles and become better known, few friends remained to me in the world. Yes, at my death almost all men alive abandoned me. Therefore do not let it grieve you that all persons will forsake you on account of perfect love and because you are living in my will."

No wonder Hadewijch says to her young Beguines (Letter 6: P. 249): "We do not live with Christ as he lived, neither do we forsake all as Christ did, nor are we forsaken by all as Christ was."

In the mysteries of Golgotha, we must "carry the cross with the Son of God"—later she remarks that "the cross we must bear with Christ is exile on earth"—but we are only too inclined to carry the cross with Simon, who received pay for carrying it. We must always persevere in all the virtues; and "this is to be crucified with Christ" (Letter 6: P. 361). Then we must hang on the cross with him (ibid.: P. 227), and finally "die with Christ."

In two different contexts Hadewijch mentions the harrowing of hell, when the Son "carried life and light where no light shall be, and his name drew his beloved ones there into clear light and full fruitfulness" (Letter 22: P. 285). The second passage is that of Vision 12: P. 112, from which we have already quoted; there Peacefulness declares that the Bride died with Christ "and freed all the prisoners with him, and bound what he bound."

For the glorious mysteries, Hadewijch states that when the soul offers to Love "noble service in all works of virtue, and a life of exile in all obedience, . . . this is . . . to rise again with him" (Letter 6: P. 361). Finally, "a short time after the fortieth day" (Vision 13: P. 241), the soul

> with him ascended to his Father; and there with him acknowledged his Father as Father, and him as Son with him; and with him she acknowledged the Holy Spirit as Holy

Spirit; and with him, like him, she knew all as One, and the Essence in which they are One. (Vision 12: P. 112)

INFLUENCE

In the fourteenth century the entire volume of Hadewijch's *Letters* was translated into High German, her name being rendered as "Adelwip." The full translation was lost, but the Berlin State Library obtained a small portion of it in two fragmentary copies, of the fourteenth and the fifteenth century respectively, both containing Letter 10, and the second adding some sentences from six other Letters.[37] Another German translation comprising parts of Letters 3 and 6 and of Poems 5 and 6 has been recently discovered at Einsiedeln in the Abbey Library, in a manuscript (codex 277) dating from the second half of the fourteenth century.[38] The Royal Library at The Hague also owns a manuscript, written probably at the end of the fifteenth century, that contains a sort of brief anthology of extracts (in the original language) from six different Letters. A full account, however, of the Hadewijch-fragments in the *Limburg Sermons,*[39] or of the relatively unimportant authors of the fourteenth to sixteenth centuries in whose works her influence can be traced, would seem to be of interest chiefly to specialists. We shall turn rather to the most prominent writer who availed himself of her thought—the great mystical theorist John of Ruusbroec (1293–1381).

Through the friendship of his uncle, John Hinckaert, who was a Canon of Saint Gudule's church in Brussels, Ruusbroec went to that city as a boy to prepare for the priesthood. After studies by which he evidently acquired a profound knowledge of theology, he was ordained priest and served as a chaplain at Saint Gudule's. A day came when the works of Hadewijch somehow fell into his hands. It may safely be conjectured that this happened rather early in his career, for evidences of his familiarity with her writings are to be found in the first of the six books he wrote before withdrawing to Groenendal in 1343, *The kingdom of lovers.*[40] Here Ruusbroec introduces the theme of the Trinity and the Unity.[41] In this work he also borrows from Hadewijch's Poem 16:31–40 the Eucharistic theme of our eating Christ and his eating us.[42]

If *The kingdom of lovers* is admittedly somewhat faltering, in his next book, *The spiritual espousals,* Ruusbroec's thought has attained full maturity. The *Espousals* further enables us to verify Porion's assertion that "the essential and specific features of his doctrine, as well as a fundamental part of his literary resources," go back to Hadewijch.[43] Although she had no system of spirituality, Ruusbroec took over the various elements of her mystical thought, deepened and enlarged them through his knowledge of theology and metaphysical psychology, and built from them his spiritual synthesis. We find in the *Espousals* her themes of living Christ by the vitues,[44] of the Trinity and the Unity already noted,[45] of conquering God,[46] and of being God with God,[47] as well as a recurring awareness of exemplarism.[48] Her image of the tree of the knowledge of God, growing upside down, reappears as the tree of faith.[49] Some striking passages are reproduced almost verbatim, such as that of the eleventh hour of Letter 20, for we read in Ruusbroec: "Here man is possessed by Love, so that he must forget himself and God, and know of nothing else but love."[50]

Lest examples grow wearisome, we add only the following: At the beginning of his last work, *The book of the twelve Beguines,* he quotes verbatim (or almost) some lines of her poems;[51] and in *The seven steps in the ladder of spiritual love* he borrows again from Letter 20, the tenth hour:

> The Holy Spirit . . . cries within us with a loud voice, yet without words, "Love the Love that ever loves you!" His cry is, as it were, an inward touching of our spirit, and his voice more terrible than thunder. . . . And his touch cries in the spirit without ceasing: "Pay your debt! Love the Love that ever loves you!" . . . Love is never silent, but ever and without ceasing cries: "Love ye Love!"[52]

LETTERS

The striking feature of Hadewijch's prose writing is its artistry. She has a sense of literary structure, of emphasis and subordination in the development of her thoughts. She has a rich vocabulary that gives both variety and a wide range in choosing the precise word; and she places no word by chance. Of the sound of each word she is keenly aware, and always uses sounds to good effect. The style of her letters is a little more finished than that of the visions, but the latter must also be recognized as artistic prose.

As has already been said, the volume entitled *Letters* includes both letters proper and a few short treatises. To speak first about the letters proper, nearly all were most probably written for the instruction and formation of the same young Beguine, the person for whom Hadewijch had a special love because she believed her to be one called by God to the highest spiritual ways.

Hadewijch's general argument, as will readily be seen, is that mystical life flows from the truths of faith, which truths she sets forth with unfaltering assurance. To point out the first appearance of some of her principal themes, that of the Trinity in Letter 1 we have already noted. In Letter 2: P. 29 she introduces the theme of self-knowledge (with which Vision 1 begins). She does not follow Bernard of Clairvaux in seeing it as the recognition that we are defaced images of God;[53] to her, as in this instance, it is an awareness of our littleness in comparison with God, arrived at by the examination of our thoughts. In the last paragraph her exemplarism should be noticed. The reference (P. 118) to the *secret word* is one of many hints of her feeling for the book of Job.

In Letter 6: P. 227, Hadewijch makes the bold statement, "We all wish to be god with God" (adopted by Ruusbroec),[54] which she here contrasts with "to live as men with his Humanity." Near the end she touches on the subject of grace, which recurs many times in both the letters and the visions.[55] In Letter 9 the theme "Who is God, and what is God?" should be compared with "What is Love, and who is Love?"[56]

Letter 12 is addressed to the superior of a men's monastery, very probably Gilbertus of Saint James' Abbey (Jacob's in Dutch) in Brussels. It urges Hadewijch's often reiterated directive that we must conquer God (or Love) so that God (or Love) may conquer us, on the model of Jacob's wrestling with the Angel (P. 174; cf. Gen. 32:22–32).

Letter 13: P. 45 brings in the concept of man's debt to God (or to Love); and Letter 14 gives us the first reference to the "land of love" where we shall travel so often with Hadewijch in the *Poems in Stanzas.* Letter 18 (which continues the thought of Letter 17) has been much spoken of because of the long quotation it contains from William of Saint Thierry.[57]

Throughout the letters, whenever Hadewijch addresses her correspondent directly, we perceive her maternal attitude of warmth and sympathy. At the same time she can reprove sternly, and she admits of no compromise. With unfailing psychological acumen she puts her finger on the grave fault, points out the causes and the remedy, and urges not the most seductive but the purest motivation for new progress.

The first of the six treatises in the volume, Letter 10, is the one that introduces, for the most part literally, several ideas taken from Richard of Saint Victor's *Commentary on the Song of Songs.* This interesting dependence was not discovered until 1943.[58] Letter 15 is a spirited allegory, in which the life in common practiced in a religious house is compared to a pilgrimage, that work of devotion so popular in the thirteenth century.

Letter 20, a fascinating piece of prose, describes the soul's mystical ascent as a series of twelve hours; they are divisible into three groups of four each, corresponding respectively to "the seeking mind," "the desiring heart," and "the loving soul." A sense of God's transcendence, as experienced by the soul, is conveyed by the very obscurity of expression and the use of negatives such as nameless, unknown, unawares, unbidden, unheard-of. Twice she uses the word *God,* but the Trinity is never mentioned, and none of the Three Persons is named. There can be no doubt, however, that in the second and third Hours she speaks of living Christ in his Humanity by union with his sufferings. This piece is often compared to *Seven ways of love* by Beatrice of Nazareth.[59]

We have already mentioned that a strophe from a Latin hymn ascribed either to Hildebert or to Abelard is the source of Letter 22. This treatise appears at first reading to be philosophical in tone, but on further consideration it is seen to be the poetical outpouring of a mystic who endeavors to express the inexpressible wonder of God's Being. Of particular interest is her use in P. 169 of the term *despair* in the ameliorative sense of a surpassing virtue. She presents the same idea at greater length in Poem 1:139–172.

Letter 28 comes back to the speculative theme of Letters 17 and 18. Without a systematic exposition, Hadewijch presents one after another a series of statements, in the form of outbursts of spiritual joy, as undefined heights in the mystical ascent.

Porion has called attention to the profound significance of Letter 30; here Hadewijch sets forth the mutual demand between the Trinity and the essential Unity in God, and also the demand between God and the soul, and seizes on the continuity between the two. This is another theme Ruusbroec takes over from Hadewijch and repeats with powerful effect.[60]

If we read through the letters to see what we can learn on the subject of Hadewijch's trouble with her young Beguines, we notice here and there references to its different phases. In the beginning, Hadewijch was accepted as mistress and guide. Gradually covert opposition to her made itself felt. In time, "false brethren" grew bold in stirring up trouble, and Hadewijch was aware that they wished to get rid of her. Then came the crisis, when separation actually took place. In the fifth and last phase, Hadewijch was forsaken by all.

Letters 8, 12, 15, and 18 allude to covert jealousy; 5 and 19 refer to the trouble caused by "false brethren"; 23, 25, and 26 are connected with the separation crisis; and 22, 29, 1, and 2 (as well as 26) belong to the phase when she was really forsaken. The arrangement in which the letters stand in the manuscripts has never been considered chronological. In a chronological list, therefore, as far as can be judged, Letter 31 would stand first; 17 and 28 would be somewhere in the group of the first nineteen Letters; and 8, 12, 15, and 18, with 5 and 19, with 23, 25–26, and with 22, 29, 1, and 2 would constitute the final group.

That Hadewijch herself placed the letters in the order in which they stand in the manuscripts can probably never be fully proved, but since it is now known that she did arrange the *Poems in Stanzas* (as will be explained shortly), it seems not improbable that she herself decided the order of all four of her volumes. In view of her literary genius one can hardly doubt that she was aware of their artistic value, and she must have considered their spiritual content as of still greater moment. Knowing in advance, as she did, that plans were being laid to send her away from the community, she would have had a certain length of time in which to ask back any significant letters of which she had no copy.

In arranging the volume she may have placed Letter 1 first because it has overtones of the first chapter of Saint John's Gospel, and it stresses her theme of living the Trinity. Its one bitter cry of pain startles us, for we are unprepared to comprehend it. Why, then, did she not choose to begin with a letter we would not have found in any way disturbing? One answer may be that if we compare this first piece with the first piece in each of her other volumes, we observe that each of them contains a strong statement about suffering encountered by the soul in its longing for union with God. Perhaps she wished to make clear from the start that anyone who undertakes with truth to perform works of justice in imitation of the Son, for the glory of the noble love that God is, must expect to meet with more than ordinary sufferings.

POEMS IN STANZAS

Hadewijch, as we have just seen, possessed no small talent for the writing of artistic prose, but the gift for poetry she displays in the *Poems in Stanzas* can only be termed lyrical genius. Since she was not a person with a religious side and a secular side but wholly centered in God, all these poems are mystical love lyrics—a new genre for which she must be given the credit.[61]

Her poems themselves are proof that she had mastered the troubadours' art. It has been said that just as Bernard of Clairvaux used the Song of Songs to express his own intimate and personal experience of God, Hadewijch used the poetry of courtly love to express the emotional tensions of the longing for God,[62] showing an unfailing mastery of all its techniques: stanza structure, the tornada,[63] meter, rhyme, assonance, concatenation, and figures of speech.

In the poetry of courtly love, she could turn everything to profit. The service of love offered to the lady became the service of love offered by the soul to God. The lady then would be God, or Love (*minne*). Sometimes Hadewijch herself would be knight errant, courting dangers and adventures in her honor, riding down the roads of the land of love. Feudal customs and modes of expression fitted readily into the pattern. The sufferings inherent in the service of the lady and the lover's many complaints over his hard lot could be effectively applied to the trials to be faced and the burdens to be borne by one whose love for God is unfaltering.

At the same time Hadewijch drew on the sequences of the Church's liturgy, not only for metrical patterns but for the Latin phrases incorporated into Stanzaic Poems 1 and 45.[64] It is also noteworthy that whenever she uses the tornada, she indicates it by R/n, the sign by which the liturgical books introduce a responsory. She draws also, and abundantly, on the beautiful words of the Scriptures.

The fact that there is a prearranged significance in the order Hadewijch assigned to the various poems in this volume remained unsuspected from the time she wrote them until as recently as 1974, when it was discovered by J. Bosch.[65] He succeeded in demonstrating that she structured this entire book according to the principles of medieval numerology, and that in the scheme she evolved (without giving the reader any hint of it), Stanzaic Poem 29, on the subject of the Virgin Mary, is the central poem of the entire series of forty-five. The discovery of this hitherto undetected aspect of Hadewijch's volume is an important addition to our knowledge of her literary artistry.

Since no one now questions that the *Poems in Stanzas* were addressed to Hadewijch's young Beguines,[66] it is to be expected that traces may be discerned in them of the same troubles alluded to in the letters, even though the demands of artistic form and poetic inspiration may make the meaning less perceptible. Scholars now tend to see Hadewijch's concern amid these disturbances as directed less to her own personal grief and suffering than to her intense desire to recall her young Beguines to their early fervor.[67]

The following passages seem to imply the activities of the "false brethren": in Stanzaic Poem 3:30, her reference in the first person to suffering "losses, defamations, oppression"; and in the last strophe of Stanzaic Poem 4, her prayer for her young Beguines ("noble souls"), who are driven from their goal by cruel aliens.

In Stanzaic Poem 13:29–32, she warns them to be on their guard, for:

> There are many who seem anxious to betake themselves
> Where they are advised to seek Love.
> But they stray away from fidelity along alien ways:
> I have watched this happen.

In Stanzaic Poem 32: stanzas 1, 2, and 6:

> Soon flowers will open to our sight, . . .
> Also men will condemn the noble hearts
> Who live under Love's dominion . . .
>
> With him who now bears true Love's chains,
> As his debt to Love requires,
> The cruel aliens before long
> Will quite openly interfere.
> Often they intimidate
> Those who trust high Love's protection . . .

I counsel them that they spare nothing,
And that they set themselves
To persevere with longing in the storm
In spite of their fault-finders,
Who are so bent on harming them.

From this perspective, H. Schottmann interprets Stanzaic Poem 1 as an appeal to her young Beguines to return to the true Love from which they have fallen away. In the refrain after every stanza, she is addressing them directly to tell them they can still reconstitute themselves as a group. While in Stanza 3 she asks her circle for pity on her own suffering, her basic theme is that of renewal, hinted in Stanza 1 by the allusions to the new year and the new spring, and strongly urged in Stanza 9:

May God give us a renewed mind
    For noble and free love,
To make us so new in our life
    That Love may bless us
And renew, with new taste,
    Those to whom she can give new fullness;
Love is the new and powerful recompense
    Of those whose life renews itself for Love alone.

The final phase, that of Hadewijch's being forsaken, is echoed in Stanzaic Poem 17:25–28, 31–34:

How life can horrify and grieve
One who has given his all for all
And in the darkness is driven the wrong way
    To a place whence he envisages no return. . . .
O proud souls who stand as if on Love's side
And live freely under her protection,
Pity one who is disowned, whom Love overwhelms
    And presses hard in despairing exile!

The mention of suffering, bitterness, blows, and death in the last two stanzas of Stanzaic Poem 45 has been associated by G. Kazemier with this final phase of Hadewijch's forsakenness. In his opinion, these stanzas strengthen the thought of danger expressed in Hadewijch's Letter 29, where she speaks of her fear of imprisonment. He argues that as Letter 29 belongs to the end of her correspondence, Stanzaic Poem 45 is the last poem she wrote, and that the final verse, *Unde mori. Amen, Amen,* shows that when she wrote this last stanzaic poem she was perhaps in prison awaiting execution.[68]

It seems as though if Hadewijch had been actually arrested or executed on a charge of heresy by the Inquisition the exhaustive efforts of the scholars to identify her would not have proved such a complete failure. The execution of the Beguine Aleydis (named in the "List") found mention in not a few contemporary chronicles.[69] That of Margaret Porete at Paris on June 1, 1310, is likewise well documented. Besides, one wonders whether the public indignation stirred up by the burning of Aleydis may not have tended to deter somewhat the prosecution of Beguines by the Inquisition. If Hadewijch's period of literary activity came to an end in 1240, only four years had elapsed since Aleydis died. It is clear in Margaret's case that the Church authorities did not wish to pursue her; she was only forbidden by the Bishop of Cambrai to circulate her book, and her failure to obey was ignored until she brought on her own fate by propagating the book in Paris.[70] As to the question of Hadewijch, one or two recent scholars think it possible she was arrested, but none definitely asserts it.[71]

VISIONS

Accounts of the visions of not a few saints, blesseds, and devout persons of the first half of the thirteenth century have been preserved, but Hadewijch's visions are distinguished from the rest by their lofty seriousness, power of imagery, and metaphysical-mystical meaning. Her visions have something of the apocalyptic character of those of Hildegard, who is mentioned in the "List," but Hildegard's vast complexity of images and moral reflections bring us the teachings of a prophetess, whereas Hadewijch's intensity and the deep impact of each phase of a vision as she tells it offer us an entrance point into her contemplative experience.

As far as the structure of the *Visions* is concerned, Hadewijch herself marks it out by the contrast between "in the spirit" and "out of the spirit." (These two terms are drawn from Richard of Saint Victor.[72])

Hadewijch did not record all her visions. She mentions, in particular, visions of the Transfiguration that she never wrote down (Vision 14: P. 85). At least some of those she has left us seem to belong to the early part of her life, for Vision 6 occurred when she was nineteen.

All things considered, it seems probable that the structure of her book of visions can be understood only by comparing it with that of her other works. The *Poems in Stanzas* are forty-five in number, and the visions are fourteen. If we add to fourteen the number of the letters, thirty-one, we have again the total of forty-five. We are inclined to believe that this second total was arrived at by design, especially when we reflect that the visions are actually only eleven in number, some of them having apparently been divided; and among the letters, Letter 6 appears to be an amalgam of sections from several distinct letters on closely related subjects.

There can be little doubt that Hadewijch chose the number fourteen deliberately. In Saint Matthew's Gospel (1:17) the genealogy of Christ is presented in three divisions of fourteen generations each, so that fourteen becomes the threefold genealogical key number of Christ. Very possibly this verse in Matthew looks back to the numerical value of the Hebrew name of David, which is fourteen.[73] A more appropriate number for Hadewijch's visions could hardly be found, since they are the source of her familiarity with the mysteries of Christ and of her teaching that we must live Christ, on which her spirituality largely depends.

In 1925 Van Mierlo stated his belief that Hadewijch wrote down the visions a considerable time after they occurred, at the request of her confessor; twenty-five years later he merely suggested the confessor, with a question mark. More recent scholarship holds that she wrote them for the benefit of her young Beguines.[74] Thus added meaning accrues to the slightly veiled expressions (for instance the vague terms *men* and *menschen,* which we have translated "persons") now and then used in the visions to designate them. It is noteworthy that in her prayer in Vision 5: P. 12, she refers to them as "those who are ours," because she has interior knowledge that these young Beguines belong both to her and to God. Very striking is the passage in Vision 8: P. 33 where she hears Christ say to her:

> "By this way I went forth from my Father to you and those who are yours, and I came again from you and those who are yours back to my Father (cf. John 16:28). With myself I have

also sent you this hour, and you must, with me, pass it on to those who are yours."

A new and important contribution on the subject of the visions and their audience has recently been made by Vekeman. Starting from the allegorical character of the visions he demonstrates that Hadewijch and her little circle of Beguines understood the difference between *allegoria in dictis* (rhetorical allegory) and *allegoria in factis* (allegory in which a genuine historical event becomes the symbol of another event), and that they therefore interpreted the graces of her visions as "the historical and spiritual manifestation of God's justifying presence."[75] Further, he points out the fact that Ruusbroec in the *Espousals* distinguishes between visions in which the soul is enlightened through the intervention of Angels, and those in which man is drawn above himself and above the spirit into an incomprehensible richness that God alone can achieve in man. This passage, which is so helpful to us for the understanding of Hadewijch, is of exceptional authority on account of Ruusbroec's perfect familiarity with her writings.[76] Vekeman also calls attention to significant passages in William of Saint Thierry, Bernard of Clairvaux, and Richard of Saint Victor on the function of the Angel in visions.[77]

Vision 1 deserves the reader's serious study, for, as Spaapen points out, "it offers the most enlightening (even if far from exhaustive) synthesis of Hadewijch's doctrine that she herself has given."[78] It falls into two parts; in the first, an Angel guides Hadewijch past seven trees that symbolize virtues; in the second part, the Angel leaves her, and in ecstasy she sees Christ, who speaks to her at considerable length; he especially commands her to live his Humanity, practicing the virtues and accepting all sufferings as he himself did in his life on earth, in order to come to live his Divinity. The two parts of the vision are explained as the life of the virtues and the life of love, or the ascetical life and the mystical life. This progress from one life to the other will be repeated later, for instance in Visions 6, 12, and 14.

Hadewijch's basic conception of life as dynamic is apparent throughout. At the beginning of the vision she is "still too childish and too little grown-up" (P. 1); but at the first appearance of the Angel, she says: "This same day, having grown up, I had come close to him, so that I had received him . . . to be my guardian" (P. 24). On leaving her, the Angel says: "I received in your regard the order to be at your service every hour, until the moment when you have outgrown me in the ways in which I have led you" (P. 199). This guardian Angel belongs to the order of Thrones, one of the three highest orders of Angels. In Vision 13, when Hadewijch has advanced in perfection, she will be given another guardian, a Seraph, belonging to the highest order of all.

It must not be passed over that Vision 1 raises a problem for the interpretation of Hadewijch. The problem arises from the complimentary speeches addressed to her by the Angel, who several times asserts that she has already attained to the heights of virtue. The reader, instinctively judging that if Hadewijch were indeed humble she would never have written down these words for the perusal of her young Beguines, may be disconcerted.

To explain this objection we might begin by distinguishing the two parts of Vision 1. The compliments are paid to Hadewijch in the first part, by the Angel. But in the second part, she hears herself reproached by Christ himself on three counts. First, she has asked him to recognize her sufferings and virtues, forgetting that he, during his life on earth, bore great sufferings and persevered in work and great love (P. 307). Second, she has said to him sometimes that it was easy for him to live as Man because he possessed the seven gifts, and his Father was with him; in saying this, she did not know that he chose to obtain the gifts at the price of suffering (P. 325). Third, she has complained of her misery and of the fact that she did not receive from him what she needed as she desired; yet at all times she possessed the seven gifts, and his Father was with her (P. 341). Now it is easy to see that Hadewijch, to save face—especially with those whom she was directing—might have concealed these reproaches by changing them into impersonal statements of principle. That she chose rather to reveal them argues in favor of her genuine humility.

Yet another explanation is possible; perhaps these extreme praises served to forwarn Hadewijch that Christ was about to single her out. He did so by a triple command. For his sake, she must be prepared for every kind of affliction (P. 281). To be like him in his Humanity, she must desire to be poor, miserable, and despised by all men (P. 288). And, finally, on earth his life in her must be so fully lived in all virtues that she may in no point fail him in himself (P. 341). Obviously Hadewijch must decide yes or no, and the Angel's words may have helped to strengthen her for this moment.

In Vision 4 we notice that Hadewijch follows the order of Ptolemaic astronomy when she speaks successively of the moon, the sun, and the stars, whereas the biblical order always places the sun first, for instance in Apocalypse 8:12, a text in some respects parallel to this vision: *The fourth angel sounded the trumpet: and the third part of the sun was smitten, and the third part of the moon, and the third part of the stars.*

The theme of the Eucharist appears several times in the visions. Visions 1, 3, and 6 all took place after she had received Communion (this is what she means when she speaks of "going to God"). Vision 1 and Vision 7 both begin with a description of the stormy longing (*orewoet*) with which she approached the Eucharist. The extreme vehemence of these two passages is clarified in Letter 22 (P. 285):

> The Son . . . imparted Christian fruitfulness to us who are called after his name, and who are fed with his name and with his Body, yes, and who partake of him and consume him as eagerly, and fruitfully, and deliciously as we ourselves wish. But in this there is greater disproportion than between the point of a needle and the whole world with the sea thrown in. One could taste and feel incomparably more fruitfulness from God—as he would rightly experience from him—if he sought him with desirous, loving confidence.

Vision 7 goes on to relate how Christ himself communicated her under both Species.

Visions 7 and 8 are actually two parts of the same vision, or at least they took place in immediate succession, as is evident from the last line of Vision 7. That there is a profound connection between them is shown by P. Mommaers, who points out that the Champion of Vision 8 is wanting in the spirituality of love for Christ (which is that of Hadewijch), and this according to his own statement prevents him from attaining the fifth way.[79]

Visions 10, 11, and 12 are strongly marked by images found in the Apocalypse; references to it of course appear in the earlier visions, but are less preponderant. The whole of Vision 10 follows from the verse: *And I, John, saw the holy city, the new Jerusalem, coming down out of heaven from God, prepared as a bride adorned for her husband* (Apoc. 21:2). This short vision seems to be more or less prophetic, revealing the ultimate reward of the soul that has been able to live Christ "as God and Man" (P. 54) in the highest possible degree.

INTRODUCTION

Vision 12, like Vision 10, is centered on the heavenly bride, whose glory in the life to come is prophetically described. Since this vision took place at Mass on Epiphany (January 6), the opening allusion to "the city" may have some relation to the fact that both the Epistle—or, as we now say, the Reading—(Isa. 60:1–6) and the Gospel (Matt. 2:1–13) for that feast mention Jerusalem.

Strongly reminiscent of the Apocalypse, the vision can be summed up in two verses from that book:

> *The marriage of the Lamb has come, and his spouse has prepared herself. And she has been permitted to clothe herself in fine linen, shining, bright, for the fine linen is the just deeds of the saints.* (Apoc. 19:7–8)

The bride is accompanied by twelve bridesmaids (twelve virtues) who give testimony to her perfection. She is

> clad in a robe made of her undivided and perfect will, always devoid of sorrow, and prepared with all virtue, and fitted out with everything that pertains thereto. And that robe was adorned with all the virtues, and each virtue had its symbol on the robe and its name written, that it might be known. (P. 58)

Then she saw herself, as veritable bride of the great Bridegroom, received in union by him, and she became one with him in the certainty of unity.

Vision 13 shows a marked structural resemblance to Vision 1. Both visions are made up of two parts. In both, the first part falls into seven sections, during which Hadewijch enjoys the help of a specially appointed angelic guide. Again, in both, Hadewijch finds herself in the second part in the presence of Christ in Vision 1, and in the presence of Mary in Vision 13. In both, Christ, or Mary, speaks to Hadewijch at some length; and in both it is evident that the wonder and mystery of the meeting call for complete reverence, and that Hadewijch can only listen without uttering a word. A striking feature of Vision 13 is the effect of constant music in the background. Hadewijch's often-repeated allusions to songs of praise, the cry and songs of the Seraphim, the songs of the spirits in the amplitude of the Countenance, and so on, all serve to create a pattern of extraordinary beauty. Her description of Love as a queen enthroned follows all the canons of twelfth-century rhetoric; she begins with Love's head and ends with her feet. In surprising contrast, Hadewijch gives us no description of Mary, stating only that all in the small company of persons among whom Mary was the twenty-ninth—that is to say, the highest—were adorned like Love as to all their attire and ornaments; and she had said previously that Love was richly arrayed, and wore on her head a crown adorned with the works of humility.

When at the end of the first part of Vision 13 (P. 195 and 198) Hadewijch alludes to Mary as the twenty-ninth in heaven, she adds that these twenty-nine saints are the full-grown perfect, and that when their number is complete, they will not be more than 107. (She goes on to give the number of other groups of saints who will be in heaven, whose perfection is great but less than that of the full-grown perfect.) That Mary should be assigned the number twenty-nine is not surprising. Traditionally the number of the lunar cycle, twenty-eight, was associated with Mary because as the moon reflects the sun's light, she reflects on men the grace streaming from God; and she is regarded as the one *beautiful as the moon* (Song 6:9).[80] To add to twenty-eight the perfect number, one, is to follow a commonplace procedure of numerology. But the other numbers Hadewijch lists here have not as yet been explained.

When Hadewijch says she knows the number of the full-grown perfect, of whom twenty-nine are in heaven and eighty-three on earth, and then concludes with these words: "Five will yet be born, and outside of these no one among all beings on earth will be full-grown," one might suppose that she meant to imply the end of the world was near at hand. But in the "List" no Joachim appears, so that there seems to be no Joachimite influence.[81] Moreover, in her four works she often speaks of time, but never alludes either directly or indirectly to its impending end. This suggests that she did not mean the number 107, on which the other numbers depend, to be taken literally.

Particularly where souls in heaven are in question, the use of a symbolic number should not surprise us. It can hardly be doubted that Hadewijch was familiar with the well-known passage of Augustine's *Expositions on the Book of Psalms* where he speaks in greater detail than in his commentary on John 21:11 of the miraculous catch of 153 fishes as symbolizing the souls of all the saved:

> You will find that the vast number of all the saints belongs to the number of a few fishes. Just as in the five virgins there are countless virgins, as in the five brethren of the man who was tormented in hell there are thousands of the people of the Jews, and as in the number of one hundred and fifty-three fishes there are thousands and thousands of saints, so on the twelve thrones there are not twelve men, but great is the number of the saints.[82]

On what basis Hadewijch could present 107 as a symbolic number, however, is a puzzle hard to solve. It is not a traditionally symbolic number like 5 and 12, or a factorial number like 153 (which is the sum of 17 plus all the numbers preceding 17). It would appear probable that the only place where we can be certain Hadewijch encountered it is in the book of Psalms. Psalm 107 may have appealed to her because it has fourteen verses (the number of David and of Christ's genealogy, as we have already said).

Because Hadewijch considered Augustine to be one of the twenty-nine already in heaven, and also because of her affinity for him, the thought suggests itself of turning to his *Expositions on the Book of Psalms* to learn what she might have read in that work about Psalm 107. We are rewarded by the discovery that among the themes Augustine's commentary builds out of the sacred text there are no less than seven that coincide with those of Hadewijch's own spirituality. They are as follows:

1. (Ps. 107:2) *My heart is ready, O God, my heart is ready: I will sing and rehearse a psalm.*[83] Augustine takes readiness here as the acceptance of the will of God (Hadewijch's general theme of doing the will of God, the will of Love).

2. As an illustration of being prepared in heart to accept the will of God, Augustine proposes Saint Paul, "because he has imitated his Lord." Paul, like Augustine, is one of Hadewijch's twenty-nine,[84] and here Augustine singles out Paul as living the Humanity of Christ.

3. The words *I will sing and rehearse a psalm,* Augustine takes to mean, "I will glory in tribulations," and he quotes Paul's words: *We glory also in tribulations . . . because the charity of God is poured forth in*

our hearts, by the Holy Spirit who is given to us (Rom. 5:3–5). Here we meet Hadewijch's principal theme, that of love. She does not quote this particular text, but she expresses the Holy Spirit's gift of love in a rather similar way. She thinks of love as a "flood," and when she speaks of the Holy Spirit as "an effusion," or as "flowing,"[85] she is saying equivalently that he pours forth love in our hearts.

4. (Ps. 107:5). This verse reads: *For thy mercy is great above the heavens, and thy truth even unto the clouds.*[86] Augustine explains these words as follows:

> The heavens are above the clouds, and the clouds below the heavens; and indeed the clouds belong to this nearest heaven; but sometimes the clouds fall back and are massed together even reaching the nearest air. There is, however, a heaven on high, which is the dwelling-place of the Angels, the Thrones, the Dominations, the Principalities, and the Powers. For in heaven the Angels praise God.

This passage can be seen in relation to certain of Hadewijch's visions where she speaks of various heavens, and especially with Vision 5: P. 1, where she gives a somewhat similar enumeration of angelic choirs in connection with the highest heavens.

5. (Ps. 107:8). *God has spoken in his holiness.*[87] Augustine comments: "Why are you afraid that what God says will not happen?" A man, he continues, may promise something and then be unable to carry it out. "But you need have no such fears with regard to God; for it is certain that he is truthful; it is certain that he is omnipotent. He cannot fail you; he has the power to do it." In two instances Hadewijch expresses a similar confidence. In Stanzaic Poem 42:14–16 she writes:

> You said—it is true, it shall happen,
> There is no doubt of it:
> If you were *lifted up*, you would *draw all things to yourself.*

And in Poem 14:150–153:

> For he has said in Scripture,
> So that he cannot fail in it:
> *He shall measure to us with the same measure*
> *With which we measure to him.*

6. (Ps. 107:8) *I will divide Sichem.* Augustine interprets the name *Sichem* as meaning "shoulders." His etymology is correct: The explanation of it, which he fails to supply, is that the city of Sichem is located in the narrow valley between the shoulders of Mount Garizim and Mount Ebal. Augustine proceeds:

> How does he divide the shoulders according to the interpretation we have given of the word? The shoulders are divided in order that some men may be weighted down by their sins, and others may take on Christ's burden. For he was looking for devout shoulders when he said: *For my yoke is sweet, and my burden is light.* (Matt. 11:30)

Hadewijch often speaks in the figurative and spiritual sense of carrying burdens, and in Stanzaic Poem 12:11–14, where she takes up this theme at some length, she quotes the same text:

> *My yoke is sweet, my burden light,*
> Says the Lover of Love himself.
> This word he had beautifully expressed in Love;
> Outside of Love one cannot experience its truth.

7. Augustine goes on to say:

> Such is Christ's burden. Let men carry it; let them not be lazy. Let no attention be paid to those who refuse to carry it. Let those who are willing, carry it; and they will find out how light, sweet, and enjoyable it is, and how by it they are rapt into heaven and snatched away from earth.

In the two Stanzaic Poems 11 and 12, Hadewijch draws a contrast between those who carry Christ's burden and those who refuse.

To sum up, it does indeed seem remarkable that as many as seven points of resemblance should be discernible between the themes drawn from Psalm 107 by Augustine in the *Exposition on the Book of Psalms* and Hadewijch's themes, especially when we consider that his commentary covers only about nine pages in the *Corpus Christianorum Series Latina*.

POEMS IN COUPLETS

The volume of *Poems in Couplets* comprises twenty-nine poems of which only the first sixteen are the work of Hadewijch. The remaining poems, however, bear so much resemblance to her work that their author is always referred to as "Hadewijch II" or "Pseudo-Hadewijch." Ruusbroec quotes both our Hadewijch and Hadewijch II. The poems of the two authors, however, are distinguishable by both vocabulary and content, for Hadewijch II is much closer to the speculative mysticism that made its appearance in the years immediately following the life span of our Hadewijch. We shall speak here only of the poems of Hadewijch I.

The *Poems in Couplets* receives this title because (with the exception of Poem 15) these poems are composed not in stanzas but in rhyming couplets. They have sometimes been named Rhymed Letters, for twelve of the sixteen are in epistolary form, and the collection, like that of prose letters, also contains treatises. A more critical survey, however, would count the purely personal rhymed letters as six (4–7, 9, and 11), and the treatises as eight (1–3, 10, 12–14, and 16), of which four (1, 2, 12, and 14) show certain characteristics of the personal letter.[88]

The *Poems in Couplets* differ completely in character from the *Poems in Stanzas.* While the former do not attain the poetic heights of the latter, they are fascinating and not devoid of aesthetic fire (the only exception being Poem 10, which, although remarkable in content, obviously lacks the balance and flawless execution of great poetry and would appear to be not a finished work but a preliminary draft). These poems show another side of Hadewijch's poetic genius, as it pours itself out in fluent improvisation. While the *Poems in Stanzas* excel in pure lyric expression, the *Poems in Couplets* impress the reader by their terse aphoristic style, which offers a wealth of memorable lines.[89]

Like the other three works, the *Poems in Couplets* are undoubtedly meant for Hadewijch's young Beguines. The only exception is the first rhymed letter, written to a person Hadewijch addresses as *Joncffer* (Maiden), who desires a reply to certain questions (line 107). The respect Hadewijch shows toward her indicates that she is a person of importance. Since "Maiden" would not be a fit title for the superior of a monastery, it seems probable that she is a Beguine Mistress.[90] Adhering consistently to the letter form, this poem is nevertheless clearly a treatise on the nature of love, intended for one who is no longer a beginner. Hadewijch enumerates, for the advanced soul, certain phases of the service of Love "according to Love's deserts," and explains how this soul should correspond to Love's action in victory, nonvictory, hope, paradoxical despair, and longing.

Because of the allusions in the other works to Hadewijch's trouble with her young Beguines, we naturally scan the poems that follow for any fresh traces they may offer. It seems certain that Poem 5, as well as Poem 6 (which really consists of two separate rhymed letters), bears on the difficulties known to us from the other works; clearly belonging to the period after Hadewijch herself was dismissed, they give fresh evidence that she was able, at least for a time, to communicate with those from whom she was separated.

In Poem 2, again a treatise that seems to have been written for one of her young Beguines in particular, Hadewijch's source is a legend (older than Christianity) of a battle of wits between three royal bodyguards of King Darius. She transforms this battle of wits into the *disputatio* practiced in the contemporary medieval schools,[91] and transforms the three bodyguards into four "masters" (equivalent to our "professors"). In the original legend, after the first two bodyguards have discussed their respective subjects, the third discusses two subjects. Hadewijch gives to each of her masters one of the four original subjects, which she spiritualizes with zest and skill. Her handling of the third subject—that the most powerful of all things is woman—would seem to be one of the most astonishing passages she ever wrote. According to the legend in 3 Esdras, Apamea, the concubine of King Darius, is named as an example of the power of woman, because on one occasion when she sat at the king's right hand, she snatched the diadem from his head and placed it on her own head, while Darius merely smiled in toleration of her audacity. Hadewijch, as she sets forth the argument for the power of woman, unhesitatingly substitutes for the concubine Apamea and her pride, the Virgin Mary and her humility (Poem 2:47–69).

The theme of Mary appears also in Poem 3, where she is referred to under the title of Mother of Love. Poem 14 is a development of the theme that the devout soul must become the mother of Christ. This theme is much older than Hadewijch, being found in Origen, Augustine, Bede,[92] and Guerric of Igny. Guerric's longest passage on the subject perhaps contributed to Poem 14.[93] In her Christmas vision, while David, Christ's ancestor, plays on his harp, Hadewijch sees "an

Infant being born in the souls who love in secret" (Vision 11: P. 1). But lest anyone should suppose that to be the mother of Christ means only sweet music, in Vision 13: P. 15 Hadewijch quotes her Seraph as crying out with a loud voice:

> "The new secret heaven . . . is closed to all those who never were Christ's mother with perfect motherhood, who never wandered with him in Egypt and on all the ways, who never presented him where the sword of prophecy pierced their soul, who never reared that Child to manhood and who, at the end, were not at his grave: for them it shall remain eternally hidden."

In Poem 14 she puts the final touches to the theme of humility, whose many aspects she has already shown us. The allusion to "a humble heart" (line 27) of course suggests Christ's humility, of which she speaks so eloquently in Letter 30: P. 84. In Poem 14:35–44 she particularly urges us to sink low in humility; for humility "brought God down into Mary" and, if we imitate her, we shall also receive him. Hadewijch presents Mary's humility to our gaze as if it were a sort of jewel she wishes us to contemplate from every angle. She displays its different facets in Poem 2, Stanzaic Poem 29, and Letter 12: P. 3. Probably the reader will longest remember the passage of haunting beauty where in Vision 13: P. 218 Mary herself speaks of the three kinds of humility, which more or less echo the three kinds of humility in Vision 1: P. 42.

With regard to Hadewijch's personal humility, we observe that on some occasions, wishing to avoid pretentiousness or perhaps a compliment, she voices a humble disclaimer of her own ability. Humility formulas were of course a common literary convention. Probably out of deference to the Joncffer, Hadewijch resorts to them four times in Poem 1.[94]

A number of Hadewijch's major themes are given prominence in Poem 16. She speaks of Christ "who is Love itself," and it can hardly be by accident that she does so in line 33, thirty-three being one of the numbers sacred to him. Singing the praises of the Eucharist she says that in it the soul can know and taste beyond its dreams the Godhead and the Manhood; and later in the poem she returns twice to the theme of the Godhead and the Manhood (lines 55–58). The Trinity theme makes its entry when (lines 123–124) she sees the soul drawn into

> That same kiss which beautifully unites
> The Three Persons in one sole Being,

an experience known to William of Saint Thierry.[95] And at the end of the poem she sees God and the soul, together, first in the Trinity of the persons (lived by the soul in its conformity to them), and then in the Unity of the Divine Essence (lines 191–193):[96] the soul is living by the rhythm of the Holy Trinity. Poem 16 forms a beautiful close not only to the *Poems in Couplets* but to the whole series of her works.

HADEWIJCH OUR GUIDE IN SPIRITUALITY

To Hadewijch's gift of lyric genius, we owe her two volumes of poems, which we can read with endless delight in their technical perfection and depth of thought. But greater than her literary endowment is the gift of spirituality that enabled her to enter the mysterious realm of visionary experience where, penetrating more deeply into the truths of faith, she learned the hidden ways by which God is attained.

This second gift was granted not merely for her own sake. She had a mission to fulfill: Probably its clearest statement occurs in the words she heard from Christ in Vision 8: P. 98: "Lead all the unled!"

This mission had in view primarily her young Beguines. Hadewijch bestowed her love and teaching on them, as a group and individually, for a number of years—but they failed to respond. In the end they were influenced against her, and she herself was dismissed from her community and forsaken by all, as we have already said. Had her mission failed?

In the next century came an unforeseen flowering of her influence. John of Ruusbroec obtained a manuscript of her works and, perceiving their wealth of meaning, transformed it into the substance of his writings. These masterpieces are his own; yet Hadewijch's voice can be heard speaking in them. Was this the final word of her mission?

Six hundred years passed, and then a little before the middle of the nineteenth century three researchers in the Royal Library of Brussels rediscovered, among its manuscripts, Hadewijch's writings and judged them deserving of publication for their philological importance. Slowly, by the efforts of these and other scholars, especially Van Mierlo, all her works were printed, edited, reprinted, and then progressively studied.

M. Brauns has said that it is to the credit of our age that we have rediscovered Hadewijch.[97] Shall we look once more at the formulation of her mission—"Lead the unled!"— Is the rediscovery of Hadewijch in reality not so much to our credit as for our rescue? Is her mission for us?

Look back to the day when Hadewijch was so overwhelmed with tumultuous longing for the infinite joy of possessing God in heaven that she fled to the seclusion of her room. There the priest, no doubt in response to an appeal from her, brought her Holy Communion. Suddenly she found herself no longer in her familiar surroundings but in a new land where spiritual sights and sounds manifested themselves to her (Vision 1: P. 1 and 15). All that she learned from those sights and sounds and from her own experience in responding to them is what constitutes her message.

The young Beguines thought they did not need Hadewijch's message. In fact they were totally unaware that they needed anything. We of today do know that we are in desperate need of spirituality, oppressed as we are on all sides by the reign of insecurity, materialism, godlessness, and sensuality. So we may be better disposed to hear.

Any strangeness we feel at first in meeting a woman of the thirteenth century will quickly wear off as we discover her real modernity. She has no distinctively medieval notions, no distinctively medieval crudity or childish naiveté.[98] She is entirely free from superstition; diabolism and melodramatic apparitions of the defunct, as found for instance in the *Dialogue of miracles* by Caesarius of Heisterbach (composed c. 1219–23), or in the "life" of Ida of Nivelles by Gosuin of Bossut (composed c. 1232),[99] are completely absent from her writings. Instead we find a wholly modern subtlety of feeling and psychological acumen. And her literary ability Van Mierlo sums up in a happy phrase: "Universally human, her art is for all times."[100]

Since Hadewijch's original mission was directed specifically to her young Beguines, it would seem to follow that, in her mission to us of the twentieth-century world, modern women with their anxious search for self-fulfillment are specially included. Her great aim had been to teach her young Beguines how to grow in love. Everything we know about these members of her circle indicates that they were insufficiently anxious to free themselves from the oppression of their culture and therefore could not move to her awareness. But perhaps, after all, her awareness was not really given her for them, but was prophetical; perhaps it is our age that can move into it. In other words, Hadewijch's teaching may enable contemporary women to escape from their cultural oppression and may provide them with hope that they can grow in love. If women of today were to grow in love, no one could estimate the happy effects that would follow in married life, in home life, in social life, in professional life.

We do not mean to say, however, that Hadewijch can lead only women. Her mystical doctrine, wholly Trinitarian and Christological, is not in itself appropriate to women rather than to men. In her numerous allusions to John the Evangelist and Augustine, the two men saints for whom she felt a pronounced sympathy, we see her recognition of the singular call of God to each of them, and of their response in faith and love. In Vision 8: P. 109 and 112, we observe her friendly attitude toward the Champion, when she shows her admiration for his knowledge of the four ways, and inquires with kindness how it is that he does not know the fifth way—eliciting his humble admission of his own failing. About her dealings with her male contemporaries in everyday life, our knowledge is limited. We do know from the "List" that Henry of Breda executed a commission abroad because she asked him to.[101] Our fullest source of information, however, is Letter 12. From Hadewijch's statement, at the beginning of the letter, that she was writing in answer to a request, it appears that she and Provost Gilbertus had already discussed together the true meaning of loving and serving God. As the letter develops, we see her recognition of Gilbertus's authority and good influence as superior; and we notice that, as with the Champion, she shows her admiration for his accomplishments. In asking his assistance for herself and her young Beguines, she approaches him on the rational level, which she obviously considers to be their area of common understanding. She finally concludes not with any subjective arguments but with illustrations based on Scripture.

From Vision 1: P. 288 and 341 stems her central teaching that we must "live Christ." She explains that in order to live Christ in his Divinity we must begin by living him in his Humanity, and that this means to live the life of the virtues. But as she herself learned from the reproaches she heard addressed to her by Christ in this same vision, we must above all live the life of the virtues *because* Christ chose to do so in his life on earth. This proviso, which Hadewijch's young Beguines disregarded, is the secret that can transform our life by shifting its center from ourself to God.

But besides this, Hadewijch continues, we must live the Trinity. This injunction of hers is of incalculable importance. Christian spirituality is not incidentally but essentially Trinitarian. The Christian must be one with Christ in sonship of the Father and in the Holy Spirit. In our time there is an admitted uncertainty as to how this theory can be brought to bear on our lives. But Hadewijch is able to tell us how, for instance in Letter 1: P. 46: We live the life of the Father when we allow his irresistible power to work in us; we live the life of the Holy Spirit when we allow his holy will to be done in us; and we live the life of the Son when we allow ourselves to be enlightened by his radiance and truth. The more we familiarize ourselves with her thought, the more fully we shall understand instructions such as this that she offers us.

From her teaching that we must live Christ in his Humanity, and consequently accept the state of human misery and suffering in which we have to practice the virtues, there follows her inveterate optimism about the final outcome of our struggles. Although she has been styled "the sublime poetess of complaints"[102] because of her many expressions—especially in her lyrics—of woe at being deserted by Divine Love, in reality she is telling us something quite different. She never relinquishes her conviction that if Christ as Man freely willed to live in human misery and sufferings, we likewise must accept human misery and sufferings *because* he did so. She well knows that the pain, grief, suffering, affliction, blows, even cruelty of which she complains are God's gifts to her, by which she participates in the sufferings of Christ's Humanity, and through which Love is being communicated to love. She invariably ends on the note of submission and acceptance in love.

After the Trinity, Hadewijch places Mary; she honors her, as we have already said, for her causal role in the Incarnation. We have seen how by her carefully designed ordering of her volume *Poems in Stan-*

zas she makes Mary its center. Visions 11 and 12 show us the Eagle—the Apostle John, mystical friend of Christ and Mary, and Evangelist of the Trinity. In Vision 13 the first mention of Mary is quite casual (P. 159); it is clearly taken for granted that she belongs to the heaven of the Seraphim, where she is united to the Trinity. It is notable that when Mary herself speaks, her phrases several times fall into the pattern of groups of three, the mode of expression implying Trinitarian reference (P. 218). This vision shows us how through Mary we can enter into Hadewijch's teaching that we must "live the Trinity."

So consistently does Hadewijch's entire presentation of Mary accord with the verification of theology and spirituality in *Lumen Gentium*[103] that it seems like a prophecy of this return to Mary, so strongly confirmed in Pope John Paul II's Encyclical *Redemptor Hominis,* 22, "in this difficult and responsible phase of the history of the Church."[104]

An area in which Hadewijch particularly reaches out to us is that of community, contrasted with present-day isolationism. Experiencing God in her life, she participated in a community of love from which she drew an understanding of her relationships in this world and saw her young Beguines as a group sharing in the riches of contemplation. Accordingly she taught them that in all contacts with others they must be guided by reason enlightened by divine Truth; they must live the life of true virtues as Christ did, constantly serving others in love; and in every circumstance they must approve or condemn, not to suit their own likes and dislikes but in union with Christ.

Hadewijch can, therefore, impart to us the secrets of true spirituality if we once accept her guidance. She understands the mystery of divine Love and Love's "modes of action," and she is able to convey this understanding to us insofar as we read her aright.

In order to read her aright, we must be aware of her explanatory procedures. On the negative side, she does not merely tell us our mistakes in our endeavor (or lack of it) to be spiritual, but she enables us to understand *why* they are mistakes. Often our aims are human or self-centered. For example, she says:

> We wish to be exalted for our patience and honored for our good deeds, and we forget the debt of Love too soon. We esteem our works to be good, and for this reason they are

> vain. . . . We exercise our charity according to need, and this is why we do not possess charity's wide power. Our humility is . . . on our face, and in appearances—and not fully motivated by God's greatness or by our perception of our littleness. (Letter 30: P. 179)

On the positive side, she does not merely catalog actions for our execution but explains *why* they establish us in spirituality. She remarks that souls of firmly established virtues

> are not awaiting sweetness but a way of ever serving Love with fidelity. They do not desire taste but seek profit; they think of what their hands are doing, not of the reward. They entrust all to Love, and are the better for it. . . . They seek only Love's will, and the only sweetness they implore of Love is that she may grant them to know in all things her dearest will. (Letter 10: P. 26)

This of course is an aspect of her principle that we must live the life of virtue because Christ chose to do so. It is not a matter of seeking perfection in virtue for its own sake; we seek it in a faith-relationship to Christ and, in Christ, to the Father.

Hadewijch can also tell us *how* to escape from a superficial life and advance toward a deep spirituality. Stanzaic Poem 9 may serve as an example of this procedure. Her instruction here, which she presents under cover of metaphors to make it more accessible, may be paraphrased something like this: The ignoble person clings to his self-centered independence; he will not even take the first step toward love of God, much less surrender himself to God. By accepting suffering this soul could reach the Beloved, but in its laziness it prefers to dress itself in the ragged garments of selfishness. We ought rather to take the trouble to put on the garments of acts of virtue performed for God's sake. The suffering this costs us will make our actions magnificent and pleasing to God. By perseverance in this suffering, we can attain such deep love of God that we will rejoice at being conquered by love and will enter into the mystery of God's love manifested in the Incarnation. Success in this undertaking will, however, be compromised by false confidence. We must beware of our shallowness and inconstancy; and above all, we must convince ourselves that the heights of spirituality will never be gained speedily, or without a full response on our part to the ever new demands of God's love.

NOTE ON THE TRANSLATION

For the translation, the Hadewijch texts edited by Van Mierlo (see Bibliography) have been utilized. As far as possible her own words are given without paraphrase, for instance the word *God* is retained in the many instances where she means "Christ."

SUBTITLES. Hadewijch's works include thirty-one *Letters*, forty-five *Poems in Stanzas*, fourteen *Visions*, and sixteen *Poems in Couplets*. She herself did not give subtitles to any of these numerous pieces. Van Mierlo, however, did propose subtitles for all those he included in his Hadewijch *Anthology* (1950). The same procedure was adopted by F. Van Bladel and B. Spaapen in their modern Flemish translation of the *Letters* (1954), and by J.-B. Porion in his French translation of the *Letters* (1972). In the present translation, conforming to the plan of these writers, we have given subtitles to all the pieces.

REFERENCES FOR THE PROSE WORKS. In the *Letters* and *Visions*, in order to facilitate cross reference to Van Mierlo's texts, we have numbered the paragraphs of the translation throughout. These paragraph numbers correspond to Van Mierlo's line numbers. This system should enable the reader to verify any particular passage in the original without loss of time. In citing references, the word "paragraph" has been abbreviated to "P."

REFERENCES FOR THE POEMS. The translation is printed in lines as far as possible identical with Hadewijch's. When citing or quoting individual poems in the Introduction and Notes, we refer to any poem from the *Poems in Stanzas* as "Stanzaic Poem," with its number, and to any poem from the *Poems in Couplets* as simply "Poem," with its number. In the Introduction, to avoid extra footnotes, we have given the line numbers immediately after the Poem number, except where a series of line numbers is required.

GENDER OF MINNE. Since the word *Minne* is of the feminine gender, we have used the feminine gender for pronouns referring to *Minne*. Despite the sometimes clumsy effect, this procedure has the advantage of keeping the reader close to Hadewijch's wording of the entire passage.

SCRIPTURE. Hadewijch quotes the Vulgate; we have therefore

followed the Vulgate text, either according to the Douay version or with our own literal translation; in references we have also retained the Psalm numbers of the Vulgate. Quotations, when literal, are italicized. For the *Letters* and the *Visions,* Scripture references are inserted in parentheses; for both *Poems in Stanzas* and *Poems in Couplets,* they are given in footnotes, to avoid interrupting the lines of poetry.

LATIN. Where Hadewijch uses Latin words, these are left standing, with her own spelling, and a translation (unless it seems superfluous) is given in the notes. For the name *Ihesus* or *Christus*, however, English is used for simplification.

LETTERS

LETTERS

LETTERS

LETTER 1

IN GOD'S RADIANCE

1. Since God has manifested by his virtues that radiant love which was uncomprehended, whereby he illuminated all the virtues in the radiance[1] of his love, may he illuminate you and enlighten you by the pure radiance with which he shines resplendent for himself and for all his friends and those he most dearly loves!

8. The greatest radiance anyone can have on earth is truth in works of justice performed in imitation of the Son,[2] and to practice the truth with regard to all that exists, for the glory of the noble *love that God is* (1 John 4:16). Oh, what great radiance it is that we may let God act with his radiance! For in it Love works—for himself and for all creatures, each one according to its rights—whatever his goodness may promise to give it, in justice (Luke 1:73) and radiance.[3]

18. This is why I entreat you, as a friend his dear friend; and I exhort you, as a sister her dear sister; and I charge you, as a mother her dear child; and I command you in the name of your Lover,[4] as the bridegroom commands his dear bride: that you open the eyes of your heart (Cf. Eph. 1:18) to see clearly and contemplate yourself in God as holiness demands.

25. Learn to contemplate what God is:[5] how he is Truth (John 14:6), present to all things; and Goodness, overflowing with all wealth; and Totality, replete with all virtues.[6] It is for these three names that the *Sanctus* is sung three times in heaven (Isa. 6:3), for they comprehend in their one essence all the virtues, whatever may be their particular works from their three distinct attributes.

33. See how God has protected you with fatherliness, and what he has given you, and what he has promised you. Behold how sublime is the love of the Three Persons for one another, and show your gratitude to God through love.[7] Do this, if you wish to contemplate what God is and to work in him, in his radiance, with fruition in glory and manifestation in radiance, in order to enlighten all things or to leave them in darkness, according to what they are.[8]

41. It is because of what God is that it is right to leave him fruition of himself in all the works of his radiance, *sicut in caelo et in terra,*

and never stop saying, both in actions and in words: *fiat voluntas tua* (Matt. 6:10)!

46. O dear child, in proportion as his irresistible power is made more clear in you, as his holy will is better perfected in you, and as his radiant truth more fully appears in you, consent to be deprived of sweet repose for the sake of this great totality of God! Illuminate your mind and adorn yourself with virtues and just works; enlarge your spirit by lofty desires toward God's totality; and dispose your soul for the great fruition of omnipotent Love in the excessive sweetness of our God!

56. Alas, dear child! although I speak of excessive sweetness, it is in truth a thing I know nothing of, except in the wish of my heart—that suffering has become sweet to me for the sake of his love. But he has been more cruel to me than any devil ever was.[9] For devils could not stop me from loving God or loving anyone he charged me to help forward; but this he himself has snatched from me. What he is, he lives by, in his sweet self-enjoyment, and lets me thus wander far from this fruition, beneath the constant weight of nonfruition of Love, and in the darkness where I am destitute of all the joys of fruition that should have been my part.

69. Oh, how I am impoverished! Even what he had offered and given me as a pledge of the fruition of veritable love, he has now withdrawn—as, in part, you well know. Alas! God is my witness that I earnestly acknowledged him as my Lord and asked of him little more than he wished to give me. But what he offered I would gladly have accepted in fruition, if he had willed to raise me to it. At first this grieved me, and I let many things be offered to me before I would receive them. But now my lot is like his to whom something is offered in jest, and when he wishes to take it his hand is slapped, and he is told: "God's wrath on him who fancied it true!" And what he supposed he held is snatched from him.

LETTER 2

SERVE NOBLY

1. Consider now all the things you have failed in, either by self-will or by unnecessary sadness.

3. It is true, as I well know: A person often grows sad when

he is without his Beloved and cannot tell whether he is approaching him or withdrawing from him; and this is sincere. But anyone who is truly faithful will know that the goodness of his Beloved is greater than his own failures. One must not be sorrowful because of suffering or sigh after repose, but give all for all and entirely renounce repose. Rejoice continually in the hope of winning love; for if you desire perfect love for God, you must not desire in return any repose whatever except Love.

14. Be on your guard, therefore, and let nothing disturb your peace. Do good under all circumstances, but with no care for any profit, or any blessedness, or any damnation, or any salvation, or any martyrdom; but all you do or omit should be for the honor of Love. If you behave like this, you will soon rise up again. And let people take you for a fool; there is much truth in that. Be docile and prompt toward all who have need of you, and satisfy everyone as far as you can manage it without debasing yourself. Be joyful with those who rejoice, and weep with those who weep (Rom. 12:13). Be good toward those who have need of you, devoted toward the sick, generous with the poor, and recollected in spirit beyond the reach of all creatures.

29. And even if you do the best you can in all things, your human nature must often fall short; so entrust yourself to God's goodness, for his goodness is greater than your failures. And always practice true virtues, with confidence, and be diligent and constant in always following unconditionally our Lord's guiding and his dearest will wherever you can discern it, taking trouble and doing your utmost to examine your thoughts strictly, in order to know yourself in all things.[10]

39. And live for God in such a way, this I implore you, that you be not wanting in the great works to which he has called you. Never neglect them for any less important work, this I implore and counsel you. For you have great motives impelling you to take trouble in God's service. He has protected you from all trouble, if you yourself will but take heed; so that your way is smoothed by grace,[11] if you will but recognize it. And all things considered, you have suffered too little to grow up,[12] as in justice you owed it to God to do—although, now and then, you willingly comply in this.

51. Although, too, you sometimes feel such affliction in your heart that it seems to you you are forsaken by God, do not be discouraged by it. For verily I say to you: Whatever misery we endure with good will and for God is pleasing to God in every respect. But if we

knew how dear this is to God, it would be premature for us, for then we should have no misery. For if a man knew God's will—that misery is dear to him—he would gladly be, by his will, in the depths of hell; but he could never make progress or grow in a place where he could taste no pains. If a person knew that God took pleasure in his deeds, he would not be grieved at anything that happened to him.

66. You are still young, and you must grow a good deal, and it is much better for you, if you wish to walk the way of Love, that you seek difficulty and that you suffer for the honor of Love, rather than wish to feel love. But take upon you Love's interests, as one who wishes to be ever in her noble service. Have no care, therefore, for honor or shame; fear neither the torments of earth nor those of hell, if by them you could prevail on Love, in order to serve this Love worthily. Her noble service consists in the care you take to recite your Hours and to keep your Rule, without wishing or receiving pleasure in any of your service. And if you find pleasure in anything at all, whatever it may be—anything that is less than this same God, who shall be yours in the union of fruition—be willingly ill at ease in it, until God illuminates you with his own Being and gives you the capacity to serve and to have fruition of Love's being wherein Love loves herself and suffices to herself.

86. Serve nobly, wish for nothing else, and fear nothing else: and let Love freely take care of herself! For Love rewards to the full, even though she often comes late. Let no doubt or disappointment ever turn you away from performing acts of virtue; let no ill success cause you to fear that you yourself will not come to conformity with God. You must not doubt this, and you must not believe in men on earth, saints, or angels, even if they work wonders (Gal. 1:8); for you were called early, and your heart feels, at least sometimes, that you are chosen, and that God has begun to sustain your soul in abandonment.

99. Rely yourself on this support so perfectly that God may make you perfect. And in future do not desire the support of any person on earth or in heaven, no matter how powerful he is. It is as I told you—you are sustained by God, and you must wish to be supported by him, with great strength and no longer with doubtful fear.

106. One thing only is excepted, to wit, we must always continue to fear that we do not serve Love sufficiently according to her dignity. This fear fills us with love because it is strongly felt and brings us into a storm of ardent endeavor. At times it seems to us that we

have done what we could for Love, and that Love helps and loves us too little, in proportion to the worthiness of our service. As long as we thus accuse Love of unfaithfulness, this fear is wanting. You should rid yourself of every other fear but this and take this one to yourself as it comes and goes.

118. Suffer gladly, in all its extent, the pain God sends you; thus you will hear his mysterious counsel, as Job says of him: *You have spoken to me a hidden word* (Job 4:12).[13]

122. There are two ways in which persons may help others. The first way consists in extending a hand to sinners in their overthrow. A man is sometimes so wounded by charity for others that he must renounce the fruition and blessedness of God for the sake of sinners who live in sin, preferring to be deprived of his Beloved until assurance is given him that these sinners are not despairing of God's grace (Rom. 9:3). Thus charity leads one man to help other men.

133. The second way is this: When God knows that a certain man is sound in virtue and established in charity, God does not spare him. When he finds him strong as a result of possessing right reason in himself, he does not let him slacken through inactivity or lose his strength through sweetness, so this man wishes rather to do without all he ought to have from God, if God does not succor sinners. Now among these sinners there are some of proud[14] and lofty nature who, however, have pampered and corrupted themselves until they can no longer return to God by their own strength. Yet even to them God is so gracious that he confides them to those strong souls he has found, in order that they may support and bring them back, in his name, to his ways where men love perfectly.

150. But you have no need of such help. For you began early and in essential matters have not so refused anything to God that he will not lead you himself to his Being, on condition that you abandon yourself to him. But I will tell you the help that is fitting for you: Follow the demand of your heart, to live in God alone. No stranger lives in God. He whom you find, or whom you believe, or whom you feel nobly dwelling in God, and who is introduced and exercises power there and is indefectibly present, is truly above you. You may follow and be submissive to such a person without self-abasement.

163. If, in fine, you wish to have what is yours (1 Cor. 3:22), give yourself completely in abandonment to God, to become what he is. For the honor of Love, renounce yourself as far as you can, to be purely obedient in all that belongs to your greatest perfection, both

in doing and in omitting. To this end you must remain humble, and unexalted by all the works you can accomplish, but wise with generous and perfect charity to sustain all things in heaven and on earth, as befits true charity, according to their order. Thus you may become perfect and possess what is yours![15]—if you wish.

LETTER 3

TO TOUCH CHRIST

1. God be with you!

2. I entreat you by the veritable virtue and fidelity that God himself is,[16] think continually of that holy virtue which he himself is, and which he was in his way of acting when he lived as Man. O sweet love! now we are living as men. Now think of those noble works by which he was so ready to assist all men according to the needs of each; and then think of the sweet nature of Love, which he is eternally—so awesome and so wonderful to contemplate.

11. Oh! wisdom leads very deep into God! So there is no security of life here except in the deep wisdom that seeks to touch him. Alas! He is always untouched, and so deep to touch that he must be moved with compassion because so few men seek or long, with eagerness or by the force of ardent works, to touch him even slightly in his mystery: who he is, and how he works with love.

19. Here below we should to a large extent understand the customs of heaven, if the chains of love drew us far enough away from the customs of this world, and if we had enough heavenly thrust toward God, and brotherly love toward men in all things where they had need.

26. Love's greatest need and love's most urgent business I attend to first. So also does the brotherly love that lives in the charity of Jesus Christ. It supports the loved brother in whatever it may be—in joy or sadness, with severity or mildness, with services or counsels, and finally with consolations or threats. In order that God may have nothing to reproach you with, keep your ability always in readiness for his sake. Thus we touch him on the side where he cannot defend himself, for we do so with his own work and with the will of his Fa-

ther, who commanded him to do the work, and whose commandment he fulfilled. And that is the message of the Holy Spirit.

38. Then Love reveals many heavenly marvels and many wonders.

LETTER 4

ROLE OF REASON

1. This I entreat you, that you consider all the points in which you have erred, and that you reform yourself in them with all your power.[17] For we err in very many things that men judge good, and that really are good; but reason errs in these things when men do not understand them properly or practice them; this is where reason fails. Then when reason is obscured, the will grows weak and powerless and feels an aversion to effort, because reason does not enlighten it. Consequently the memory loses its deep notions, and the joyous confidence, and the repeated zealous intentions by which its confidence taught it to endure more easily the misery of waiting for its Beloved. All this depresses the noble soul; but when it reaches this state, hope in God's goodness consoles it once more. But one must err and suffer before being thus freed.

18. Now consider all the things I shall say to you about where reason errs, and reform yourself in these things with all your ardor. And do not let it grieve you then that you fall short in some things. For the knight who is humble will not be concerned about his gashes if he looks at the wounds of his holy Lord.[18] When God judges the time has come, everything will be quickly restored to order, so suffer with patience. To the reason, God will give light, constancy, and truth; the reason will gain over the will, and thus new strength will remain with it. And the memory will find itself courageous when God with his omnipotence drives away every sort of anguish and fear.

32. To put it briefly, reason errs in fear, in hope, in charity, in a rule of life one wishes to keep, in tears, in the desire of devotion, in the bent for sweetness, in terror of God's threats, in distinction between beings, in receiving, in giving—and in many things we judge good, reason may err.

39. Reason well knows that God must be feared, and that God is great and man is small. But if reason fears God's greatness because of its littleness, and fails to stand up to his greatness, and begins to doubt that it can ever become God's dearest child, and thinks that such a great Being is out of its reach—the result is that many people fail to stand up to the great Being. Reason errs in this and in many other things.

49. In hope many people err by hoping God has forgiven them all their sins. But if in truth their sins were fully forgiven, they would love God and perform works of love. Hope leads them to count on things that never eventuate, for they are too lazy and do not pay their debt either to love or to God, to whom they owe pains to the death. In hope reason errs, and they who are of this mind also err in many things. But on this point I need say much less to you than on the other points.

60. In charity men err through injudicious service, for instance when they give out of mere liking where there is no need, or render superfluous service, or weary themselves when there is no need. Often emotional attraction motivates what is called charity.

64. In keeping a rule of life, people encumber themselves with many things from which they could be free; and that causes reason to err. A spirit of good will assures greater interior beauty than any rule of life could devise.

69. In tears, people err a great deal. Although reason remonstrates with us, that we should weep because we lack what is ours, yet it is often self-will; in this we err extremely.

73. In desires for devotion, all souls err who are seeking anything other than God. For we must seek God and nothing else. And anything he gives in addition, we must gladly take.

77. In seeking spiritual sweetness, people err greatly; for there is very much emotional attraction in it, whether toward God or toward men.

80. God's threats or all sorts of torment that we fear cause reason to err, if we are often more influenced by fear than love in what we do or omit.

84. Making distinctions in a multiplicity of occupations to be undertaken or rejected greatly curtails the liberty of love.[19]

86. In accepting what could be dispensed with, outwardly or inwardly, reason errs.

88. In possession of any sort, in repose without cares, and in imperturbable peace with God and men, reason errs.

91. As for the gift of oneself, one errs greatly if he wishes to make it before its time, or lend himself to many alien things for which he is not destined or chosen by Love.

95. In grief, in pain, in repose, in quarreling, in reconciliation, in sweetness or bitterness—to spend too much time in all these things, reason errs.

98. In yielding obedience to various and sundry claims, reason errs extremely: All the other points are included in this one. To be obedient to fear according to our whims, and to the other points without control; to be obedient in fear, hope, emotional attraction, and all the other things we obey that do not belong to perfect love: Reason errs in all this.

106. My motive for telling you that reason errs in all these points, which people try to present in a favorable light, is that they are important points, and reason by its nature throws light on each of these points according to their value.

LETTER 5

FALSE BRETHREN

1. God be with you, dearly beloved, and give you consolation and peace in himself!

2. What I was now most glad to see is that God supported you with peace, consoled you with his own goodness, and enlightened you with the noble-mindedness of his Spirit; this he will do, and willingly, if you will entrust things to him and rely sufficiently on him.

8. O dear child, lose yourself wholly in him with all your soul! And lose in him likewise whatever befalls you (apart from all things love is not); for our adversities are many, but if we can stand firm, we shall reach our full growth.

13. It is great perfection to suffer all things from all people. But, God knows, the greatest perfection of all is to suffer from false brethren who seem to be *members of the household of the faith* (Gal. 6:10). Oh, do not be surprised if it pains me that those we had chosen to rejoice with us in our Beloved are beginning to interfere with us here

and to destroy our company in order to disband us, and especially me, whom they wish to leave with no one! Alas, how unspeakably sweet Love makes me find her being and the gifts that come to me from her! Oh, I can refuse Love nothing! And you, can you wait for Love and withstand her, this Love that is said to conquer all things?[20]

28. O beloved, why has not Love sufficiently overwhelmed you and engulfed you in her abyss? Alas! when Love is so sweet, why do you not fall deep into her? And why do you not touch God deeply enough in the abyss of his Nature, which is so unfathomable? Sweet love, give yourself for Love's sake fully to God in love. Necessity requires it, for your not doing so is hurtful to us both; it is hurtful to you and too difficult for me.

37. O dear love, do not be remiss in virtue, no matter what the suffering! You busy yourself unduly with many things, and so many of them are not suited to you. You waste too much time with your energy, throwing yourself headlong into the things that cross your path. I could not persuade you to observe moderation in this. When you want to do something, you always plunge into it as if you could pay heed to nothing else. It pleases me that you comfort and help all your friends, yes, the more the better—provided you and they remain in peace; I willingly allow that.

49. I entreat and exhort you, by the true fidelity of Love, that when there is question of doing or omitting anything, you follow the counsel I have given you; and that, for the sake of our unconsoled sorrow, you console to the best of your power all who are sorrowful. I charge you above all fully to observe the commandments of love, eternally laid on us (Matt. 22:37–40), and to keep them inviolate from all alien cares and all sadness.

LETTER 6

TO LIVE CHRIST

1. I wish to put you on your guard this time against one thing from which much harm results. I tell you that this is now one of the most pernicious evils that are found among souls, of all the evils found there, which are still numerous everywhere: Everyone wishes to demand fidelity from others and to test his friend, and continually complains on the subject of fidelity. These are the occupations souls

are now living in, when they ought to be tendering high love to the God of all greatness!

11. If someone desires the good and wishes to uplift his life in God's sublimity, why is he preoccupied about who treats him with fidelity or infidelity, and whether he should be thankful or reproachful toward one who does evil or good to him? The man who fails in fidelity or justice toward another is the one who suffers the greatest harm; and the worst of it is that he himself lacks the sweetness of fidelity.

19. If anyone, no matter who, behaves toward you with fidelity and helps you in the things you need, do not fail to thank him and to render him service in return; but serve and love God more heartily because someone is faithful, and as far as thanking or not thanking goes, leave that to God. For he is just in himself, and it lies in his power to take and give what is right: For he is in the height of his fruition, and we are in the abyss of our privation. I mean you and I, who have not yet become what we are, and have not grasped what we have, and still remain so far from what is ours.[21] We must, without sparing, lose all for all; and learn uniquely and intrepidly the perfect life of Love, who has urged on both of us to her work.

36. O dear child! First and above all I entreat you that you keep yourself from instability, for nothing could or can separate you from our Lord so quickly as instability.

40. And, also, do not be so self-willed in yourself at any unpleasantness that you ever let yourself doubt, in future, that anything less than the great God totally shall be yours in the being of love, so that doubt or self-will makes you neglect any good action. For if you abandon yourself to Love, you will soon attain full growth. And if you remain in doubt, you will become slothful and unwilling, so that everything you ought to do will be unwelcome to you. Do not be anxious about anything; and amid the tasks that lead to your goal, do not think there is anything so high that you cannot surely surmount it, or so remote that you cannot surely reach it. So you must be ardent and persistent, with ever new strength.

54. If you see a man who meets the needs of love and wishes eagerly to come to it, and consequently suffers misery and many griefs, be generous to him so far as lies in you, and pour yourself out in helping him—your heart in merciful kindness, your reasoning power in consolation, and your members in energetic service. Toward sinners be compassionate, with fervent petitions to God; but do not take on

yourself to keep reciting prayers for them or earnestly wish that God withdraw them from that state; for you would waste your time, and in other respects it would not be of much use.

67. Those who already love God, you can sustain with love, helping to strengthen them so that their God may be loved; this is profitable, but nothing else is. And for the lowest, who are sinners and estranged from God, neither efforts nor prayers to God are profitable, but rather the love we give to God. And the stronger that love is, the more it frees sinners from their sins and gives security to those who love.

76. To live sincerely according to the will of Love is to be so perfectly one in the will of veritable Love, in order to content her, that—even if one had another wish—one would choose or wish nothing except to desire above all what Love wills, no matter who is condemned or blessed by it. And a person should consent to be deprived of repose and pleasure for no other reason than that he knows he has not grown sufficiently in love.

86. We must be continually aware that noble service and suffering in exile are proper to man's condition; such was the share of Jesus Christ when he lived on earth as Man.[22] We do not find it written anywhere that Christ ever, in his entire life, had recourse to his Father or his omnipotent Nature to obtain joy and repose. He never gave himself any satisfaction, but continually undertook new labors from the beginning of his life to the end. He said this himself to a certain person who is still living, whom he also charged to live according to his example, and to whom he himself said that this was the true justice of Love:[23] where Love is, there are always great labors and burdensome pains. Love, nevertheless, finds all pains sweet: *Qui amat non laborat;* that is, he who loves does not labor.[24]

102. When Christ lived on earth as Man, all his works had their time (John 7:6). When the hour came (John 2:4), he acted; in words, in deeds, in preaching, in doctrine, in reprimands, in consolation, in miracles, and in penance; and in labors, in pains, in shame, in calumny, in anguish, and in distress, even to the passion, and even to death. In all these things he patiently awaited his time. And when the hour came in which it befitted him to act, he was intrepid and powerful in consummating his work; and he paid, by the service of perfect fidelity, the debt of human nature to the Father's divine truth. Then *mercy and truth met together, and justice and peace kissed each other* (Ps. 84:11).

117. With the Humanity of God you must live here on earth, in the labors and sorrow of exile, while within your soul you love and rejoice with the omnipotent and eternal Divinity in sweet abandonment.

120. For the truth of both[25] is one single fruition. And just as Christ's Humanity surrendered itself on earth to the will of the Majesty, you must here with Love surrender yourself to both in unity. Serve humbly under their sole power, stand always before them prepared to follow their will in its entirety, and let them bring about in you whatever they wish.

128. Do not, then, undertake anything else. But serve the Humanity with prompt and faithful hands and with a will courageous in all virtues. Love the Divinity not merely with devotion but with unspeakable desires, always standing with new ardor before the terrible and wonderful countenance in which Love reveals herself[26] and engulfs all works. Read in that most holy countenance all your judgments[27] and all you have done in your life. Set aside all the melancholy to which you have yielded, and renounce the cowardice that is in you; prefer wandering in continual exile far from the Beloved to coming out (after the enjoyment of much happiness) somewhere below him. All your perfection depends on this: shunning every alien enjoyment, which is something less than God himself; and shunning every alien suffering, which is not exclusively for his sake.

146. O be most compassionate in all things! For myself this is urgently necessary. And turn with an upright will toward the Supreme Truth.[28] We have an upright will when we wish no object or enjoyment, in heaven or on earth, in our soul or in our body, except those alone for which God has loved and chosen us (cf. Col. 3:2).

153. And count this the most important thing for you, without needing to question anyone: to stand always ready for God's good pleasure, sparing no trouble, without fearing that anyone might remark it, whether in mockery or reproach, anger or zeal.

158. Whether you make a good impression or a bad impression, do not renounce truth in your good works. We can willingly put up with derision when it is aimed at good works in which we recognize God's will; we can also willingly put up with praise that follows on virtues in which the sublimity of our God is honored. The affliction of our sweet God which he suffered when he lived as Man, merits our gladly bearing for his sake all affliction and every sort of derision; and it even merits our desiring every sort of affliction. And the eternal

Nature of his sweet love also merits that each of us should perform with perfect good will the virtues in which God our Beloved is honored.

172. Do not shirk, therefore, either disgrace or honor. For all that we can suffer or accomplish is welcome to Love's insatiableness. For Love is that burning fire which devours everything[29] and shall never, never cease in all the endless ages to come.

178. And since you are still young and as yet have had nothing to suffer, you must make the strongest efforts to grow as if out of nothing, like one who has nothing and who can attain nothing unless he struggles from the depths of his being. And whatever works you are able to accomplish, always fall back into the abyss of humility. That is what God wishes of you: that you walk at all times in humility of behavior with all the people with whom you associate on the way. And rise above all the low things that are something less than God himself if you wish to become what he wills you to be: that is your peace in the totality of your nature.

191. If you wish to follow your being in which God created you, you must in noble-mindedness fear no difficulty; and so in all hardihood and pride[30] you must neglect nothing, but you should valiantly lay hold on the best part—I mean, the great totality of God—as your own good. And so must you also give generously, according to your wealth, and make all the poor rich: for veritable Charity never fails to prevail over those who began with the pride of their whole will; so that she gives truly what she wishes to give, overcomes what she wishes to overcome, and maintains what she wishes to maintain.

204. O dear child! I entreat you now that you will always work without grumbling, purely with your will accompanied by all the perfect virtues, in every good work small or great. And do not wish or demand any favor from God, either for your needs or for your friends; do not ask him for spiritual joys in any sort of repose or consolation, unless this is as he himself wills. Let him come and go according to his holy will, and let him do, as his sublimity demands, all his will with you and with all those whom you long to instruct in his love.

215. Both for your interests and for theirs you must desire his will; if you pray for them, do not pray for what they choose in accordance with their own sense of values. Under cover of holy desires, the majority of souls today go astray and find their refreshment in an inferior consolation that they can grasp. This is a great pity.

222. Be careful therefore to choose and love God's will aright in all things, in what concerns you or concerns your friends, as well as in what concerns God, whereas you would most gladly receive from him something that gave you pleasure, by which you might live out your time in consolation and repose.

227. Nowadays this is the way everyone loves himself; people wish to live with God in consolations and repose, in wealth and power, and to share the fruition of his glory. We all indeed wish to be God with God,[31] but God knows there are few of us who want to live as men with his Humanity, or want to carry his cross with him, or want to hang on the cross with him and pay humanity's debt to the full. Indeed we can rightly discern this as regards ourselves, in that we are so little able to hold out against suffering in all respects. An unexpected sorrow, though slight, goes to our heart; or a slander, or a lie that people tell about us; or someone's robbing us of our honor, or our rest, or our own will: How quickly and deeply any of this wounds us all! And we know so well what we want or do not want, there are so many things and kinds of things for which we have an attraction or an aversion: now alike, now different; now sweetness, now bitterness; now here, now there; now off, now on; and as regards everything, we are so ready to provide for ourselves where any repose for us is in sight!

249. This is why we remain unenlightened in our views, inconstant in our whole manner of acting, and unreliable in our reason and our understanding. So we wander, poor and unhappy, exiled and robbed of everything, on the rough roads of a foreign land (Luke 15:11–20). And we all had little need of doing so, were it not that illusions assail us on every side. By this we show plainly that we do not live with Christ as he lived; neither do we forsake all as Christ did, nor are we forsaken by all as Christ was. We can discern this in many ways: for we strain every nerve in our own interests where anything can fall to our share, and we strive after honor wherever possible; we gladly carry our own will into effect, we esteem and love ourselves in our pleasure, and we gladly seize our outward and inward advantages. For every advantage fills us with delight and convinces us that we are something; and precisely through this conviction we become nothing at all. And thus we ruin ourselves in all respects: We do not live with Christ, and we do not carry that cross with the Son of God, but we carry it with Simon who received pay because he carried our Lord's cross (Matt. 27:32).

274. So it is with our struggles and our suffering: for we demand God as a reward for our good works, and we wish to feel him present in this life, on the supposition that we have truly merited this, and consequently that he, in his turn, should rightly do what we want him to. We hold in great esteem what we do or suffer for him, and we never resign ourselves to being left without recompense, or without knowing and feeling that it pleases God; we very quickly accept from him pay in the hand, namely satisfaction and repose; we also accept pay a second time in our self-complacency; and a third time, when we are satisfied that we have pleased others, and we accept commendation, honor, and praise from them.

290. All this is to carry that cross with Simon, who carried the cross a short time; but he did not die on it. Thus it is with the people who live as I have just said—even if in their neighbor's eyes their behavior may be lofty and their works glorious and manifest, so that at times they appear to lead a life sincere and holy, nobly ordered and adorned with the moral virtues—God, all the same, has little pleasure in it; for they do not stand firm, and they do not go all the way to the end. Just when they shine forth, they quickly break down; the smallest obstacle they encounter shows what their soul's depths really are. In sweetness they are quickly elated, and in bitterness they are dejected, because they are not established in the truth; the depths of their soul continue untrustworthy and unstable. Whatever they erect on such a foundation, they remain inconstant and untrustworthy in their works and in their being. They neither stand firm nor go to the end, and they do not die with Christ.[32] For although they practice virtues, their intentions are neither pure nor trustworthy; for there is an intermingling of many untruths, which so falsify the virtues that they no longer have the power to direct man aright, or enlighten him, or keep him in firm and constant truth, in which he must possess his eternity.

316. For it is man's obligation to practice virtues, not in order to obtain consideration, or joy, or wealth, or rank, or any enjoyment in heaven or on earth, but solely out of homage to the incomparable sublimity of God, who created our nature to this end and made it for his own honor and praise, and for our bliss in eternal glory.

324. This is the way on which the Son of God took the lead, and of which he himself gave us knowledge and understanding when he lived as Man. For from the beginning to the end of the time he spent on earth, he did and perfectly accomplished, amid multiplicity, the

will of the Father in all things and at all times, with all that he was, and with all the service he could perform (Matt. 20:28), in words and works, in joy and pain, in grandeur and abasement, in miracles, and in the distress of bitter death. With his whole heart[33] and his whole soul, and with all his strength (Deut. 6:5), in each and every circumstance, he was ready to perfect what was wanting on our part. And thus he uplifted us and drew us up by his divine power and his human justice to our first dignity, and to our liberty[34] (Gal. 4:31), in which we were created and loved, and to which we are now called (Gal. 5:13) and chosen in his predestination (Eph. 1:4–5), in which he had foreseen us from all eternity.

344. The sign that anyone possesses grace is a holy life. The sign of predestination is the pure and genuine impulse by which the heart is borne, in living confidence and unspeakable desires, toward God's honor and toward what befits the incomprehensible divine sublimity.

350. That cross which we must bear with the Son of the living God (Matt. 12:38) is the sweet exile[35] that we bear for the sake of veritable Love, during which we must await with longing confidence the festival when Love shall manifest herself and reveal her noble power and rich omnipotence on earth and in heaven. In this she shows herself so unreservedly to him who loves that she makes him beside himself; she robs him of heart and mind, and causes him to die to himself and live in devotion to veritable Love.

361. But before Love thus bursts her dikes, and before she ravishes man out of himself and so touches him with herself[36] that he is one spirit and one being with her and in her, he must offer her noble service and the life of exile—noble service in all works of virtue, and a life of exile in all obedience. And thus we must always persevere with renewed ardor: with hands ever ready for all works in which virtue is practiced, our will ready for all virtues in which Love is honored, without other intention than to render Love her proper place in man, and in all creatures according to their due. This is to be crucified with Christ (Gal. 2:19), to die with him, and to rise again with him (Col. 3:1). To this end he must always help us; I pray him for this, calling upon his supreme goodness.

LETTER 7

ASSAULT ON LOVE

1. Oh, I greet you, dear, with the love that is God himself (1 John 4:16)! And with what I am, which is also somewhat what God is. And I congratulate you insofar as you are that, and I do not congratulate you insofar as you are not.

4. O my dear! We must seek everything by means of itself:[37] strength by means of strength, knowledge by means of knowledge, riches by means of riches, love by means of love, the all by means of the all, and always like by means of like: This alone can content the Beloved, nothing else can. Love alone is the thing that can satisfy us, and nothing else; we must continually dare to fight her in new assaults[38] with all our strength, all our knowledge, all our wealth, all our love—all these alike. This is how to behave with the Beloved.

14. O my sweet love, Do not cease to abandon yourself to our Love with new works, and let her work, even if we cannot have sufficient fruition of her! She suffices to herself in herself, even if she is wanting to us in her outward manifestations. Love always rewards, even though she often comes late. Each person who gives her everything he has shall possess her wholly—one shall possess her in joy, another in sorrow.

LETTER 8

TWO FEARS ABOUT LOVE

1. In proportion as love grows between these two, a fear also grows in this love. And this fear is of two kinds. The first fear is, one fears that he is unworthy, and that he cannot content such love. And this fear is the very noblest. Through it one grows the most, and through it one submits to Love. Through this fear one stands at the service of Love's commandments. This fear holds men in love and in the dispositions they most need. It maintains them in humility when it is needful that they be awakened so they become fearful. For when they fear that they are not worthy of such great love, their humanity is shaken by a storm and forbids them all rest. For indeed to suffer pain through love makes a person courtly in speech, because he fears

that all he says about Love will be of no account to her. This fear makes a man free, for he can no longer think of anything or feel anything except that he would gladly please Love. Thus this fear adorns the one who loves. It gives clarity to his thought, instructs his heart, purifies his conscience, gives wisdom to his intellect, confers unity on his memory, watches over his works and his words, and permits him not to fear any sort of death. All this is done by the fear that is afraid it does not content Love.

27. The second fear is, we fear that Love does not love us enough, because she binds us so painfully that we think Love continually oppresses us and helps us little, and that all the love is on our side. This unfaith[39] is higher than any fidelity that is not abysmal, I mean, than a fidelity that allows itself to rest peacefully without the full possession of Love, or than a fidelity that takes pleasure in what it has in the hand. This noble unfaith greatly enlarges consciousness. Even though anyone loves so violently that he fears he will lose his mind, and his heart feels oppression, and his veins continually stretch and rupture, and his soul melts—even if anyone loves Love so violently, nevertheless this noble unfaith can neither feel nor trust Love, so much does unfaith enlarge desire. And unfaith never allows desire any rest in any fidelity but, in the fear of not being loved enough, continually distrusts desire. So high is unfaith that it continually fears either that it does not love enough, or that it is not enough loved.

47. He who wishes to remedy this inadequacy must keep his heart ever vigilant, so as to maintain perfect fidelity in all things. And all pain for the sake of Love must be pleasing to him. He shall silence good answers he would have regretted to silence were it not for love. He shall be silent when he would gladly have spoken, and speak when he would gladly have fixed his thought on divine fruition, in order that no one blame the Beloved on account of his love.[40] He ought rather to suffer woe beyond his strength than to fail on any point relating to the honor of Love.

58. Anger we must have nothing to do with, if we want the peace of veritable love—even if he whom we loved were the devil in person! For if you love, you are bound to renounce everything and despise yourself as the last of all, in order to content Love according to her dignity. He who loves gladly lets himself be condemned without excusing himself, because he wishes to be freer in Love. And for Love's sake, he will gladly endure much. He who loves gladly lets

himself be beaten in order to be formed. He who loves is glad to be rejected in order to be utterly free. He who loves gladly remains in aloneness, in order to love and to possess Love.

72. I cannot say much more to you now, because many things oppress me, some that you know well and some that you cannot know. Were it possible, I would gladly tell you. My heart is sick and suffering; that comes partly because my fidelity is still not abysmal. When Love wells up in my soul, I will tell you more about these things than I have yet said to you.

LETTER 9

HE IN ME AND I IN HIM

1. May God make known to you, dear child, who he is, and how he deals with his servants, and especially with his handmaids—and may he submerge you in him![41]

4. Where the abyss of his wisdom is, he will teach you what he is,[42] and with what wondrous sweetness the loved one and the Beloved dwell one in the other, and how they penetrate each other in such a way that neither of the two distinguishes himself from the other. But they abide in one another in fruition, mouth in mouth, heart in heart,[43] body in body, and soul in soul, while one sweet *divine Nature* flows through them both (2 Pet. 1:4), and they are both one thing through each other, but at the same time remain two different selves—yes, and remain so forever.

LETTER 10

VIRTUES THE MEASURE OF LOVE[44]

1. He who loves God loves his works. His works are noble virtues; therefore he who loves God loves virtues. This love is genuine and full of consolation. Virtues and not sweetness are the proof of love, for it sometimes happens that he who loves less feels more sweetness. Love is not in each person according to what he feels, but according as he is *grounded* in virtue *and rooted in charity* (Eph. 3:17). Desire for God is sometimes sweet; nevertheless it is not wholly di-

vine, for it wells up from the experience of the senses rather than from grace,[45] and from nature rather than from the spirit. This sweetness awakens the soul more to the lesser good and less to the greater good, and lays deeper hold on what it likes than on what it needs: for it has the nature of what gave it birth.

19. Such sweetness is experienced by the imperfect man as well as by him who is perfect. And the imperfect man imagines he is in greater love because he tastes sweetness; yet it is not pure but impure. Besides, even if the sweetness is pure and wholly divine, and this is a delicate question to decide, love is not to be measured by sweetness but by the possession of virtues together with charity, as you have heard.

26. For we discover in these souls that as long as sweetness endures in them, they are gentle and fruitful. But when the sweetness vanishes, their love goes too; and thus the depths of their being remain hard and unfruitful. The reason is that they are not yet equipped with virtues; for when virtues are early planted in the soul and firmly established by long practice, even if sweetness then diminishes, the virtues still follow their nature and continually work the work of love. These souls are not awaiting sweetness but a way of ever serving Love with fidelity. They do not desire taste but seek profit; they think of what their hands are doing, not of the reward. They entrust all to Love, and are the better for it. Love is so noble and liberal, she withholds no man's reward (Tob. 4:15). No man should clamor for a reward; if he did his part, Love would do her part. The wise souls who strive continually after virtue are well aware of this. They seek only Love's will, and the only sweetness they implore of Love is that she may grant them to know in all things her dearest will. If they are in consolation, let it be as Love wills; if they are disconsolate, again as Love wills.

51. But those other souls are poor in virtues. When they experience sweetness, they love; and when the sweetness vanishes, their love vanishes likewise. In the day of grace they are valiant, but in the night of tribulation they turn their back. These are fainthearted folk; they are easily elated when all is sweet and distressed when anything is bitter. A small heavenly favor makes their heart exceedingly joyful, and a small sorrow exceedingly afflicts it. This is why it sometimes happens that quickly moved hearts are stirred more than those that are serious, and hearts poor in grace more than those that are rich. For when God comes with his grace and wishes to console their pu-

sillanimity, help their weakness, and arouse their will, they are greedy and eager for his sweetness; in a word, they are more affected than those who are habitually penetrated with divine things. And it is sometimes supposed that people of this kind have great graces and great love, when in reality they suffer a deep privation of God. Sometimes, for this reason, an insufficiency of divine things is more the cause of sweetness than abundance is.

73. Sometimes also the evil spirit is the cause of sweetness. For sometimes when a man experiences sweetness, he feels so much pleasure of the senses in it and yields so far to this pleasure that he falls into bodily illness and thus lets slip more profitable things. In may happen also that when a man sees he possesses overflowing sweetness, he begins little by little to believe in his own perfection, so that he takes insufficient care to uplift his life.

83. Hence it follows that every man should be observant of the grace he has and augment with wisdom that grace of our Lord. For the gifts of grace do not make a man just, but lay obligations on him. For if he works with his grace, he pleases God; but if he does not do so he becomes culpable. He must also use wisdom in exercising his grace. For as virtue becomes vice when it is practiced out of its time, so grace is no longer grace except under the influence of grace.

93. Therefore is it needful that he whom God has set up as a merchant to trade with his goods should be wise and so guard his grace that it may remain with him (Matt. 19:13–27). For as he who is without grace must needs pray to God for grace, so he who is in grace must needs pray to God that he may preserve it. For anyone who ever allowed that good of our Lord to diminish in him instead of seeking to augment it would have forfeited all had not God's goodness intervened. This is why the bride of whom we read in the Song of Songs sought her Bridegroom not only with desire but with wisdom; and when she had found him, she was no less anxious to hold him (Song 3:4). Every wise soul who has been strongly stirred by love should do likewise. We therefore should continually increase our grace with desire and wisdom, and carefully cultivate our field, rooting out weeds and sowing virtues; and we should build the house of a pure conscience, in which we may worthily receive our Beloved.

LETTERS

LETTER 11
INCIDENTALLY ABOUT HADEWIJCH

1. O dear child! May God give you what my heart desires for you—that God may be loved by you worthily.

3. Yet I have never been able, dear child, to bear the thought that anyone prior to me should have loved him more than I. I do believe, however, that there were many who loved him as much and as ardently, and yet I cannot endure it that anyone should know or love him so intensely as I have done.

10. Since I was ten years old I have been so overwhelmed by intense love that I should have died, during the first two years when I began this, if God had not given me other forms of strength than people ordinarily receive, and if he had not renewed my nature with his own Being. For in this way he soon gave me reason, which was enlightened to some extent by many a beautiful disclosure; and I had from him many beautiful gifts, through which he let me feel his presence and revealed himself. And through all these tokens with which I met in the intimate exchange of love between him and me—for as it is the custom of friends between themselves to hide little and reveal much, what is most experienced is the close feeling of one another, when they relish, devour, drink, and swallow up each other—by these tokens that God, my Love, imparted to me in so many ways at the beginning of my life, he gave me such confidence in him that ever since that time it has usually been in my mind that no one loved him so intensely as I. But reason in the meantime made me understand that I was not the closest to him; nevertheless the chains of love that I felt never allowed me to feel or believe this. So that is how it is with me: I do not, finally, believe that he can be loved the most intensely by me, but I also do not believe there is any man living by whom God is loved so much. Sometimes Love so enlightens me that I know what is wanting in me—that I do not content my Beloved according to his sublimity; and sometimes the sweet nature of Love blinds me to such a degree that when I can taste and feel her it is enough for me; and sometimes I feel so rich in her presence that I myself acknowledge she contents me.

LETTER 12

THE JACOB LETTER

1. May God be God for you, and may you be love for him![46] May he grant you to experience Love's work in all things that belong to Love.

3. Therefore I begin with the veritable humility where his loveress began, and with which she drew him into herself (Luke 1:48).[47] So must anyone always do if he wishes to draw God into himself and to possess him fruitively in love. He must remain unassuming in all things and unconquered by any kind of service, always equally valiant in the storm, equally fierce in the assault, and equally intrepid in the encounter. Although you ask me to write to you about this, you yourself know well what one must do for the sake of perfection in God's sight.[48]

13. They who strive and desire to content God in love begin here on earth that eternal life by which God lives eternally. For to give him love to the full and content him according to his sublimity, heaven and earth are busy every instant in new service, and this they will never perfectly fulfill. For the sublime Love, indeed, and the grandeur that is God (cf. 1 John 4:16) are never satisfied or known by all that man can accomplish; and all the denizens of heaven shall burn in love eternally in order to give Love satisfaction to the full.[49] So they who here on earth accept no other pleasure or alien consolation but strive at every moment to content Love begin here that eternal life in which the denizens of heaven belong to God in fruitive love.

31. All that man comes to in his thought of God, and all that he can understand of him or imagine under any outward form, is not God. For if men could grasp him and conceive of him with their sense images and with their thoughts, God would be less than man, and man's love for him would soon run out, as now low-minded men are the ones who so soon come to the empty bottom of their love.

40. To put it briefly, low-minded men are all those who are not enthralled by eternal Love and are not continually watchful in their hearts to content Love. But they who stand ready to content Love are also eternal and unfathomable. For their *conversation is in heaven* (Phil. 3:20), and their souls follow everywhere their Beloved (Apoc. 14:4), who is unfathomable. But even if they also were loved with eternal

love (Jer. 31:3), they also are never attained by the depths of Love, so that they can never attain the one they love or content him; and nevertheless they will nothing else—either to content God or to die in the attempt—nothing else matters.

53. Therefore I entreat you earnestly, and exhort you by the true fidelity that God is (cf. 1 Cor. 1:9)—make haste to Love, and help us in order that God may be loved; I ask you this first, above all things. Think at all hours of God's goodness, and regret that it is so untouched by us, while he has full fruition of it; and that we are exiled far from it, while he and his friends, in mutual interpenetration, enjoy such blissful fruition, and are flowing into his goodness and flowing out again in all good.[50] Oh, he is God, whom none of us can know by any sort of effort unless veritable Love comes to our aid! Love brings him down to us and makes us feel so tenderly who he is; in this way we can know from him who he is. This is an unspeakably delightful bliss but, God knows, in the bliss there always remains woe. For the heart of the courtly lover, however, that is the law of chivalry: The only rest of such a heart is to do its utmost for the sake of its Beloved and to render him love and honor in view of his sublimity; and to offer him noble service as a gift—not for pay in the hand, but because Love herself at all times is satisfaction and pay enough.

76. But nowadays Love is very often impeded, and her law violated by acts of injustice. For no one wishes continually to renounce his emotional attractions for the honor of Love. All wish to hate and to love at their pleasure,[51] and to quarrel and to be reconciled in accordance with their whims, not in accordance with the justice of brotherly love. They also depart from justice out of human respect; this is also a personal leaning. And they destroy justice by anger; this is a passion from which many ills take their rise. The first ill is: Wisdom is thereby forgotten. The second: The common life is thereby destroyed. The third: The Holy Spirit is thereby driven away. The fourth: The devil is thereby strengthened. The fifth: Friendship is thereby troubled and, while remaining in abeyance, is forgotten. The sixth: The virtues are thereby neglected. The seventh: Justice is thereby destroyed.

95. Further, the emotional attraction of hate and of nonvirtuous anger—which is not holy anger—deprives us of love and proud desires, drives away purity of heart, makes us look at everything with

suspicion, and causes us to forget the sweetness of brotherly love; and anger has nothing to do with what exists in heaven, but envy readily accords with what exists in hell.

103. By the emotional attraction of worldly joy one forgets the narrow ways (cf. Matt. 7:14) that belong to high Love, and the beautiful behavior, the gracious bearing, and the well-ordered service that belong to sublime Love.

108. By the emotional attraction of frivolous love, we forget humility, which is the worthiest place and the purest palace in which we receive love. And in this emotional attraction we lose enlightened reason, which is our rule[52] and teaches us how to observe Love's right, when we wish to content Love. For enlightened reason casts light on all the ways of service which are welcome to the will of sublime Love and show clearly all the things that content Love. Alas, poor souls! That these two should have been driven out by the emotional attraction of frivolous love! This seems to me the most pitiable ill I know of.

121. All these emotional attractions I have singled out impede and destroy the excellence of Love. Along with these principal deviations I have mentioned, many lesser but countless ones creep in and take away the radiance of Love. While no harm is caused you and the others by most of these matters, many of them do, alas, creep in among your group disguised in fancy dress, so that no one takes the trouble to get rid of them. Baseness is dressed up as humility; anger, as just zeal; hate, as fidelity and reason; worldly joy, as consolation and abandonment; and frivolous love as prudence and patience, with an appearance of unearthly elevation, and fine words referring to other things than God. No one can safeguard from these dangers souls whom the chains of veritable Love do not inwardly protect.

139. Be sure that I have not said all this for your sake, but because of the harm that befalls us on account of this, here and elsewhere, and that we cannot surmount. To all of us it seems pitiable that people should be leading one another astray, so as to charge us with their errors instead of helping us to love our Beloved. But because your position in the community is such that on some occasions you can promote or hinder what takes place, I invite you to watch with care that in all things the excellence of Love be promoted, in yourself as in the others. And continually hold up to them, by all that you are, the blazon of Love, in all and above all.

151. For it seems to me that the commandment of love that God spoke to Moses is the weightiest I know in Scripture: *You shall love your Lord your God with all your heart, with all your soul, and with all your strength* (Deut. 6:5). When he had said this, he continued: These words you shall never forget, sleeping or waking. If you sleep, you must dream of them; if you are awake, you must think of them, and recite them, and carry them into effect. These words you shall write on the threshold, and on the lintel, and on the wall, and in all the places where you shall be, that you may not forget what you must do there (cf. Deut 6:6–9).

163. In other words, God himself commands that we nevermore forget Love, either sleeping or waking, in any manner, with all that we are, with heart, with soul, with mind, with strength, and with our thoughts. He gave this commandment to Moses and in the Gospel (Matt. 22:37; Mark 12:30; Luke 10:27), that in this way we should live wholly for Love. Woe indeed! How dare we then give Love short measure in anything? Alas, is it not fearful robbery (Isa. 61:8) that we spare anything for Love, or hold back anything? Alas! Think about this, and work without neglect to promote Love above all things.

174. Consider also what Obadiah the prophet says: *The house of Jacob shall be a fire; the house of Joseph shall be a flame; the house of Esau shall be stubble* (Obad. 5:18). Jacob is everyone who conquers; by the power of Love, he conquered God, in order to be conquered himself.[53] After having conquered, so that he was conquered and received the blessing, he will further help those who are also conquered but not yet wholly conquered, and still walk upright on their two feet and do not limp, as do those who have become Jacob. For Jacob remained infirm from wrestling and, ever after, went limping on one side; when he was conquered and limped, he was first given the blessing (Gen. 32:24–31). So must he fare who wishes to be Jacob and wishes to receive God's blessing. Whoever wishes to wrestle with God must set himself to conquer in order to be conquered; and he must start to limp on the side on which there is anything else for him besides God alone, or on which anything else is dearer than God. He then to whom anything is more than God, and who is not united with God in his one sweet blessing, stands on two feet and remains unconquered, and he tastes no blessing. You must leave all for all so exclusively, and burn so ardently in your soul, and in your being, and in all your works, that nothing else exists for you any more but God

alone—no pleasure and no pain, nothing easy and nothing difficult. If you live in this condition without cessation, *the house of Jacob* is *a fire.*

204. *The house of Joseph shall be a flame.* And as Joseph was a savior and a leader of the people and of his brethren, so you and they who have become Joseph must be leaders and protectors for the others who have not yet reached this state, but are still in want caused by the sadness of estrangement. With the great fieriness of the unified burning life, they will be enkindled; and with the flames of burning charity, they will be illuminated.[54]

214. The aliens among the common people are Esau. Their house is stubble, which is rapidly ignited by fiery flames; so shall the others be ignited by you, when you are a flame. This pertains to your function of prelacy in the monastery: that you kindle the dry stubble by your good example, by your way of life, and by your commands, counsels, and admonitions. And you should also lead your brethren on the right way by fervent love and help them to love, so that they may love in God and in veritable works, for God and for veritable virtues. And always remember what Scripture says: *Sobrie, pie, iuste viuamus in hoc seculo*[55] (Tit. 2:12). This pertains to your function.

228. O help us with pure and unmixed love, so that our Beloved may be loved! To put it briefly, this is what I wish from you above all things: veritable love for God. This I exhort you and entreat you to offer God—and that you may satisfy him where we fall short.

232. God be with you: make haste to Love!

LETTER 13

LOVE UNAPPEASABLE

1. Man must so keep himself pure from sin among all vicissitudes that he will seek his growth in all things and work, according to the manner prescribed by reason, above all things. And so God will work all things for him and with him, and he with God will *fulfill all justice* (Matt. 3:15) and will desire that, in himself and in all of us, God may accomplish the just works of his Nature.

9. To choose and will this above all is the law of the loving heart, whether condemnations or blessings follow. And this is always its desire and prayer, to be in exclusive union with Love, as we read

in the Song of Songs: *Dilectus meus mihi et ego illi* (Song 2:16).[56] Thus shall there be a single meeting in the one will of unitive love.

17. He who wishes all things to be subject to him must himself be subject to his reason, above whatever he wills or whatever anyone else wills of him. For no one can become perfect in Love unless he is subject to his reason. For reason loves God on account of his sublimity, noble men because they are loved by God, and ignoble men because they are in want of Love. Therefore one must exert his uttermost power in all things according to the perfection of Love, who is ever unappeasable no matter how much trouble one takes for her. For even should it happen that a man in all men's eyes seems to satisfy God by his behavior, nevertheless he falls so short when it comes to perfect satisfaction of Love that he must live more and more in accord with Love's demands, and his longings must far surpass what he has.

34. What satisfies Love best of all is that we be wholly destitute of all repose, whether in aliens, or in friends, or even in Love herself. And this is a frightening life Love wants, that we must do without the satisfaction of Love in order to satisfy Love. They who are thus drawn and accepted by Love, and fettered by her, are the most indebted to Love, and consequently they must continually stand subject to the great power of her strong nature, to content her. And that life is miserable beyond all that the human heart can bear.

45. For nothing in their life satisfies them—either their gifts, or their service, or consolations, or all they can accomplish. For interiorly Love draws them so strongly to her, and they feel Love so vast and so incomprehensible; and they find themselves too small for this, and too inadequate to satisfy that Essence which is Love. And they are aware that they themselves owe such a heavy debt, which they must pay by contenting Love in all manners, that with relation to everything else they can experience neither pleasure nor pain, either in themselves or in other people, except where Love herself is concerned. Only in this case could they experience pleasure or pain: pleasure in proportion as Love was advanced or grew in themselves and in others; pain, in proportion as Love was hindered or harmed in those who love—in themselves and in others—whom aliens gladly hinder and harm insofar as they can.

65. Take the trouble to labor for the progress of Love and of sublime charity; for charity understands all God's commandments without error and fulfills them without labor. For he who loves does

not labor, because he does not feel his labor. And he who loves ardently runs faster and attains more quickly to God's holiness, which is God himself, and to God's totality, which is God himself. In view of his totality may all your service be perfect, like the zeal befitting perfection, which contents him in his whole Nature wherein he is all-loving. May God grant you to realize the whole debt you owe him: pains that are merited, but principally the single love with which, as he himself has commanded, men should love God above all.

LETTER 14

SERVING WITH WISDOM

1. May God be to you vast and eternal Love, and may he give you the wise life and the excellent virtue through which you may content his holy Love.

3. Work to this end every moment without sparing. Always be fervent in humility and serve with wisdom. May God be your help and your consolation in your whole being; and may he teach you the veritable virtue by which we render Love the most honor and justice. God must teach you that well-pleasing oneness which he offered to his Father, when as Man he lived for him exclusively and purely. And may he teach you the holy oneness he taught and prescribed for his holy friends, who for the love of God rejected all alien consolation. And may he also make known to you, in truth and reality, that sweet and delightful union the experience of which he still gives to his dear friends who conform to his holy sweet love above all things.

19. Take care that you become renewed and fresh without growing tired; and consider the lofty essence of eternal charity, the characteristics Saint Paul ascribes to it (1 Cor. 13:4–13), all that it embraces, and all that it is capable of; and apply yourselves to it. This you must always do, if you wish to live for God; for anything we did without charity would be simply nothing. Make haste therefore to pursue charity with the strength of burning desire for veritable love. Be fervent in this charity and persistent in the pilgrimage of life, in order to carry the pursuit of Love into effect and then to attain fruition in the land of Love where charity shall abide eternally.

32. Charity must owe something to humility, for he who knows he has not sought the kingdom of God's love must humble himself

under God's mighty power. Oh, it is truly fitting, if anyone belongs exclusively to his Beloved, that his Beloved, in return, belong exclusively to him! As the Bride says in the Song of Songs: *My Beloved to me, and I to him!* (Song 2:16). Oh, to whom else should anyone belong exclusively but to his Beloved? For all that anyone does for another, unless as one beloved for the other Beloved, is estranged from Love. But only what comes from the Beloved is sweet and welcomed in all respects.

13. If you wish to experience this perfection, you must first of all learn to know yourselves: in all your conduct, in your attraction or aversion, in your behavior, in love, in hate, in fidelity, in mistrust, and in all things that befall you. You must examine yourselves as to how you can endure everything disagreeable that happens to you, and how you can bear the loss of what gives you pleasure; for to be robbed of what it gladly receives is indeed the greatest sorrow a young heart can bear. And in everything pleasant that happens to you, examine yourselves as to how you make use of it, and how wise and how moderate you are with regard to it.[57] In all that befalls you, preserve your equanimity in repose or in pain. Continually contemplate with wisdom our Lord's works; from them you will learn perfection.

57. It is truly fitting that everyone contemplate God's grace and goodness with wisdom and prudence: for God has given us our beautiful faculty of reason, which instructs man in all his ways and enlightens him in all works. If man would follow reason, he would never be deceived.

LETTER 15

THE PILGRIMAGE OF LOVE

1. Nine points are fitting for the pilgrim who has far to travel. The first is that he ask about the way. The second is that he choose good company. The third is that he beware of thieves. The fourth is that he beware of gluttony. The fifth is that he don short dress and tight belt. The sixth is that when he climbs a mountain, he bend far forward. The seventh is that when he descends the mountain, he walk erect. The eighth is that he desire the prayers of good people. The ninth is that he gladly speak of God.

13. So it is likewise with our pilgrimage to God, in which we

shall *seek the kingdom of God and his justice* (Matt. 6:3) in perfect works of love.

16. The first point is: You must ask about the way. He himself says this: *I am the way* (John 14:6). Oh, since he is the way, consider what ways he went—how he worked, and how he burned interiorly with charity and exteriorly in works of the virtues for strangers and for friends. And hear how he commanded men how greatly they should love their God—*with all* their *heart, with all* their *soul, and with all* their *strength* (Matt. 22:37; Luke 10:27); and that they nevermore forget this, sleeping or waking (Deut. 6:6–7). Now consider how he himself did this, although he was himself God—how he gave all, and how he lived exclusively for veritable love of his Father and for charity toward men. He worked with vigilant charity, and he gave to Love all his Heart,[58] and all his soul, and all his strength. This is the way that Jesus teaches, and that he himself is, and that he himself went, and wherein is found eternal life and the fruition of the truth of his Father's glory.

36. Next ask about the way from his saints, those he has taken to himself, and those who still remain here below, who are following after him in perfect virtues, who have followed him up the mountain of the noble life from the deep valley of humility, and have climbed the high mountain with strong faith and perfect confidence in the contemplation of the Love so sweet to our heart.

45. And further, ask about the way from those who are close to you, and who you see are now going his ways in the manner most like his, and are obedient to him in all works of virtues. Thus follow him who himself is the way, and those who have gone this way and are now going it.

51. The second point is: You must choose good company—that is, the holy devout community, where you participate in so many advantages, and where especially you are with holy lovers of God, by whom God is most loved and honored, and from whom you feel that you receive the greatest help, and through whom your heart is most united and elevated to God, and whose words and society most draw you and advance you toward God. But with these persons shun your repose and the inclination of your senses. And closely observe, with regard either to myself or to others in whom you seek sincere practice of virtue, who they are that help you to improve, and consider what their life is. For there are all too few on earth today in whom you can

find true fidelity; for almost all people now want from God and men what pleases them and what they desire or lack.

69. The third point is: You must beware of thieves. These are subtle temptations from without and from within. If a man can learn no trade without a master, never be so reckless as to undertake anything exceptional without counsel from persons of spiritual wisdom.

75. The fourth point is: You must keep yourself from gluttony, that is, from any worldly self-satisfaction; let nothing outside of God ever suffice you or have any taste for you, before you have tasted how wonderfully sweet he is (Ps. 33:9). Oh, remember this, and bear it always in mind: Whatever anyone takes pleasure in, other than God alone, is all gluttony.

108. The fifth point is: You must don short dress and tight belt; that is, you must be preserved from all earthly stain and from all baseness, and be so tightly girded with the chain of the Love that is God (cf. 1 John 4:16) that you never let yourself sink into something else.

88. The sixth point is: When you climb a mountain, you must bend far forward, that is, you must give thanks in all the pains that come to you on account of Love; and you must humble yourself with all your heart and, even though you alone were to practice all the virtues that all men alive could practice, you must think all these virtues small and nothing whatever in comparison with God's greatness and with the debt you owe God in service and in love.

97. The seventh point is: When you descend the mountain, you must walk erect, that is, although you must at times come down to the level of supplying your needs and feeling the exigencies of your body, you must nevertheless keep your desires lifted up to God, with the saints who lived high-mindedly and said: All *our conversation is in heaven* (Phil. 3:20).

104. The eighth point is: You must desire the prayers of good people, that is, you must wish to be helped on to God's supreme will by all the saints and all good men, and in order to be united with them in God, you must renounce all things.

109. The ninth point is: You must gladly speak of God. This is a criterion of Love, that the name of the Beloved is found sweet. Saint Bernard speaks of this: "Jesus is honey in the mouth."[59] To speak of the Beloved is exceedingly sweet; it awakens Love immeasurably, and it lends ardor to works.

115. Now I exhort you in the name of God's holy Love that you

make your pilgrimage with beauty and purity, without sadness or any hindrance from willfulness, in a sweet spirit of peace and joy. Pass through this place of exile so upright and so pure and so ardent that you may find God your Love at the end. In this may your help be God himself and his holy Love!

LETTER 16

LOVING GOD WITH HIS OWN LOVE

1. God be with you! And may he teach you the true ways that belong to high Love.

2. For your part be vigilant and discerning in what you are doing, attentive to yourselves and your quest, and firm in your faith. Provided you seek in truth—following not your emotional attraction but God's will—you shall obtain everything for which, in his love, he has destined you.

9. You must also live in joyful hope and strong confidence that God will allow you to love him with that great love wherewith he loves himself, Three and One, and wherewith he has eternally sufficed to himself and shall so suffice eternally.

14. In contenting him with that love, all the denizens of heaven are and shall be eternally engaged. This is their occupation, which never comes to an end; and the incompletion of this blissful fruition is yet the sweetest fruition. According to this, men on earth must strive for it with humble hearts and realize that, as regards such great love, and such sublime love, and this never-contented Beloved, they are too small to content him with love. Oh, this never-completed work must stir every noble soul like a storm, causing it to cast aside all superfluity and all that is either unlike or less than that which can content Love.

28. If two things are to become one, nothing may be between them except the glue wherewith they are united together. That bond of glue is Love, whereby God and the blessed soul are united in oneness. To this lofty surrender, holy Love at all times exhorts the noble, proud souls who are willing to understand it and cast away all things for the sake of Love, as he himself cast away all when he was sent by his Father, and when he finished the work Love had commanded him

to do, as he said in the Gospel: *Father, the hour is come* (John 17:1). After that he said to his Father: *I have finished the work which you gave me to do* (John 17:4).

41. Now consider how he lived, and the saints who remained here below after him, as well as the good people now alive who wish to practice that great Love which God is (1 John 4:16); they live constantly in humility of heart and the unremitting pursuit of good works. Live according to justice, not according to your pleasure or satisfaction in any way whatever, unless you know that to God accrue the glory and right that are his due. Entrust yourself to his sovereign goodness as to a Father. Be ready to follow good counsel given you by your friends who were glad to see you make progress. And listen gladly to good counsel in matters of virtue, whoever he be that gives it; and suffer everything gladly in the exercise of virtue for Love's sake.

56. You are too weak of heart and too childish in all your behavior. You are too quickly saddened, and you lack moderation in all your activity. What is the use of taking everything to heart? Master yourself as you ought, for the sake of God's purest sublimity. And see to it that you have work to do; idleness is very risky for one who wishes to become like to God. *For idleness is the teacher of all evil* (Ecclus. 33:29). *Pray without ceasing* (1 Thess. 5:17), or do a charitable deed, or perform an act of some other virtue, or serve the sick. For the honor of Love, bear with the angry and the ignorant. Rejoice in the Spirit of God (cf. Phil. 4:1), for he alone suffices to himself and is Love. Always be joyous among your companions, and let all their sufferings be yours, as Saint Paul says: *Who is weak, and I am not weak?* (2 Cor. 11:29). Watch over all your words as sincerely as if they were spoken in the presence of Christ who is truth itself (John 14:6).

73. It may grieve you that I preach to you so much about modes of action you yourself well know and possess. But I do it as a reminder of the truth that anyone who wishes to gain Love must begin with the virtues, with which God himself began, as did his saints. So we read of the martyrs, that *by faith they conquered kingdoms* (Heb. 11:33). It is not said, by love. That is because faith gives firmness to love; but love enkindles faith. Therefore works with faith must precede love; then love will set them on fire.[60] Be satisfied with my assurance, therefore, for I wrote this for your good.

LETTER 17

LIVING IN THE RHYTHM OF THE TRINITY

Be generous and zealous for every virtue,
But do not apply yourself to any one virtue.
Fail not with regard to a multitude of things,
But perform no particular work.
Have good will and compassion for every need,
But take nothing under your protection.[61]
This I wished long since to tell you,
For it lies heavy on my heart;
May God give you to understand what I mean,
Solely in the one nature of Love.

11. The things I order you in these verses were ordered me by God. Therefore I desire in my turn to order you the same things, because they belong perfectly to the perfection of Love, and because they belong perfectly and wholly in the Divinity. The attributes I mentioned here are perfectly the divine Nature. For to be generous and zealous is the Nature of the Holy Spirit; this is what is his proper Person. And not to apply oneself to a particular work is the Nature of the Father; through this he is the one Father.[62] This pouring out and keeping back are the pure Divinity and the entire Nature of Love.

Fail not with regard to a multitude of things,
But perform no particular work.

26. The first of these verses expresses the power of the Father, whereby he is God almighty. The second verse expresses his just will, with which his justice works its unknown mighty works. These works are deep and dark, unknown and hidden for all who, as I said, are below this Unity of the Godhead[63] but nevertheless render service (and, indeed, chivalrously) to each of the Three Persons, according to the verses I placed first in each couplet:

To be favorable and zealous for every virtue,
And not to fail with regard to a multitude of things,
And to have compassionate good will for every need.

This seems indeed to be the most perfect life one can attain on earth. And you have heard this continually, for I always recommended it above all; and I also experienced it above all, and rendered service accordingly and worked chivalrously until the day it was forbidden me.

44. The verses that come second in each of the three couplets I have composed express the perfection of the Unity and of Love, and according to justice treat of Love as one being, one sole Love, and nothing else. O *Deus!* This is a frightening being who, at one and the same time engulfs in unison such hatred and such charity!

Have good will and compassion for every need.

That was the Son in what is proper to his Person. He was purely this and did purely this.

But take nothing under your protection.

Thus his Father engulfed him in himself; this cruel great work ever belongs to the Father.[64] Yet it is the Unity of purest love in the Divinity: so that this Unity is also just with the justice of love and includes this Devotion, this Manhood, and this Power; nor would it have anyone left in need. And it includes one's charity and compassion for those in hell[65] and purgatory; for those unknown to God (Matt. 25:12; Luke 13:25), or who are known to him but still stray outside his dearest will; and for loving souls, who have more sorrow than all the rest, since they lack what they love. Justice takes up all this into itself. And yet each Person separately has given out what is proper to him, as I have said.

67. But the just nature of the Unity, in which Love belongs to Love and is perfect fruition of herself, does not seek after virtues, virtuous tendencies, or particular works, however pure or of however pure authority they are; and it does not give its protection, out of mercy, to any need, mighty though it is to enrich.

74. For in that fruition of Love there never was and never can be any other work than that one fruition in which the one almighty Deity is Love.

78. What was forbidden me (as I told you it was forbidden) was to have on earth any undueness of love; that is, to stand in awe of nothing outside of Love, and to live in love so exclusively that everything outside of Love should be utterly hated and shunned; therefore

for those outside of Love, to have no inclination and no virtuous acts, to perform no particular works that might assist them, and to have no mercy that might protect them, but to remain constantly in the fruition of Love. But when this fruition grows less or passes away, all three of the forbidden works should indeed be performed, as justly owed. When anyone seeks Love and undertakes her service, he must do all things for her glory, for during all this time he is human and needy; and then he must work chivalrously in all things, be generous, serve, and show mercy, for everything fails him and leaves him in want. But when by fruition man is united to Love, he becomes God, mighty and just. And then will, work, and might have an equal part in his justice, as the Three Persons are in one God.[66]

101. These prohibitions were laid upon me on Ascension Day, four years ago, by God the Father himself, at the moment when his Son came upon the altar. At this coming, I received a kiss from him;[67] and by this token I was shown what follows. Having been made one with him, I came before his Father. There the Father took the Son to himself with me and took me to himself with the Son. And in this Unity into which I was taken and where I was enlightened, I understood this Essence and knew it more clearly than, by speech, reason, or sight, one can know anything that is knowable on earth.

112. This seems wonderful indeed. But although I say it seems wonderful, I know indeed it does not astonish you. For earth cannot understand heavenly wisdom. Words enough and Dutch enough can be found for all things on earth, but I do not know any Dutch or any words that answer my purpose. Although I can express everything insofar as this is possible for a human being, no Dutch can be found for all I have said to you, since none exists to express these things, so far as I know.

123. Although I forbid you some works and command the others, you will in either case have to serve much.[68] But lack of discrimination regarding the things I have said, this I forbid you as those works were forbidden me by God's will. But you must still labor at the works of Love, as I long did, and as his friends did and still do. For my part I am devoted to these works at any hour and still perform them at all times: to seek after nothing but Love, work nothing but Love, protect nothing but Love, and advance nothing but Love. How you are to do or omit each of these things, may God, our Beloved, teach you.

LETTERS

LETTER 18
GREATNESS OF THE SOUL

1. O sweet, dear child, be wise in God![69] For you have great need of wisdom, as has every man who wishes to reach conformity with God; for wisdom leads very deep into God. But nowadays no one either will or can acknowledge what he needs in the service of love he owes. O you have much to do if you are to live the Divinity and the Humanity and come to full growth, according to the measure of the dignity in which you are loved and destined by God![70] Conform wisely and valiantly, as one undaunted, to all that is meet for you, and act in all things according to your free nobility.

13. God, who is powerful and sovereign above all power, gives enough to all men out of his omnipotence and pure benevolence. This he does not by his own exertion, or procurement, or gifts from his own hand, but through his rich omnipotence and mighty messengers, that is, his divine perfections. They serve him, govern his kingdom, and give to all men what they need, according to the glory and rights of him who is Lord over them. And each of his perfections gives according to the condition of its birth and function. Mercy gives God's gifts to all the indigent people who are utterly poor and ensnared in all sorts of vices, because of which they remain infamous and ragged. Charity guards the common people of the kingdom and gives each of them what he needs. Wisdom arrays all the noble knights who, in burning desire, labor with great combat and fierce assault for noble Love. Perfection gives the peers of the kingdom the lordship over their land, like the sovereign dominion of the sovereign soul I am speaking of who, with a sovereign and perfect will and perfect works, has obtained her noble mode of living by all the will of Love.

37. Justice directs these four virtues, in order to condemn or commend what they do.[71] In this way the emperor himself remains free and in peace, because he commands the officials to administer the law and invests the kings, dukes, counts, and chief peers with the high feudal tenure of his domain and the true legal rights of Love. This same Love is the crown of the blessed soul,[72] who can help all according to their needs while, at the same time, seeking after nothing of its own except in the love of its Beloved. This is what I meant when I last wrote you about the three virtues:

To have compassion for all,
But to take nothing under your protection,

and the other things I told you.

51. In this manner earnestly maintain the noble perfection of your invaluable and perfect soul. But consider the meaning of this. Remain undivided and withhold yourself from all meddling with good or bad, high or low; let everything be, and keep yourself free to devote yourself to your Beloved and to content him whom you love in Love. This is your real debt, which, according to the truth of your nature, you owe to God and to those with whom you live in him—thus to love God in simplicity and seek after nothing but this single Love who has chosen us for herself alone.

63. Now understand the deepest essence of your soul, what "soul" is. Soul is a being that can be beheld by God and by which, again, God can be beheld. Soul is also a being that wishes to content God; it maintains a worthy state of being as long as it has not fallen beneath anything that is alien to it and less than the soul's own dignity. If it maintains this worthy state, the soul is a bottomless abyss in which God suffices to himself;[73] and his own self-sufficiency ever finds fruition to the full in this soul, as the soul, for its part, ever does in him. Soul is a way for the passage of God from his depths into his liberty; and God is a way for the passage of the soul into its liberty, that is, into his inmost depths, which cannot be touched except by the soul's abyss. And as long as God does not belong to the soul in his totality, he does not truly satisfy it.

80.[74] The power of sight that is created as natural to the soul is charity. This power of sight has two eyes, love and reason. Reason cannot see God except in what he is not; love rests not except in what he is. Reason has its secure paths, by which it proceeds. Love experiences failure, but failure advances it more than reason. Reason advances toward what God is, by means of what God is not. Love sets aside what God is not and rejoices that it fails in what God is. Reason has more satisfaction than love, but love has more sweetness of bliss than reason. These two, however, are of great mutual help one to the other; for reason instructs love, and love enlightens reason. When reason abandons itself to love's wish, and love consents to be forced and held within the bounds of reason, they can accomplish a very great work. This no one can learn except by experience. For wisdom does not interfere here or try to penetrate this wonderful and fathomless longing, which is hidden from all things; that is only for the fruition of love. *In this joy the stranger shall not intermeddle* (Prov. 14:10)—or anyone outside of Love. To gain it the soul must be nursed with motherly care, in the joy of the blessedness of great love, and disciplined by the rod of fatherly mercy; moreover it must cling inseparably to God, read its judgments in his countenance, and thereby abide in peace.

112. Now when this noble soul turns back to men and human affairs, it brings a countenance so joyous and so wonderfully sweet from the oil of charity that in all things willed by charity it turns to men with mercy. But from the truth and justice of the judgments it has received in the divine countenance, it appears to ignoble men awesome and unheard-of (Exod. 34:29–30). And when these ignoble men see that the soul is then wholly arrayed according to truth and well-regulated in all ways, how fearful and alarming it is to them! They must give way to it under the pressure of Love. But they who have been chosen for such a state in union with Love and are not yet full grown for it possess already, in their capacity, the omnipotence of eternity; yet this is unknown to themselves and also to others.

130. Thus reason secretly gives its light. This power of sight of the soul enlightens the soul in all the truth of God's will. For he who reads his judgments in God's countenance works becomingly, in conformity with the truth of the laws of Love. The law of Love is to be obedient; this is contrary to the way of acting of many aliens. And he must work not like anyone else, but according to truth. He is subject to no one save Love alone, who holds him fettered in love. No matter what anyone else would have said, he speaks according to Love's will. And he does service and performs the works of Love according to her will night and day in all liberty, without delay or fear and without counting the cost, according to the judgments he has read in Love's countenance. These judgments remain hidden from all who, on account of alien motives or alien things, forsake the works of Love because they are scorned among aliens, who prefer and judge it better that their will, rather than Love's will, be done. For they have not come to the great countenance of omnipotent Love, by which we may live free in the midst of every kind of distress.

154. You must know this liberty, and you must also know those who serve for its sake. People judge all sorts of things for themselves, and in this way, under the delusion of greater liberty, they scorn the works of Love; they do so indeed with great worldly wisdom. And

so as to neglect the commandments of Love, some issue contrary commands.[75] But a noble person who wishes to keep his rule of life, following what enlightened reason teaches him,[76] does not fear the aliens' commands or counsels, no matter what torment befalls him in consequence, be it scandal, disgrace, indictments, insults, desertion, imprisonment, homelessness, nakedness, or utter want of every sort of thing man ought to have. He is not afraid to be ready to show obedience to Love in all that she wills, and to devote himself to her in truth, in all things and through all troublesome works, in the joy of his heart with all the power of Love.

174. By your whole life, then, you should gaze fixedly at God with the sweet eyes of single affection, which always seeks the service of the Beloved with delight. That is, you should contemplate your dear God cordially, yes, much more than cordially, so that the eyes of your desire, both together, remain fixed to the countenance of your Beloved by the piercing nails of burning encounters that never cease. Then for the first time you can rest with Saint John, who slept on Jesus' breast[77] (John 13:23–25). And this is what they do who serve Love in liberty; they rest on that sweet, wise breast and see and hear hidden words (Job 4:12)—which are ineffable and unheard-of by men—through the sweet whisper of the Holy Spirit.

189. You should always look fixedly on your Beloved whom you desire. For he who gazes on what he desires becomes ardently enkindled, so that his heart within him begins to beat slowly because of the sweet burden of love. And through perseverance in this holy life of contemplation, wherein he continually gazes on God, he is drawn within God. Love ever makes him taste her so sweetly that he forgets everything on earth. Then he is determined that, whatever befalls him at the hand of aliens, he will deny himself nine hundred times rather than neglect to perform one iota of the service of that worthy love of which *Christ is the foundation* (1 Cor. 3:11).

LETTER 19

TO HAVE NOTHING BUT GOD

God be with you and give you
True knowledge of the methods of Love;
May he enable you to understand

What the Bride says in the Song of Songs:
I to my Beloved, and my Beloved to me![78]
If anyone allowed Love to conquer him,
He would then conquer Love completely.
I hope this will be your experience;
And although we are waiting long for the event,
Let us thank Love for everything.
He who wishes to taste veritable Love,
Whether by random quest or sure attainment,
Must keep to neither path nor way.
He must wander in search of victory over Love,
Both on the mountains and in the valleys,
Devoid of consolation, in pain, in trouble;
Beyond all the ways men can think of,
That strong steed of Love bears him.
For reason cannot understand
How love, by Love, sees to the depths of the Beloved,
Perceiving how Love lives freely in all things.
Yes, when the soul has come to this liberty,
The liberty that Love can give,
It fears neither death nor life.
The soul wants the whole of Love and wants nothing else.
—I leave rhyme: What mind can say eludes me.

27. For with nothing the mind says can one put into words the theme of Love, which I desire and want for you. I say no more; here we are obliged to speak with our soul. Our theme is boundless; for this theme—Love—which we take, is God himself by Nature (cf. 1 John 4:16). Veritable Love never had the restrictions of matter, but is free in the rich liberty of God, always giving in richness, and working with pride,[79] and growing in nobleness.

37. Oh, may you fully grow up according to your dignity, to which you were called by God from all eternity![80] How can you endure it that God has fruition of you in his Essence, and you do not have fruition of him? How I feel about that is something I must be silent about; read what you have here; as you will, I shall keep silence. God must work according to his pleasure. I can say as Jeremiah said: *You have deceived me, O Lord,* and I am glad to have been deceived by you (Jer. 20:7)![81]

46. The soul who is most untouched is the most like to God.

Keep yourself untouched by all men in heaven and on earth, until the day when God is lifted up above the earth and draws you and all things to himself (John 12:32). Some say that he meant by this, upon the cross on which he was lifted up. But when God and the blessed soul are united he, together with the blessed soul, will be exalted from the earth in all beauty. For when the soul has nothing else but God, and when it retains no will but lives exclusively according to his will alone; and when the soul is brought to nought and with God's will wills all that he wills, and is engulfed in him, and is brought to nought—then he is exalted above the earth, and then he draws all things to him; and so the soul becomes with him all that he himself is.[82]

62. The souls engulfed in God who are thus lost in him are illuminated on one side by the light of Love, as the moon receives its light from the sun. The simple knowledge then received by them in this new light, from which they come and in which they dwell—this simple light then catches their darker half, so that the two halves of the soul become one; and then there is full light.

69. If you had demanded this light to choose your Beloved, you would be free. For these souls are united and clothed with the same light with which God clothes himself (Ps. 103:2).[83]

73. How these two halves of the soul become one—there is much to say on this point. I do not dare to say anything more about it, for my sad lot with regard to Love is too hard; and besides, I fear that the aliens may plant nettles where roses should stand.

77. Here we now drop the subject. God is with you.

LETTER 20

TWELVE NAMELESS HOURS[84]

1. That nature from which veritable Love arises has twelve hours,[85] which fling Love forth from herself and carry her back again into herself. And as Love then returns into herself, she gathers in everything for the sake of which the nameless hours had driven her outside: a seeking mind, a desiring heart, and a loving soul.[86] And when Love brings these in, she casts them into the abyss of the strong nature from which Love is born and on which she is nourished. Then the nameless hours come into the unknown nature. Then Love has

returned to herself and has fruition of her nature, beneath, above, and all round her. And all they who then remain beneath this experience shudder for those who have passed into it, and who must work, live, and die in it, as Love and her nature bid.

19. The first nameless hour of the twelve that draw the mind into the nature of Love is that in which Love reveals herself and makes herself felt, unawares and unlonged for when, in view of Love's dignity, this is least expected; and the strong nature that Love is in herself remains to the soul incomprehensible. And therefore this is rightly called a nameless hour.

26. The second nameless hour is that in which Love makes the heart taste a violent death and causes it to die without being able to die. And yet the soul has only recently learned to know Love and has scarcely passed from the first hour into the second.

32. The third nameless hour is that in which Love teaches by what means one can die and live in Love, and reveals that there can be no loving without great pain.

36. The fourth nameless hour is that in which Love permits the soul to taste her secret judgments, which are deeper and darker than the abysses (Ps. 35:7).[87] Then she makes known to it the misery of being without love. And nevertheless the soul does not experience the essence of Love. This is rightly called a nameless hour when, before the soul knows Love by experience, it accepts her judgments.

44. The fifth nameless hour is that in which Love allures the soul and heart and makes the soul ascend out of itself and out of the nature of Love, into the nature of Love. And then the soul loses its amazement at the power of Love and the darkness of her judgments, and forgets the pain of Love. And then it experiences Love in no other way but in Love herself. This seems to be a lower state, yet it is not. Therefore it may well be called a nameless hour when, although nearest to knowing, one is poorest in knowledge.

56. The sixth nameless hour is that in which Love disdains reason and all that is in, above, or below reason. What belongs to reason is altogether at variance with what suits the true nature of Love, for reason can neither take anything away from Love nor give anything to Love. For the true law of Love is an ever-increasing flood without stay or respite.

64. The seventh nameless hour is that nothing can dwell in Love, and nothing can touch her except desire. The most secret name of Love is this touch, and that is a mode of operation that takes its

rise from Love herself. For Love is continually desiring, touching, and feeding on herself; yet Love is utterly perfect in herself. Love can dwell in all things. Love can dwell in charity for others, but charity for others cannot dwell in Love. No mercy can dwell in Love, no graciousness, humility, reason, fear; no parsimony, no measure, nothing.[88] But Love dwells in all these, and they are all nourished on Love. Yet Love herself receives no nourishment except from her own integrity.

81. The eighth nameless hour is that the nature of Love in her countenance is most mysterious to know. What one is, is usually best revealed by one's countenance. In Love, however, this is what is most secret; for this is Love herself in herself. Her other parts and her works are easier to know and understand.

88. The ninth nameless hour is, that where Love is in her fiercest storm, sharpest assault, and deepest inroad, her countenance shines the sweetest, most peaceful, and loveliest, and she shows herself the most lovable. And the more deeply she wounds him at whom she rushes, the more gently, with the dignity of her countenance, she engulfs this loved one within herself.

97. The tenth nameless hour is that Love stands on trial before none, but all things stand on trial before her (cf. 1 Cor. 2:15). Love borrows from God the power of decision over those she loves. Love will not yield to saints, men here below, Angels, heaven, or earth. She has vanquished the Divinity by her nature.[89] She cries with a loud voice, without stay or respite, in all the hearts of those who love: "Love ye Love!" This voice makes a noise so great and so unheard-of that it sounds more fearful than thunder (cf. Apoc. 6:1). This command is the chain with which Love fetters her prisoners, the sword with which she wounds those she has touched, the rod with which she chastises her children, and the mastership by which she teaches her disciples.[90]

113. The eleventh nameless hour is that in which Love powerfully possesses him whom she loves, so that his mind cannot wander for an instant, his heart desire, or his soul love, outside of Love. Love renders his memory so unified that he can no longer think of saints, men here below, heaven or earth, Angels or himself, or God, but only of Love,[91] who has taken possession of him in an ever-new presence.[92]

123. The twelfth nameless hour is like Love in her highest nature. Now Love first breaks out of herself; and she works by herself

and always sinks back into herself, for she finds all satisfaction in her own nature. So she is self-sufficient: Were no one to love Love, Love's name would give her enough lovableness in her own splendid nature. Her name is her being within herself; her name is her works outside herself; her name is her crown above herself; and her name is her depths beneath herself.

135. These are the twelve nameless hours of Love. For in none of these twelve hours can anyone understand the love of Love, except, as I have said, those who are cast into the abyss of Love's strong nature, or those who are fitted to be cast into it. These last rather believe in Love than understand her.

LETTER 21

GAINING AND POSSESSING LOVE

1. God be your Love, dear heart!

Be fervent in God, and let nothing grieve you, whatever you encounter. For *the time is short* (1 Cor. 7:29), and here is much to do, and *the reward is great* (Luke 6:23). I have not complained much, and I do not wish you to grow discouraged or complain: Consecrate yourself to our Love, who is self-sufficient in fruition. Be wise, and take the trouble to understand what the virtues are with which one pursues veritable Love; have compassion, and do not abandon anyone in need. People think that if they acted thus they would lose all—their property, and their peace, and everything they might obtain. Thus they prefer their own peace to that of others. You, however, must keep yourself so naked before God, and so despoiled of all repose outside of him, that nothing can ever satisfy you but God alone. And if this is not the case, you should feel as much pain for his sake as a woman who cannot bring her child into the world.

21. So it is with those who love: They can neither have fruition of Love nor do without her, and this is why they live in anguish and are ruined. Before the soul possesses the Beloved, therefore, in order to court him, it must do everything in a distinguished and becoming manner, in all business and with all people, strangers or acquaintances, according to the sublimity of its Beloved, and for the good and the high renown that its Beloved will hear of it. For the Beloved is courtly and understands courtliness in love. And therefore when he

acknowledges the great pains and the grievous exile that the soul he loves has suffered for him, and the noble price it has paid, certainly he cannot fail to *mete out the same measure* of love and give himself completely in return (Luke 6:38).

35. This is how we court the Beloved: As long as we do not possess him, we must serve him with all the virtues. But when we are admitted to intimacy with the Beloved himself, all the things by which service was previously carried on must be excluded and banished from remembrance.

40. As long as we serve in order to attain Love, we must attend to this service. But when we love the Beloved with love, we must exclude all the rest and have fruition of Love with all the promptings of our heart and all the surrender of our being, and stand ready to receive the exceptional wisdom the loving soul can win in love. For this the powers of our soul and all the veins of our mind must always stand ready, and toward it our eyes must always gaze; and all the floods of the sweet flood shall all flow through and into one another. So must love live in Love.

LETTER 22

FOUR PARADOXES OF GOD'S NATURE

1. He who wishes to understand and know what God is in his name and in his Essence must belong completely to God—yes, so completely that God is all to him and he is free from himself. For *charity does not seek her own* (1 Cor. 13:5), and Love applies herself only to herself. Therefore let a man lose himself if he wishes to find God and to know what God is in himself.

8. "He who knows little can say little": so says wise Augustine. This is my case, God knows. I believe and hope greatly in God, but my knowledge of him is small; I can guess only a little of the riddle of God; for men cannot interpret him with human notions. But one who was touched in his soul by God could interpret something of him for those who understood this with their soul.

17. Enlightened reason interprets a little of God to the interior senses, whereby they can know that God in his wondrousness is an alarming and fearfully sweet Nature to contemplate, and that *he is all things* to all, and wholly *in* all (1 Cor. 15:28). God is above all, and un-

elevated; God is beneath all, and unabased; God is within all, and entirely uncircumscribed; God is outside all, and completely comprised.[93]

25. That God is above all and unelevated means that he eternally exalts, and will exalt in the highest, the infinite Nature that he himself is in his Nature. But since he himself is what he exalts,[94] he does not exalt himself and remains unelevated.

31. And because the eternity of God effects his Being without end, and with this Being from all eternity it also acts in one fruition of his own love, the depth of his Being from the beginning brings it to pass that his height remains unelevated. His own fearfully sweet Nature satisfies him completely, and so his nonelevation falls into the depth of his fathomlessness; thus he remains unelevated.

39. Moreover he constantly invites men to unity in the fruition of himself; and they are all stirred and set in commotion by the force of his fearful invitation. The spirit of some of them is frightened by his just warning, and they go astray. But others, the proud souls, he awakens, and they stand up with a violent new will and raise themselves toward his nonelevation, which eternally escapes us and, in its highest height, is beyond our reach.

47. And because we pray for his kingdom to come in us (Matt. 6:9–10), we in our turn demand unity with him according to the Three Persons. We demand of him his power and his rich Essence, in unitive surrender to the Father. We demand his mercy and his wise teaching; and we desire his Love, as our Brother, in order to serve our Father and with him to be the same child, in love and right of inheritance, that he is (cf. Rom. 8:14–17). We demand him in his goodness, and in his clarity, and in his fruition, and in his wonderful mystery. And so with the strong cement of union we become *one spirit* with God (1 Cor. 6:17), because we, with the Son and with the Holy Spirit, thus invite the Father—even the Three Persons with all that they are.

61. Because this is so, God likewise remains unelevated; and although we ask his kingdom for ourselves (Matt. 6:10), we likewise cannot elevate him; for he alone can move himself; and that is how all creatures come into movement in their being. Thus God remains unelevated, for God is above all and even and equal in all respects. Thus he is the highest of all, but unelevated.

69. Then anyone whom—yes, with *the earthly man* (1 Cor. 15:47)—God elevates with himself, he shall draw most deeply within

himself (John 12:34) and have fruition of him in nonelevation. O *Deus!* What a marvel takes place then—when such great dissimilarity attains evenness and becomes wholly one without elevation! Oh, I dare write no more here about this; I must always keep silence about the best, because of my sad lot, and besides no one can truly reproach himself because he knows nothing about God. People think the mystery is easy enough; and if they hear anything they do not understand, they doubt immediately. And therefore I am distressed that I dare not say or write to persons what is worth the trouble, or write any words about the depths of my soul.

84. The second point, that God is beneath all and yet unabased, means that the depths of his eternal Nature sustain all beings and nourish them and enrich them with such wealth as that in which God lives—with divine wealth. But because the most profound of the divine depths and the very highest of the divine heights are on the same level, God is beneath all, and unabased.

90. All men also praise him according to his supreme height, which is Love, and not for anything less; they love him also, from all eternity, in his eternal Nature, with which he will eternally satisfy all those who are to become God with God. So shall he also there with them be beneath all things, in order to sustain and nourish all. And so he remains unabased, for these souls exalt him eternally and in every hour with new desires of alluring, burning love. But again, I dare not say more about it, because we do not know regarding God how he is all in all.

102. The third point, that God is within all and uncircumscribed, means that he is, in the eternal fruition of himself, in the dark power of his Father,[95] and in the wonder of his love for himself, and in the radiant, overflowing flood of his Holy Spirit. He is also in the storms that arise in the Unity and condemn or bless all things according to their deserts.[96] In this Unity he has fruition of himself, in the glory he is in himself. He has fruition of his blessed wonders in all men who were, and are, and shall be,[97] in the state that is their due in all the plenitude of glory. Oh, this interior reality must above all be kept silent, for no ways of aliens lead to it!

116. Although God is within all, he is nevertheless uncircumscribed, for he pours forth his Unity in Persons, and has inclined them toward us in four ways.[98]

119. He lavishes the eternal time, which he himself is,[99] in unattainable Love and in inscrutability as far as every spirit that is not

one spirit with him (1 Cor. 6:17) is concerned. He lavishes eternal time so totally that he inspirits souls with his Spirit and gives all that he has, and is all that he is. When God leads a man along this way, no one else can follow him, either by his own power or by cleverness—with the exception of those whom by his sublime Spirit he has inspirited to be *one spirit* with him. This is the first of the four ways, and the highest, about which, by reason, nothing can be said, unless one speaks with inspirited soul to inspirited soul. This way lies where God is the way beyond our being.

133. The other three ways by which he has inclined himself to us are as follows: The first is, that he gave us his Nature; the second, that he delivered up his substance to death; and the third, that he relaxed time.

137. He gave us his Nature in the soul, with three powers whereby to love his Three Persons: with enlightened reason, the Father; with the memory, the wise Son of God; and with the high flaming will, the Holy Spirit. This was the gift that his Nature gave ours to love him with.[100]

143. He delivered up to death his substance, that is to say his holy Body, which fell into the hands of his enemies for the love of his friends; and he gave himself to be eaten and drunk, as often as we will and with the dispositions we will. Yes, much smaller than an atom compared to the entire world is what we receive from God compared to what we could have from God, if we trusted in him and would receive it from him. Alas, how very many souls now remain thus unfed, and how few consume him among those who have the right to eat and drink![101]

155. He relaxed time; that is, he is patient to wait for our advance to a good life when we will. We see his mouth brought close to us to kiss him who wishes it (cf. Song 1:1).[102] His arms are outstretched: He who wishes to be embraced may throw himself into them. Yes, to put it briefly, God has inclined himself toward us, in time, in all we can have and wish to have from him, and all we can understand, as much as we wish and according as we wish, in order that he may be with us in Love and in fruition.

165. They who follow the first way, according to which he gave us his Nature, live on earth as if in heaven: They apply themselves to Love without great woe, and in devotion, and in delight, and in abundance, for they can have these things without great woe.

169. They who follow the second way, according to which he de-

livered up his substance to death, live as if in hell: That comes from God's fearful invitation. It is so fearful to their mind; their spirit understands the grandeur of conformity to the delivering up of the Son, but their reason cannot understand it. This is why they condemn themselves at every hour. All their words, and works, and service seem to them of no account, and their spirit does not believe that it can attain that grandeur. Thus their heart remains devoid of hope. This way leads them very deep into God, for their great despair[103] leads them above all the ramparts and through all the passageways, and into all places where the truth is.

183. They who in the third way follow time, which has been relaxed, live as if in purgatory. They burn with interior desires without ceasing, because everything is inclined toward them: The mouth is open; the arms are outstretched; and the rich Heart is ready.[104] That fearful outstretching renders the depth of their souls so deep and so vast that they can never be filled. The fact that God opens himself so wide for them invites them at all hours to surpass their faculties. For with his right arm he embraces all his friends, both heavenly and earthly, in an overflowing wealth. And on the left side he embraces the strangers who with naked and scanty faith come to him for the sake of his friends, so that there may be fulfilled in them the full and unitive bliss in him that has never been lacking to him. For the sake of his good friends and his beloved ones, he gives the strangers his glory and makes them all friends of the house.

201. Oh, this sweet invitation and that open Heart make them invite him, in order to obtain fruition! The rich wonders overflowing out of his rich Heart cause them to experience desires above reason and to burn with inextinguishable fire. Therefore this is purgatory, for although they burn from being so unburned by the blaze (perfect love is a fire), they burn in order to content him. And the truth of his rich open Heart says to their spirit that he shall be totally theirs. With this confidence they fly through all the heights of Love. These souls consume without being satisfied.

213. Since God has put forth all these ways by which to love him fully as he is in himself, he is within all and totally uncircumscribed; for by these four ways we can come into his inmost secret.

218. There is a fifth way trodden by ordinary people with simple faith, who go to God through all kinds of outward service.

221. They who enter by the first way, that of time, which is God himself in his unfathomable power and incomprehensible Love, pen-

etrate within him from depth to depth. They walk outside all the ways open to representation.

224. They who go to God by the way of heaven consume and are fed, for he has given them his Nature, and they accept it freely. They live on earth in the land of peace.

228. They who go to God by the way of hell are fed without consuming, for they can neither believe nor hope that they would ever be able to content Love in her substantial being. They live in the land of debt, and reason penetrates all their veins and invites them to lift themselves up to this divine self-offering and to the height of all men who are beloved. They cannot believe what they feel: Thus God stirs them interiorly in a madness without hope.

237. They who go to God in his depths by the way of purgatory live in the land of holy anger; for what was given them in trust is soon devoured by their deep, anxious longing. What causes the soul's wrath to increase continually is that she knows with her interior spirit what of God is lacking to her—that he has something that she does not have to the full, and that is not given her fully. This is the wrath of the soul. There is besides a more intense anger in certain souls, about which I must be silent.

247. Since we enter within God by all these ways—through himself, through heaven, through hell, and through purgatory—God is uncircumscribed, although he is within all.

251. The fourth point is that God is outside all, but entirely comprised. He is outside all; for he rests in nothing but the tempestuous Nature of his profusely overflowing flood, which flows back and forth over all. This is what is said in the Song of Songs: *Oleum effusum, et cetera. Your name is as oil poured out; therefore the young maidens love you* (Song 1:2). Oh, how truly the bride speaks! She understands this well and says of him that his name is poured out above all ways, to make every soul fruitful according to its need, according to its worthiness, and according to the office of the service God awaits from it.

264. That emanation of his name has enabled us to know his unique name in the properties of the Persons. The flood of his one eternal name pours out with fearful storminess of invitation which they, one and triune, claim for one another. The Father has poured out his name in powerful works, and rich gifts, and just justice. The Son has poured out his name in revelations of burning affection, in veritable doctrine, and in cordial tokens of Love. The Holy Spirit poured out his name in the great radiance of his Spirit and of his

light, and in the great fullness of overflowing good will, and in the jubilation of sublime, sweet surrender on account of the fruition of Love.

279. The Father poured out his name and gave us the Son, and called him again into himself. The Father poured out his name when he recalled the Holy Spirit, that he should return to him with all that he had inspirited.

285. The Son poured out his name when he was born Jesus, when with this name he wished to make all our barrenness fruitful, and to save all who wished to be saved. The Son poured out his name when he was baptized Jesus Christ. Thereby he imparted Christian fruitfulness to us who are called after his name, and who are fed with his name and with his Body, yes, and who partake of him and consume him as eagerly, and fruitfully, and deliciously as we ourselves wish. But in this there is greater disproportion than between the point of a needle and the whole world with the sea thrown in. One could taste and feel incomparably more fruitfulness from God—as he would rightly experience from him—if he sought him with desirous, loving confidence. Anyone who wishes proudly to accept this outpouring of his name should join the company of the *young maidens* of the Song of Songs (Song 1:2) and love him. The Son poured out his name in a wonderful way when by his death he bore life and light into hell, which indeed is death without life. He carried life and light where no light shall be, and his name drew his beloved ones there into clear light and full fruitfulness. This same name burned those who remained there with the eternal fire of dark death. Oh, how dark is death where his name is not known! The Son poured out his name when he said: *Father, glorify me with the glory which I had with you, before the world was* (John 17:5). Not that glory was lacking to him at any hour, but he wished, when he had drawn all things to himself (cf. John 12:34), to glorify them with him. Also he then said: *I will, Father, that they may be one in us, as you, Father, in me and I in you* (John 17:21). This is the loveliest word of his love God ever revealed—of all the words anyone reads in Scripture. Then he returned with his name, which he had poured forth very greatly and which, now very luxuriantly multiplied, he now again poured into him.[105] His name was multiplied although nothing was added to it; for all things are poured out and multiplied by the fructifying oil of his sublime name, and were as great in him from all eternity[106] as they shall be without end.

328. The Holy Spirit poured out his name, since all the holy

spirits and Angels who reign on high in glory flow from him. The names under which they are ordered are called their choirs,[107] and they are poured forth from this name. And the holy spirits of heaven and earth, and the good spirits who have not yet been brought to holiness, even those who will not be brought to it, and all spirits individually and together—all these his name has inspirited, each one according to the measure in which his spirit is loved. His name has inspirited all wise spirits, and all swift spirits, and all strong spirits, and all sweet spirits: he inspirits them all. His name is poured out over all the earth, over men at large, to sustain and lead each of them, according to how much he is loved.

345. Thus God is outside all [and nevertheless comprised],[108] for something of God is God in his entirety. And because everyone has from God what befits him, so each one comprises God wholly in what he has from him. Thus God is entirely comprised.

348. And because the power of the Father at all hours so fearfully invites to his unity for fruition, in which he suffices to himself: so he comprises himself at all hours—yes, and therewith the being of every creature; whatever its name, he comprises it in his own Unity, and invites it to the fruition of his Being. And these interior spirits of the four first ways also comprise him; they enter within his Being, and wish to be in all things what he is, and wish to give him no advantage but to obtain him wholly in confidence and love, and to be all that he himself is, nothing less. These loving, interior spirits comprise him totally.

362. And above all, jubilation over his wondrousness comprises him with full wealth. And the Father comprises the Godhead in justice, in his own right:[109] that is why his judgments are deep and dark as abysses (Ps. 35:17);[110] dark above all are the justice of the Father and the jubilation of his Spirit.[111]

368. And the Father also comprises the justice of the Son and of the Holy Spirit—and he comprises justice in all spirits whom he has inspirited in jubilation and in the full fruition of Love. and it is wondrous that, in this, God is fully comprised.

371. Thus God with all the floods of his name is overflowing in all, and around all, and beneath all, and above all; and yet he is comprised in the fruition of Love.

376. The four attributes of God now meet in one total fruition.[112] This totality sits with splendor in the middle of a circle with *four living creatures* (Ezech. 1:5; Apoc. 4:6–7, 5–6).[113] The eagle on its

sailing wings flies incessantly toward the heights: This shows that God is above all and unelevated. The ox attends the place: This shows that God is beneath all and unabased. The lion guards this place: This shows that God is within all and uncircumscribed. The man contemplates this place: This shows that God is outside all and yet comprised.

385. The interior soul, which is to be an eagle, must fly above itself in God, as we read of the four living creatures that the fourth flew the highest of the four—just what Saint John did when he said: *In principio,* etc. (John 1:1). The eagle fixes its eyes on the sun without turning from it, and the interior soul does the same; it does not turn its eyes from God.[114] The wise soul must be John in this circle, that is, in its application to God in Love. There we shall think no longer of the saints or of men, but only fly in the heights of God.

395. The eagle, if its eaglet cannot fix its eyes on the sun, throws it out.[115] Thus the wise soul also must throw from it all that might obscure the clarity of its spirit: for the wise soul, as long as it is an eagle, does not stop to rest; it flies continually toward the unelevated heights.

401. *The living creatures went and returned;* and they went but did not return (Ezech. 1:14, 17). That they did not return signifies that the divine height is never absolutely reached; their return signifies life and vision in the breadth, and in the depth, and in these four balanced attributes.

LETTER 23

TRUTH, NOT LIES

1. May God be God for you in truth, in which he is God and Love at once!

2. If he is yours in love, you must live for him, by yourself being love. In that expectation, abandon yourself to the truth that he himself is. Live thus exclusively for holy Love out of pure love, not because of the satisfaction you might find by communing with his love in your devout exercises, but in order to devote yourself to God himself in the works that content Love. And whatever God bestows on you, however beautiful it is, do not give your kiss before the day when you know it will last eternally.

11. Behave yourself wisely where you now are; this is certainly needful for you. Above all things I counsel you to withhold yourself there very prudently from eccentricities, which are there very numerous; yield they pain or pleasure, have nothing to do with them. Always and in every way be humble, yet not so humble that you become foolish and neglect truth and justice wherever you can put them into practice. For verily I say to you: He who tells a lie for the sake of humility shall be punished for it. In this respect they are capable of almost everything. Look after yourself, spend your time well, be faithful, and grow with us. They would gladly draw you away from us and attach you to themselves; their hearts suffer from our exceptional fidelity. Do not let yourself now be too greatly engrossed in anything. Do everything with reliance on Love. Live in the same fervor as we; and let us live in sweet love. Live for God; let his life be yours, and let yours be ours.

LETTER 24

LOVE THROUGH VIRTUES

1. I will tell you without beating about the bush: Be satisfied with nothing less than Love. Give reason its time, and always observe where you heed it too little and where enough. And do not let yourself be stopped by any pleasure through which your reason may be the loser. What I mean by "your reason" is that you must keep your insight ever vigilant in the use of discernment. Never must any difficulty hinder you from serving people, be they insignificant or important, sick or healthy. And the sicker they are, and the fewer friends they have, the more readily must you serve them. And always bear with aliens willingly. As for all who slander you, contradict them not. And be desirous to associate with all who scorn you, for they make the way of Love broader for you.

15. Leave not anyone in need out of spite. And never fail to ask about any wise teaching you are ignorant of, out of spite or shame that you do not know it. For you are bound before God to acquire a knowledge of all the virtues and to learn them by exertion, questioning, study, and earnest purpose.

22. And if by your fault you have offended anyone, wait not too long to set it right with him.[116] You are bound to this by the death

of our Lord, in order to content him. Take whatever means you think the quickest and best to make peace with the one you have offended. To fall at his feet,[117] and to answer peaceful words, or to seal a reconciliation—these actions you must not omit because of spite, loss, or shame, if you wish to obtain God as your Love and your Bridegroom. Should you neglect this out of pride, you would thereby expose yourself to many evils.

34. Do not become so stubbornly attached to anything that God may, in consequence, refuse you his grace. Do not, through pride, spare any service. Do not, through pride, refrain from giving little gifts to the poor. Do not, through pride, fail to ask for anything you need and cannot well do without. Do not, through pride, be ashamed that you are hungry, thirsty, drowsy, or cold, or be ashamed of a repulsive illness, or of having shown a lack of good understanding or courtliness. For it is great honor and the finest courtly behavior if one acknowledges outwardly what one is ashamed of; but it is great pride not to tell it; and it is outrage and shame to see more evil than is truly to be seen. Moreover toward God, our Beloved, it is guileful insincerity and odious infidelity. For it is the law of high troth and love, that loved one be revealed to beloved in all that he or she is, lowly or sublime.

53. Also I say to you, for all you do amiss before God alone, you should humble yourself before him; and also avow it lovingly and lament it before him with consciousness of your guilt, until he has heard the lament, forgiven the misdeed, and moreover granted you grace before you can come to confess it in the priest's presence.

59. For all your misdeeds that were seen by men, humble yourself publicly. What you do amiss only in your heart, avow, as I said to you before, between yourself and God in confession.

64. With your eyes you should contemplate God, simply, exclusively, and purely, never henceforward to regard anything else or receive consolation except in him. You should bear God in your heart with constant remembrance, and embrace him lovingly with an open and expectant heart; and always long for the sweetness coming from his Heart, and the inner affection of his inner sweet Nature.[118]

72. By all you do or omit, therefore, bear yourself thus outwardly pure and perfect, according to the precepts you are under, as is meet. Do without whatever you can dispense with; and in all things take what you need with a frugal hand. Be outwardly so humble that God may have nothing to reproach you with, and inwardly so free

that you are always longing for him with a miserable, rueful heart. And pray more earnestly his loving, sweet Heart and his strong love, that he may give you himself to love and may be mindful what it is for a young heart to be obliged to do without love; for he is the God of love and knows perfectly our need of love.

86. Since therefore, he perfectly knows the hard life of love, how can God fail to impart himself to you, if you keep yourself as pure as I have told you? He is so sweet and imparts himself to the soul so deeply, yes, takes full possession of it, if it longs for him. Forget not to keep crying inwardly to your tender Love: "O great God, almighty and rich in all gifts, leave me not so poor in you!" Whenever you begin to perform any work, say to him earnestly that you will not go away empty and without fruit. Desire no thanks or praise for any service, but from all things and in all things, humbly accept him himself.

99. And you should wish to have God from creatures; but from no one should you receive him except from the plenitude of his simple Essence, to which you must lovingly devote yourself. For his sweet name makes him pleasing to all men, in the ears of the rational soul. And give entrance into your heart to all the words you hear from him in the Scriptures, whether you read them yourself, or I, or some one else repeats them to you in Dutch or Latin. And take care you do your utmost to live as his sublimity demands. Apply yourself thus to all I have told you. For no one can teach a person love; but these virtues lead one fully to love.[119]

112. May God give you success in achieving this! Amen.

LETTER 25

SARA, EMMA, AND MARGRIET

1. Greet Sara also in my behalf, whether I am anything to her or nothing.

2. Could I fully be all that in my love I wish to be for her, I would gladly do so; and I shall do so fully, however she may treat me. She has very largely forgotten my affliction, but I do not wish to blame or reproach her, seeing that Love leaves her at rest and does not reproach her, although Love ought ever anew to urge her to be busy with her noble Beloved. Now that she has other occupations and

can look on quietly and tolerate my heart's affliction, she lets me suffer. She is well aware, however, that she should be a comfort to me, both in this life of exile and in the other life in bliss. There she will indeed be my comfort, although she now leaves me in the lurch.

16. And you, Emma and yourself—who can obtain more from me than any other person now living can, except Sara—are equally dear to me. But both of you turn too little to Love, who has so fearfully subdued me in the commotion of unappeased love. My heart, soul, and senses have not a moment's rest, day or night; the flame burns constantly in the very marrow of my soul.

24. Tell Margriet to be on her guard against haughtiness, and to be sensible, and to attend to God each day; and that she apply herself to the attainment of perfection and prepare herself to live with us, where we shall one day be together;[120] and she should neither live nor remain with aliens. It would be a great disloyalty if she deserted us, since she so much desires to satisfy us, and she is now close to us—indeed, very close—and we also so much desire her to be with us.

34. Once I heard a sermon in which Saint Augustine was spoken of. No sooner had I heard it than I became inwardly so on fire that it seemed to me everything on earth must be set ablaze by the flame I felt within me. Love is all!

LETTER 26

COPING WITH SEPARATION

1. In God may greeting come to you, and perfect fidelity be sent you from me, and offered from me; and may it be demanded that at every moment, in veritable love, you live for truth (cf. Eph. 4:15) and perfection, in order to give God satisfaction and contentment, and honor and right, in himself first of all and then in the good men who are loved by him, and he by them—and to give them everything they need, in whatever situation they may be.

10. I invite you to do this continually; and I myself have ever done this since I lived in your house. For that is the best and most beautiful work that I know of for God's sake. Scripture teaches you this (cf. Eph. 4:15), and it is true. And above all, think of this unitive Love, whom I love and intend, although I cannot content her. Oh, feel and understand how gladly I would see that you also did this!

And feel also and taste how much woe it causes me that this is still lacking. It makes our misery and the sufferings occasioned by our exile from Love the greater, that we can find joy neither in our mutual society nor in him. I wish you would live so as to grow in your perfection.

24. But I, unhappy as I am, ask this, with love, from all of you—who should offer me comfort in my pains, solace in my sad exile, and peace and sweetness. I wander alone and must remain far from him to whom I belong above all that I am, and for whom I would so gladly be perfect love. And—God knows—he has fruition of all, and I lack everything through which my soul might repose in him.

31. Alas! Why does he permit me to serve him thus and to have fruition of him, and of those who are his—and yet hold me so far from him, and from those who are his?

34. Farewell, and live a beautiful life!

LETTER 27

ULTIMATE MOTIVES FOR HUMILITY

1. God be with you and make known to you all the hidden ways (cf. Job 3:23) you are under obligation to follow and live by in veritable love, so that he may make known to you the unspeakable, vast sweetness of his ardent sweet Nature, which is so deep and so unfathomable that in wondrousness and unknowableness he is deeper and darker than the abyss. May God grant you yourself to know in all things what you are in want of, and may you thus attain to a knowledge of the sublime Love that he himself, our great God, is (cf. 1 John 4:16).

12. Be submissive to all creatures in perfect humility, and never glory in anything. Look at your littleness and his greatness; your lowness and his sublimity; your blindness and his clear sight, penetrating all things: how he sees through everything in heaven and on earth, and the bottomless abyss and the hidden depths. And if you reflect also on the perfection of his Being, how he fully suffices to himself in love and in glory; and if you see that you are so exiled from all interchanges of love that lovers receive from each other—in the embrace, in the kiss, in union, in knowledge, in receiving, in giving, in humility, in mutual greeting, and in gracious welcome—and that the

Beloved can hide so little from his loved one, while whether he loves you or not is so hidden from you and so concealed by him: Oh, all these things can well cause you to be humble! For you would not know what to glory in if you thought of the great darkness and privations in association with Love I have told you about, which in fact are three times greater than I will tell you. This is true, I acknowledge it; I should have told you much more about it than I have until now. But you are so little aware of lacking anything that you do not know what its importance is, or what is missing, or what the sweetness is that the loved one has from her Beloved.

38. I spoke of the Beloved's kiss:[121] that means, to be united with him apart from all creatures, and to accept no appeasement except what one receives in the delight of unity within him.

41. And for the embrace: that means the support he gives to our disinterested abandonment to him *in charity unfeigned* (2 Cor. 6:6).

44. This is the meaning of the embrace and the kiss of the Beloved, as far as it can be expressed in words. But how much sweetness is found in the interior feeling and fruition of the Beloved, all those who were ever born in the human shape could not fully explain to you. One could tell you much more about it, if it would be of any use. Here I break off.

50. But if now you knew this lack—that you do not have, from God who has loved you, what you would have deserved to have if you had loved him above all, as we are under obligation to love him—if you were to love him thus and truly be his loved one, you would experience all the unspeakable wonders overflowing from him that I have made mention of. As you now know that you are this and he is that—and, because of your lowness, what he is must remain out of your reach—it is truly needful for you to humble yourself to the extreme about this and not to glory in it. These are the ultimate motives for which one must be humble.

LETTER 28

TRINITARIAN CONTEMPLATION CAUGHT IN WORDS

1. In the riches of the clarity of the Holy Spirit, the blissful soul celebrates wonderful feasts.[122] These feasts are holy words exchanged in holy rapture with the holiness of our Lord. These words give every soul who hears them and understands them essentially four things in full holiness: They give her pleasure, and sweetness, and joy, and bliss, and all in veritable spiritualness.

10. So whenever God gives the blissful soul this clarity, which enables it to contemplate him in his Godhead,[123] it contemplates him in his Eternity, and in his Greatness, and in his Wisdom, and in his Nobility—and in his Presence, and in his Effusion, and in his Totality.[124] It sees how God is in his Eternity: God through his own Divinity. It sees how God is in his Greatness: powerful in his own power. It sees how God is in his Wisdom: blissful in his own bliss. It sees how God is in his Nobility: glorious in his own glory. It sees how God is in his Presence: sweet with his own sweetness. It sees how God is in his Effusion: rich with his own riches.[125] It sees how God is in his Totality: happy in his own happiness.

26. In all this, it contemplates God in his Godhead. And in each of these attributes, nevertheless, it contemplates God in the manifoldness of the divine riches. Whenever it is in this contemplation, it is needful that it remain in repose of heart, even if it is busy outwardly. This is what the sweet soul says when, full of love and suffering great pains, it has awaited its Lord with confidence, and its Lord has enlightened its heart, and in this radiance it has come into a total manifestation. And it speaks of its feasts and says in its delights: "What have I except God (cf. Ps. 72:25)? God is disclosed to me as Presence; God is to me an Effusion; God is to me Totality. God is present to me with the Son, in sweetness; God with the Holy Spirit is an Effusion for me in richness; God is for me, with the Father, Totality with bliss.[126] Thus God is to me in Three Persons one Lord, and one Lord in Three Persons, and in these Three Persons he is to my soul in the manifoldness of the divine riches."

48. And this soul itself says further: "The soul who walks *with God* (Gen. 5:22) in his Presence gladly speaks of his pleasure, and of his sweetness, and of his greatness. The soul who walks yet farther

with God in his Effusion speaks gladly of his love, and of his bliss, and of his nobility. The soul who walks yet farther with God in his Totality speaks gladly of heavenly riches, and heavenly joy, and heavenly happiness. This blissful soul who walks in God (cf. Col. 2.6) with all these, and walks *with God* (Gen. 5:22) in all these, knows every kind of grace; and it is master and blissful with the same bliss in divine riches as God, who is one eternal Lord, and who is all good, and who is God, and who created all things.

65. "God is greatness, and power, and wisdom.[127] God is goodness, and presence, and sweetness. God is subtlety, and nobility, and happiness. God is eminent in his greatness, and perfect in his power, and blissful in his wisdom. God is wonderful in his goodness, and total in his presence, and joy in his sweetness. God is true in his subtlety, and blessed in his nobility, and wholly overflowing in his happiness. Thus is God in Three Persons with himself in the manifoldness of the divine riches. God is one blessed Beatitude, and he subsists with the fullness of his omnipotence in wonderful exalted riches."[128]

80. These are words that come surging up in the soul with bliss from God's excellence. And what is God's excellence? It is the Being of the Godhead in the Unity, and the Unity in the totality, and the totality in the manifestation, the manifestation in glory, and glory in fruition, and fruition in eternity. God's graces are all excellent. But he who understands this—how this is in God, and in the throne of thrones,[129] and in the riches of heaven—possesses the excellence of all kinds of graces. He who wishes to say more about this must speak with his soul.

93. God abides in bliss and is present in the midst of his glory. And therein he is, within himself, ineffable in his goodness, riches, and wondrousness. God by himself pronounces himself within himself in full beatitude; and the beatitude of his creatures consists in what he is. This is why heaven and earth are full of God; anyone spiritual enough to know God by experience can understand this.

101. A blessed soul saw with God according to God; and it saw God enclosed and yet overflowing. And it saw God overflowing in totality, and total in overflowingness. And this soul spoke with its totality and exclaimed: "God is a great and unique Lord in eternity, and he has in his Godhead the Being of Three Persons: He is Father in his power; he is Son in his knowableness; he is Holy Spirit in his glo-

ry. God gives, in the Father; and he reveals, in the Son; and he enables us to taste, in the Holy Spirit. God works with the Father in power; with the Son in knowableness; and with the Holy Spirit in subtlety. Thus God works with Three Persons as one Lord; and with one Lord as Three Persons; and with Three Persons in a manifoldness of the Divine riches; and with the manifoldness of the divine riches in the souls he has blessed, whom he has led into the mystery of his Father, and all of whom he has made blissful."

121. Between God and the blissful soul that has become God with God, there reigns a spiritual charity. So whenever God reveals this spiritual charity to the soul, there rises within it a tender friendship (cf. Rom. 8:28). That is, it feels within it how God is its friend[130] before all pain, in all pain, and above all pain, yes, beyond all pain, in fidelity toward his Father. And this tender friendship gives rise to a sublime confidence. In this sublime confidence there rises a genuine sweetness. In this genuine sweetness rises a veritable joy. In this veritable joy rises a divine clarity. Then the soul sees, and it sees nothing.[131] It sees a truth—Subsistent, Effusive, Total—which is God himself in eternity. The soul waits; God gives, and it receives. And what it then receives in verity, and spiritualness, and pleasure, and wonder can be communicated to no one. And it must remain in silence, in the liberty of this bliss. What God then says to it of sublime spiritual wonders, no one knows but God who gives it, and the soul who, conformed to God's spiritual Nature, is like God above all spiritualness.

146. Thus spoke one person[132] in God: "My soul is completely torn by the power of eternity, and melted by the friendship of Paternity; and it is streamed through by God's greatness. This greatness is without measure. And the Heart of my heart is that rich wealth which my God and Lord is in his eternity."[133]

153. Thus spoke one person in God's friendship: "I have heard the voice of bliss (Bar. 2:23); I have seen the land of clarity; and I have tasted the fruit of joys. Since this has happened, all the senses of my soul await lofty spiritual wonders, and all my prayers in the presence are continually filled with a sweet confidence that is God himself in veritable truth. Because this is so, I am immeasurably enriched with the same bliss as God is in his Godhead."[134]

165. God is a torrent of holiness above all the saints, in his own Paternity. And from it he gives to all his dearest children new riches,

all full of glory. Because God is this, he can—today, and tomorrow, and always—give new riches that were never heard of, except by the Three Persons who heard of them from himself in his eternity.

172. God is in his Persons and in his attributes. In his attributes, God is above without end; and he is beneath without end; and he is around all without end. God is in the midst of his Persons, filling all his attributes with divine riches. Thus God is in the Persons with himself in the manifoldness of the divine riches. Something of God is God; and this is why in his least gifts God sets in motion all his attributes. Yes, something of God is God himself; he is in himself.

182. God's riches are manifold, and God is manifold in unity, and he is onefold in manifoldness. Because God is this, all his children are filled with bliss, and one of them is ever in greater bliss than the other, and all his children are filled with bliss.

188. The blissful soul speaks of spiritual wisdom with love; and she speaks sublimely with truth; and she speaks powerfully with riches. God gives love, and truth, and riches out of the fullness of his Godhead. God gives love with comprehension; God gives truth with great clearness; God gives riches with fruition.

196. Thus spoke a soul in the presence of God: "There is one God of all the heavens; and the heavens are open, and the attributes of the great God appear in the hearts of his secret friends with pleasure, and with sweetness, and with joy. Then the blissful soul is led into a spiritual inebriation,[135] in which she must play[136] and surrender herself according to the sweetness she feels from within. No one blames her for this;[137] she is the child of God and is blissful."

207. There is another soul my soul calls yet more blissful. That is the soul who is led through truth, and nobility, and clarity, and sublimity, into a blissful silence. And in this blissful silence she hears a great noise (cf. Job 26:14) of the wonders that God himself is in eternity.[138]

213. Both[139] are children of God, and they are blissful already in this life.

214. The soul that has come so far with God that it possesses love and practices wisdom in divine truth is most of the time blissful with the same bliss as God himself is, because it loves with love as much as it can see with wisdom, and sees with wisdom as much as it can love with love. And most of the time it is working with love and with wisdom in the richness of God. And that is a sublime bliss.

224. The soul that has stood so long with the God-Man that it understands such a wonder as God is in his Godhead appears most of the time—for the God-fearing men who are not acquainted with this experience—ungodly through too much godliness, unsteadfast through too much steadfastness, and ignorant through too much knowledge.

231. I saw God was God, and man was man; and then it did not astonish me that God was God, and that man was man. Then I saw God was Man, and I saw man was conformed to God. Then it did not astonish me that man was blissful with God.

236. I saw how God gave the very noblest of men insight through adversity, and through adversity withdrew this insight. And where he withdrew this insight, he gave him the sharpest insight of all. When I saw that, I found my consolation with God in all adversity.

242. Thus spoke a soul in the richness of God: "Divine wisdom and perfect humility, that is great bliss in the clarity of the Father, and that is great perfection in the truth of the Son, and that is great play in the sweetness of the Holy Spirit. Since God's holiness has caused me to keep silence, I have heard many things. And since I have heard many things, why have I retained them? Not in folly did I retain what I retained. I retained everything before and after. So I kept silence then and reposed in God, until the time when God bade me speak. I have integrated all my diversity, and I have individualized all my wholeness. And I have enclosed all my individuality in God until the time when someone will come with such discernment as to ask me what I mean. And since I feel with God in God, that nothing separates me more from him than having to speak, for this reason I keep silence."

262. Thus spoke a soul in the liberty of God: "I have understood all diversity in the pure Unity. Since then I have stayed to play in the Lord's palace, and I have left his vassals to attend to his kingdom. Oh, at this time all the provinces of the lands have flowed into this Land!

267. "I called this the time of bliss. I remained there, standing above all things and yet in the midst of all things, and I looked out above all things into the glory without end."[140]

LETTER 29

HADEWIJCH EVICTED

1. God be with you! and may he give you consolation with the veritable consolation of himself, with which he suffices to himself and to all creatures according to their being and their deserts. O sweet child, your sadness, dejection, and grief give me pain! And this I entreat you urgently, and exhort you, and counsel you, and command you as a mother commands her dear child, whom she loves for the supreme honor and sweetest dignity of Love, to cast away from you all alien grief, and to grieve for my sake as little as you can. What happens to me, whether I am wandering in the country[141] or put in prison—however it turns out, it is the work of Love.

14. I know well, also, that I am not the cause of such grief to you; and I am close to you in heart, and trusted; and for me, you—after Sara—are the dearest person alive. Therefore I well understand that you cannot easily leave off grieving over my disgrace. But be aware, dear child, that this is an alien grief. Think about it yourself; if you believe with all your heart that I am loved by God, and he is doing his work in me,[142] secretly or openly, and that he renews his old wonders in me (cf. Ecclus. 36:6), you must also be aware that these are doings of Love, and that this must lead aliens to wonder at me and abhor me. For they cannot work in the domain of Love, because they know neither her coming nor her going. And with these persons I have little shared their customs in their eating, drinking, or sleeping; I have not dressed up in their clothes, or colors, or outward magnificence. And from all the things that can gladden the human heart, from what it can obtain or receive, I never derived joy except for brief moments from the experience of the Love that conquers all.

38. But from its first awakening and upward turning, my enlightened reason (which, ever since God revealed himself in it, has enlightened me as to whatever in myself and in others was lacking in perfection) showed me and led me to the place where I am to have fruition of my Beloved in unity according to the worthiness of my ascent.

44. This place of Love which enlightened reason showed me, was so far above human thought that I was obliged to understand I might no longer have joy or grief in anything, great or small, except

in this, that I was a human being, and that I experienced Love with a loving heart; but that, since God is so great, I with my humanity may touch the Godhead without attaining fruition.[143]

52. This desire of unattainable fruition, which Love has always given me for the sake of fruition of Love, has injured me and wounded me in the breast and in the heart: *in armariolo et in antisma.*[144] *Amariolo*—that is, the innermost of the arteries of the heart, with which we love; and *antisma*—that is, the innermost of the spirits by which we live, and the one sensitive to the greatest preoccupation.

61. I have lived with these persons nevertheless with all the works I could perform in their service. And they found me prepared with ready virtue for all their needs. This was no doubt unjustifiably.[145] I have also been with them in all things; since God first touched me with the totality of love, I have felt everyone's need according to what he was.[146] With God's charity I have felt and given favor to each one according to that person's needs. With his wisdom I have felt his mercy, and why one must forgive people so much, and how they fall and get up again; and how God gives and takes away (Job 1:21); and how he strikes and heals (Job 5:18); and how he gives himself gratuitously. With his sublimity I have felt the sins of all those whom in this life I have heard named and have seen. And this is why ever since, with God, I have passed just judgments according to the depths of his truth, on us all as we also were. With his unity in love I have felt constantly, since then, the experience of being lost in the fruition of Love, or the suffering of being deprived of this fruition, and the ways of veritable Love in all things, and its mode of operation in God and in all men.

85. In love I have experienced all these attributes, and I have acted with justice toward these persons, however much they have failed me. But if I possess this in love with my eternal being, I do not possess it yet in fruition of Love in my own being.[147] And I remain a human being, who must suffer to the death with Christ in Love; for whoever lives in veritable Love will suffer opprobrium from all aliens, until Love comes to herself, and until she is full-grown within us in virtues, whereby Love becomes one with men.

LETTER 30

ANSWERING THE DEMAND OF GOD'S TRINITY AND UNITY

1. God, who ever was and evermore shall be the foundation of veritable Love and perfect faith, is for us the perfect pledge of the most perfect Love with which he loves himself in himself, and with which all his friends, whom he loves, must love him in pure perfection.[148] For this perfection they whom he has called, and chosen, and marked out for his service should live. They could do great works and progress rapidly if they were what they seem to be and what they ought to be, according to the just debt of perfect faith and of veritable Love.

14. He who loves works great works. And he spares nothing, and he never becomes discouraged at any distress that befalls him, or any torments that confront him; but in adverse situations he shows himself continually active and cheerful. And it is the same in all things, small and great, easy and difficult, whereby he may win virtues that truly give pleasure to Love.

22. Alas! Few people nowadays wish to live according to the pleasure of Love; most of them live according to their own pleasure. They wish to receive much from Love, but to live in a manner little worthy of her. For we are weak in virtue but zealous in pleasure. Some insignificant thing can annoy and grieve us to such a point that we put Love away and forget to serve her. This is great baseness. For at all hours we must content Love by our life: that may mean to be lost in the sweetness of Love, or to be in great tormenting pain—according to Love's dignity and for the sake of contenting Love.

35. The most sublime life and the most rapid growth lie in dying away and wasting away in the pain of Love. And in the experience of sweetness one is on a lower level, for people easily allow themselves to be conquered by it, and so the strength of desire diminishes. And what they experience, they find so great that they cannot come to the knowledge of the greatness and perfect Being of Love. For when the heart and the lower feelings, which are easily satisfied, are touched according to our emotional attractions, they think they are in the highest heaven. And in this delight they forget the great debt—payment of which is being demanded every hour—that Love demands of Love.

49. I mean the demand that the Father demands in eternal fruition from the Unity of the Son and the Holy Spirit, and the debt that the Son and the Holy Spirit demand from the Father in the fruition of the Holy Trinity. And that demand is eternally new in one possession and one Being; and from the need to satisfy the demand of the Father's Unity, the justice of all judgment is derived.

57. By the demand of the Father's omnipotence, through the wisdom of the Son and the goodness of the Holy Spirit, in the Trinity, man was created. But because man did not answer the demand of the Unity, he fell. By the demand of the Trinity God's Son was born, and to satisfy the debt to the Unity he died.[149] By the demand of the Trinity he rose again among men; and to satisfy the debt to the Unity he ascended to his Father.

68. So it is also with us. When payment of the debt we owe is demanded of us by the Trinity, grace is given us to live worthily according to the noble Trinity, as is fitting.

72. But if, because our will is estranged, we thwart this and fall back from this unity into our own self-complacency, we no longer grow and no longer make progress in that perfection which was thus demanded of us from the beginning by the Unity and the Trinity. But if rational man's noble reason would recognize its just debt and follow Love's leading into her land—that is, follow Love according to her due—then he would be capable of attaining that great object and being enriched in God with divine riches.

84. He who wishes to clothe himself, and to be rich (cf. Apoc. 3:18), and to be one with the Godhead must adorn himself with all the virtues that God clothed and adorned himself with when he lived as Man; and one must begin this by the same humility with which he also began it. For he was destitute of all alien consolation, and he was unexalted by all his nobility, and all his virtues, and his works, and his power, through which he stood first among all. And he remained unexalted until the time when he was exalted by the fearful and wonderful demand of the Unity. We are now under Love's demand toward the Holy Trinity. Therefore we ourselves must make a demand on Love, and we must do this with all ardor; and we must demand nothing else but his Unity.

100. And we must live according to the pleasure of Love, who at all hours has demanded this Unity, and has adorned unexalted humility with just works; and according to the demand of the Holy Trinity, which always demands perfect virtues according to its pleasure, by

which one grows, here, and becomes perfect in a life in accordance with the Trinity and in accordance with the Unity.

107. There are three things through which one lives for Love, here with the Trinity and, in the beyond, in the Unity. First, here, one desires Love under the guidance of reason, and one desires to content her with all just works of perfection, and to be perfect and worthy of all perfection. In this manner one lives the Son of God.

114. Second, at all hours one wills in this way the will of Love with new ardor, and exercises all the virtues with overflowing desire, and enlightens all creatures according to what they are[150] and according to the due of the nobility he recognizes in them, be it in nobility or in lowness; so shall we, for the honor of love, do the pure will of our God in our works and love. In this manner one lives the Holy Spirit.

123. Third, one is held by sweet constraint to be in perpetual exertion; and with never-conquered power[151] to be a match for this Being; and—strong and unconquered and joyful—by ardent striving to grow up as loved one in the Beloved in every respect: to work with his hands; to walk with his feet; to hear with his ears where the voice of the Godhead never ceases to speak through the mouth of the Beloved, in all truth of counsel, of justice, of sweet sweetness, of consolation for everyone according to each person's need, and of caution against sin; to appear like the Beloved, unadorned and without beauty (cf. Isa. 53:2), live for no one else but for the Beloved in love alone, live in him as the loved one in the Beloved, with the same way of acting, with one spirit, and with one heart; and in one another to taste the unheard-of sweetness he merited by his sufferings. Oh yes! To feel heart in heart, with one single heart and one single sweet love,[152] and continually have fruition of one full-grown love. And lastly, that one must ever know certainly, without any doubt, that one is wholly in the Unity of Love. In this state one is the Father.[153]

145. Thus one pays off here on earth the debt that the Trinity demands, and that it has always demanded of the Unity from all eternity. It is true, they who thus live according to Love make many a beautiful ascension in their Beloved, with their Beloved. But what happens when they have wholly grown up to this Unity, when they make their ascent without returning, and when they reach union there on the heights where first the great light, the brilliant lightning, has flashed, and then the loud thunder has resounded?

155. Lightning is the light of Love, which shows her in one flash

and confers grace in many things, in order to show who Love is and how she can receive and give—in the sweetness of clasping, in the fond embrace, in the sweet kiss, and in heartfelt experience when Love actually speaks: "I am the one who hold you in my embrace! This is I! I am the all! I give the all!"

162. But after that comes the thunder. Thunder is the fearful voice (cf. Apoc. 1:6) of threat: and it is retraction; and it is enlightened reason, which holds up before us the truth, and our debt, and our failure to grow up to conformity with Love, and our smallness compared to Love's greatness.[154]

167. When therefore the soul is brought to union out of the multiplicity of gifts, it becomes all that that is.[155] And then the Unity for the first time obtains what it has demanded, and then the demand is first truly actualized,[156] and then the soul can have, through the Trinity, the fruition that until now had been withheld. Then shall the Three Persons forever demand and eternally render—at one and the same time—their Unity in one will, one possession, and one fruition.

177. How this is, I do not dare to tell you now, for I am too far from having obtained full growth, and the love I possess is too small.

179. If this life in Unity is wanting to me and to any others who are destitute of it, that comes from having falsified the truth: We began excellently, but our works are small, and we wish to live on them without delay and to rely on them. We wish to be exalted for our patience and honored for our good deeds, and we forget the debt of Love too soon. We esteem our works to be good, and for this reason they are vain. We are conscious of our distress, and for this reason we do not find our Beloved in it. We make a great stir about our labors, and for this reason we find in them no rich inn of consolation and sweet repose, in which the Beloved entertains his loved one who has journeyed to him from afar and with great risky ventures. We wish that our virtues be known; for this reason we *do not have on* that *wedding garment* (Matt. 22:11). We exercise our charity according to need, and this is why we do not possess charity's wide power. Our humility is in our voice, on our face, and in appearances—and not fully motivated by God's greatness or by our perception of our littleness.

200. Therefore we do not carry God's Son maternally[157] or suckle him with exercises of love. We have too much self-will, and we want too much repose, and we seek too much ease and peace. We are too easily tired, and dejected, and disconsolate. We seek too much consolation from God and men. We will not endure any setback. We

wish to know too exactly what we have not got, and then we are too concerned with obtaining it, and we will suffer nothing. It offends us if men scorn us, or cast doubt on our experiences of God, or rob us of our repose, or of our honor, or of our friends.

214. In church we wish to be holy, but at home and elsewhere we wish to know about all the worldly things that help us or harm us. And there we find time to spend with our friends, in talk and association, and in quarreling and reconciliation. We wish to have a good reputation with little service of Love, and we are concerned about fair clothing, choice food, beautiful things, and worldly amusements that no one needs. For no one ought to seek amusement in order to escape from God, who comes incessantly with new force. And if we are sick because of our weakness, with better sense and greater profit we can ridicule it. But because we relieve this sickness too early, and comfort it with weakness, and deceive ourselves, and forget the *wisdom from above* (James 3:15), we do not equal God's valiant warriors (cf. 2 Tim. 2:4), and therefore we are not upheld, or consoled, or nourished by God. For we fall away from God, not he from us; and because we ourselves withhold something from Love, we do not wear her crown, and we are not exalted or honored by her.

238. On account of this we are hindered in all directions, and veritable fidelity and Love remain out of our reach. And because all these defects in us are so numerous, we remain not fully grown in the spiritual life and imperfect in all virtues. And for this reason no one can help others.

244. Alas the day, how hard this is for us! May God now correct everything within us and grant us such perfect being that we may live in conformity with the Trinity, and that we may become united to the Unity of the Godhead. Amen.

LETTER 31

INVITATION TO JOIN HADEWIJCH

1. O dear child! The best possible life is this: to do our utmost to content God with love, and above all to trust in him. For we come closest to him by confidence; for he said himself to one person that true prayer is nothing else than pure abandonment to him, with perfect fidelity to trust him in all that he is. For he himself said: "People

who do not know me and my goodness, who I am, serve me with fasting, and vigils, and sundry labors. And with these labors they entrust themselves to me. But nothing has so much power over me as the perfect abandonment of lofty fidelity." He added: "Your soul's hunger disposes me to prepare everything for you, so that I, what I am, shall be yours. Through your striving to satisfy your hunger for me, you grew up to full perfection, and you became like to me: your death and mine shall be one, and therefore we shall live with one life, and one love shall satisfy the hunger of us both."[158]

21. I am imparting to you these glad tidings, which our Lord uttered, so that you may better believe, and think, and know that abandonment in fidelity is the quickest way to perfection, by which we may content God most perfectly and best.

26. By this I exhort you to all the most perfect liberty of Love,[159] for I saw in a dream-vision in the past that you would rally to my blazon; so I urge this on you, for I hold it dearest to me above all things. Make haste to virtue in veritable Love; and take care that God be honored by you and by all those whom you can help, with effort, with self-sacrifice, with counsel, and with all that you can do, unremittingly.

POEMS IN STANZAS

POEMS IN STANZAS

1 VALE MILLIES

1

If now, alas! it is cold winter,[1]
    With short days and long nights,
Bold summer speedily walks in
    To set us free from distress
5 In a short time: that is plainly seen
    From this new year;
The hazelnut tree offers us fair blooms,
    The season's public token.
—Ay, vale, vale, millies—
10 All you who in the new spring
—Si dixero non satis est[2]*—*
    Wish to be joyful for Love's sake![3]

2

So truly chivalrous souls,
    Whatever storms they encounter for Love's sake,
15 Accept them in a perfect manner,
    As if to say: "This is where I win
And shall win everything! God send me all
    That best suits Love,
According to the way she pleases,
20 Even if affliction be my greatest profit!"
—Ay, vale, vale, millies—
    All you who do not fear
—Si dixero non satis est—
    Pain and adventure for the sake of Love!

3

25 Alas! what shall I do, unhappy woman?
    I can rightly hate good fortune.

My life grieves me sorely:
I can neither love nor cease to love.
Rightly do I face as foes
30 Good fortune and adventure alike;
I am not in tune, and no one else is:
That seems contrary to nature.
—Ay, vale, vale, millies—
Are you not all deeply touched
35 *—Si dixero, non satis est—*
That Love lets me moan thus?

4

Alas! I gave full trust to Love,
Since first I heard her named,
And I left myself to her free power;
40 For this all wish to condemn me,
Friends and strangers, young and old,
Whom I always served in every way—
Giving them my heart's affection—
And favored their success in Love.
45 *—Ay, vale, vale, millies—*
I counsel them to spare nothing,
—Si dixero, non satis est—
No matter how badly I have fared.[a]

5

Alas, poor me! I cannot cause
50 Myself to live or die![4]
O sweet God, what has happened to me
That these people bring me to ruin?
But let them leave you alone to strike me;
You should best decide
55 In justice, all I have done ill,
And they would be left without loss!
—Ay, vale, vale, millies—
They do not let God act,

a. Cf. Job 19:13–19.

—Si dixero, non satis est—
60 And they do not love but hate.

6

While they are busy scanning me,
Who shall be loving their love?
Better had they gone their free way,
Where they might have learned to know you.
65 They wish to help you deal with me,
A labor obviously wasted;
To scourge or pardon, you know best,
And to search with pure truth.
—Ay, vale, vale, millies—
70 All who hold with God,
—Si dixero, non satis est—
In pardoning and in justice!

7

Solomon would dissuade us from this attempt:
That we search not
75 *Into things above our ability,*
And that we seek not
Things that are too high for us—
That we be not inquisitive about them,[b]
But we should let true Love
80 Set us free or chain us fast.
—Ay, vale, vale, millies—
Whoever to the mystery of sublime Love
—Si dixero, non satis est—
Ascends from degree to degree.[5]

8

85 Man's thoughts are so limited,
God passes infinitely above them;

b. Ecclus. 3:22, 24.

God alone is wise without limit:
    This is why men shall praise him for all,
And verdict they must leave to him,
90   Be it vengeance or acquittal.
Never deed so far remote
    That it can escape his eyes.
—Ay, vale, vale, millies—
    Souls who surrender totally to Love,
95 *—Si dixero, non satis est—*
    And perfectly give pleasure in Love's sight!

9

God must give us a renewed mind
    For nobler and freer love,
To make us so new in our life
100   That Love may bless us
And renew, with new taste,
    Those to whom she can give new fulness;
Love is the new and powerful recompense
    Of those whose life renews itself for Love alone.
105 *—Ay, vale, vale, millies—*
    That renewing of new Love
—Si dixero, non satis est—
    Which renewal will newly experience.

2 TRIUMPH HARD-WON

1

Now in a short time
The sap will flow upward from the roots;
Through its vitality, far and wide,
Meadow and plant will don their foliage.
5   Of this we have an infallible presentiment:
    The birds are growing joyful.
    He who for love turns warrior
    Will soon triumph,
    If he is half-hearted in nothing.

2

10 Whoever spares nothing for sublime Love's sake
Is wise in all his work.
Love is noble maiden and queen;
When she gives anyone loftiness of mind,
He fulfils her every wish
15 And does his utmost with strength and forethought,
So that Love acknowledges his work:
However much she resists at first,
It is he who conquers Love.

3

But in this it appears she is Love and lady,
20 That she is the mother of the virtues:[6]
She is fertile, and she alone bears the fidelity
From which all you who love are endowed with power.
Fidelity alone has consoled us
And has rewarded all our griefs.
25 I pray fidelity to look upon us
And cause our youth to prosper
By entrusting to us the fulness of all love.

4

Love is so sweet in her nature
That she conquers every other power.
30 He who serves Love has a hard adventure
Before he knows Love's mode of action,
Before he is fully loved by her.
He tastes her as bitter and sour;
He cannot rest for an instant,
35 So long as Love does not fetter him completely in love
And bring him into the union of fruition.

5

Whoever strives for the fruition of Love
Shall conquer all his distress;

He whom Love touches cannot die—
40 Her name is *a-mor,* "delivered from death"—
If he has done what Love commanded
And in this has failed in nothing.
She is the wealth of all things;
Love is that *living bread*[7]
45 And above all sweet in taste.[a]

6

Now great lamentation
Replaces my new songs,
Which I have sung so long,
Poetizing Love so beautifully.
50 Although I have striven too little,
It causes me woe and pain
That I am not in possession
Of Love's unconquered power
In the fruition where I become controlled by Love.

7

55 In the days left me, it were plainly best
I hush the songs of true love
With which I was accustomed to be joyful
In singing or reciting in the past,
When her rich teaching
60 Gave me indubitable joy,
Whereas I now suffer pain
And heartache:
I wither like an old man and waste away.

8

So greatly has the pain of love worn me out
65 That I am now unfit for anything.
She first led me to her school,[8]

---

a. John 6:41; Wisd. 16:20.

Where I sought her wise secrets,
Whereas she has withdrawn them from me since then
And has hidden many from me.
70 Yet I will gladly suffer all things,
For Love has never revoked
The promises she held out to me.

9

Would that Love might give me new days,
As these I have are so old!
75 Then I would silence my complaint,
Which now counts so many themes,
And live free from care, in full trust of Love,
Where now I am confronted by risky ventures.
However joyful I'd then find myself,
80 May Love nonetheless make her free disposal
Of me, according to her pleasure.

10

Although it causes me such smarting pain
That I know myself forsaken by Love,
Love shows honor to all her friends
85 Who are prompt to serve her with fidelity,
So that in pleasure or pain
They understand her rich teaching.
They who work without growing fainthearted,
And whom Love completely fetters in love,
90 Remain in her glorious kingdom.

11

As the beautiful rose
Appears to us in the dew between the thorns,
So shall he who loves, in spite of all disasters,
Endure Love's storms with confidence.
95 Free and assured

He shall grow amid all that is harmful;
That is why the heartless have abandoned
This role quickly enough,
Whereas they who love are free.

100 He who wishes to possess Love completely
Must shun all false teachers;
Although their coaxing is sweet now,
Very soon it will be clear
That their deceitful teaching is false.

3 MY BEST SUCCESS

1

News is spread by many tokens—
The birds, the flowers, the fields, the daylight—
That these beings one and all will triumph over the pains
That oppressed them sorely in winter.
5 Because summer can console them,
They are sure of undelayed joy,
While I must suffer bitter adversity.
I too would be joyful if Love gave me good fortune,
But good fortune never has been mine.

2

10 O what did I do to good fortune
That it was always so merciless to me?
That to me it did such violence—
More than to a thousand other souls?
That it did not reward my fidelity,
15 Unless now and then with a half smile?
And yet perhaps this was my fault.
I will not, therefore, stand my ground:
Love may make her free disposal of me!

3

If I could trust myself to Love,
20 It might still be my rescue:
If with regard to what Love made me suffer in fidelity
I were established in good expectation
That in fidelity she had done this,
And that she would consider my sorry plight,
25 I should regain courage none too soon:
For my shield has warded off so many stabs
There's no room left on it for a new gash.

4

Whoever could understand all this as good
Would possess the ability I lack:
30 In losses, defamations, oppression,
To suffer all without bitterness, for Love;
And to be pleased at any price
And say: "This is my best success!"—
Like one for whom this is the highest wisdom.
35 He who behaved thus would be named wise;
I lack wisdom, and this is my grief.

5

Love holds many gifts in store;
Sometimes she gives consolation, then again wounds;
After heavy blows she bestows health.[a]
40 How can anyone protect himself from this?
One man employs all he ever had,[9]
Yet she hides from him all knowledge of her;
While to another her pleasure gives
The sweet *kisses of* her *mouth*;[b]
45 And yet a third she puts under the ban.

---

a. Job 5:18.
b. Cf. Song 1:1.

6

O *Deus!* Who shall acquit those
Whom Love places under the ban?
No one but Love! He who wishes to bring a lawsuit against her
Must oppose her so bravely
50 That he counts the whole exploit a great success—
Pains and joys intermingled—
And finds them all good without distinction:
So Love teaches him to shout for joy,
And acquaints him with all her splendors.

7

55 When storms are spent, the weather's fair,
Of this we see repeated proof;
Anger and reconcilement in succession
Make Love enduring.
He whom Love by all this proves to be noble
60 Becomes, thanks to the pains of love, so bold
That he proclaims: "Love, I am all yours!
I have nothing but you to revive me.
O noble Love, be all mine!"[c]

8

If good fortune, with its constant hatred for me,
65 Would let me be cured in love,
I should yet be all love to belong to Love,
Could my woe but bear its fruit.
So would I in her deep, perilous waters
Read all my judgments,
70 And give Love room in my love.
If my nature were to mount so high,
My hunger would be satisfied.[10]

---

c. Cf. Song 2:16.

We are too half-hearted in our spending for love.[11]
As long as this lasts, we are aliens in her sight.
75 Therefore we remain poor.—Know, everyone:
To him who pleased her,
Love gave her kingdom and her treasure.

4 FIDELITY

1

Now shall the season and the birds be sad;
But winter need bring no sadness to one
Who wishes to conform himself with truth
So as to work by lofty fidelity's counsel:
5 He will satisfy his Beloved with fidelity;
That is the very best surrender.

2

However it may be with the season,
Anyone who is accompanied by works in truth
Finds himself ever face to face
10 With blossoms, joy, summer, and daylight.
He is always new and afire with longing;
Winter no longer molests him.

3

To one who gives himself with fidelity in truth
And then with truth lives fidelity,
15 The *hidden word*[a] is spoken,
Which no alien can understand
But only he who has had a taste of it
And has experienced silence amid great noise.[b]

---

a. Job 4:12.

b. Cf. Job 26:14, *The Anchor Bible, Job,* trans. M. Pope (Garden City: Doubleday, 1965), pp. 164, 166–167.

4

After deep stillness, loud noise,
20 After perfect consolation, anxious search;
Anyone who is apprehensive is blameworthy,
Since it is all great gain.
On these noble flowers with their fruit,[c]
Fix your thought and understanding, O free, noble soul!

5

25 O noble souls, where are you wandering off to?
How could you thus lower yourselves,
Since you have long appeared as though
You must always live on fidelity alone?
If you had ever been touched by fidelity,
30 How could you find peace in anything less?

6

Many are called and are shown beautiful things,
But few are chosen:[d] what use to gloss it over?
But the false shall themselves be the most taunted,
When fidelity shall repay all men according to their works
35 And shall crown all its friends
With what it is and shall be.

7

But, O free, noble, and highborn souls,
Not only called but chosen,
Spare no trouble or pain in your approach
40 To live in the ardor of lofty fidelity!
Let your whole life be holy affliction,
Until you are master of your Beloved.

---

c. Cf. Song 7:12.
d. Matt. 20:16, 22:14.

8

O hearts, let not your many griefs
Distress you! You shall soon blossom;
45 You shall row through all storms,
Until you come to that luxuriant land
Where Beloved and loved one shall wholly flow through each
other:
Of that, noble fidelity is your pledge here on earth.

9

God must give noble souls an insight
50 That will enlighten for them the life of exile,
Since they are now wounded and driven from their goal
Under the blow of cruel aliens.
If the loved one shall be *lifted up*[e] in the Beloved,
How blessed that will be for him!

5 LOVE'S MODE OF ACTION

1

However sad the season and the birds,
The valiant heart that wills to suffer pain
For Love, has no need of sadness;
It shall know and understand all—
5 Sweetness and cruelty,
Joy and sorrow—
That must be encountered for Love's sake.

2

Valiant souls who have come so far
That they endure unsatisfied Love
10 Shall in all ways, toward her,

e. Cf. John 12:32.

Be bold and undaunted,
And ever ready to receive
Be it consolation, be it blows,
From Love's mode of action.

3

15 Love's way of acting is unheard of,
As anyone who has experienced it well knows.
For Love withdraws consolation midway;[12]
He whom Love touches
Cannot hold out:
20 He tastes
Many nameless hours.[13]

4

Sometimes afire and sometimes cold,
Sometimes cautious and sometimes reckless,
Love is full of fickleness.
25 Love summons us all
To pay our great debt
For her rich power,
Which she invites us to share.

5

Sometimes gracious and sometimes fierce,
30 Sometimes aloof and sometimes close by:
For him who understands this in fidelity to Love
It is matter for jubilation:
How Love knocks down
And seizes
35 At one stroke.

6

Sometimes stooping low and sometimes mounting high,
Sometimes hidden and sometimes revealed:
Before Love cherishes anyone,

He suffers many adventures
40 Ere he arrives
Where he tastes
The nature of Love.

7

Sometimes indulgent and sometimes harsh,
Sometimes dark and sometimes bright:[14]
45 In liberating consolation, in coercive fear,
In accepting and in giving,
Must they who are
Knight-errants in Love
Always live here below.

6 CONQUEST OF LOVE—AT A PRICE

1

When March begins, we see
All beings live again,
And all plants spring up
And in a short time turn green.
5 It is the same with longing,
Particularly that of the true lover:
In his lawsuit with Love he wishes to win,
And to become so bold against her
That she will give herself wholly in love
10 And live wholly as Love with love;
If he could not conquer her entirely,
It would be a great pain to him.

2

He who begins to make progress
Must see that he does not lose
15 Zeal for good works,
But serve for the honor of Love

And live in high hope
Of what his heart has chosen.
Love will indeed strengthen him:
20 He shall conquer his Beloved;
For Love can never
Refuse herself to anyone;
Rather she gives him what she is willing he possess,
And more than she herself promised him.

3

25 He who endures Love with doubt
Is a branch blighted by the frost,
So that he cannot grow
As it pleases Love; therefore he feels
The burden of noble Love;
30 There is no foliage springing up from him:
Moreover he cannot bear flowers and fruit
When the sun is absent—
That sun is veritable Love, who calls forth
Flowers and fruit from the mind.
35 Whether he loses or wins,
He always finds the outcome joy.[15]

4

He who in his spiritual youth
Makes his beginning in Love,
And is wholly submissive to her,
40 And gives all his strength,
And proves his gift by virtue,
And employs in this all his understanding:
Such a one shall receive in full freedom
Love's unheard-of power;
45 This he will truly carry into effect,
And it will not escape him:
He shall yet subdue Love
And be her lord and master.

5

Love makes me wander outside myself.
50 Where shall I find something of Love
According to my heart's delight,
So that I may sweeten my pain?
Although I follow her, she flies;
Although I attend her school,
55 She will not agree with me in anything.
In a moment this becomes all too clear to me.
Alas! I speak from heart's distress;
My misfortune is too great,
And for me, to do without Love is a death,
60 Since I cannot have fruition of her.

6

Since I ought to love totally,
Why did she not give me total love?
Yet according to my small desires
That would be small pleasure for me;
65 To win Love's favor, however,
I have brought all my understanding to nought;
I no longer know what to live on.
She knows well what I imply.
For I have so spent what is mine,
70 I have nothing to live on—or she must give it.
But even if she gave something, hunger would remain,
For I want the whole.

7

How, alas, can it be bearable to me[16]
(And to the others with the same experience)
75 That Love precedes us on the way
And still withholds herself thus?
O sweetest of all that exists!
Your refusal to give yourself to me
As fully as is my right

80 Does not embolden me so much:
But I complain for your friends,
Who ever served you faithfully,
And ever gladly denied themselves
For the sweetness of your nature.

85 Now they are in heavy chains,
Exiled in their own land;
There they wander, subject
To alien adventures.

7 THE NEW PATH

1

At the new year[17]
We hope for the new season
That will bring new flowers
And new joys manifold.
5 He who for Love's sake suffers fears
May well live joyful:
She shall not escape him;
For Love's rich power
Is new and indeed friendly
10 And sweet of demeanor,
And sweetens with a recompense
Every new sadness.

2

Oh, how new in my eyes was anyone
Who served new Love
15 With new veritable fidelity—
As the tyro should rightly do
When Love first reveals herself to him.
So even if he had few friends,
That could have saddened him little
20 Had he kept close to Love;

For Love gives the new good
That makes the new mind,
That renews itself in all
Wherein Love newly touched it.[18]

3

25 Oh, Love is ever new,
And she revives every day!
Those who renew themselves she causes to be born again
To continual new acts of goodness.
How, alas, can anyone
30 Remain old, fainthearted at Love's presence?
Such a person lives truly old in sadness,
Always with little profit;
For he has lost sight of the new path,
And he is denied the newness
35 That lies in new service of Love,
In the nature of the love of new lovers.

4

Alas, where is new Love now
With her new good things?
For my distress brings me
40 Into many a new woe;
My soul melts away
In the madness of Love;[19]
The abyss into which she hurls me
Is deeper than the sea;
45 For Love's new deep abyss
Renews my wound:
I look for no more health
Until I experience Love as all new to me.

5

But old souls, they of new wisdom,
50 Who newly give themselves away to Love
And spare themselves no new trouble—

These I call renewed and old.
They live high-mindedly;
For they become attached to Love
55 And constantly gaze on her with ardor.
This is why their power in love grows,
For they must exercise themselves as tyros
And, as old, lean upon Love
To go where their Beloved will lead them,
60 With mind renewed by new violent longing.

6

They who come to Love's new school
With new love,
According to new Love's counsel
In honor of new fidelity,
65 Often seem outside of themselves;
Then they are deepest swallowed up
In Love's disfavor,
Where they yearn painfully for her;
And so comes that new clarity
70 With all new truth,
And brings newly to light
What it had announced to me in secret.

7

Oh, how sweet is proclaiming the renewal!
Although it occasions new vicissitudes
75 And many new sufferings,
It is a new security;
For Love will truly repay us
With great new honors;
Love shall cause us to ascend
80 To Love's highest mystery,
Where that new totality shall be
In new glorious fruition,

And we shall say: "New Love is wholly mine!"[a]
Alas, this newness happens too seldom!

85 All who shun this renewal
And renew themselves with newness not that of Love
Shall be distrusted by the new,
And condemned by both the new and the newly reborn.

8 LAYING SIEGE TO LOVE

1

Spring comes in new; and the old winter season,
After its long reign, vanishes.
Were anyone ready in Love's service,
He would receive from her a reward:
5 New consolation and new power;
And if he loved Love with the power of love,
He would speedily become love with Love.

2

It is unheard of to become Love.
He who wishes to become Love shall spare nothing;
10 For this state of being is above all conception;
He shall sail long and far through the storm.[20]
Love dwells so deep *in the bosom of the Father*,[a]
Our service must be exceedingly great
If we wish Love to reveal her work.

3

15 Service in works of mercy, and the debt of the law,
The lover pays off at the start;
After he possesses this power,

a. Cf. Song 2:16.
a. John 1:18.

He comes into immense profit:
He performs all his works with no sign of effort,
20 And suffers all griefs without pain;
This is life above human comprehension.

4

He who wishes to become Love performs excellent works,[21]
For nothing can make him give way;
He is unconquered, and equal in strength
25 To the task of winning the love of Love,
Whether he serves the sick or the well,
The blind, the crippled or the wounded—
He will accept this as his debt to Love.

5

To serve strangers, to give to the poor,
30 To comfort the sorrowful as best he can,
To live in the faithful service of God's friends—
Saints or men on earth—night and day,
With all his might, beyond possibility—
If he thinks his strength will fail,
35 Let him trust henceforth in reliance on Love.

6

By valiant confidence in Love
We attain all that is needful for us:
Love gives counsel to the sorrowing.
And comforts those who are sorrowing.
40 If anyone places his reliance in Love alone
And wishes to trust no other,
That is a sign that he contents Love.

He who wishes to serve Love alone,
With all his heart and all his powers,
45 Has wisely laid out the whole siege,
So that he may wholly capture Love.

9 THE KNIGHT OF LOVE

1

To sing of Love is pleasant in every season,[22]
Be it autumn, winter, spring, or summer,
And to plead our case against her power,
For no courageous man keeps out of her way.
5 But we lazy ones often say in anxiety:
"What, would she tyrannize thus over me?
I had rather share the lot of those
Who manage to secure quiet,
And remain at home! Why should I
10 Sally forth to meet my doom?"

2

Ignoble persons of small perception
Fear the cost will be too high:
Therefore they withdraw from Love,
From whom all good would have come to them.
15 If they withdraw from Love's service,
They will be the conquerors, so they think.
But fidelity will show they are poor and make them known as they are,
All naked before Love's magnificence;
These are they who consumed everything they had,
20 But without coercion from Love.

3

He who would gladly suffer sweet exile[23]
(The roads to the land of high Love)
Would find his beloved and his country at the end;
Of this, Fidelity gives seal and pledge;[a]
25 Many a yokel, however, is such a beggar
That he takes what lies nearest his hand,

a. Cf. Eph. 1:13–14.

Remaining before Love unknown
With his beggar's garment;[24]
So he has not the form or badge of honor
30 By which Love recognizes what is hers.

4

A fine exterior, fine garments,
And fine language adorn the knight:
To suffer everything for Love without turning hostile
Is a fine exterior for him who has such ability;
35 His garments then are his acts,
Performed with new ardor, not with self-complacency,
And with regard for all the needs of strangers
Rather than of his own friends:
This is the colored apparel, best adorned
40 With blazons of nobility, to the honor of high Love.

5

Veracious words and great expenditures
In public, and fair splendor at home,
Most give the knight honor and luster;
By these signs can he best be recognized.
45 So it is also with them who love,
If they are established in the truth
And if they arrange their inner life with fair splendor,
As best pleases Love,
And give their whole love for Love's sake:
50 This gift is best pleasing to Love.

6

I speak of Love; and I counsel
Adorned splender and noble deed.
That fidelity must pay back what Love consumed
Is small consolation for many a one
55 Who stands in the chains of Love,
In nonfruition and disgrace.
"Love always rewards, even though she comes late."

Here is my answer to that:
They who follow her suffer
60 From night in the daytime![b]

7

Who would be ever singing the praises of Love,
Since she gives night in the daytime?
Those she ought to clothe, honor, and nourish,
She robs of all their strength:
65 Anyone who would gladly pay the tribute of love,
She ought to teach according to all justice,
And under the seal of fidelity raise to the height
Where the loved soul both encounters
And, with the whole fruition of love,
70 Honors and adorns the Beloved.

8

What seems to the loved soul the most beautiful encounter
Is that it should love the Beloved so fully
And so gain knowledge of the Beloved with love
That nothing else be known by it
75 Except: "I am love conquered by Love!"
But he who overcame Love was rather conquered[c]
So that he might in love be brought to nought:[d]
In this lies the power that surpasses everything,
That from which Love
80 Was born from the beginning.[25]

9

But we who are shallow, of frivolous mind,
Find the fears of Love harsh;
We are inconstant with small gains;
Therefore we are deprived of Love's clear truth.

---

b. Cf. Job 5:14.
c. Cf. Gen. 32:22–32.
d. Cf. Phil. 2:7.

85 I know (although I know not all the joys
That one experiences in Love's wealth,
Still enlightened reason teaches all this)
    How to correspond with Love to the full.
    Reason does not reach this truth:
90 No task too hard, and all is prepared anew.

They who early
Catch sight of Love's beauty,
And are quickly acquainted with her joy,
And take delight in it—
95 If things turn out well for them,
Will have, God knows,
A much better bargain in love
Than I have found so far.

10 KNIGHT ERRANT

1

Long hushed are the birds
That sang so joyously before:
Their joy is ended
Simply because they have lost summer.
5 They would soon have turned up in triumph
If they had got summer back again
With their favorite halcyon days,
For birds are born for summer:
You know this when you hear their song.

2

10 I say nothing of the birds' complaint:
Their joy, their pain are soon over;
But I complain of what displeases me more:
That Love, whom we should strive for,
Oppresses us with her noble burden,
15 And we grasp alien things close at hand,

So that Love cannot admit us to her good graces.
Alas, what our baseness has done to us!
This is disloyalty—who will oust it for us?

3

I know brave knights, strong of hand,
20 In whom I place my fullest trust.
They ever serve in the chains of Love,
And they fear no pain, grief, or vicissitudes,
But they wish to fare through all that land
Which the loving soul ever found with Love in Love;
25 Their noble heart is of lordly turn:
They know what Love teaches with love,
And how Love honors the loyal lover with love.

4

Why then should we miss the opportunity
(If we can conquer Love with love),
30 And not with ardent longing fare through the storms
In confidence and reliance on Love,
And give ourselves to the service of Love?
So should nobility become known to us.
Lo! the day of love is dawning
35 When men will never fear pain for Love's sake,
And the pain of Love will never be oppressive.

5

Often I cry for help like one in despair:
"Beloved, when you come,
Seek me with new consolation!"
40 Then I ride my proud steed
And consort with my Beloved in supreme joy,
As if all beings of the North, the South, the East,
And the West were captive in my power.
And suddenly I am unhorsed, on foot.
45 —What use is it, alas, to recount my misery?

HADEWIJCH

11 CARRYING STONES

1

Now has the new year
Arrived, that is evident,
With beautiful new weather.
A great fear manifests itself to us;
5 Very grave fear seizes us,
Both far and wide;
And I sing with heavy grief:
That where formerly noble fidelity was exercised,
I now behold treachery.
10 On account of this my heart is afflicted.
Is it any wonder, then, that I am sad
And lament on account of Love?
Love is the Lady of all—
And we at her side swerve from fidelity!

2

15 Here and everywhere
I see uncordiality
Toward supreme Love,
Of which I shall now complain.
The mountain is degraded to a valley,
20 In my way of thinking.
For although adversity has pursued me,
And I admit that I complain of my wants
And am one who carries light burdens alone,
That is merely the urge of my nature:
25 But he who grows fainthearted,
And to whom Love's pain is unwelcome,
And who asks for alien consolation,
Will surely be late in conquering.

3

Although I lament in the new season
30 That I am afflicted—

The days have long been lengthening,
And we see on every side
The sheep running about—
Yet that can occur.
35 But the souls to whom Love revealed herself,
Giving a foretaste of all they longed for,
Who then found they must carry stones, not feathers,
Were laid low by disappointment.
If they held themselves ready
40 And free for the fief of Love,
And craved no other consolations,
Love would truly give them love.

4

It is not so much I
Or the common people as well
45 Who thus go far astray;
But those possessed of rich fiefs
Are the ones I mean,
Whom Love day after day
Has led to her school
50 And has taught them the secrets of combat,
And knight-errantry in reliance on Love,
And the pains she has required of them;
But they seek their own satisfaction
And hunt worldly spoils
55 That can harm them;
So they remain out of sweet Love's ken.

5

Thus we hunt worldly goods
On account of their more perceptible taste:
That is a great loss to us.
60 This hunger grieves us,
As does the long, miserable watch
For satisfaction through Love;
But could we ascend the highest summits
In the first days,

65 And did we see what we loved,
We would (so we think) speedily be wise in counsel.
But because it grieves us
To carry burdens at Love's beck and call,
We lay hold on the nearest consolations
70 And shun the deeds of Love.

6

A soul would be only too foolish
If, for the sake of a poor pleasure,
It made itself so miserable
That it did not know in the slightest degree
75 What high Love means.
But he who sailed the sea of Love
Dwelt in her uttermost depths,
And she made herself wholly known to him,
So that in a short time
80 She healed all the wounds of his desires.
And if anyone at law would speak against Love,
And take Love prisoner with his love,
I tell him that he would find
The veritable love which he lacked.

7

85 If we let ourselves be lacking to Love
And thus hate ourselves,
And if for our part we view Love as pain,
Love will surely avenge herself on us
And let us stray in strange streets,[26]
90 So that it may become clear to us
That we, by our fault,
Have lost the noble affection
That Love would give us,
And with which she satisfies her valiant servants,
95 While we are seeking repose.
Now I have made bold to voice my disapproval,
I suppose I hardly long
That Love touch us further.

Since our cowardly manner of life
100 Shows us so cold toward Love—
How would it help if I longed for her touch,
Since our behavior ever keeps us poor?

12 TO BEAR THE YOKE

1

Now is born the noble season
That will bring us *flowers in the land.*[a]
So it is for the noble hearts, chosen
To bear the yoke, the chains of Love:
5 Fidelity ever blossoms in their hands
With flowers and fruits of nobleness;[b]
Among them the word is experienced by fidelity;
Among them Love remains constant
Through one friendship, intimately united
10 In the highest counsel of Love.

2

My yoke is sweet, my burden light,[c]
Says the Lover of Love himself.
This word he had beautifully expressed in Love;
Outside of Love one cannot experience its truth,
15 To my way of thinking.
So for them the light burden is heavy,
And they suffer many an alien fear
Since they live outside of Love;
For the servants' law is fear,
20 But love is the law of sons.[27]

a. Song 2:12.
b. Cf. Song 7:12.
c. Matt. 11:30.

3

What is this light burden of Love
And this sweet-tasting yoke?
It is the noble load of the spirit,
With which Love touches the loving soul
25 And unites it to her with one will
And with one being, without reversal.
The depth of desire pours out continually,
And Love drinks all that outpouring.
The debt Love summons love to pay
30 Is more than any mind can grasp.

4

No heart or mind could ever guess
How anyone looks with love on his Beloved
When Love has heavily burdened him with love;
He will not waste an instant's time
35 Until he passes with love through all,
To gaze with fidelity on true Love;
For all his judgments must be
Read[d] in Love's countenance.[28]
And there he sees clear truth without illusion
40 In many a sweet pain.

5

He sees in clarity that one who loves
Must live with full truth;
When he then understands with truth
That he does too little for Love,
45 His noble mind is forcibly stirred;
For in Love's face he learns fully
How love shall practice love;
And this judgment sweetens his pain
And makes him give all for all,
50 In order to content Love.

---

d. Cf. Ps. 16:2.

6

To those who give themselves thus to content Love,
What great wonders shall happen!
With love they shall cleave in oneness to Love,
And with love they shall contemplate all Love—
55 Drawing, through her secret veins,
On the channel[e] where Love gives all love,[29]
And inebriates all her drunken friends with love
In amazement before her violence:
This remains wholly hidden from aliens,
60 But well known to the wise.

7

To all who desire love, may God grant
That they be so prepared for Love
That they all live on her riches
Until, after themselves becoming Love, they draw Love into themselves
65 So that nothing evil, on the part of cruel aliens,
Can befall them more; but they shall live free
To cry: *I am all Love's, and Love is all mine!*[f]
What can now disturb them?
For under Love's power stand
70 The sun, moon, and stars!

13 SEEMING AND TRUTH

1

In the new season
On New Year's day
One may surely hope, from every side,
Spring weather will now be continual.

---

e. Cf. Ecclus. 22:41.
f. Cf. Song 2:16.

5 Love knows the repeated blows
That I suffer for her.
So I live henceforth in reliance on Love,
With a sad heart, joyful.

2

Even if I had new years
10 And a new and verdant season,
I would still live with fear
In whatever I do,
With unrelieved new disquiet,
So long as Love does not reveal herself to me
15 And give herself wholly that I may live on her
In all new clarity.

3

He who now wishes to be faithful
Will have a difficult holiday;
Harm will befall him:
20 With many bitter griefs
The cruel aliens will harass him
In many a bitter feud,
Before he can behold that land
To which Love carries off her friends.

4

25 Alas! listen, you newcomers
Who now wish to serve Love,
And pay heed to what I say to you,
And be on your guard.
There are many who seem anxious to betake themselves
30 Where they are advised to seek Love,
But they stray away from fidelity along alien ways:
I have watched this happen.

5

Some people think that in love
They have great success;
35 It seems to them that in all directions
Mountain and valley burst into bloom.
But if we find out the truth,
There is little in it:
By works of fidelity it is fully proved
40 Whether we gain anything in love.[30]

6

It is a miserable life
To be so long without the Beloved.
This often makes us fall short
And brings us into many a doubt.
45 Could it be, I should offer thanks to fidelity
For giving us the frame of mind
That would lead us under Love's control,
To cleave as one to her nature.

7

We can indeed make bold to say:
50 "You are mine, Beloved, and I am yours!"[a]
But we say this because pleasure moves us,
And self-enjoyment sets us free.
While we could not be at peace, ah me!
If Love once let us understand
55 What a noble being she is;
We could never forget it!

8

Now pay heed, all you wise ones,
And learn how great is Love's power:

---

a. Cf. Song 2:16.

She wields the almighty scepter
60 Over all that God created;
She brought him himself to death!
Against Love there is no defense.[31]
He who serves in the fidelity of Love becomes her partner,
And tastes to the full her noble goodness.

65 If anyone is inwardly shot by Love's arrow,[32]
He is so high-minded
That what he has suffered in adversity
He regards as the best success.

14 SCHOOL OF LOVE

1

The most joyous season of the year,
When all the birds sing clearly,
And the nightingale publicly
Makes its joy known to us,
5 Is the time of greatest sadness
For the heart noble Love has wounded.

2

How can the noble soul keep on—
Yes, it is the noblest of all creatures,
Which of its nature must love in the highest degree—
10 When it does not have its Beloved?
As Love's arrows strike it,
It shudders that it lives.

3

At all times when the arrow strikes,
It increases the wound and brings torment.[a]

---

a. Cf. Job 6:4.

15 All who love know well
That these must ever be one:
Sweetness or pain, or both together,
Tempestuous before the countenance of Love.

4

How they who love can shudder
20 When they know themselves thus lost in love!
They are conquered so that they may conquer
That unconquerable greatness,[33]
And this at all times causes them to begin
That life in new death.

5

25 Here the soul that loves Love cannot defend itself;
We must sustain her kingdom and her power,
However we fear to go to ruin in love;
This is unknown to aliens;
So the higher the palace of desire is,
30 The deeper yawns the abyss.

6

In the law of Love,[34] it is written:
He who strikes shall himself be struck;[35]
Light and heavy are judged equal;
Power is the first conquered;
35 The kingdom itself comes here to meet us.
This holds good for all who can love.

7

But there are few who, for the sake of all love, love all,
And fewer still long for Love with love.
All too late, therefore, shall they attain
40 That kingdom and that sublime mystery,
And that knowledge Love imparts
To those who go to school to her.

8

It is a great pity that we thus stray,
And that high wisdom remains hidden from us
45 Which Love entrusted to the masters
Who give lessons on true Love;
In the school of Love the highest lesson
Is how one can content Love.

9

But they who early leave off,
50 And then nevertheless jubilate
And feast their Beloved
For a brief while with salutations—
Provided they live in concord with the virtues—
Can still master the course of study.

10

55 But they who wish to enjoy the Beloved here on earth,
And dance with feelings of delight,
And dwell in this with pleasure,
I say to them in advance:
They must truly adorn themselves with virtues,
60 Or the course of study is a loss to them.

11

But those who arrange their lives with truth in Love
And are then enlightened by clear reason,
Love will place in her school:
They shall be masters
65 And receive Love's highest gifts,
Which wound beyond cure.

12

In those whom Love thus blesses with her wounds,
And to whom she shows the vastness knowable in her,

Longing keeps the wounds open and undressed,
70 Because Love stormily inflames them;
If these souls shudder at remaining unhealed,
That fails to surprise us.

13

Anyone who has thus waded through Love's depths,
Now with deep hunger, now with full satiety,
75 Neither withering nor blossoming can harm,
And no season can help:
In the deepest waters, on the highest gradients,
Love's being remains unalterable.

15 SURE REWARD

1

Although the season is joyful everywhere,
And mountain and valley are all verdant,
That would seem a truly small matter to him
Who has met mischance in love;
5 I know not what he can rejoice at;
All joy is pain to him.
That is no wonder:
When he is without
His Beloved for whom he longs,
10 And he finds nothing
By which to live—
What then should he live on?

2

He who lives on love with no success
Endures, in the madness of love,
15 Suffering that can only be known
By him who sincerely forsakes all for Love,
And then remains unnourished by her.

He is in woe because of Love;
For he sorely burns
20 In hope and in fear
Incessantly renewed;
For all his desire is
To partake of and to enjoy
And to have fruition of Love's nature.

3

25 They who live thus in hunger for Love
And yet lack fruition,
O who can praise them enough?
For they as one cleave wholly to Love;
And instead of receiving everything from her,
30 They are robbed of everything:
And so she stirs up in them such a fear!
O *amabar*
What must I—poor woman—do?
Before it came to this point,
35 Alas, *utinam*[36]
Her touch had been death to me!

4

This is truly an unknown woe,
One never welcomed by aliens;
Also it is too hard for satisfaction,
40 Which continually endeavors
To become attached to fruition
In liberty without fear.
But resistance
Is offered by clear reason.
45 Regression is all reason sees
So long as it does not ascend
Where it fully finds
Its Beloved in his highest glory.

5

The loving soul wants Love wholly, without delay;
50 It wishes at all hours to delight in sweetness,
In opulence according to its desire.
Reason commands it to wait until it is prepared;
But liberty wishes to lead it instantly
Where it will become one with the Beloved.
55 Storms of this kind
Impart a calm resignation.
That is incomprehensible to aliens
Who never condescended
To taste every kind of death
60 At the urging of Love.[37]

6

Because Love consoles the young lovers anew,
They fancy then they are fully free;
So they are as if at court,
And live well satisfied with themselves
65 And fancy they have fought in the joust
With the fullest praise.
If reason then disillusions them,
And holds up before them the work
They have to do,
70 With a change of mood
They experience fear
And lose their first boldness.

7

O may Love—the true virtue
Who is guardian of all things
75 And can subdue all things—
Show herself openly!
Then she will repay us;
She shall not elude us.

They who bear
80 All pains with fidelity
Can surely sing joyfully.

That anyone doubts this is a great shame:
Love always rewards, even though she comes late.
Those who forsake themselves for her,
85 And follow her highest counsel,
And remain steadfast in longing,
She shall compensate with love.

16 COMPLAINT AND SURRENDER TO LOVE

1

Far and wide we can perceive
The new season:
The birds are in raptures,
While mountain and valley burst into bloom.
5 All living things
Loose themselves
From the torment of cruel winter.
But it is all over with me
Unless Love quickly
10 Consoles me for my cruel destiny!

2

Now has my cruel destiny
Marched its army against me,
Recruited from every side.
My highways, but lately free,
15 Are heavily occupied.[a]
Peace is refused me:
See whether my sad lot can find any counsel?
If I am led on

a. Cf. Job 19:12.

By Love to victory,
20 O noble Love, I thank you for it!

3

Love conquers all things:
May she help me to conquer in my turn!
And may she who knows every need
Grant that I may learn
25 How hard it is for me
(Had I the chance)
To wait for the fruition of Love:
Cruel reason,
Which helps against it,
30 Introduces confusion in my mental powers.

4

Through Love I can fully conquer
My misery and exile;
I know victory will be mine.
But I have so many misfortunes,
35 Which drive me to the verge of death
Many a time,
Since Love's arrow first inwardly shot me.
I am willing to do without everything,
Until Love wills to place me
40 In possession of the magnificence with which she satisfies me.

5

In the days of my youth,
When Love first fought against me,
She showed me great advantages—
Her wisdom, her splendor, her goods, her power.
45 When I associated with her,
And took it upon me
To pay the full tribute of Love,
Gladly above all things,

She bound me to herself in union of love.
50 But the storm of happiness now seems fully calmed!

6

Thus Love left me in the lurch
With many things she had promised me,
With many a sweet dainty
By which inexperienced youth was fed.
55 Choice tidbits
With new delight
For which I have gladly suffered all—
I complain and accuse her
With new indignation:
60 She refuses the happiness that had consoled me.

7

I truly know that Love
Lives,[b] although I thus die often.
Because I know she is living,
I endure everything with joyfulness in play:[38]
65 Affliction or mercy,
What is evil, or what is good,
I hide them carefully from aliens.[39]
My high-mindedness
Is wise with regard to this:
70 That Love will compensate with love.

8

To sublime Love
I have given away all that I am.
Whether I lose or win, let all
That is owed her be hers without diminution.
75 What has happened now?
I am not mine:

b. Cf. Job 19:25.

She has engulfed the substance of my spirit.
Her fine being
Gives me the assurance
80 That the pain of Love is all profit.

9

I realize that Love deserves it:
If I lose, if I win, it is all one to me.
What I have most desired,
Since Love first touched my heart,
85 Was to content her
According to her wish,
As was always apparent:
For I endured
Her blows:
90 For her sake this was my richest feudal estate.

10

If anyone wishes to content Love,
I counsel him to spare himself in nothing.
He shall give himself totally,
So as to live in the performance of the noblest deeds,
95 For lovers, secret:
To aliens, unknown,
For they do not understand the essence of Love.
That sweet attendance
In the school of Love
100 Is unknown to him who never enters there.

However cruelly I am wounded,
What Love has promised me
Remains irrevocably.

17 UNDER THE BLOW

1

When the season is renewed,
Although mountain and valley
Are everywhere dark and colorless,
The hazelnut tree is already in bloom:
5 While the lover of Love has a sad lot,
He too shall grow in every way.

2

What use are joy or springtime to him
Who gladly took delight in Love
And never finds in the wide world
10 One whom he can trust or rest in—
To whom he can freely say: "Beloved, it is you
Who can utterly satisfy me!"

3

What joy can surround
Him whom Love has thrown into close confinement,
15 When he wishes to journey through Love's immensity
And enjoy it as a free man in all security?
More multitudinous than the stars of heaven[a]
Are the griefs of love.

4

The number of my griefs must be unuttered,
20 My cruel burdens must remain unweighed:
Nothing can be compared to them,
So it is best to give up the attempt.
Though my share of griefs is small, I have borne it;
I shudder that I exist.[b]

---

a. Cf. Gen. 15:5.
b. Cf. Job 10:1.

5

25 How can life horrify and grieve
One who has given his all for all,
And in the darkness is driven the wrong way
To a distance from which he envisages no return,
And in a storm of despair is wholly crushed?
30 What grief can compare with this pain?

6

O proud souls who stand as if on Love's side
And live freely under her protection,
Pity one who is disowned, whom Love overwhelms
And pursues in a despairing exile!
35 Alas! let whoever can observe reason live free with reason:
My heart lives in despair.[40]

7

For I saw a shining cloud rise
Over all the dark sky; and its form seemed so beautiful,
I fancied I would soon with full happiness
40 Play freely in the sunlight:[41]
But my joy was only a fancy!
If I should die of it, who would blame me?

8

Then for me night fell over the daylight.[c]
Oh, woe that I was ever born!
45 But if one gives his all in reliance on Love,
Truly Love will compensate him with love.
Although I am again under the lash,
God consoles all noble souls.

---

c. Cf. Job 5:14.

9

In the beginning Love always contents us.
50 When Love first spoke to me of love,
O how with all that I was I greeted all that she is!
But then she made me resemble the hazelnut trees
That bloom early in the dark season,
And for whose fruit one must wait a long time.

10

55 Fortunate is he who can wait
Until Love gives him all in exchange for his all.
O God! what is patience to me?
To wait, on the contrary, gives me greater joy,
For I have abandoned myself wholly to Love.
60 But woe has treated me all too harshly.

11

This is all too hard for the lover:
To stray after Love without knowing where,
Be it in darkness or in daylight,
In wrath or in lovingness: Were Love
65 To give her true consolation unmistakably,
This would satisfy the exiled soul.

12

Oh, if my Beloved let me obtain what is lovable in love,
Love would not be completely exhausted by it,
And so there would be no joy but a delusion;
70 And if this happened it would be a pity.
O may God make noble spirits understand
What harm would come of it!

13

Oh, what I mean and have long meant,
God has indeed shown to noble souls,

75 To whom he has allotted the torments of love
To give them fruition of Love's nature;
Before the All unites itself to the all,
Sour bitterness must be tasted.

Love comes and consoles us; she goes away and knocks us down.
80 This initiates our adventure.
But how one grasps the All with the all,
Alien rustics will never know.

18 LONGING FOR ETERNITY

1

The New Year has come to us.
God be blessed for it.
Springtime can be gladly received
By him who has the delight of Love;
5 But if he realizes in his mind
That he suffers because of sublime Love,
He will suffer gladly in every season.

2

In every season suffering must befall
Him who wishes to serve sublime Love
10 And to increase his service in Love,
If he is to have success from her,
And if he is to experience that nature
In which he is loved with love
By Love who has robbed him of his mind and heart.

3

15 A new springtime and the ever new Love
Strike together one single wound.
My newly re-experiencing this

Has wounded my heart anew:
That this noble being
20 Remains hidden from us
In her subtle nature such a long time.

4

In this new spring it seems that now
Something new and wonderful should make headway in
Love;
For few people are now to be found
25 Who strive after the taste of veritable Love;
For to the cruel aliens it remains hidden
How the spring of eternity I continually long for
Has robbed me of my heart.

19 DEFENSE OF LOVE

1

At great favors before the time,
And at great promises before the gift,
No one can rejoice overmuch.
Both have largely failed us:
5 False joys
That implied the possession of Love's being
Have swept me far from myself.

2

From pure dawns
We expect serenely clear days.
10 Love's offer of promises has heavily burdened
Both me and many another I do not name
(He to whom this applies knows it);
And for myself I know
I must constantly complain of Love.

3

15 "Wait for evening," says the peasant,
"Before you praise the fair day."
That I understood this so late
Now makes me cry: "Woe is poor me!"
Where is now the consolation
20 And the peace of Love
With which she provided me so splendidly at first?

4

How she first made me beautiful promises
And then grew cruel, I now know.
That Love did not deceive or mock me
25 In that woe, would I might understand it!
But she meant to make clear
And reveal to me
How reason illuminates the entire abyss of Love.[42]

5

Enlightened reason gives approval
30 And counsel, in the name of sublime Love,
To scrutinize with her the whole garden of Love
To see whether all is abundant there:
If anything fails,
Let it be thought of,
35 So that fidelity may provide it by virtuous deeds.

6

If I could so maintain fidelity
That Love uttered no reproach against me
And thus, with all that I am and have, pay my debt
perfectly—
Yes, pay all I can, human being as I am—
40 I who merely invited Love at first
Would then give her a summons,
To obtain full and free fruition of her.

7

Alas, noble Love! in what season, when,
Will you restore serene days to me
45 And a change from my darkness?
How glad I'd be to see the sun!
You alone know
How I mean this:
Whether I wish anything but your pleasure.

8

50 O powerful, wonderful Love,
You who can conquer all with wonder!
Conquer me, so that I may conquer you,
In your unconquered Power.[43]
In the past I knew this conquering:
55 In conquering there is a knowledge
That always oppressed me most sorely.

9

But you are still, Love, what you always were:
They who are with you in all know this.
I admit it; to spare oneself is useless.
60 The misfortune that barred my way
Was my not yet knowing
And not yet loving this work
By which fidelity will help me attain the end.

10

Since I have followed in her train with strong fidelity,
65 That Love might stand me in good stead,
I have renounced all alien sadness,
And I am firm in confidence
Through which I know
That Love one day
70 Will embrace me in oneness.

11

That is mighty Love's mode of action:
If she wholly lures someone to her hand,
Although she forces him with violence,
She contents him and sweetens his chains.
75 For this reason
She is highly renowned
And greatly praised in all lands.

12

When Love first traps someone, she shuts his eyes
With all her sweets: he thinks his fortune made
80 And fancies he will meet nothing but joys:
Thus she lures all with her cleverness.
Then comes reason, in force,
And with new works of obligation:
So is desire's intensity allayed.

13

85 What I sang so often of Love
Did not avail me much—in fact, very little.
Yet the minds of old and young
Are enlightened by a song of Love.
But my good fortune holds
90 So small a share of love:
My song, my weeping seem without success.

I cry out, and I lament:
Love has the days—
And I, the nights and the madness of love!

20 LOVE'S SUBLIMITY

1

This new year has begun for us.
Now must God grant us with love
That we may be able so to begin it
That it may be of value for Love.
5 No living man under the sun
Can content Love.

2

I know that a new year and a new day
Are truly pleasing to anyone
Who has always been eager to see joy
10 Under his eyes and in his hand:
But to him who loves, all this is a burden
So long as he does not live in Love's chains.

3

With sincere, brave, and free mind,
We must beg the goodness of Love
15 That she may bring us successfully to her,
For we have need of it:
He who lives outside Love's authority
Is worse than one actually dead.

4

Death is more tolerable than bitter life.[44]
20 Pray, O Love, fully grant us
To be uplifted above all
That's baseness!
We are too far driven away
From you: for this cause, have mercy!

5

25 God, who created all things
And who, above all, is particularly Love,[a]
I supplicate to consent,
According to his pleasure,
That Love now draw the loving soul to herself
30 In the closest union possible to Love.

6

The union possible to Love is very close,
But how close, I am the one who does not understand.
But he who is ardent for the sake of Love
Shall yet understand
35 How Love is always possessed in violent longing:
Here one cannot find repose.

7

O noble soul dowered with reason, where else could you rest—
You, noblest of all creatures,
Chosen for the nature of Love
40 Wherein rich fruition is tasted?
Renewal, joy, and continual blossoming
Almighty Love will give as the reward.

8

And if they shudder who are blind
And unfamiliar with the taste of love,
45 I ask you, noble soul, for what do you strive?
If you wish to serve Love, say: "I will gladly
Go where she sends me,
Be it to combat, be it to weeping!"

---

a. Cf. 1 John 4:16.

9

For Holy Church proclaims to us—
50 Her lofty, her lowly, her priests, her scholars—
That Love is of the highest works
And the noblest by nature:
Even though she conquers us, she conquers all strength,
And her power shall last.

10

55 When all things have passed away,
Noble Love shall remain[b]
And reveal her whole clarity,
When you, in a new beginning,[c]
Shall contemplate Love with love:
60 "Behold, this is what I am!"

11

When Love thus draws the soul in resemblance to her,
And the loving soul shows love to Love,
I know not how, for it remains unspoken
And also past understanding;
65 For no comparison is adequate for this—
How Love can embrace the loving soul.

12

All who love must be moved to pity
That Love lets me moan thus
And cry so often: "Woe is me!"
70 In what season and when
Will Love reach out to me
And say: "Let your grief cease"?

---

b. Cf. 1 Cor. 13:8.
c. Apoc. 21:5.

"I will cherish you;
I am what I was in times past;
75 Now fall into my arms,
And taste my rich teaching!"[45]

21 THE NOBLE VALIANT HEART

1

When the flowers of summer are with us again,
We look forward to the fruit.
So also does the noble, valiant heart
That wishes to endure every storm of Love,
5 And says with brave mind:
"I greet you, Love, with undivided love,
And I am brave and daring;[46]
I will yet conquer your power,
Or I will lose myself in the attempt!"

2

10 What evil could ever befall a brave heart
That stakes everything on the conquest of Love?
This could never actually happen
If you, Love, gave all you should have given,
Entirely as it might be;
15 Alas, if your mountains were valleys,
And we then could see
Our journey toward you pressed to the end,
All would be well with us!

3

He must march far who presses on to Love—
20 Through her broad width, her loftiest height, her deepest abyss.
In all storms he must explore the ways;

Then her wondrous wonder is known to him:
    That is—to cross her desert plains,
    To journey onward and not stand still;
25   To fly through and climb through the heights,
    And swim through the abyss,
    There from Love to receive love whole and entire.

4

Alas! sublime Love, though she seems so sweet
That her sweetness consumes all other sweetness,
30 Wounds heart and mind; yet he whom she stormily touches
Always desires new assaults,
    So that he shrinks from no difficulties,
    No pain, no anguish, no death,
    All the while he has no success in the service of Love.
35   O may God, who brings this about, bless him!
    Noble heart was never cowardly.

5

I let Love be all that she is.
I cannot understand her fierce wonders;
Although I can recover from this in my own case,
40 She has greatly troubled many.
    This disaster must be borne by one
    Who addresses words of protest to her,
    If he does not ward off her power by his power.
    For he who has never fought against Love
45   Has never lived a free day.

6

I bid farewell to Love now and forever.
He who will may follow her court; as for me, I have had too
        much woe.
Since I first chose her, I expected to be the lady of her court;
I did everything with praise: I cannot hold out.
50   Now her rewards
    Seem to me like the scorpion

That shows a beautiful appearance,
And afterwards strikes so cruelly.[47]
Alas! What does such a show mean?

7

55 If in love I had good fortune (which ever fled from me
And during my whole life was not at hand),
I should still conquer and live in joy,
While I now stray in too cruel misery.
Were it possible, I'd gladly make an end of this!
60 I stray with courage and ardor
Where Love requires of me
To follow her without success,
And where, for me, she remains too unattainable.

8

May God give good success to all lovers, as is fitting.
65 Though I and many others have so little part in Love,
They who know her fully give all for all.
She gives herself wholly to whom she pleases.
He who was empowered always attained her.
What use is it for anyone to fear
70 What must invariably happen?
All her blows are good.
But it takes a warrior to keep up the fight!

9

To make any complaint against Love is now unheard of;
Her name is so loved that, from her, men suffer everything.
75 I counsel them whom she now confuses to say nothing;
This state is unknown to him whom she does not so oppress.
But let him who is high-minded and daring
Look to himself
And ward off blow with blow;
80 So shall he still see the day
When Love herself offers him reconciliation.

To him who dares to fight against her,
Love grants full pardon
And makes him perfectly free of her.
85 So we can well say: "Woe is me!
How dare we cling to our repose?"

22 TO LIVE OUT WHAT I AM

1

My distress is great and unknown to men.
They are cruel to me, for they wish to dissuade me
From all that the forces of Love urge me to.
They do not understand it, and I cannot explain it to them.
5 I must then live out what I am;[48]
What Love counsels my spirit,
In this is my being: for this reason I will do my best.

2

Whatever vicissitudes men lead me through for Love's sake,
I wish to stand firm and take no harm from them.
10 For I understand from the nobility of my soul
That in suffering for sublime Love, I conquer.
I will therefore gladly surrender myself
In pain, in repose, in dying, in living,[a]
For I know the command of lofty fidelity.

3

15 This command which I come to know in Love's nature
Throws my mind into bewilderment:
The thing has no form, no manner, no outward appearance.
It can only be tasted as something actual;
It is the substance of my joy,

a. Cf. Rom. 14:8.

20 Which I long for in every season
And because of which I spend my days in much bitterness.

4

I do not complain of suffering for Love:
It becomes me always to submit to her,
Whether she commands in storm or in stillness.
25 One can know her only in herself.
This is an unconceivable wonder,
Which has thus filled my heart
And makes me stray in a wild desert.

5

Never was so cruel a desert created
30 As Love can make in her land!
For she impels us to long desiringly for her
And to taste her without knowing her being.
She shows herself as she takes flight;
We pursue her, but she remains unseen:
35 This makes the miserable heart ever exert itself.

6

If I spared any effort in following Love's counsel,
All who love know that I was offending.
Then I implored what I can now be master of;
Otherwise I could never have overcome such great harm.
40 Now in acting as what I am, I find delight
That gives me love and new ascent;
Therefore in my fiery longing I will never be appeased.

7

It weighs me down that I cannot obtain
Knowledge of Love without renouncing self.
45 Even if desire crushes my heart,

Even if strength slips away from me through Love's coercion,
I shall yet know what draws me
And awakens me so mercilessly
If for a moment I seek pleasure for myself in repose.

8

50 Were there someone to be my judge, I would complain to him
On my own behalf: Indeed I cannot bear
Love ever should have led me to such summits,
And now I meet her with her cruel blows.[b]
I have neither good fortune nor success.
55 I know not whether it is Love's own doing;
I fear a trick on the part of false and cruel disloyalty.[49]

9

Small wonder I am afraid of disloyalty:
It has hurt me more than is ever guessed;
For my being withheld from the aim I intend,
60 Disloyalty and no other must take the blame.
It has done me such harm!
If I escape it in future,
This can only be by lofty fidelity.

10

What use is it for me to sing of Love,
65 And newly prolong for myself my torment?
With whatever distress Love fetters me,
Before her might I am unable to plead.[c]
I avow what must be avowed by anyone
Whose heart Love's power has stolen.
70 What use is it for me to force my nature?

b. Cf. Job 30:21.
c. Cf. Job 5:19.

For my nature shall always remain
What it is and conquer what belongs to it,
However men may narrow its path.

23 PRAYER FOR ASSISTANCE

1

The season offers us good success,
And if with success we did good,
We could conquer.
And if we were wise in care,
5 We would be caring for the unwise,
Who do not yet know themselves
And arc inwardly blind;
For they do not know what they love.
Thus we go astray in all directions.[50]
10 May God now come to our assistance![a]

2

Our fickleness assails us hard,
And if we assailed fickleness,
We might put fickleness to death;
If we understood Love's noble teaching,
15 And if thanks to that teaching we were noble,
We should win Love,
And inherit all her riches
Of which we have now been all too long deprived,
To our great harm.
20 May God now come to our assistance!

3

We had great need of power,
That we might drive away

a. Ps. 69:2.

With power the greatness of our needs,
Which offer us resistance with threat of death.
25 If we struck resistance a deathblow,
It could not survive,
And we should certainly please Love
And become strong against all aliens
Who could oppress us.
30 May God now come to our assistance!

4

If someone submits enough to the power of Love,
I say that he is empowered by submission;
Fidelity guarantees this to him.
For this lover so evidences conformity to Love,
35 And by this evidence is so conformed inwardly to her,
That they are found to be both one,
So that no mind might separate them;
He would live in hunger for the depths of Love,
In all full satisfaction.
40 May God now come to our assistance!

5

If anyone strives to gain the heights of Love,
What he heightens by this strife
Is clearly seen to be done for Love;
For he suffers it with all obviousness
45 And makes it fully obvious through his suffering
That with love of Love
He contemplates Love and all her truth
And with full liberty, without fear,
Can wade through her deepest river bed.
50 May God now come to our assistance!

6

If I had thought of my noble birth,
I would have given birth to noble thoughts

And would have given myself all to Love,
My whole self, with the devotion of all powers,
55 And I would have succeeded, by the power of devotion,
In cleaving as one to Love's nature.
So could I live love with Love—
What I have missed now too long
On account of my base deeds.
60 May God now come to our assistance!

7

We find valleys in Love's heights;
Whoever finds heights in these valleys
Is of rich insight.
Since Love first commanded torment for me,
65 He who gives me any other commands torments me:
I place torment before all profit.
For I know this is the best life for me,
Since Love has commanded me to wander about
In the climb to the highest summits.
70 May God now come to our assistance!

8

He who is ready to seize high expectation,
Shall with high expectation seize
Love with Love's service,
And so with storm take his stand
75 And stand persistent against Love
And become equally strong,
As closely as I can estimate.
It is to this that Holy Church invites
All who are docile to her.
80 May God now come to our assistance!

9

Obviously fears of Love are stalking us:
It is right that we obviate Love's fear.

For we gladly withdraw from Love,
Who offers us her truth so clearly,
85 And clearly with full, inviolate truth
Teaches all her highest customs.
Hence for our own benefit, as far as we can,
We set aside the strange whims of truth,
Contrary to Love's good pleasure.
90 May God now come to our assistance!

10

A long time I have shown my grief;
Rightly should Love show me her fidelity.
I often grieve that I must live!
I have shown regard for fidelity;
95 That I have not been regarded as faithful
By Love is my great misery.
But if I wish to give myself wholly to her
And, with confidence, to cleave wholly to her,
She shall not escape me.
100 May God now come to our assistance!

11

In the considerations of all the Church's scholars,
I say no scholar is able to consider
How fortunate will be the state
Of him who has wrought deeds of strength in Love:
105 He will have become so strong by these deeds,
And will have conquered without fatigue;
Then, in the madness of Love,
He will burn in her deepest flood
And melt away like tallow:
110 May God now come to our assistance!

We are too remiss in our care,
And we accept consolation at the first success.
Love must scorn us for this;
May God now come to our assistance!

24 SUBJUGATION TO LOVE

1

The birds sing clearly,
And the wide-open flowers
Announce to us the season.
Voices silent not long ago,
5 And buds that were colorless,
Now are full of delight
That they have the new season again,
For which they pined so long.
So may all fare
10 Who are fettered in Love's distress.

2

In the distress of veritable Love
We taste many a death;
This is my conviction:
That he whom she touches in herself
15 Must be continually
In painful longing
And in great disfavor.
Unless Love helps me with her counsel,
I am one of those
20 Who, from Love, have pain as their fief.

3

What counsel can be given
To one Love has thus oppressed
With her heavy burdens?
To one whom she led in the beginning
25 And to whom she showed great advantages
On her high summits,
And has now flung down so low
That he imagines he will never rise again—
Unless it be unexpectedly,
30 By the madness of Love perhaps?

4

This is the best counsel
That can be given on the subject:
To one whom Love has thus captured
And bound with her chains,
35 That he surrender himself into her hands
And always be submissive
To all the lordship that Love exercises;
He who refuses any pain of love—
This is clearly evident—
40 Shall remain without love for a long time.

5

Love has subjugated me:
To me this is no surprise,
For she is strong, and I am weak.
She makes me
45 Unfree of myself,
Continually against my will.
She does with me what she wishes;
Nothing of myself remains to me;
Formerly I was rich,
50 Now I am poor: everything is lost in love.[a]

6

Not only from aliens but from friends
Whom I served formerly,
I now stay away:
I have given up honor and repose,
55 Because I wish to live
Free, and receive in love
Great riches and knowledge.
He who disputes them with me has it on his conscience.
I cannot do without this gift,
60 I have nothing else: I must live on Love.

a. Cf. 2 Cor. 8:9.

7

And I am now forsaken
By all creatures alive:[51]
This is clearly evident.
If in love
65 I cannot win,
What will become of me?
I am small now; then I would be nothing.
I am disconsolate unless Love provides a remedy.
I see no deliverance; she must give me
70 Enough to live on freely.

8

The cruel aliens
Afflict me immoderately
In this weary exile
By their false counsel:
75 They allow me no repose
And frighten me many a time.
For in their blindness they condemn me.
They will never reach the point
Where they can understand Love,
80 Who has captured my heart with desire.

9

He who wishes to conquer Love
Must not neglect
To give himself continually to Love.
And he must suffer
85 Incessantly
For what his heart has chosen,
And surrender himself in pain or in defamation,
In sorrow or in joy, in Love's chains:
Thus shall he come to know
90 The noblest Being in the depths of Love.

25 REASON, PLEASURE, AND DESIRE

1

In all seasons of the year,
Whatever season it may be,
Both joy and fear are experienced by him
Who suffers distress for lavish Love's sake.
5 And then he would gladly be with his Beloved
In order to sweeten his distressed days.
Because such happiness is not yet his, he cries: "Woe is me!"
Because it will surely come, he softens his complaint:
"Alas! I am all yours: Beloved, be all mine,[a]
10 If it please you!"

2

He who wishes to serve Love must surrender himself
Into her power, in accord with her commands,
Be it in dying or in living[b]—
In whichever Love wills him.
15 Nothing can befall him except
In liberating consolation or coercive fear.
Love always gladly fulfilled what she promised
With her clear truth.
Alas! What Love commands to hide
20 Is what imparts knowledge of her sweetness.[52]

3

What amazes me about sweet Love
Is that her sweetness conquers all things,
And yet she subjugates me from within
And so little knows my heart's distress.
25 She has brought me into such woe,
I feel I am not match for it.

---

a. Cf. Song 2:16.
b. Cf. Rom. 14:8.

The *bidden ways* by which Love sends me[c]
Are such as completely rob me of myself.
That great noise, that loud gift
30 Of soft stillness makes me deaf.

4

Love's soft stillness is unheard of,
However loud the noise she makes,
Except by him who has experienced it,
And whom she has wholly allured to herself,
35 And has so stirred with her deep touch
That he feels himself wholly in Love.
When she also fills him with the wondrous taste of Love,
The great noise ceases for a time;
Alas! Soon awakens Desire, who wakes
40 With heavy storm the mind that has turned inward.

5

Pleasure would certainly close her eyes
And gladly enjoy what she possesses
If fierce Desire, who always
Lives in fury, would tolerate it.
45 For every hour Desire begins anew
To cry: "Alas, Love! Be all mine!"
Thus she awakens Reason, who says to Pleasure:
"Behold, you must first reach maturity!"
Alas! That Reason should refuse Pleasure
50 Cuts more than all other pains.

6

Desire cannot keep silence,
And Reason counsels her clearly,
For she enlightens her with her will
And holds before her the performance of the noblest deed.

c. Cf. Job 3:23.

55 Pleasure would gladly have a safe place
Where she may consort with her Beloved in sweet repose.
So Reason shows her the highest degree in Love
And overcharges her with the heaviest burdens.
Pleasure, alas, even if she had had to kill Reason,
60 Would certainly not have picked them up.

7

But when the loved soul attains to the Beloved so closely
That it cannot be parted from the dear Beloved,
And the soul with love so tastes its Beloved to the full
That it lives for the Beloved on the Beloved's word,
65 And Reason then proposes an impediment,
Showing the soul's lack of growth,
Because of which Reason judges the loved soul and the
Beloved ever unequal;
By this the loving soul is ever most wounded;
Alas! Too heavy is the blow
70 When the soul experiences all—itself loved, the Beloved, and
the Beloved as loved.

8

What will become of the wounded soul?
How can anyone give it counsel:
What physician shall cure the soul
That would gladly live as loved one for the Beloved
75 But is so hard pressed by Reason,
Who addresses it with new storm
And shows it where it falls short:
"Behold, this is still wanting to you!"
Alas! who will give me counsel on the subject of Love,
80 And avenge me on Reason?

9

Alas! God knows no one exists
Who can be avenged of anything on Reason:

She herself is Love's surgeoness:
She can best heal all faults against her.
85 To him who adroitly follows all Reason's moves,
In all the ways in which she leads him,
She will speak of new wonders:
"Behold! Take possession of the highest glory!"

Alas! No alien conciliator dares attempt
90 To conciliate feuds;
And they who know this understand
Well enough Reason's teaching.

26 LOVE'S INEXORABLE DEMAND

1

Although daylight and the season are drear,
May God be blessed for everything!
We shall soon behold better.
Love, your being so far from me—
5 Whereas all my delight must come from you—
Remains a constant grief.
But that is self-evident:
All that gives light to my heart,
By which I should live,
10 Searches for you in your totality.
See what must befall me:
Nothing whatever is left to me!

2

Alas, how should anything content me, Love, save you in your totality?
It is my lot that I do not possess you fully,
15 And that I cannot fully content you with
Veritable, high-minded, and lavish love.
Were anyone to give you anything less,

That would be a great insult to you.
For you ask total love,
20 *With heart and with mind*
And with the *whole soul.*[a]
They who thought they had love
Without ever beginning their course
Could only be expected to fall.

3

25 The Queen of Sheba
Came to Solomon;[b]
That was in order to gain wisdom.
When she had found him, indeed,
His wonders streamed upon her so suddenly
30 That she melted in contemplation.
She gave him all,
And the gift robbed her
Of everything she had within—
In both heart and mind,
35 Nothing remained:
Everything was engulfed in love.

4

It is right that she had given him everything.
If she had once lingered on alien ways,
Among the poor rabble,
 That high wonder would not have befallen her.
Now she was utterly brought to nought[c] in love.[53]
Many people still go without this:
Too early they accept
What turns to their advantage
45 Among the run of men.
It will therefore be late

a. Mark 12:30.
b. 3 Kings 10:1.
c. Cf. 3 Kings 10:1–13.

Before their deeds of love
Are proclaimed as wonderful.

5

But of those who find repose in lavish love
50 And do not break down in the way,
But cleave wholly to Love
And suffer her miserable tricks,
Amazing wonders can be related.
For they surrender themselves,
55 As ready to pass through everything
Without any sparing,
Only to please Love,
In fear to the death
Lest for them the great good
60 Of Love should remain out of reach.

6

See! Thus all is lost in the power of Love;
Yes, and then the tribute of Love is all paid,
As one should pay all according to equity:
That is one of the most beautiful imprisonments
65 And an unconquered new power,
And indeed what God fully willed.
For the truest full gift of Love
Is exactly this inner inability.
For souls in this state can do nothing to the full,
70 And what they do for her is quickly over
When it is received by high Love.
In this way they come out of the spirit.

7

When mighty reason opens their eyes to Love
And shows them their great good,
75 Which Love is by nature,
And that if they content her in love

Love can give them all that good in return—
    This awakens souls,
        And causes them to arise
80   And dare all
    With ardent happiness,
        And promises them a glory
        Without rival
    In eternal bliss.

85   They who thus conquer
        In the storm of love
        Are veritable heroes;
        But they who take any rest
        And do not continue to the end
90   Are rightly condemned.

27 OLD IN LOVE

1

By the short days
    We can perceive the passing of the summer.
Birds and men may complain that it passes;
    But lovers find another grievance,
5   For theirs is a different subject of complaint:
    That man is so unreasonable toward Love;
Her rich teaching becomes sorely laid waste,
Whereas it ought to be an honor to us.
Love complains of this to loftiest Fidelity,
10 And Fidelity must look down on us with love.

2

Indeed, many a glory
    Of Love has been taught us:
That she is mighty over all
    And has possessed everything,
15 And has swayed everything that lives.

Who possesses Love but he to whom she gives herself?
He to whom she gives something can receive it.
Surely we will be submissive to her with noble service
And pray to mighty Love
20 That she make known to us her power.

3

It is a very beautiful prayer
To implore the power of high Love.
But when Love gives love to anyone according to her pleasure,
She *throws him into* such *a prison*
25 That *he cannot come out from it*[a] again.
He who conquers Love is vanquished himself:
So he is served;
And when she nourishes anyone, she consumes in a new chase all he owns.
So, being old, he learns through the power of Love to conquer peace,
30 Where he discovers the price of Love in misery.

4

That misery I know by guess
And not from experience.
When Love has made anyone old by the burden of knowledge,
In what woe he sees himself!
35 That is, he sees himself so small, and Love so great,
And the joy Love bestowed on him at the start,
And the happiness of his childish youth.
Love gives gifts to the young who do not know her,
And lets the noble souls who are old wander in exile,
40 Whereas the young, still yokels, never knew Love.

a. Luke 12:58–59.

5

You, young souls, have lost much,
    Once you have lost your youth!
Then you would live for Love old, in sadness,
    Whereas now you may live young
45 And in the happiness of lavish Love,
    And say: "I am all Love's, and Love is all mine."[b]
Now all you have to endure is this:
Wise old souls little remember those joys;
For they know the cost of the years of Love
50 In which we must live sparingly.

6

There is scarcely any peasant so stupid
    That he does not know when he will
Increase his profits or use up his store.
    All of us have the bad attitude
55 That we wish to remain young,
    Loved in joy at no cost to us.
Our decision amounts to this:
Now we forsake Love's high mansion for the valley!
Let us pray Love to lead us
60 In her ways and in her high adornments.

7

I do not condemn our gladly acepting
    Success in sweet Love.
But they who dare to serve their Love sparingly in love
    Never derive profit from it;
65 And of this we can be certain:
    They who love their love perfectly to the end are noble,
And not only old but wise,
Provided no impatience or frivolity makes them unstable;
Then they can be certain:
70 The deeper sunk in Love, the higher ascended.

---

b. Cf. Song 2:16.

Deeds are the proof of Love.
He who loves says: "Love, what is mine is yours;[c]
For your sake I shall never more spare mind or will,
Power, or marrow, or heart's blood!"
75 For it stands in the code of Love:
The deeper wounded, the easier cured.

28 THE MADNESS OF LOVE

1

Joyful now are the birds
That winter oppressed.
And joyful in a short time will be
(We must thank Love for that)
5 The proud hearts who too long
Have borne their pain
Through confidence in Love.
Her power is so effective
That she will give them in reward
10 More than they can conceive.

2

He whose wish it is
To receive all love from high Love
Must seek her gladly,
No matter where,
15 And dare the worst death
If Love destines him for it,
Being always equally bold—
Whatever noble Love commands—
That he may not neglect it
20 But be ready to perform it.

c. John 17:10.

3

Alas! What then will happen to him
Who lives according to Love's counsel?
For he shall find no one
Who understands his distress.
25 With unfriendly eyes
Men will show him a cruel look;
For no one will understand
What distress he suffers
Until he surmounts his distress
30 In the madness of love.

4

The madness of love
Is a rich fief;
Anyone who recognized this
Would not ask Love for anything else:
35 It can unite opposites
And reverse the paradox.
I am declaring the truth about this:
The madness of love makes bitter what was sweet,
It makes the stranger a kinsman,
40 And it makes the smallest the proudest.[54]

5

The madness of love makes the strong weak
And the sick healthy.
It makes the sturdy man a cripple[55]
And heals him who was wounded.
45 It instructs the ignorant person
About *the broad way*
Whereon many[a] inevitably lose themselves;
It teaches him everything
That can be learned
50 In high Love's school.

---

a. Matt. 7:13.

6

In high Love's school
Is learned the madness of Love;
For it causes delirium
In a person formerly of good understanding.
55 To one who at first had misfortune,
It now gives success;
It makes him lord of all the property
Of which Love herself is Lady.
I am convinced of this,
60 And I will not change my mind.

7

To souls who have not reached such love,
I give this good counsel:
If they cannot do more,
Let them beg Love for amnesty,
65 And serve with faith,
According to the counsel of noble Love,
And think: "It can happen,
Love's power is so great!"
Only after his death
70 Is a man beyond cure.

High-minded is he
Who becomes so fully ruled by Love
That he can read
In Love's power her judgments on him.

29 TO LEARN MARY'S HUMILITY

1

Because of fidelity to high Love,
All my senses are
In manifold pain;
To bear my distress
5 Without complaint

Will truly be a sign for me.
He for whom I languish
And suffer so many afflictions
Has given me to understand
10 That by high Love I shall escape from them.

2

Certain as I am that high Love
Will not lead me into error,
I am certain of this,
With inward understanding,
15 That the Lover of our love
Is indeed perfect.
For all he does is without measure;
He is not satisfied to give any gift but love.
This is well known
20 To those who are filled with high Love, but to no one else.

3

They who are filled with high Love
Shall complain little,
Whatever pains befall them.
They shall be like the wise—
25 Always in deep humility,[56]
Ready for high Love
Whatever Love commands, be it far, be it nigh,
In dying, in living, whatever it is,[a]
In liberty without fear:
30 So it is that high Love is first revealed to us.

4

No matter what benefits God ever conferred on us,
There was no one who could
Understand veritable Love

a. Rom. 14:8.

Until Mary, in her flawlessness,
35 With deep humility,
Had received Love.
Love first was wild and then was tame;
Mary gave us for the Lion a Lamb.[b]
She illuminated the darkness[c]
40 That had been somber for long ages.

5

The Father *in the beginning*[d]
Kept his Son, Love,
Hidden in his bosom,[e]
Until Mary,
45 With deep humility indeed,
In a mysterious way disclosed him to us.
Then the mountain flowed down into the deep valley,[57]
And that valley flowed aloft to the height of the palace.
Then was the castle conquered
50 Over which long combat had taken place.

6

Each prophet gave us
A beautiful promise beforehand:
That he[58] was rich and beautiful
And would bring us the peace
55 Of Love; and moreover he was mighty.
Moses and Solomon
Praised his boundless power,
His wisdom and his wonders,
Together with Tobias, Isaiah, Daniel,
60 Job,[59] Jeremiah, and Ezechiel.

b. Cf. Apoc. 5:5–3.
c. Cf. John 1:5.
d. John 1:1.
e. Cf. John 1:18.

7

They saw visions:
They spoke beautiful parables,
Concerning all that God would give us later on.
But, in my opinion,
65 Genuine, lavish Love
Remained wholly unpracticed by them.
For their manner of life was commonplace,
Now here, now there, now off, now on;[60]
Mary, however, said no words but these:
70 *Be it done to me* as God wills.[f]

8

David said that when he remembered
God, he was moved
And his *spirit swooned away.*[g]
He indeed was called strong in work,
75 But Mary wrought a work of greater strength.
Truly David bore the largest share of that great work
Save for Mary, who received him totally.
As God, and as Man, and as Infant.
There can we first perceive
80 The genuine work of Love.

9

It was by deep longing
That this mystery happened to her,
That this noble Love was released
To this noble woman
85 Of high praise
In overflowing measure;
Because she wished nothing else and owned nothing else,
She wholly possessed him of whom every Jewish woman had read.

---

f. Luke 1:38.
g. Ps. 76:4.

Thus she became the conduit[h]
90 Open to every humble heart.

10

The prophets and all their disciples
Offered up sheep and cattle:
That was their sacrament.
They sprinkled themselves with blood.
95 Their sacraments were only symbolic rites;
Until to Mary that sublime gift,
The Son, was sent by the Father.
Now to the rich repast, all together
—*The marriage is ready*—
100 Come they whom Love finds adorned with the *wedding garment.*[i]

11

The virtue of our friends the prophets
Must not be forgotten:
It was beautiful and bright.
They suffered the misery
105 And great bitterness
Of the Law, for long ages.
Their sacraments were only symbolic rites.
Because they were ready to submit to their role,
We must truly thank them—
110 Although, as I said, for Mary it was different.[61]

12

You who are humble and noble,
If you wish Love all unaltered,
As Love lives for herself,
I counsel you: For the sake of fidelity
115 (Although you suffer pain)

---

h. Cf. Ecclus. 24:41.
i. Matt. 22:8, 12.

Forsake and give up everything.
Then your hearts will become wide and deep;
Then shall come to you that conduit[j] which flowed
To Mary without measure.
120 Pray lofty Fidelity to let it flow to you.[62]

For lofty Fidelity is given charge
Over all who pass through humility,
That she lead them without fail
To where Mary is one with Love in all.

30 LOVE AND REASON

1

We must at all seasons
Be joyful because of Love,
And follow her everywhere
By all the ways where she leads;
5 We must live joyful for her sake
And then also be ready for affliction.

2

May Love be favorable to me!
I have begun to love;
What the aliens blame me for,
10 They cannot wrest from me.
I have begun to love:
God grant that to Love I may become true!

3

Since I gave myself to Love's service,
Whether I lose or win,
15 I am resolved:
I will always give her thanks,

j. Cf. Ecclus. 24:41.

Whether I lose or win;
I will stand in her power.

4

He who wishes to please Love
20 Shall not complain
Of his manifold burdens,
Which he must bear for Love,
He shall not complain:
To suffer for Love's sake is pure advantage.

5

25 He who wishes to love with fidelity
Must perceive virtue
And perform works,
If he wishes to live in the chains of Love.
This could be perceived in him
30 Who first brought us Love on earth.

6

I came so close to Love
That I began to know
What is won by all those
Who give themselves wholly to Love;
35 When I came to know this by experience,
What was wanting in me gave me pain.

7

Would that Love might content me!
I sought to conform myself to her,
Until joy flowed through my veins.
40 Then came Reason and gave me insight:
"Behold what conformity you are after,
And all that you must undergo beforehand!"

8

In the beginning Love enriched me.
She added to my sensible joy
45 And showed me all the winnings.
Why does she now run away like a vagabond?
She added to my sensible joy,
But now I wander in a strange land.

9

It is truly no easy risk
50 To ask Reason's counsel about Love.
Yet on this it depends to receive
Love in her entirety and thus to win.
To ask Reason's counsel about Love
If unheard of, and too hard for the sensual man.

10

55 Love came to hold out to me the promise of all love.
Now it seems to me this was a provocation.
When I wanted to send Love a summons,
Reason said: "If you are making a wish now—
It was a provocation of Love—
60 Reflect that you are still a human being!"

11

Then Reason did me an injury.
I thought it a feud,
That she took from me the attire
Love herself had given me.
65 I thought it a feud;
Yet Reason taught me to live the truth.

12

It was high charity
Love showed me in outward complaisance

When, without moderation,
70 She took my heart wholly to her;
But what she meant in outward complaisance
She has now shown me to some extent.

13

No matter how Love has disappointed me,
I must yet follow her;
75 For she has utterly engulfed
My soul, from the depths of my heart.
I will follow her totally,
However much Reason has wounded me.

14

By Reason one can win
80 Veritable fruition of Love,
Regarding which Reason clearly makes known
That one has satisfied both Love and Reason.
Veritable fruition of Love
Then, from Love, Reason lets us receive.

15

85 May God grant to all who love
That they may win the favor of Reason,
By which they may know
How fruition of Love is attained.
In winning the favor of Reason
Lies for us the whole perfection of Love.

31 MELODY AND SONG

1

I wish to devote all my time
To noble thoughts about great Love.
For she, with her infinite strength,
So enlarges my heart
5 That I have given myself over to her completely,
To obtain within me the birth of her high being.
But if I wish to take free delights,
She casts me into her prison!

2

I fancied I would suffer without harm,
10 Being thus fettered in love,
If she willed to make me understand
All the narrowest paths of her requirements.
But if I think of reposing in her grace,
She storms at me with new commands.
15 She deals her blows in a wonderful way:
The greater her love, the more crushing her burden!

3

This is a marvel difficult to understand—
Love's robberies and her gifts;
If she gives me any consolation to taste,
20 It becomes *fear and trembling.*[a]
I pray and invite Love
That she may incite noble hearts
To sing in tune the true melody of Love
In humble anxiety and high hope.

---

a. Ps. 54:6.

4

25 Consolation and ill treatment both at once,
This is the essence of the taste of Love.[b]
Wise Solomon, were he still living,
Could not interpret such an enigma.
We are not fully enlightened on the subject in any sermon.
30 The song surpasses every melody!
That springtime of eternity I continually long for
Keeps in store for me the reward.

5

Yearning, delaying, and long awaiting
This springtime, which is Love itself,
35 Makes us despise associations with aliens
And shows losses and great gains.
The pride[63] of Love counsels me to hold
So firmly to her that I may encompass
Union above comprehension:
40 The melody surpasses every song!

6

When I speak of the melody that surpasses every song,
What I mean is Love in her might.
I say a little, yet it serves not to enlighten
The alien hearts that are cold
45 And have met small suffering for the sake of Love:
They do not know that Love reveals
Her glory to the noble-minded, who are bold
And are cherished in Love.

7

Love's invincible might
50 Is unheard of by our understanding:

---

b. Cf. Job 30:31.

It is nearby when we are lost, and far away when we grasp
 it;
It is a peace that disturbs all peace:
A peace that is conquered in love,
By which he who sets his whole mind on Love
55 Is cherished by her consolation,
And thus she loves him with love in love.

8

He who wishes thus to progress in love
Must not fear expense, or harm,
Or pain; but faithfully confront
60 The strictest commands of Love,
And be submissive with faultless service
In all her comings and in all her goings:
Anyone who behaved thus, relying on Love's fidelity,
Would stand to the end, having become all love in Love.

32 NOBILITY IN LOVE

1

Soon the flowers will open for us,
And other plants in great numbers.
But at the same time men will condemn the noble hearts
Who live under the dominion of Love.
5 In Love I place my salvation,
And my power in her hands;
I demand no other compensation from her
Than to remain wholly in her chains.

2

With anyone who now bears the chains of veritable Love,
10 As man's debt to Love requires,
The cruel aliens before long
Will quite openly interfere.

They find many ways to intimidate
Those who trust high Love's protection;
15 But any harm they cause them,
Thanks be to God, amounts to very little.

3

He who is to serve high Love
Must fear no pain;
He shall give himself all for all,
20 To content high Love;
But if it happens that he delays somewhat,
He will indeed learn this truth:
That he will positively never become
Master of veritable Love.

4

25 Love is master of contraries;
She is ready to give bitter and sweet;
Since I first experienced the taste of her,
I lie at her feet continually;
I pray her it may be her pleasure
30 That I endure, for her honor's sake,
Suffering to the death, without recovery,
And I will not complain of it to aliens.

5

If anyone made known to aliens
What we suffer for the honor of Love,
35 He would truly break her heart
And deeply wound her being;
For aliens understand nothing at all
Of what we must suffer for veritable Love—
What adventures and changes of destiny—
40 Before she will rejoice in our love.

6

When souls truly wish to please Love,
I counsel them that they spare nothing,
And that they accord with her
So as to persevere in the storms with longing
45 In spite of their fault-finders,
Who are so bent on harming them.
No matter how such foes may oppress them,
These souls are privileged to be ever free.

7

A free man's nobility we can recognize
50 In jousts and in noble deeds;
With the pride of noble minds, he wades through
Where the storm of Love withstands him.
For in jousts a knight receives praise
Of which he appears worthy because of love.
55 Love is so strong a buttress:
It is right that men suffer for her sake.

8

People afraid of any pains in love
Certainly cannot understand
What can be won by souls
60 Who are always submissive to Love,
Who receive from her hand heavy blows
Of which they remain wholly unhealed,
And who mount on high and are knocked down again
Before they please Love.

9

65 From slothful hearts and ignoble minds
Remains hidden the great good
Which those well understand
Who live in the madness of love;
For they make many a gallant stand

70 In storm and in adventure:
It is right that they should have success
In the high nature of Love.

10

God grant success to those who strive
To please the will of Love,
75 Who for her sake gladly receive
Great burdens with heavy weights,
And who always endure on her account many sufferings,
Of which they judge Love worthy.
I truly wished they should yet behold
80 The wonders of Love's wisdom.

33 HUNGER FOR LOVE

1

The season is renewed with the year;
The days, dark a short time ago, grow lighter.
When souls desire Love but possess her not,
It is a wonder they do not go to wrack and ruin.[64]

2

5 The new year already begins.
For anyone who has resolved
To spare neither much nor little
For Love, his pain becomes pure profit.

3

But he who spares any pain for Love,
10 Thus betraying his baseness,
And expects profit from joys unrelated to love,
Inevitably finds his service burdensome.

4

But lovers who are true-born
And chosen to bear Love's likeness
15 Spare no pain in her service
And live continually in holy affliction.

5

He whom high Love's nature touches
Always suffers gladly,
As in his deeds clearly appears;
20 He ever thinks them imperfect.

6

For the perfect man it would be a pity
If he, by the counsel of baseborn aliens,
Ceased to perform those noble deeds,
Which create hunger in new satisfaction.

7

25 Inseparable satiety and hunger
Are the appanage of lavish Love,
As is ever well known by those
Whom Love has touched by herself.

8

Satiety: for Love comes, and they cannot bear her;
30 Hunger: for she withdraws, and they complain.
Her fairest enlightenments are heavy burdens;
Her sharpest assaults, renewed pleasures.

9

How does Love's coming satiate?
Filled with wonder, we taste what she is;

35 She grants possession of her sublime throne;
She imparts the great treasure of her riches.

10

How does Love's refusal create hunger?
Because we cannot come at what we wish to know
Or enjoy what we desire:
40 That increases our hunger over and over.

11

How does Love's enlightenment overwhelm us?
Because we cannot receive her great gifts,
And we can elaborate nothing so beautiful as she:
So we do not know where to seek rest.

12

45 How does noble Love make assault and blow
Always welcome, night and day?
Because we can fall back on nothing else
But confidence with reliance on Love.

13

To holy Love I now recommend
50 All of you who wish to know Love,
And who therefore spare nothing
So as to dwell in Love with new ardor.

14

May new light give you new ardor;
New works, new delights to the full;
55 New assaults of Love, new hunger so vast
That new Love may devour new eternity!

34 BECOMING LOVE WITH LOVE

1

In all seasons new and old,
If one is submissive to Love,
In the hot summer, the cold winter,
He will receive love from Love.
5 He shall satisfy with full service
    In encountering high Love;
So he speedily becomes love with Love;
    That is bound to happen.

2

Bitter and dark and desolate
10 Are Love's ways in the beginning of love;
Before anyone is perfect in Love's service,
He often becomes desperate:
Yet where he imagines losing, it is all gain.
    How can one experience this?
15 By sparing neither much nor little,
    But giving himself totally in love.

3

Many are in doubt about Love;
Love's labor seems to them too hard,
And at first they receive nothing in it.
20 They think: "Should you wander there?"
If their eyes clearly saw the reward
    That Love gives at the end,
I dare indeed say openly:
    They would wander in Love's exile.

4

25 In love no action is lost
That was ever performed for Love's sake;
Love always repays, late or soon;

Love is always the reward of love.
Love knows with love the courtly manners of Love;
30 Her receiving is always giving;
Not least she gives by her adroitness
Many a death in life.

5

It is very sweet to wander lost in love
Along the desolate ways Love makes us travel.
35 This remains well hidden from aliens;
But they who serve Love with truth
Shall in love walk with Love
All round that kingdom where Love is Lady,
And united with her receive all that splendor
40 And taste to the full her noble fidelity.

6

As for the tastes that fidelity gives in Love—
Whoever calls anything else happiness
Has always lived without happiness,
To my way of thinking.
45 For it is heavenly joy, free,
To the full, devoid of nothing:
"You are all mine, Beloved, and I am all yours"[a]—
There is no other way of saying it.

7

I can well keep silent about how it is
50 With those who have thus become one in love:
Neither to see nor to speak is my part;
For I do not know this in itself,
How the Beloved and the loved soul embrace each other
And have fruition in giving themselves to each other.
55 What wonder is it that grief strikes me
Because this has not yet fallen to my share?

---

a. Cf. Song 2:16.

8

That I was ever short of love
Causes me sadness; that is no wonder.
Rightly do I suffer pain for it,
60 That I ever descended so low.
For Love promised me all good,
    If I would conceive the high plan
Of working in the realm she assigned me,
    In her highest possible service.

9

65 That realm to which Love urges me on,
And the service she commands us to perform,
Is to exercise love and nothing else,
With all the service this entails.
He who truly understands this,
70   How to work in every respect with fidelity,
Is the one whom Love completely fetters
    And completely unites to herself in love.

10

To this I summon all the perfect,
Who wish to content Love with love,
75 Thus to be in Love's service
In all her comings and in all her goings.
If she lifts them up, if she knocks them down,
    May it all be equally sweet to them;
So will they speedily become love with Love:
80   In this way may God help us!

35 UNLOVED BY LOVE

1

The season is dark and cold:
On this account, bird and beast grow sad.
But sufferings of a different kind envelop hearts
Who know Love's proud nature
5 And that she will remain out of their reach.
Whoever ascends, I stay in the valley,
Robbed of rich consolation,
Continually burdened with heavy loads.

2

The load is all too heavy for me,
10 And is never laid down, though need be great.
How could a heart keep on
When it must endure as many deaths
As one experiences who knows that he
Is ever unloved by Love,
15 And that everyone she receives is refused
Help and consolation and confidence?

3

If Love will not admit me to favor as her loved one,
Why was I ever born?
If I am thus ill-starred before Love
20 I am lost and no mistake;
So I can complain bitterly,
All my time from now on.
I hope for no prosperity,
Since Love will thus be out of my reach.

4

25 I showed Love my pains;
I prayed her to have pity on them;
By her behavior she gave me to understand

That she had neither inclination nor time.
What becomes of me is all the same to her.
30 How she ever showed herself favorable to me,
Her strange fickleness has put out of my head.
Therefore I must live in night by day.

5

Whereabouts is Love? I find her nowhere.[a]
Love has denied me all love.
35 Had it ever happened to me by Love
That I lived for a moment
In her affection, supposing I did,
I would have sought amnesty in her fidelity.
Now I must keep silence, suffer, and face
40 Sharp judgments ever anew.

6

I am brought to ruin by these decrees
That Love must thus remain out of my reach.
Even if I wished to secure her affection,
I have no good fortune or success in the attempt.
45 Disheartenment has so set itself against me,
I cannot receive any comfort
That may ward off from my heart
This unheard-of adversity.

7

Love, you were present at the council
50 Where God called me to become a human being.
You willed me to exist in disquiet;
All that happens to me, I impute to you!
I fancied I was loved by Love;
I am disowned, that is clear to me.
55 My confidence, my high false assurance,
Is all concluded in grief.

a. Cf. Job 23:8–9.

8

Sweet as Love's nature is,
Where can she come by the strange hatred
With which she continually pursues me
60 And transpierces the depths of my heart with storm?
I wander in darkness without clarity,
Without liberating consolation, and in strange fear.
Give love to noble spirits, O Love,
And perfect all you have begun in me!

9

65 It is plain that Love has dealt with me deceitfully.
From whom shall I now seek remedy?
I shall seek it from Fidelity, if she will receive me
And, for the sake of her high achievement,
Lead me before Love, that I may give myself up
70 Fully to her, in the hope she will show some concern.
I do not pray for her consolation or any remedy,
But only that she may acknowledge me as hers.

10

Alas, Love, do all your pleasure!
Your law is my best consolation;
75 I will wholly conform myself to it,
Whether I am a prisoner or liberated.
I will abide above all by your dearest will,
In torment, in death, in disaster.
Grant, Love, that I may acknowledge you as Love:
80 That is richness above all gain.

HADEWIJCH

36 DARING THE WILDERNESS

1

Whatever season of the year it is,
O you who are lovers!
So control your ardor
5 That nothing too much depress or too much gladden you,
But everything be in the just middle—
Whatever Love does with you or omits to do,
Whether it be misfortune or benefit.
For these are attitudes
Through which Love blesses
10 Your abiding
In Love.

2

Let him whom Love has ever blessed
Be—according to the season of the year—
Sad or joyful,
15 And always on Love's side,
And let him be continually available
Where he knows the will of Love
In ease, in harshness,
In pleasure, in pain:
20 That wilderness
He dares
In Love.

3

He who wills to dare the wilderness of Love
Shall understand Love:
25 Her coming, her going,
How Love shall receive love with love,
Perfectly.
So Love has kept nothing hidden from him,
But she shows him her wilderness and her highest palace

30 —Know well, everyone—
Because he has kept on to the end
With his suffering
In Love.

4

35 He who wishes that Love heal his suffering
Shall behave himself toward Love
According to her pleasure,
With confidence that disregards all that befalls him,
According to true love:
He suffers all grief indeed without pain
40 In order to content high Love.
He lets it appear
That he shall read
All judgments passed on him
In love.

5

45 Judgment of Love
Pierces deep within
Through the inward senses;
This cannot be known by the ignoble heart
That spares anything for Love;
50 But he who fares high-mindedly
Through all Love's nature—
Where the loving soul with love gazes upon Love—
Because he has conquered
55 Remains enlightened
In love.

6

O soul, creature
And noble image,
Risk the adventure!
Consider your law and your nature—
60 Which must always love—

And love the best good of Love.
To have fruition of her, defend yourself boldly;
Thus you will have success.
65 And spare no hour,
But ever keep on to the end
In love.

7

He who, according to love,
Understands Love's counsel
And who dares through Love
70 Many a great exertion for Love's sake,
All perseveringly,
Finds that to be less than love is great pain;
On this subject Love shows him her rich teaching
Ever new.
75 Irrevocably
He remains high-minded
In love.

8

But you who reject Love's counsel
In which fidelity lies,
80 And on whom pain weighs heavy,
I take it that you will be grieved again,
And without avail.
For you never did what Love urged
While Love promised you love with love,
85 And this you fled;
So you remain cast out
Of what Love provides
In love.

9

Let him whom Love provides with any favor
90 Live, from then on, free,
And in this liberty say:

"I am all Love's, and Love is all mine!"[a]
High-minded and bold,[65]
He summons all the love of Love as owing to him.
95 For this she gives diverse riches;
She is kind to him in all things.
He alone
Has full power
In Love.

10

100 Of herself, Love is good.
What she does to this person
Makes him wise:
How Love causes the high mind to love
She so teaches him
105 That he can nevermore forget it.
So Love has taken possession of him with love.
What happened to him then?
By the fury of Love
He is all devoured
110 In Love.

11

Alas! Where then is Love,
When someone cannot find her[66]—
Someone, that is,
Who employs all he ever had[67]
115 And nevertheless does not find Love—
Someone to whom Love sends love
So that Love keeps him revolving in woe,
And yet he cannot experience her?
But another to whom she gives favor
120 Has quickly become perfect
In love.

---

a. Cf. Song 2:16.

12

Love is indeed there,
Beyond, I know not where,
Free, without fear.
125 That for me Love is inaccessible
Causes me anguish,
And still more woe to anyone who clings fast
To Love in her oppressive power.
But this did not last long;
130 Love gave unmistakably
Her embraces
In love.

13

Now may God help those
Who would gladly do all things
135 According to Love's wishes,
And who will gladly traverse the deep wilderness
To the land of love,
Where they are often placed in afflictions
And are subject to Love in all things
140 In heavy chains:
Thus Love holds them heavy laden
In the continual fire
Of Love.

Here is Love's guarantee:
145 When Love with love finds fidelity in anyone
Who for Love's sake undergoes all pains,
Sweet and harmless,
Full satisfactions shall be known to him
In love.

37 LOVE'S GREAT POWER

1

The season approaches us rapidly
When Summer will set up for us
His banner with all sorts of flowers;
Many noble lovers will rejoice at this.

2

5 For the days become long for us,
And the birds raise their song;
He for whom Love sweetens all his distress
Can give her his grateful thanks.

3

I also would thank you, Love, had you deserved it
10 To the full—just like one of your poor friends.
But since you first bowed me under your yoke,
You have always spoiled my happiness.

4

You do good to those whom you favor;
I think you can never bear anyone's success.
15 At this my heart is sad; at this my mouth complains;[a]
At this my strength is truly broken.

5

O Love, if you were love, as you actually are,
Where would you have come by the strange hatred
With which you transpierce him
20 Who gives you his kiss at all times?

---

a. Job 23:4.

6

Yes, you are all, Love, you are so wise;
Your name is Love, and it is of high renown;
All you do ever gives delight,
No matter who remains under oppression.

7

25 Your name adds grace, your mien breathes joy;
Your refusal annihilates, but your gift crowns.
However sorely you have distressed us,
With one kiss you give us full reward.

8

Thus Love's work surpasses all,
30 And all things are beleaguered by her powers;
Her burden has outweighed all burdens;
There is no escaping her: we must go out to meet her!

9

God bless Love!
If anyone so will, let Love make him free in a different way.
35 As for her wonders and her cunning tricks,
I cannot avow many in my favor.

10

Since you, O Love, can do all with love,
Give me, for the sake of love, the fruition
That delights the loving soul through your highest goodness!
40 But you have consumed all my youth.

11

Love wills that the loving soul lovingly demand total love.
She has set up her highest banner.

From this we learn what kind of works she requires,
With clear truth and without doubt.

12

45 O noble souls! Apply yourselves to the exercise of love,
And adorn yourselves with the light of truth,
So that no darkness may assail you,
But you may consort with your Beloved according to the law
of love.

13

Love wills all love from noble spirits,
50 And that they bring their works into conformity with it,
And that they rejoice with memory
And delight in Love with joy.[68]

Praise and honor be to Love,
To her great power, to her rich teaching;
55 And by her consolation may she heal the pain
Of all who gladly brave Love's vicissitudes.

38 NOTHINGNESS IN LOVE

1

Now that Spring is born for us,
We look forward to fairer days,
With the blossoming of grass and wheat
On which many can set their hopes.
5 If a man has formed this expectation of success,
Resentment will remain in his heart because of it;
But he who dares to fight Love with love
Very quickly comes to his goal.

2

Flowers bloom in the summer as well,
10 But many are followed by little fruit.
We wish to confess to Love our many deeds
That veritable Love never constrained.
A poet composes a new love song
And wishes to boast of his good fortune in love;
15 Anyone Love is good to may thank her—
From her I have little else but condemnation!

3

Alas! Since Love has thus decreed
That I bemoan her verdicts and my heart's distress,
I have nothing that will serve me to plead against her:
20 My right is minimal, her power is great.
The swan, they say, sings[69]
When it is about to taste death.
Whatever Love desires in my regard,
I wish her to fulfill without fail.

4

25 Alas, Love! Although you thus oppress me,
And make the hours so weary for me,
To your favorites you reveal
Your clear word without number.
Alas! Often I know not what will become of me
30 When you so oppress me with woe in fear.
Whoever ascends with you, I remain in the valley.
I often shudder at how I fare.

5

Alas, Love, that after all you could forget
The sharp pains you cause us,
35 Or what to many you have been known as—

Cruel to one and generous to another:
One you possess in your madness
So that, from within, he is utterly devoured;
Others you nourish tenderly—
40 Without making them yours for an instant!

6

Concerning Love we can relate many a wonder
Of what the work of her wonder is.
On one she adroitly tries her tricks,
Saying: "I am all yours, and you are all mine!"[a]
45 On another she rushes so swiftly
That she touches him and breaks his heart;[70]
Still another she leaves entirely free of her:
Thus she can throw us off the scent and bring us back again.

7

To be reduced to nothingness in Love
50 Is the most desirable thing I know
Among all the works I have experience of,
Although I know it is beyond my reach.
And if anyone then dares to fight Love with longing,
Wholly without heart and without mind,
55 And Love counters this longing with her longing:
That is the force by which we conquer Love.

Thenceforward, whether with joy or pain,
If anyone can dare to fight Love with ardor,
Love cannot resist the violence of the assault:
60 But he shall abide firm in the storm, conformed to Love.

---

a. Cf. Song 2:16.

39 LOVE'S BLOWS

1

Nearly all creatures are
In the power of the cold winter.
Much more he who loves is, from his nature,
In the power of Love's might.
5 If anyone were noble and bold of mind[71]
And would risk all adventures,
The sweet with the bitter,
He should send Love summons for debt:
He should touch Love wholly with love.

2

10 Who is able to praise the touch of Love?
He who can make sense of it may praise her!
To some she gives an ace for a six;
To others she passes off a six for an ace.
She makes the unlettered a wise man,
15 And she robs the wise man of his wisdom.
She makes one in the lower place go up higher,
Saying: "This is my sweet friend!"[a]
And nourishes him with her food.

3

Love's mode of action cannot be grasped
20 By any man, however wise;
She wounds to the heart
Someone who never sought the chains of Love;
While one who gladly lived under Love's protection
She drives completely out of his mind;
25 And another who would gladly have had fruition
Of all love, she keeps without success,
Making him uncertain how to approach her.

---

a. Cf. Luke 14:10.

4

Let him who finds these modes of Love's action
A source of pleasure make the most of them!
30 But let him take good care he judges accurately
Whatever Love passes herself off for, late or soon.
Someone, supposing this a game, fancies he loves:[72]
But at once she shows him such hostility,
In that woe with which she strikes him,
35 He can no longer do anything other
Than what Love tells him.

5

Abasement and hard adventure
Have I suffered many a day.
Bitter to me are all things
40 That my eyes ever looked upon.
How can I get off cheaply?
Love, sweetest above all that is sweet,
And who can give all things,
Detains me indeed in woe and bitterness.
45 I shudder how I keep on.

6

I will let Love be,
From my side, what she wishes.
Someone fancies he reads his judgments in her;
She has quickly silenced the great noise of his words,
50 And quickly ended all his praise of her,
With which he was enraptured:
She can, according to her pleasure,
Adroitly fence under the shield,[73]
Inflicting wounds from which no one can recover.

7

55 Although in love I have fared differently,
God bless those who are bent on Love!

And who, as her burdens are light or heavy,
Can follow or flee her according to the case.
If one can wait until good befalls him,
60 And in the meantime fence with Love,
She will make known what he is
Who can wait till that day
When Love shall reveal all.

8

I know well that if Love wanted to,
65 She would be able to console my sad mind.
Alas! Did she think any harm of me,
Thus to send me to wrack and ruin?
She holds me with great woe,
Wholly without success, desperate.
70 Unless she quickly has mercy on me
And lets me become wiser in her,
She will come to me perhaps too late.

9

However painfully I stray in Love's path—
And for me, experience of her has been delayed too long—
75 However deep I wade in her dangerous waters,
I will always give her thanks.
For I depend wholly on her,
If I shall ever ascend clear to her summit.
Whatever else I did,
80 My hunger would remain as strong as ever:
Did she not give me full satisfaction in her.

10

So I remain on Love's side,
Whatever may happen to me after that:
The pain of hunger for her, the joy of satisfaction in her,
85 No to desires, or yes to delight.
The valiant lover himself strikes before Love strikes:
Thus he comes bravely to the combat.

He who dares to fight Love with longing,
Whatever cruelty he meets with,
90 Shall possess her immensity.

I counsel the valiant lover who dares to fight Love
In the time of his youth
Not to give way to her,
But to see that he entirely catches hold of her
95 Before she passes him by.

40 LOVE'S REMOTENESS

1

As this new year begins for us,
We hope for the rapid coming
Of the season many await,
Which causes mountain and valley to burgeon,
5 Although the joy is not yet ripe.
So is it, likewise, with him who gives his all
At high Love's alluring promise,
Before he measures the remoteness of Love.

2

Who then shall be that swift one
10 Who shall measure the remoteness of Love?
The noble soul that accepts what Love grants it,
That lives by deliberation and works with forethought,
And employs all it ever had,[74]
Until enlightened reason acknowledges
15 It can spare nothing for Love—
This is the one who shall measure the remoteness of Love.

3

That Love is so remote from us,
When by right she should be so near us,
Is held by many—of whom I am one—

20 Who depend on worldly consolation.
But the noble soul in Love's service lives so free
That it dares to fight her with passion
To the death, or nearly,
Until it conquers the power of Love.

4

25 Anyone who thus conquers the power of Love
May well be called a champion,[75]
For we read of the power of Love
That she conquers all other things.
The wise man pays all the tribute of Love
30 And takes care to manage things grandly,
With continual urge of new pursuit,
Until he conquers the power of Love.

5

Love conquers him so that he may conquer her;[76]
To anyone who succeeds in this, her sweet nature becomes known.
35 When he experiences this sweet Love,
He is wounded with her wounds;
When in amazement he beholds her wonders,
He imbibes eagerly from Love's deep veins,
With continual thirst for a new beginning,
40 Until he enjoys sweet Love.

6

So for the soul things go marvellously;
While desire pours out and pleasure drinks,
The soul consumes what belongs to it in love
And sinks with frenzy in Love's fruition.
45 So in love the loving soul has full success,
When Love with love fully gives her love;
Thus is the loving soul well fed by Love alone,
Where it enjoys sweet Love.

7

The fruition of Love is a game
50 That no one can explain truly.
And although he who has felt it can truly explain something,
He who has never felt it could not understand it:
How Love wishes love and nothing else
From all that the daylight ever shone upon.
55 The course of the firmament is not so swift
As is the course of love in Love.

8

The course of the firmament and of the planets,
And of the signs that stand in the firmament,
We can know to some extent by a similitude,
60 And count the number by calculation.[77]
But no master can presume this—
That he can give understanding of Love to the minds
Of all who ever knew and shall know Love,
And shall run the course of Love.[a]

65 People have forgotten Love's immensity
If they fancy they dare to fight Love with their minds.
Alas, *Deus!* What has God brought upon those
Who must run the course of Love!

41 LOVING LOVE'S WILL

1

Although this new year has begun—
Both month and year together—
But little joyousness is gained by the fact,
For we lack clear days
5 And all the other joyousness
That makes young hearts happy.

a. Cf. 2 Tim. 4:7.

But nothing equals the woe of one
Who desires Love and never tastes her to the full.

2

Alas! He who must journey into distant exile
10 Is wearied by the deeply worn roads;
He wanders after Love and suffers reverses;
His sad lot causes him woe,
In that he does not know enough about Love
To ascertain by clear evidence
15 What gives her pleasure or displeasure;
Truly he often experiences sorry days.

3

Alas, Love, your wrath or your favor
We cannot distinguish—
Your high will and our debt,
20 Why you come, or why you fly?
For you can give, in response to small service,
Your sweet splendors in great clarity;
But for small faults this seems withheld,
And then you give blows and bitter death.

4

25 Alas, Love, how shall we learn
The why of your comings and goings?
Where shall we stop your escape,
And the storms by which you strike us down?
And by what exertions will your sweet splendors
30 Remain for us in wise clarity?
So that we may not by baseness deprive ourselves,
It may be, of what would otherwise protect us!

5

Alas! On dark roads of misery
Love indeed lets us wander,

35 In many an assault, without safety,
Where she seems to us cruel and hostile;
And to some she gives, without suffering,
Her great and multiform joy:
For us these are truly strange manners,
40 But for connoisseurs of Love's free power, they are joy.

6

Alas, Love! In whatever you do,
Your departure seems to be wrath;
But he who is high-minded and wise
Had best follow you perfectly
45 In sweet, in bitter, in consolation, and in fear,
Until he fully knows what you will for him:
When you show him your will so clearly,
His woe is silenced in peace.

7

Oh! He who sets sail for afar must suffer
50 What adventure brings him.
So he who loves must strive anxiously
Before he lives perfectly to Love's contentment.
In every season he must seek
Nothing but her high will,
55 And be saddened or gladdened by nothing else,
Whatever happens to him besides.

8

Oh! If anyone thus totally loves the will of Love—
In mounting tumult, in lowly silence,
Through everything Love ever inflicts on him—
60 In him Love ever has her fullest contentment.
This is one of the strongest fortresses,
The fairest rampart ever man saw,
And the highest walls and the deepest moat,
In which to guard Love prisoner forever.

42 THE SOUL'S WINTER

1

The sad season has come
Outdoors, but much more in the heart.
That you, Beloved, have left us in the lurch,
Is for us an insuperable grief.
5 That good, which you gave in times past,
Through strange vicissitudes escapes us,
    Together with your rich teaching
And the knowledge that you are excellent.

2

If you, Love, wish to deny us your inheritance,
10 We do not know where to fly;
So we should go to utter wrack and ruin;
We could not tell in what to find support.
But we will seek consolation in the words
You said—it is true, it shall happen,
15 There is no doubt of it:
If you were *lifted up*, you would *draw all things* to yourself.[a]

3

Alas, Love! who will raise you in himself to your full height,
So that you, all that you are, may draw him?
Who will struggle through the deep valleys,
20 The high mountains, the wide fields,
With deep humility in new ardor,
With confidence in high delight,
    Strong in the combat?
Help quickly in this, O Love; there is need, it is high time!

a. John 12:32.

4

25 It is your lofty name,
Like oil poured out,[b] Love,
Sweet and soft, very good and pleasing;
But above all, you are the delight of the inward senses.
Too few souls, however,
30 Nourish themselves with this oil's strength,
And become well acquainted, Love,
With the rich profit of your name.

5

Since, Love, your name is poured out,
And since it overflows with a flood of wonder,
35 *The young maidens*[c] are melted away in you
And love with violent longing, above counsel;
So they perform many a tremendous deed
And cry: "Total liberty in confidence
Is counsel enough for me!"
40 Alas, that success should lead to destruction!

6

He does not fight who never parries a blow.
He wishing to grow up must exert himself.
If anyone wastes away through neglecting to eat,
He seldom happens to receive honor.
45 Cowardly is the hunter who flies before
What urged him on to the chase—
That is Love, who promised us her splendor.
Alas! Nothing less than all is worth our while.

7

If the heart can be refreshed by anything
50 That is not Love's totality alone,

b. Song 1:2.
c. Song 1:2.

That passes beyond the taste of the soul;
For nothing less shall content it
Than the upsurge of the birth of Love,
And the great and *wonderful things without number*[d]
55 That lead to the mutual merging
In which Love never conceals love from the loving soul.

8

For Love to conceal anything from love
Were a heavy blow for the soul;
It would waste away perforce in the fury of hunger,
60 Since nothing but Love can satisfy it.
But heart and mind do something quite different:
Into trivial pastime and play
And contemptible pleasure
They successfully transform their grief themselves.

43 THE NEED OF ALL NEEDS

1

When we meet harsh wintertime,
Which makes many a heart heavy,
The season, as everyone knows,
Brings round the feast of All Saints.
5 I have suffered many fears,
But this fear troubles me above all:
How I shall attain to Love.

2

Love cannot console me;
But, for her sake, all bitterness is gain to me;
10 She is the power of my mind;
For she is herself enlightenment and judgment.

d. Job 5:9.

Whether I lose or win,
Love shall be my gain;
For she is herself satisfaction in all things.

3

15 Alas, Love! Might you find this a fit time
(I have long felt the hour was come)
To pity my misery's broad extent,
Which for me is too long and too wide,
And to confer joy on my heart,
20 Which all too rarely has been gladdened
Since I first came to long for you.

4

How gladly should I see that book,
To know where, Love, *in your book*
You have set down your very ardent loveress,
25 And how with love you love *your friends.*[a]
That I, your loveress, may glory with them
For I, your loveress, have never gloried
As now do they who taste you.

5

Alas, true Love! you alone are pure Love;
30 When will you so make me pure love
That I shall be conformed to you in nature?
For all I have is contrary to nature:
All other things are bitter to me;
But what is bitter to me above all
35 Is that I cannot touch you.

6

Alas! I was never willingly without Love,
For that is the need of all needs.

a. Ps. 138:16–17.

They who live without Love are dead.
But the worst of all deaths is this—
40 That the loving soul be cowardly toward Love;
For perfect Love is never cowardly,
But claims its rights, which it lacks.

7

O sublime nature, true Love,
When will you make my nature so fair
45 That it will be wholly conformed to your nature?
For I wish to be wholly conformed.
If all that is other in me were yours,
Everything that is yours would be altogether mine:
I should burn to ashes in your fire!

8

50 O Love, those who are of your lineage
You nourish with your nature according to your lineage;
Whoever spared his nature, keeping back something from you,
Was left remote from your nature;
But he whom your nature ever enlightened
55 Remained enlightened in your nature,
So that he lives according to perfection.

9

Let him who wishes to be perfect have humility,
And subject all his powers to humility;
Then all his work will yield good results,
60 But otherwise it will fall short of goodness,
Wanting both power of action and success;
For no one ever had success in love
If in anything he ascribed Love's work to himself.

10

We must always, in misfortune,
65 For Love's sake choose misfortune;
Love's powers, with which she to herself is all,
Will then help us all;
In her great and *wonderful things without number,*[b]
Of which there never was a number,
70 We can take delight with Love.

11

From Love I have night by day,[c]
Whereas she should cause me to have day by night.
Desire makes me lament;
Pleasure constantly speaks to me of woe;
75 But Reason counsels me that I be patient,
And says: "Through Love, work and be patient,
Until your own work helps you to take revenge."

12

By Reason's counsel, work is noble;
I do not say that it cannot be nobler;
80 Reason promises us great rewards,
But Love herself has rewarded at once.
At times she shows such false hopes
To someone from whom she takes those hopes after showing
them
That they were spears, which wounded deeply.

13

85 A noble heart goes questing the depths of Love:
Love, however, is depthless;
Doing without Love is the heart's suffering,

---

b. Job 5:9.
c. Job 5:14.

Of which it may be healed too late.
When the heart is on the point of knowing Love,
90 Love first becomes wholly unknown by it.
So it is by desire that the heart's veins are rent.

14

We must wholly forsake love for Love;
He who forsakes love for Love is wise.
It is all one whether we die or live:
95 To die for Love's sake is to have lived enough.
Alas, Love! You have long driven me to extremity;
But in this very extremity to which you have driven me,
I will keep vigil, Love, in service of your love.

15

O Love, if you also wish my ruin,
100 No matter how unwillingly I have ever been ruined,
I will suffer all in order to attain you.

All who shrink in fear before the greatness of Love
And live in hope, outside her greatness,
Love shall render purer than white samite.

44 PLAYING THE NIGGARD

1

When the fruits of the year
Are harvested under our gaze,
Without either trouble or anxiety,
Everyone has reason to live in joy.
5 Only our heart suffers and sorely hungers—
The heart desiring but not possessing Love.

POEMS IN STANZAS

2

What anyone desires, he gladly accepts.
But to be robbed of Love is the greatest woe.
Against this I caution all men
10 To forearm themselves wisely.
All other pains are negligible
Compared to that of desiring Love without success.

3

They who succeed in other things
Than that of straying in the madness of Love
Seem wise in the eyes of aliens
15 To whom any misery of Love is unknown.
He who can succeed in Love is protected:
He has no return in which to lose himself.

4

I know one person who in the beginning
20 Applied himself to Love as a game;
Until he so far lost himself in it
That there is no more game for him.
Whether he loses or wins,
For him withdrawal is truly impossible.

5

25 In serving Love one cannot lose,
Although it is true that she brings help late.
She always gladly repays her promises.
If anyone believes this, he is awaiting
The kind of joy expressed in the proverb:
30 "Let the man who is hanged wait till they cut him down!"

6

The man who is hanged, much though he enjoy waiting,
And he who lives in the chains of Love

And for Love's sake gives up all—these two are in the same case.
Alas, Love, see to it yourself!
35 However far you apparently drive him who serves you,
See that your nature satisfies him.

7

It may be well that Love satisfies;
But for the poor, the gleanings suffice.
That Love partake of her fare with her beloved friends
40 Is but equitable, she is so great,
And that she compensate us continually;
For her niggardliness is worse than any death.

8

Alas, Love, if you play the niggard with me,
I vow I will play the niggard with you!
45 I wonder how it comes to pass
That you stay a great distance off?
You are far from me, and I am near you;
Therefore I live continually in the sad season.

9

Alas, Love, temper your mighty power!
50 You have the days, and I the nights.
Why, when you force me to go out hunting for you,
Do you flee so far ahead of me?
You make me pay such a tribute,
I shudder that ever I was born a human being.

45 LOVE ALONE

1

No matter what the time of year,
Nothing exists anywhere in the world
That can give me delight
    Except: *verus amor!*[78]
5 O Love! In fidelity (since you are all
My soul's joy, my heart's goal),
Pity distress; look upon struggle;
    Hear: *cordis clamor!*

2

However I cry out and complain of my woe,
10 May Love do with me according to her pleasure;
I wish to give her, throughout my life,
    Laus et honor.
Alas, Love, if the eyes of fidelity but saw you!
For by mentioning fidelity I become valiant;
15 For when I first glimpsed your high summits,
    Your: *traxit odor.*[a]

3

O Love! Indeed you have never deceived:
For you showed me in my youth
What I request (for it is in your power)—
20 Be *medicina!*
O Love! since all things are in your disposition,
Give me for Love's sake what most delights me;
For you are the mother of all virtues,
    Lady and *regina.*

---

a. Song 1:3.

4

25 O dearest Love, true and pure,
Why do you not see how I suffer,
And be in my smarting bitterness
Condimentum?
Amid hardships I go in quest of adventure.
30 All other things, apart from you, are bitter to me;
Give me fully, Love, your sublime nature,
Sacramentum.

5

Whether I am in plenty or in want,
35 Let all, Love, be according to your counsel;
Your blows show me the grace I owe
Redemptori.
Whether I wade the deep or climb the summits,
Or find myself in hunger or in satiety,
40 All I wish, Love, is fully to content you,
Unde mori. Amen, Amen.

VISIONS

VISIONS

VISION 1

THE GARDEN OF PERFECT VIRTUES

T was a Sunday, in the Octave of Pentecost,[1] when our Lord was brought secretly to my bedside, because I felt such an attraction of my spirit inwardly that I could not control myself outwardly in a degree sufficient to go among persons; it would have been impossible for me to go among them.[2] And that desire which I had inwardly was to be one with God in fruition.[3] For this I was still too childish and too little grown-up; and I had not as yet sufficiently suffered for it or lived the number of years requisite for such exceptional worthiness. That is what was shown me then and still seems the same to me. 15. When I had received our Lord, he then received me to him, so that he withdrew my senses from every remembrance of alien things to enable me to have joy in him in inward togetherness with him. Then I was led as if into a meadow, an expanse that was called the space of perfect virtue. In it stood trees, and I was guided close to them. And I was shown their names and the significance of their names.

24. The first tree had a rotten root, which was very brittle, but a very solid trunk. And above this bloomed a charming, very beautiful flower; but it was so frail that if a storm had ever blown up, this flower would have fallen and faded. He who guided me was an Angel belonging to the choir of Thrones (cf. Col. 1:16), the very ones who are charged with discernment.[4] And this same day, having grown up, I had come close to him, so that I had received him; and from then on he was to be my guardian and the companion of all my ways. And this Angel said: "Human nature, understand and know what this tree is!" And I understood, just as he revealed it to me, that the tree was the knowledge of ourselves.[5] The rotten root was our brittle nature; the solid trunk, the eternal soul; and the beautiful flower, the beautiful human shape, which becomes corrupt so quickly, in an instant (cf. James 1:11).

42. Then he led me farther to where a tree stood that was very low and had beautiful leaves, graceful and multicolored, that were pleasing to the sight. And above all these beautiful leaves hung withered leaves that concealed all the beautiful leaves. And then the Angel said again: "Chosen soul of high aspirations, you have been drawn from such ignobility to such loftiness, from such dark ignorance to such light (cf. 1 Pet. 2:9), and from such great poverty to the greatest wealth—understand what this is!" And he showed me, and I understood that it was humility that had recognized God's greatness and its own unworthiness, and now with wise fear hid all the virtues by which it was truly adorned, because it felt and knew that it lacked fruition of its Beloved, and that it did not know how to remedy this lack. This is pure humility.

60. After that he led me farther to where a tall tree stood, a strong tree adorned with big, wide leaves. And then the Angel said again to me: "O powerful and strong one, you have conquered the powerful and strong God, from the origin of his Being, which was without beginning; and with him you shall wield power over eternity in eternity! Read, and understand!" And I read and understood. On each leaf was written: "I am the power of the perfect will; nothing can escape me."

71. And nearby stood a tree with many branches; it was tall and extended all its branches through those of another tree. And the Angel said to me again: "O wise one, instructed by reason, even by the reason of the great God,[6] read and understand the wise and long-sighted lesson that teaches those who grow up through one another!" And I understood that it could be read on each leaf: "I am discernment: *without me you can do nothing*" (John 15:5).

80. After that he led me farther where a very beautiful tree stood that had three sorts of branches, and three of each sort: three above, three in the middle, and three below. And the Angel said to me again: "O soul, apprehensive lest disastrous adventures occur in your future! O soul, sighing as you behold the vagaries of the persons[7] who were created to love God but go astray from him and finally end elsewhere! O soul, dying of the death your Beloved died of![8] Understand these three lowest branches, for it is thanks to them that you have climbed to the highest ones!" Then I understood that all these leaves were a bright green color, and sharp and long; and on each leaf a heart was etched. On the lowest branches, the hearts on

each leaf were red; on the middlemost, white; on the highest branches, they were gold.[9]

100. And the Angel said to me again: "O pure *pillar* (Apoc. 3:12) *in the church of the saints* (Ps. 88:6), you have kept your body undefiled by all things unbefitting the holy *temple of God* (1 Cor. 3:17)! O sinless soul, consoler for every sin, through you the pure will of our great God shall be and is strengthened! O soul perceiving with perception the noble Nature of our sweet God, for which reason you so early chose pure chastity above all that was and is, and have never fallen short in any situation![10] Now understand these three middlemost branches!" And I understood.

112. And the Angel said to me again: "O seeker of veritable love solely in your God, acting perfectly in all things according to the customs of the holy law, which God sanctified by the holy life he lived, and by his great commandments and his sublime counsels! O loving soul, observant of the holy customs by loving service according to the good pleasure of the omnipotent God! O being of constancy, since God always finds in you the fidelity of veritable Love,[11] and in you he will eternally possess it! Understand these three highest branches!" And I understood.

124. This tree was wisdom. The first lowest branch, which had the red hearts on its leaves, signified the fear of not being perfect and of forsaking perfect virtues. The second branch was the fear that persons do not show God many marks of homage,[12] and that such a number go astray from the Truth, which is himself. The third branch was the fear that each person must die by the same death whereby our Beloved died,[13] with wisdom to be perfect in each and every virtue in order to die of that death every hour, and to carry that cross, and to die on it each day, and to die with all those who go astray and die.

138. The first of the middlemost branches—those with the leaves etched with the white heart—signified chastity: of body, in deportment, in words, and in deeds. The second branch was to desire that everyone's work be innocent and pure, and to watch over one's works in order that they may please our Beloved. The third branch was to remain so pure of all stain in spirit, in desire, and in soul that no baseness may penetrate there by error, haughtiness, vainglory, despair, or excessive hope of what one does not yet possess; and that one may not fall into joy over possessing something, or grief over lacking something, or into emotional attractions; or that one may not be fully sat-

isfied before the day when one has carried Love long enough, according to what she deserves, and until Love is carried so full-grown and is so fully nourished by appropriate works that one rises above the carrying of Love to that feeling which is much higher than carrying Love.[14] For to carry Love means a propensity, a longing, a desire, a service, and incessant exercise of burning will. But to feel Love means the awareness of being in the liberty of Love.[15] But to be Love surpasses all.[16]

163. The first of the three highest branches—which had the gold heart on their leaves—signified: by many perfect virtues to seek Love in her inmost being, where she is to be found in totality.[17] The second branch is: to accomplish with love God's high will,[18] according to the pleasure with which he himself gives with prodigality to everyone who lives for him in this manner. The third branch is to be steadfast and thus always to be wholly with Love, above the multiplicity of virtues in the wholly unique Virtue[19] that engulfs the two lovers[20] in one and casts them into the abyss where they shall seek and find eternal fruition.

177. Then the Angel led me farther, to where we found a chalice all full of blood. And the Angel said to me again: "O great one with a great will, having surmounted, without being bruised, and with sweet quietude, all afflictions heard of or unheard of! Drink!"

181. And I drank, and it was the chalice of patience; by this I made the vow to content God steadfastly by patient fidelity.

185. Then the Angel led me farther, into the center of the space where we were walking. There stood a tree with its roots upward and its summit downward. This tree had many branches. Of the lowest branches, which formed the summit, the first is faith, and the second hope, by which persons begin. The Angel said to me again: "O mistress, you climb this tree from the beginning to the end, all the way to the profound roots of the incomprehensible God! Understand that this is the way of beginners and of those who persevere to perfection!"[21] And I understood that it was the tree of the knowledge of God, which one begins with faith and ends with love.

199. Near this tree stood another, which had large round leaves. And the Angel said to me: "Remain here as a prisoner until the moment when he who had you called to come here sends you back. And understand his secret will,[22] and why he wishes to make use of you. I am going elsewhere, in order to serve in your mighty service. Today I received in your regard the order to be at your service every hour

(cf. Heb. 1:14), until the moment when you have outgrown me in the ways by which I have led you; and these you can perfectly pursue, and experience the hidden counsel[23] that our great and powerful God will reveal to you at this moment. I am going elsewhere to watch over your pure body in order that it may remain in the noble worthiness in which I found it and wish to keep it."[24]

214. And then he said: "Turn from me, and you will find the one whom you have always sought (cf. Matt. 28:5), and for whom you have turned away from all things of earth and heaven." And I turned from him, and I saw standing before me a cross like crystal, clearer and whiter than crystal. And through it a great space was visible. And placed in front of this cross I saw a seat like a disk, which was more radiant to see than the sun in its most radiant power (cf. Apoc. 1:16); and beneath the disk stood three pillars. The first pillar was like burning fire. The second was like a precious stone that is called topaz; it has the nature of gold and the brightness of the air, as well as the colors of all gems. The third was like a precious stone that is called amethyst and has a purple color like the rose and the violet. And in the middle under the disk, a whirlpool revolved in such a frightful manner and was so terrible to see that heaven and earth might have been astonished and made fearful by it.

236. The seat that resembled a disk was eternity. The three pillars were the three names under which the wretched ones who are far from Love understand him. The pillar like fire is the name of the Holy Spirit. The pillar like the topaz is the name of the Father. The pillar like the amethyst is the name of the Son. The profound whirlpool, which is so frightfully dark,[25] is divine fruition in its hidden storms.

246. At this mighty place sat he whom I was seeking, and with whom I had desired to be one in fruition. His appearance could not be described in any language. His head was grand and broad, with curly hair, white in color (cf. Apoc. 1:14), and crowned with a crown that is like a precious stone that is called sardonyx and has three colors: black, white, and red.[26] His eyes were marvelously unspeakable to see and drew all things to him (cf. John 12:32) in Love. I cannot bear witness to it in words, for the unspeakable great beauty and the sweetest sweetness of this lofty and marvelous Countenance rendered me unable to find any comparison for it or any metaphor. And my Beloved gave himself to me, both in spiritual understanding of himself and in feeling. But when I saw him, I fell at his feet, for I divined

that I had been led toward him the whole way, of which so much was still to be lived.

265. And he said to me: "Stand up (cf. Ezech. 2:1)! For you are standing in me, from all eternity, entirely free and without fall.[27] For you have desired to be one with me,[28] and in all respects you have done what you could to this end. And since you are so shaken by the storm of inquietude, because you possess testimony from me and from the obvious acts you have performed in all things where you believed you discerned my will, and because of your wise works, *I have sent you* this *Angel* (Apoc. 22:16)—from the choir of Thrones—who is wise in leading those of good will to perfection.[29] He found you so arrayed inwardly that he actually led you by all the ways, which he had wished merely to show to you, as to a child. He likewise gave you such exalted names that they have beautified you in my sight.

281. "Now I shall make known to you what I wish of you. I wish you for my sake to be prepared for every kind of affliction. I forbid you ever, even for the twinkling of an eye, to dare to strike back for any reason or take revenge for any cause. If you dare to do that in any way whatever, you will be the one who wishes to supplant my right, and who mars my greatness."

288. He continued: "Moreover *I give you a new commandment* (John 13:34): If you wish to be like me in my Humanity, as you desire to possess me wholly in my Divinity and Humanity, you shall desire to be poor, miserable, and despised by all men; and all griefs will taste sweeter to you than all earthly pleasures; in no way let them sadden you. For they will be beyond human nature to carry. If you wish to follow Love, at the urging of your noble nature, which makes you desire me in my totality,[30] it will become so alien to you to live among persons, and you will be so despised and so unhappy, that you will not know where to lodge for a single night, and all persons will fall away from you and forsake you, and no one will be willing to wander about with you in your distress and your weakness,[31] whatever the state in which you find yourself. You will still for a short time lead such a life of suffering, and I shall find my pleasure in it. For your hour has not yet come.

307. "But I have one thing against you (cf. Apoc. 4:2), and consequently I am incensed on one point, which I wish to show you. You are young in days, and you want me to recognize the sore pain of your body, and the fidelity of your handiwork, and your new will always overflowing with charity for others, and the desires of your

heart, and the languishing of your senses, and the love of your soul. All this I do recognize. But recognize also on your side that I lived merely as Man, and that my body suffered sore pain, and that my hands worked faithfully, and that my new will overflowed with charity for men through the whole world, upon strangers and upon friends, and that my senses languished, and that my Heart desired, and that my soul loved. And during my whole time I persevered in all this until the hour came when my Father took me up to him.

325. "You have said to me at times that it was easy for me to live as Man because I possessed the seven gifts (cf. Isa. 11:2–3);[32] that is true, and not only did I have the gifts, but I was myself the Giver of the spirits (cf. Apoc. 1:4) that are called the gifts. And you have also said that *my Father* was *with me* (John 16:32); that is true, not one single hour were we separated. But I make known to you a hidden truth concerning me, perceptible however for one who knows how to understand it: this is, that never for a single instant did I call upon my power to give myself relief when I was in need, and never did I seek to profit from the gifts of my Spirit, but I won them at the price of sufferings and through my Father, for he and I were wholly one—as we now are (cf. John 10:30)—before the day when my hour came of my full-grownness. Never did I dispel my griefs or my pains with the aid of my omnipotence.[33]

341. "Now you have complained of your misery and of the fact that you did not receive from me what you needed, according to your desire; and I ask you, when did this fail you without your having the seven gifts of my Spirit? And I ask you also, when were you forsaken by my Father in any state of soul, so that my Father was not always with you, as he was with me and I with him, while I lived as Man? Since, then, you are a human being, live in misery as man. I wish that on earth my life in you should be so fully lived in all virtues that you may in no point fail me in myself.[34] Possess the seven gifts of my Spirit and the power and help of my Father in the perfect works of virtues with which man becomes and remains God eternally. But feel yourself as man in all the hardships proper to the human condition, except sin alone. All the suffering that belongs to the human race I experienced while I lived as Man, *except sin* alone (Heb. 4:15). I never cheered myself by my inner power, except with the consolation that I was certain of my Father.

364. "You have also known that I lived a long time on earth before men learned to know me among that people, and before I worked

miracles. And when I had worked miracles and became better known, few friends remained to me in the world. Yes, at my death almost all men alive abandoned me. Therefore do not let it grieve you that all persons will forsake you on account of perfect Love and because you are living in my will. Beautiful revelations and miracles have happened to you during your days, by free favor, more than to any person who was born since I died. Exterior miracles and gifts that had indeed begun to be worked in you, you refused to accept from me, and you renounced them and did not want them. You forsook them because of Love, and you want nothing else than myself. For my sake you have rejected everything, and you wish to have fruition of me in feeling (this is beyond all). For that, however, the number of days you have lived is still insufficient."

383. He continued: "I will give myself to you secretly, dearest beloved, when you desire to possess me, since you do not wish aliens to console you or come to know you. Thus I will give you understanding of my will, and the art of veritable Love, and the faculty of feeling me in union—sometimes—in the storms of Love, in those moments when you cannot hold out without feeling me, and your grief becomes too heavy for you.

391. "With understanding you shall wisely carry out my will, in all those who need to know, through you, my will, which is still unknown to them. You have not failed anyone until now; never fail anyone until the day when I say to you: 'Your work is totally accomplished' (cf. John 19:30)! With Love you shall live and persevere and accomplish my hidden will by which you belong to me and I to you (cf. Song 2:16). And to feel yourself in me will be sufficient for you, and you will be sufficient for me. Thus fulfill my will with understanding, my most desired beloved! Thus give yourself to me with Love, you who enjoy me the closest in my nearness. Thus you shall have fruition of me.

404. "This is the tree described by the words I have now spoken to you: It is called the knowledge of Love. For as so many things were preached to you that might incline you to lowness,[35] I have shown you myself what I expect of you.

408. "You must go back quietly and do what I have commanded you. If you wish, take from this tree a leaf to symbolize the knowledge of my will. And if you are saddened, take a rose from its summit and one petal from the rose to symbolize Love.[36] And if you cannot bear it, take from the rose what is within it. This signifies that I will

grant you myself in fruition. You shall always have knowledge of my will, and experience Love; and at the expedient time you shall feel me in fruition. So my Father did for me although I was his Son; he left me in affliction but never abandoned me; I felt him in fruition, and I served those to whom he had sent me. The heart that is found so full in the rose symbolizes the fruition of Love through feeling. My beloved, help all persons in their affliction impartially, whether they do you good or evil. Love will make you capable of it. Give all, for all is yours!"

VISION 2

EXPERIENCE OF PENTECOST

NCE on Pentecost Sunday I received the Holy Spirit in such a manner that I understood all the will of Love in all, and all the modes of this will of the heavens and of heavenly things, and all the perfection of perfect justice, and all the shortcomings of the lost; and with regard to all, I saw the will in which they then were, either of truth or of falsehood. And since then I have felt in the same way the love of all the persons I saw, in whatever degree they then were. And then I understood all the languages that are spoken in seventy-two ways.[37] The multiplicity of all these things was hidden from me and has vanished. But that simple gazing upon him, and the burningness of Love, and the truth of his will, from that time onward have never been extinguished, and have never been silent, and have never been appeased within me. 18. In the old days, before this time, with regard to all my acts, I constantly wished to know, and kept thinking of it, and repeated ceaselessly: "What is Love? And who is Love?"[38] 20. I had spent two years in this occupation.

VISION 3

WHAT AND WHO IS LOVE

ATER, one Easter Sunday, I had gone to God; and he embraced me in my interior senses and took me away in spirit. He brought me before the Countenance of the Holy Spirit, who possesses the Father and the Son in one Essence. And from the total Being of that Countenance I received all understanding, and thus I read all my judgments.[39] 8. A voice issuing from this Countenance resounded so fearfully that it made itself heard above everything. And it said to me: "Behold, ancient one, you have called me and sought me, what and who I, Love, am, myriads of years before the birth of man! See and receive my Spirit! With regard to all things, know what I, Love, am in them! And when you fully bring me yourself, as pure humanity in myself, through all the ways of perfect Love, you shall have fruition of me as the Love who I am. Until that day, you shall love what I, Love, am. And then you will be love, as I am Love.[40] And you shall not live less than what I, Love, am, from that day until the death that will make you alive.[41] In my unity, you have received me and I have received you. Go forth, and live what I am; and return bringing me full divinity, and have fruition of me as who I am."[42]

25. Then I returned into myself, and I understood all I have just said; and I remained to gaze fixedly upon my delightful sweet Love.

VISION 4
TWO KINGDOMS, TWO HEAVENS

sat one day in May, ready to hear the Mass of Saint James, as was right, for that was his feast day. Then during the Epistle (Wisd. 5:1–5)[43] my senses were drawn inwards with a great tempestuous clamor by an awe-inspiring spirit that from within drew me within myself. From within I was then wholly drawn into the spirit. 9. Then a wonderful symbolic vision was shown me: two kingdoms as of the same opulence, and the same birth, and the same race, and the same power in all dominion. And then came a burning Angel completely enkindled with ardent fire. And he opened his wings wide and struck with them seven mighty claps, like a herald who wishes to silence everything for his voice, to make his will listened to. At the first clap, the moon[44] stood motionless in her rotation, for this silence, which was commanded there. At the second clap, the sun stood motionless in its rotation, for this silence. At the third clap, all the stars (cf. Apoc. 8:12) ceased their rotation. At the fourth clap, the dwellers in paradise were awakened from their repose to wonder at this, because it was something new. At the fifth clap, the rotation of the throne ceased. At the sixth clap appeared all the saints, all holy men, living and dead, all who are in heaven, and in purgatory, and on earth, each one as he shall be perfect in all. At the seventh clap, all the heavens of each kingdom of heaven opened in eternal glory.

33. When the Angel had struck thus with his wings and caused silence, he emitted a voice like thunder or like the mighty trumpet with which the highest command is commanded. And then he said: "All you who have been brought to a standstill in your service, and all you who, having been served thereby, appeared, be herewith witnesses to me of what I shall reveal to this soul, who is in wonder and fear of you that stand here!" At that instant I was encompassed in his wings and in the midst of his kingdom that was himself.

44. Then he said to me: "You, unknown to all your friends and to all your enemies! You, ever loved as I myself! Choose now one of the two heavens you saw as kingdoms!" Then I sank into him as en-

compassed by a sweet new fidelity that was full of knowledge with the taste of veritable Love.[45]

50. In this penetrating taste of sweet Love he said to me: "You are touched[46] by the perfect fidelity, which eternally shall *make all things new* (Apoc. 21:5): Taste and understand what the difference between the two heavens is, and choose the richest and the most powerful!"

56. And I said:[47] "Lord, I understand them fully, for you by making me perfect have taken from me all my lowness because of which I doubted."[48]

58. And then I saw her to whom one heaven pertained[49] and my Beloved, each possessed of a heaven[50] and each of them equally powerful, in the same service, the same glory, the same omnipotence, and the same long-suffering mercy in all eternal being. And all the heavenly bodies that had come to a standstill in their rotation—moon, sun, stars, and throne—and all that had appeared in order to bear witness—paradise, men, and all the heavens that serve them—all said: "Amen!" and bore witness to the unity of them both. And to all of them was permission given each to be in its being as it was before.

72. Then the Angel said to me further: "Now see me united in unity with your Beloved[51]—and you are my loved one, loved with me. These heavens, which you behold, are wholly hers and mine; and these you saw as two kingdoms that were separated were our two humanities before they attained full growth. I was full-grown before; and nevertheless we remained equal. And I came into my kingdom yesterday, and you became full-grown afterwards; nevertheless we remained equal. And she shall become full-grown today and come tomorrow with you into her kingdom; and nevertheless shall remain equal with me. You have wished, dear strong heroine and lady, with your doubts, to know from me how it might come to pass, and through what works, that she should attain full growth so as to be like me, so that I should be like her and you like myself. Let this be in me,[52] and let it be announced to you by my mouth; it is my understanding of my rich Nature.

90. "Her first great work,[53] by which she shall attain to full growth, is that she shall exercise all the virtues that are shown her by me in Scripture, in counsel, in the taste of Love between her and me, in the command that you have laid on her with the chain of Love, and through the wide knowledge you have of my will, which gives fruition.

97. "Her second great work[54] shall be to be miserable and unstable while she exercises many great virtues that we have loved in her, so that she shall exercise them with violent zeal in the highest likeness.

101. "Her third work[55] and her still greater virtue shall be her discouragement that will visit her incessantly and say within her: 'What does God intend? What does this maiden intend?[56] What is ahead, how can it happen that I shall become full-grown like him and like her, so as to content both of them according to their dignity?'

107. "She knows me as perfect God; and she will wish to know you as the most perfect person who lives by all similar virtues according to my modes of action. The fear and the torment how she should content us with such defective modes of action as hers are, and her sweetest haste with earnest desire that she may ever be perfect, without failing in anything, whatever the cost—and then relapsing into faults that condemn her and cause her to despair,[57] whereas she so gladly remained noble and without stain, according to the likeness of both of us, and felt herself far removed from it, with all the judgments passed on her: realize it now yourself—what more can she do?

120. "Her fourth work[58] and the greatest of all, which she shall lead to the end in us, is the privation—which each of us feels from the other—of our sweet nature, and the knowledge and the perception of it that we have twofold in ourself while she, not full-grown, must do without him, whom she must love above all, and must consequently experience as all-darkness. This shall be her work, with which tomorrow she shall present herself as wholly conformed to us."

VISION 5

THREE HEAVENS AND THE TRINITY
(Digression on Lucifer)

T Matins on the day of the Assumption, I was taken up for a short while in the spirit: and I was shown the three highest heavens,[59] after which the three highest Angels are named—the Thrones, the Cherubim, and the Seraphim. Then came to me the eagle from among *the four living creatures* (Ezech. 1:5–6; Apoc. 4:6–8), sweet Saint John the Evangelist,[60] and he said: "Come and behold the things I saw as man; all that I saw only in symbol, you have seen disclosed and entire; you have understood them, and you know what they are like."[61] 12. And in thinking about what Saint John had said to me here, I fell on my face in great woe, and my woe cried aloud: "*Ah, ah!* (Jer. 1:6) Holy Friend and true Omnipotence, why do you let those who are ours wander off to alien things, and why do you not flow through them in our oneness? I have my whole will with you besides, and I love and hate with you, like you.[62] For now—since you once again gave me assurance—I am no longer a Lucifer, like those who are now Lucifer and wish that good and grace be given them, when they offer entry neither in their lives, nor in their works, nor in their service; and they wish to get rid of their labor, and they wish to enjoy grace; and they exalt themselves and, because you show them a little of your goodness, they wish to have it as their right. And they fall from your heavenly honor; this you made known to me.

30. "In one thing I did wrong in the past, to the living and the dead, whom I with desire would have freed from purgatory and from hell as my right. But for this be you blessed: Without anger against me, you gave me four among the living and the dead who then belonged to hell. Your goodness was tolerant of my ignorance, and of my thoughtless desires, and of the unrestrained charity that you gave me in yourself for men. For I did not then know your perfect justice. I fell into this fault and was Lucifer because I did not know this, although on that account I did no evil in your eyes. This was the one thing because of which I fell among men, so that I remained un-

known to them, and they were cruel to me. Through love I wished to snatch the living and the dead from all the debasement of despair and of wrongdoing, and I caused their pain to be lessened, and those dead in hell to be sent into purgatory, and those living in hell to be brought to the heavenly mode of life. Your goodness was tolerant of me in this and showed me that for this reason I had fallen in that way among those people.

52. "Then you took my self into yourself and gave me to know what you are, and that you hate and love in one same Being. Then I understood how I must hate and love wholly with you, and how I must be in all respects. Because I know this, I desire of you that you will make those who are ours all one with us."

59. And he who sat on the throne in heaven said to me: "These three thrones I am in Three Persons—Throne, Man; the Cherubim, the Holy Spirit; and the Seraphim, in my fruition, in which I am all."[63] And he took me out of the spirit in that highest fruition of wonder beyond reason; there I had fruition of him as I shall eternally.

65. The time was short, and when I came to myself he brought me again into the spirit and spoke to me thus: "As you now have fruition of this, you shall have fruition of it eternally."

68. And John said to me: "Go to your burden, and God shall renew his old wonders (cf. Ecclus. 36:5) in you."[64]

71. And I came back into my pain again with many a great woe.

VISION 6

TO CONDEMN AND BLESS WITH CHRIST

T was on a certain feast of the Epiphany: I was then nineteen years old, as was mentioned to me that day.[65] Then it was my will to go to our Lord; for at this time I experienced desires and an exceedingly strong longing—how God takes and gives with regard to persons who, lost in him and taken up in fruition, are conformed to his will in all circumstances.[66] On this day, because of my longing, I was again strongly moved in Love. 9. And then I was taken up in a spirit and carried on to where a vast and awe-inspiring place was shown me, and in this strong place stood a seat. And he who sat upon it was invisible and incomprehensible in the dignity of the jurisdiction he exercised on that height. To be seated in such a place is ununderstandable to either heavenly or earthly beings. Above that high seat in this lofty place, I saw a crown that surpassed all diadems. In its great breadth it embraced all things beneath it, and beyond the crown was nothing.

22. And an Angel came with a glowing censer, which glowed all red-hot with fire and smoke. He knelt before the highest place of the seat above which the crown hung, and he paid him honor and said: "O unknown Power and great almighty Lord, receive herewith honor and dignity from this maiden who resorts to you in your secret place: This place is unknown to all those who do not send you such an enkindled offering with such sharp arrows as she sends you with her new burning youth, for she has now ended her nineteenth year, so people say. And it is she, Lord, who comes to seek you in the spirit—who you are, in your incomprehensibility. For that mysterious life, which you with burning charity have aroused in her, has led her to this place. Now reveal to her that you have drawn her here, and transport her wholly within yourself."[67]

40. And then I heard a Voice speaking to me; it was terrible and unheard-of. It spoke to me with imagery and said: "Behold who I am!"

43. And I saw him whom I sought. His Countenance revealed itself with such clarity that I recognized in it all the countenances and

all the forms that ever existed and ever shall exist,[68] wherefrom he received honor and service in all right. I saw why each one must receive his part in damnation and in blessing,[69] and by what each one must be set in his place; and by what manner of acting some persons wander away from him and return to him again, finer and more beautiful than they were before; why still others seem always wandering and never came back—they remained standing entirely still, and almost devoid of consolation at all times. And others have remained in their place since childhood, have known themselves at their worth, and have held out to the end.

59. I recognized all these beings there in that Countenance.

60. In his right hand I saw the gifts of his blessing; and I saw in his hand heaven in its vastness opened, and all those who will be with him there eternally. In his left hand I saw the sword of the fearful stroke, with which he strikes all down to death. In this hand I saw hell and all its eternal company.

67. I saw his greatness oppressed under all. I saw his littleness exalted above all. I saw his hiddenness embracing and flowing through all things: I saw his breadth enclosed in all. I heard his reasoned understanding and perceived all reason with reason. I saw in his breast the entire fruition of his Nature in Love. In everything else I saw, I could understand that in the spirit.

76. But then wonder seized me because of all the riches I had seen in him, and through this wonder I came out of the spirit in which I had seen all that I sought; and as in this situation in all this rich enlightenment I recognized my awe-inspiring, my unspeakably sweet Beloved, I fell out of the spirit—from myself and all I had seen in him—and, wholly lost, fell upon the breast, the fruition, of his Nature, which is Love. There I remained, engulfed and lost, without any comprehension of other knowledge, or sight, or spiritual understanding, except to be one with him and to have fruition of this union. I remained in it less than half an hour.[70]

90. Then I was called back again in a spirit, and again I recognized and understood all reasoning as before.

92. And once again it was said to me by him: "From now on you shall never more condemn or bless anyone except as I wish;[71] and you shall give everyone his due, according to his worth. This is what I am, in fruition and in knowledge, and in entrancement for those who wish to content me according to my will. I direct you—to live in conformity with my Divinity and my Humanity—back again into

the cruel world, where you must taste every kind of death—until you return hither in the full name of my fruition, in which you are baptized in my depths."

103. And with this I returned, woeful, to myself.

VISION 7

ONENESS IN THE EUCHARIST

N a certain Pentecost Sunday I had a vision at dawn. Matins were being sung in the church, and I was present. My heart and my veins and all my limbs trembled and quivered with eager desire and, as often occurred with me, such madness and fear beset my mind that it seemed to me I did not content my Beloved, and that my Beloved did not fulfill my desire,[72] so that dying I must go mad, and going mad I must die. On that day my mind was beset so fearfully and so painfully by desirous love that all my separate limbs threatened to break, and all my separate veins were in travail. 14. The longing in which I then was cannot be expressed by any language or any person I know; and everything I could say about it would be unheard-of to all those who never apprehended Love as something to work for with desire, and whom Love had never acknowledged as hers. I can say this about it: I desired to have full fruition of my Beloved, and to understand and taste him to the full. I desired that his Humanity should to the fullest extent be one in fruition with my humanity, and that mine then should hold its stand and be strong enough to enter into perfection until I content him, who is perfection itself, by purity and unity, and in all things to content him fully in every virtue. To that end I wished he might content me interiorly with his Godhead, in one spirit, and that for me he should be all that he is, without withholding anything from me. For above all the gifts that I ever longed for, I chose this gift: that I should give satisfaction in all great sufferings. For that is the most perfect satisfaction: to grow up in order to be God with God.[73] For this demands suffering, pain, and misery, and living in great new grief of soul: but to let everything come and go without grief, and in this way to experience nothing else but sweet love, embraces, and kisses. In this sense I desired that God give himself to me, so that I might content him.

42. As my mind was thus beset with fear, I saw a great eagle flying toward me from the altar, and he said to me: "If you wish to attain oneness, make yourself ready!"

45. I fell on my knees and my heart beat fearfully, to worship the Beloved with oneness, according to his true dignity; that indeed was impossible for me, as I know well, and as God knows, always to my woe and to my grief.

50. But the eagle turned back and spoke: "Just and mighty Lord, now show your great power to unite your oneness in the manner of union with full possession!"

53. Then the eagle turned round again and said to me: "He who has come, comes again; and to whatever place he never came, he comes not."

57. Then he came from the altar, showing himself as a Child; and that Child was in the same form as he was in his first three years. He turned toward me, in his right hand took from the ciborium his Body, and in his left hand took a chalice, which seemed to come from the altar, but I do not know where it came from.

64. With that he came in the form and clothing of a Man, as he was on the day when he gave us his Body for the first time; looking like a Human Being and a Man, wonderful, and beautiful, and with glorious face, he came to me as humbly as anyone who wholly belongs to another. Then he gave himself to me in the shape of the Sacrament, in its outward form, as the custom is; and then he gave me to drink from the chalice, in form and taste, as the custom is. After that he came himself to me, took me entirely in his arms, and pressed me to him; and all my members felt his in full felicity, in accordance with the desire of my heart and my humanity. So I was outwardly satisfied and fully transported. Also then, for a short while, I had the strength to bear this; but soon, after a short time, I lost that manly beauty outwardly in the sight of his form. I saw him completely come to nought and so fade and all at once dissolve that I could no longer recognize or perceive him outside me, and I could no longer distinguish him within me. Then it was to me as if we were one without difference. It was thus: outwardly, to see, taste, and feel, as one can outwardly taste, see, and feel in the reception of the outward Sacrament. So can the Beloved, with the loved one, each wholly receive the

other in all full satisfaction of the sight, the hearing, and the passing away of the one in the other.

94. After that I remained in a passing away in my Beloved, so that I wholly melted away in him and nothing any longer remained to me of myself; and I was changed and taken up in the spirit, and there it was shown me concerning such hours.

VISION 8

THE MOUNTAIN

saw a great mountain, which was high and broad and of unspeakably beautiful form. Five ways went steeply upward to the mountain; they all led to the highest seat of the noble mountain, which was there on high. But they went high, and higher, and still higher, and to the highest, so that the summit itself was the highest of all and the highest Being himself. And I was taken up and carried upward to the mountain. There I saw a Countenance of eternal fruition, in which all the ways terminate, and in which all those who have followed the ways to the end become one. 14. Someone who carried me upward showed himself to me, and when I was on high he said to me: "Behold how I am the champion and vassal of this true Countenance, which sees to the depths of all things and irradiates perfect service, leads to perfection, teaches both the science of God and wisdom, and gives the riches of all fruition of all the taste of full cognition. I have the appearance of a champion; see that my beauty is that of one who conquers everything and has in his power the Thing heaven, hell, and earth serve. I have ascended on these ways to the highest; I guide you, and I am your trustworthy finger post on the four ways. The fifth, however, which is yours, will be made known to you by the just God who sent you this way and sends it to you."

30. Then he showed me again that ineffably beautiful Countenance, which was in appearance like a great fiery flood, wider and deeper than the sea.

33. And out of the flood I heard a great Voice, that said to me: "Come,[74] and be yourself the highest way,[75] and be one with the beings who are perfect in it, and who with short hours retrieve all long hours. Your great privation of Love has given you the highest way in the fruition of me. I have longed for this from the beginning of the world, and you have often paid for it with painful desire, and you will yet pay for it. This privation of what you desire above all, and this reaching out to me who am unreachable: This is the short hour that outvies all long hours. This is also the way that leads to my Nature, by which I came to myself and went forth. And by this way I went forth from my Father to you and those who are yours, and I came again from you and those who are yours back to my Father (cf. John 16:28). With myself I have also sent you this hour, and you must, with me, pass it on to those who are yours.[76]

51. "This hour, which outvies the efforts men might make in a year, is you yourself; and it is those who are always in new ardor of increasing desires and who, because of this, suffer great opprobrium in unheard-of measure and are complained of by all; and they doubt themselves in spite of all their good works; men condemn them, and almost no one is merciful to them. For godly men doubt them, their neighbors wonder, and a few hate them; but the hour outvies the year.

61. "The month, which outvies the year, is you yourself; and it is those who, in their pain and in their outward or inward privations, have little consolation but suffer this gladly for my sake, relying on my consolation when I shall come to them. They are closer to overtaking me in a month than those who have consolation are in a year.

68. "The instant, which outvies the month, is you and those who, for my sake and for the sake of others who have need of them, live in torment for my sake and because of their offense, their mischief, and their loss, outwardly and inwardly in all their need, while they themselves labor continually in order to possess knowledge of Love.

75. "The days that retrieve the week are you and those who, although without guilt they fall into distress, retain their longing for God, because no guilt was attributed to them.

79. "And because you alone placed your charity for all men in unity with me, you touched me in this hour with the way of my Nature, which I came and went; so I bear to you the true witness (cf.

Apoc. 1:5) with which I am the Truth (cf. John 14:6) of my Father. And my Father bears witness to me that you are the highest way and have brought with you this way of life, which I have awaited in my *hidden way* (Job 3:23). And because you have knowledge of this in the sanctity of us both, now be holy in us; and all who come to us and have knowledge of it through you shall at least be holy! Till they are so unified that they know you in this highest way above all things, trust you, and serve you because you are what this way is; and that they desire me in this highest way, and speak aright in what concerns you, and give you their approval, until the day when they will lead so high a life that I and my Father and you can bear true witness that their short hour outvied so long a time.[77]

98. "Now you have tasted me and received me outwardly and inwardly; and you have understood that the ways of union wholly begin in me. Now, as the unconquered one who has conquered all heavenly, earthly, and hellish champions, turn to me, and be adorned as victor! Lead all the unled according to their worthiness, in which they are loved by me and with which they love and serve me according to my Nature, wherein I am everything that all creatures need and lack."

109. And I came again into the presence of the spirit who had brought me there, and I asked him: "Lord Champion, how did you come to the beauty of your high witness, so that you led me upward and yet not to the end?"[78]

112. He told me who he was.[79] After that he said to me: "I bear witness to you concerning the four ways, and I travel them to the end; in these I recognize myself, and I conquer the divisions of time. But the Beloved gave you the fifth way; you have received it where I am not. For when I lived as man, I had too little love with affection, and followed the strict counsel of the intellect. For this reason I could not be set on fire with the love that creates such a great oneness, for I did the noble Humanity great wrong in that I withheld from it this affection."

123. And he continued: "Return again into your material being, and let your works blossom forth. The blows of enmity are drawing near you. But you return as victor over all, for you have conquered all."

127. Then I came back to myself as someone in new severe pain, and so I shall remain until the day when I am again recalled to the experience from which I then turned away.

VISIONS

VISION 9
QUEEN REASON

was at Matins on the feast *In nativitate beatae Mariae*, and after the Third Lesson something wonderful was shown me in the spirit.[80] My heart had been moved beforehand by the words of love that were read there from the Song of Songs (Song 1:1–16), by which I was led to think of a perfect kiss.[81] 6. Shortly afterwards, in the Second Nocturn, I saw in the spirit a queen come in, clad *in a gold dress* (Ps. 44:11);[82] and her dress was all full of eyes; and all the eyes were completely transparent, like fiery flames, and nevertheless like crystal. And the crown she wore on her head had as many crowns one above another as there were eyes in her dress; you shall hear the number when she herself declares it. Before the queen walked three maidens. One had on a red cloak of state and carried two trumpets in her hands; and she blew on one of them and said: "Whoever does not hearken to my Lady will be eternally deaf to happiness and nevermore hear or see the highest melody and the wonder of powerful Love." And the other trumpet sang and said: "Whoever flies and goes the ways my Lady loves shall be powerful in the kingdom of Love."

25. The second maiden had on a green cloak of state and had in her hand two palm branches, each of which was sealed with a book. With these she fanned from her Lady the dust of the days and of the nights, and of the moon and of the sun,[83] for from none of these did she wish to be dusty.

32. The third maiden had on a black cloak of state and in her hand something like a lantern full of days, by which her Lady saw the profundity of the depths, and the height of the highest ascent.

37. The queen approached me dreadfully fast and set her foot on my throat, and cried with a more terrible voice, and said: "Do you know who I am?"[84]

40. And I said: "Yes, indeed! Long enough have you caused me woe and pain! You are my soul's faculty of Reason,[85] and these are the officials of my own household with whom you walk abroad in such fine style! The trumpeter is my Holy Fear, who has examined

my perfection in all that belongs to the life of Love. The second maiden is Discernment between you and Love, and she has tried to distinguish Love's will, kingdom, and good pleasure from yours. The third maiden is Wisdom, through whom I have acknowledged your power and your works when you let yourself be led by Love, and through whom I learned to know God alone as God, and all things as God in God's knowledge,[86] and each thing as godlike, when in the spirit I am united with God." Then I added: "What tidings do you bring me now?"

55. And she said, "It is true, with this eye-covered dress you yourself are adorned, and you have clothed me with heavenly glory. The number of these eyes is one thousand, the full number of every virtue. The fieriness of the eyes comes from each eye's knowledge of Love. The crystallinity of the eyes is past and quenched a hundredfold in painful mystical knowledge. And every eye of knowledge, either of love or of pain, had the crown of Love, formed according to its significance. Thus every eye had a mighty crown."

65. When Reason had thus spoken to me, she ordered me to acknowledge the whole number of my company; and I truly acknowledged it. Then Reason became subject to me,[87] and I left her. But Love came and embraced me; and I came out of the spirit and remained lying until late in the day, inebriated with unspeakable wonders.[88]

VISIONS

VISION 10
THE BRIDE IN THE CITY

was taken up in the spirit on the feast of Saint John the Evangelist in the Christmas Octave. There I saw prepared a new city of the same name as Jerusalem and of the same appearance. It was being adorned with all sorts of new ornaments (cf. Apoc. 21:2) that were unspeakably beautiful. They who served in the city were the most beautiful of heaven, and all belonged among those called Auriolas and Eunustus. And all who had been sanctified by Love, together with all the living, adorned it and evoked all the new wonders that gave rise to new admiration. 12. And in the midst of the high city flew an eagle crying with a loud voice: "All you lords and wielders of power, here shall you learn the eternity of your domain!" 15. And he flew a second time through the city, crying: "The time is at hand! All you living, find joy in her who possesses the true life!"

18. And a third time he cried and said: "O you dead, come into the light and into the life! And all you who are unready, insofar as you are not too naked to attend our marriage (cf. Matt. 22:1–14), come to our abundance and contemplate the bride, who by love has experienced all needs, heavenly and earthly! She is so experienced with need in the alien land that I shall now show her how she has grown in the *land of darkness* (Job 10:33). And she shall be great, and she shall see her repose, and the voice of power shall be wholly hers."

29. After this an Evangelist came and said: "You are here, and you shall be shown the glory of your exile. The city you here see adorned is your free conscience; and the lofty beauty that is here is your manifold virtues with full suffering; and the adornment is your fiery ardor, which remains dominant in you in spite of all disasters. Your unknown virtues with new assiduity are the manifold ornaments that adorn the city. Your blessed soul is the bride in the city. Here is that highest society which wholly lives in love and in the spirit of the highest virtue. All those whom you see here, Eunustus and Auriolas, and the whole multitude who are highest in power, have come here to participate in your marriage. Moreover all the living,

both of heaven and earth, shall renew their life in this marriage. The dead sinners—who have come without hope, and are enlightened by the knowledge of your union,[89] and desire grace or entrance into purgatory—cling somewhat to virtue and are not altogether naked. If only they believe in the oneness of you both, they will find full contentment through your marriage."

54. Then I heard a Voice loudly crying: "New peace be to all of you, and all new joy! Behold, this is my bride, who has passed through all your honors with perfect love, and whose love is so strong that, through it, all attain growth!" And he said: "Behold, Bride and Mother, you like no other have been able to live me as God and Man! What do you think they who are Eunustus to all earthly repose become? That is what you are for all of them collectively. You alone have never tasted earthly poison; you like no other have superhumanly suffered much among men. You shall suffer everything to the end with what I am, and we shall remain one. Now enjoy fruition of me, what I am, with the strength of your victory, and they shall live eternally contented through you."

70. The Voice embraced me with an unheard-of wonder, and I swooned in it, and my spirit failed me to see or hear more. And I lay in this fruition half an hour; but then the night was over, and I came back, piteously lamenting my exile, as I have done all this winter. For truly the whole winter long I have been occupied with this kind of thing. I lay there a long time and possessed love, or revelations, or anything else in particular that Love gave me.

VISIONS

VISION 11
THE ABYSS OF OMNIPOTENCE

was in a very depressed frame of mind one Christmas night, when I was taken up in the spirit. There I saw a very deep whirlpool, wide and exceedingly dark; in this abyss all beings were included, crowded together, and compressed. The darkness illuminated and penetrated everything. The unfathomable depth of the abyss was so high that no one could reach it. I will not attempt now to describe how it was formed, for there is no time now to speak of it; and I cannot put it in words, since it is unspeakable. Second, this is not a convenient time for it, because much pertains to what I saw. It was the entire omnipotence of our Beloved. In it I saw the Lamb (cf. Apoc. 5:6) take possession of our Beloved. In the vast space I saw festivities, such as David playing the harp, and he struck the harp strings.[90] Then I perceived an Infant being born in the souls who love in secret, the souls hidden from their own eyes in the deep abyss of which I speak, and to whom nothing is lacking but that they should lose themselves in it.[91] I saw the forms of many different souls, according to what each one's life had been. Of those whom I saw, the ones whom I already knew remained known to me; and those I did not know became known to me; I received interior knowledge about some, and also exterior knowledge about many. And certain ones I knew interiorly, having never seen them exteriorly.

28. Then I saw coming as it were a bird, namely the one called phoenix.[92] It devoured a grey eagle that was young, and a yellow eagle with new feathers that was old.[93] These eagles kept flying about incessantly in the deep abyss.

33. Then I heard a voice like thunder (cf. Apoc. 6:1) that said: "Do you know who these different-colored eagles are?"

36. And I answered: "I should like to know this better."

37. And although I asked to know this, I nevertheless perceived the essence of all the things I saw. For all that is seen in the spirit when one is ravished by Love is understood, tasted, seen, and heard through and through. So was it also here. I wished, however, to hear

the Voice that came to my hearing from the Beloved. And indeed the truth was told me concerning all this, in particular the natures and perfections comprised in my vision. All this would take too long; I pass over it. For a great book would be required if one were to write everything perfectly in full truth![94]

49. One of the eagles who were swallowed was Saint Augustine, and the other myself. The old feathers that were grey, and the eaglet that was young—this was I, for I was attaining to perfection, beginning, and growing in love. The feathers that were yellow and old—this was the full-grownness of Saint Augustine, who was old and perfect in the love of our Beloved.[95] The old age I had was in the perfect nature of eternal being, even though I was youthful in created nature.[96] The young feathers of the old eagle were the renewed splendor he received from me in the new heavenly glory of my love, with which I loved him and so greatly desired with him to pour forth one single love in the Trinity, where he himself was burning so totally with an unquenchable love. The youth that the old feathers that were yellow had signified also the renewal of Love, which continually grows in heaven and on earth (cf. Ps. 102:5).[97] The phoenix that swallowed the eagles was the Unity in which the Trinity dwells, wherein both of us are lost.

72. When afterwards I returned to myself, where I found myself poor and miserable, I reflected on this union with Saint Augustine to which I had attained. I was not contented with what my dearly Beloved had just permitted, in spite of my consent and emotional attraction; it weighed on me now that this union with Saint Augustine had made me so perfectly happy, whereas previously I had possessed union far from saints and men, with God alone. From this I understood that neither in heaven nor in the spirit can one enjoy one's own will, except in accordance with the will of Love. And as I thought about this attitude, I asked my Beloved to deliver me from it. For I wished to remain in his deepest abyss, alone in fruition. And I understood that, since my childhood, God had drawn me to himself alone, far from all the other beings whom he welcomes to himself in other manners. But I well know that whatever was in him is, in highest measure, eternal glory and perfect enjoyment, but I likewise wished to remain in him alone. I understood this when I asked for it, and so greatly desired it, and suffered so much; then I remained free. No doubt I continued to belong to God alone while being united in Love to this creature. But my liberty I gained then was given me

moreover for reasons of my own, which neither Augustine nor many others had.

98. I did not suggest this as a claim to be more privileged than Saint Augustine; but in the time when I knew the truth of Being, I did not want to receive any comfort from him insofar as he was a creature, or to accept any joy amid my pains, and so I would allow myself no satisfaction in the security that was given me in this union with Saint Augustine. For I am a free human creature, and also pure as to one part,[98] and I can desire freely with my will, and I can will as highly as I wish,[99] and seize and receive from God all that he is, without objection or anger on his part—what no saint can do. For the saints have their will perfectly according to their pleasure; and they can no longer will beyond what they have. I have hated many great wonderful deeds and experiences, because I wished to belong to Love alone, and because I could not believe that any human creature loved him so passionately as I—although I know it is a fact and indubitable, still I cannot believe it or feel it, so powerfully am I touched by Love.

121. In this wonderful way I belong to God alone in pure love, and to my saint in love, and then to all the saints, each one according to his dignity, and to men according to what each one loved and also according to what he was and still is. But in striving for this I have never experienced Love in any sort of way as repose; on the contrary, I found Love a heavy burden and disgrace. For I was a human creature, and Love is terrible and implacable, devouring and burning without regard for anything. The soul is contained in one little rivulet; her depth is quickly filled up; her dikes quickly burst. Thus with rapidity the Godhead has engulfed human nature wholly in itself.

134. I used to love the blessedness of the saints, but I never ceased to desire the repose in which God within them had fruition of himself; their quietude was many a time my inquietude; yes, truly, it was always forty pains against one single pleasure. I could not but know that they were smiled at, while I wept; that they boasted themselves fortunate, while I pitied myself; and that they were honored by God, and that God was honored because of them in every land, while I was an object of derision. All this, nevertheless, was my greatest repose, for he willed it—but this was such repose as comes to those who desire love and fruition, and who have in this desire such woe as I do.

147. Now for persons, my repose lay in loving each of them in what was proper to him, and wishing for each of them that only what he held desirable and good might happen to him; whether this good

was that of their will or of the divine will was a question with which I did not meddle. But what they had in love, I loved for God, in order that he might strengthen it for himself and cause it to grow to perfection; such was my desire. Because I loved God's being loved, I wished no pleasure from it but that.

156. As for persons who failed God and were strangers to him, they weighed heavy on me. For I was so laden with his love and captivated by it that I could scarcely endure that anyone should love him less than I. And charity for others wounded me cruelly, that he should let these souls[100] be such strangers to him and so deprived of all the good that he himself is in love. This was such an intolerable burden to me in many an hour that it happened to me as it did to Moses because of his love for his sister: I would have wished that he give his love to others or withdraw it from me. I would gladly have purchased love for them by accepting that he should love them and hate me. And sometimes, too, because he did not do this, I would willingly have turned away from him in love and would have loved them in spite of his wrath (cf. Rom. 9:3); seeing that these unfortunates could not know the sweet and ardent love that dwells in his holy Nature, I would most gladly have loved them, had I been able.

174. Also, charity has wounded me the most—except for actual Love. What is actual Love? It is the divine power that must have priority; and it does so in me. For the sovereign power that is actual Love spares no one, either in hate or in love; favor is never found in it. This power held me back once again when I had wished to free all men in the twinkling of an eye, otherwise than in accordance with how God had chosen them. When I could thus turn myself against him, it was a beautiful and free expression of life as a human being. Then I could desire what I wished. But when I did the opposite, I was more beautiful and taken up into a fuller participation in the Divine Nature.

188. Thus I have lived quietly as a human being, so that I have taken repose neither in saints nor in men on earth. And so I have lived in misery without love, in the love of God and of those who are his; and while I do not receive from him what is mine,[101] and what God does not yet give me—I have it nevertheless, and it shall remain mine! Hence I never felt love, unless as an ever-new death—until the time of my consolation came, and God granted me to know the perfect pride of love;[102] to know how we shall love the Humanity in order to come to the Divinity, and rightly know it in one single

Nature.[103] This is the noblest life that can be lived *in the kingdom of God* (Col. 4:11). This rich repose God gave me,[104] and truly in a happy hour.

VISION 12

THE PERFECT BRIDE

NCE on Epiphany, during Mass, I was taken up out of myself in the spirit; there I saw a city, large, and wide, and high, and adorned with perfections. And in the midst of it there sat Someone upon a round disk, which continually opened and closed itself again upon hidden mysteries. And he who sat there above the disk was sitting in constant stillness; but in the disk his Being circled about in unspeakable swiftness without stopping. And the abyss in which the disk ran as it circled about was of such unheard-of depth and so dark that no horror can be compared to it. And the disk, seen from above, was set with all kinds of precious stones and in the color of pure gold; but on the darkest side, where it ran so fearfully, it was like fearful flames, which devoured heaven and earth and in which all things perished and were swallowed up. 21. And he who sat upon the disk was One whose Countenance none could perceive without belonging to the terrible flames of this disk and being thrown into the deep abyss which lay underneath. And that Countenance drew all the dead to it living; and everything that was withered blossomed because of it; and all the poor who saw it received great riches; and all the sick became strong; and all who were in multiplicity and division became one in that Countenance.

29. And he who sat in this high place was clothed with a robe whiter than white (cf. Mark 9:2), on the breast of which was written: "The Most Loved of all beloveds" (cf. Apoc. 19:16). That was his name.

33. Then I fell down before that Countenance in order to adore the truth of that terrifying Being whom I there saw revealed.

35. Then came a flying eagle, crying with a loud voice, and said: "The loved one does not yet know all she shall become!"

38. And a second eagle said: "The loved one does not yet know what her highest way is!"

40. And a third said: "The loved one does not yet know what the great kingdom is that she as bride shall receive from her Bridegroom!"

42. And the fourth said to me: "Have patience, and watch, and do not fall down before that Countenance! They who fall down before the Countenance and adore receive grace; they who contemplate the Countenance standing receive justice and are enabled to fathom the deep abysses that for those unacquainted with them are so terrifying to know."

49. At that moment I was taken up, through the voice of this eagle who spoke to me. And then there came into the city a great crowd in festive apparel, and each one rich in her own works. They were all virtues; and they were conducting a bride to her Beloved. They had served her nobly and had looked after her so proudly that they could present her as worthy to be received by the mighty great God as his bride.

58. And she was clad in a robe made of her undivided and perfect will, always devoid of sorrow, and prepared with all virtue, and fitted out with everything that pertains thereto. And that robe was adorned with all the virtues, and each virtue had its symbol on the robe and its name written, that it might be known.[105]

65. The first of the virtues was Faith: She had lifted her up from her lowness.

67. The second, Hope, had raised her above herself to great confidence of attaining eternal joy.

70. The third, veritable Fidelity, bore witness that she was noble; for she never departed from fidelity because of any distress, however great it was.

73. The fourth, Charity, bore witness that she was rich, for she never gave up her works outward or inward, and she never lacked rich gifts by which she honored Charity; for she practiced rich liberality because of lofty abandonment.

78. The fifth, Desire, bore witness how vast she was in her territory, and how beautiful and splendid in her full wealth, so that she might well entertain all the greatness of heaven.

82. The sixth, Humility, bore witness that she was so deep and so unfathomable that she could truly receive greatness to the full in her unfathomableness.

85. The seventh, Discernment, bore witness that she was so clear-sighted that she set every being in its place: heaven in its height, hell in its depth, or purgatory in its manner of being;[106] the Angels in their orders; or men, each according to what befits him, when he falls, and when he gets up again. Thus to let God act accorded well with the robe of the undivided will.

93. The eighth, her veracious mighty Works, bore witness that she was so strong that nothing could hold her back, so that she alone would not have conquered all opposition and made all lowness lofty and all loftiness low.[107]

98. The ninth, Reason, showed that she was well ordered and that Reason was her rule,[108] by which she always performed works of justice, and which enlightened her with regard to all the dearest will of her Beloved, so that like him she gave blessing and condemnation in all that he loved and all that he hated;[109] and she gave all that he gave, and she took all that he took.

105. The tenth, Wisdom, showed her to be familiar with all the power of every perfect virtue that must be encountered in order to content the Beloved perfectly. Wisdom showed that she also had profound knowledge of each Person of the Trinity, in the Unity that was the very deep abyss beneath the wonderful, terrifying disk on which sat the One who was to receive the Bride.

112. The eleventh, Peacefulness, showed and bore witness to her, as pleasing in appearance and beautiful, and as possessing knowledge of the total embrace and of a perfect kiss (cf. Ps. 84:11), and of all the honor and all the encounter the loved one must offer to the Beloved in love; and that she had been announced and born with him;[110] and that her body was born from the other; and that she grew up with him and lived together with him as man in all like pains, in poverty, in ignominy, and in compassion for all those with whom justice was angry; and that her body was nourished interiorly and exteriorly from the other, and never received alien consolation; and that she died with him,[111] and freed all the prisoners with him, and bound what he bound; and with him rose again, and one with him ascended to his Father; and there with him acknowledged his Father as Father, and him as Son with him; and with him she acknowledged the Holy Spirit as Holy Spirit; and with him, like him, she knew all as One, and the Essence in which they are One. To all this her Peacefulness bore witness for her, that she has thus lived and that, later on, she will live perfectly as his, truly with love in love.

135. The twelfth was Patience, who had protected her from all evil, without any sorrow in all sorrow, and was as it were an instrument of good works,[112] through which she was as if in a new embrace. And Patience showed her as conformed to God, in one Being and in one work.

140. Thus is the robe of undivided will wholly adorned through the divine Nature. Thus festively attired comes the bride, with all this beautiful company represented in symbols. She wore on her breast an ornament with the divine seal (cf. Apoc. 7:2, 9:4), by which she had knowledge of the undivided divine Unity. This was a symbol that she had understood the *hidden word* (Job 4:12) of God himself out of the abyss. So in this company she came into the city, led between Fruition of Love and Command of the Virtues; Command accompanied her there, but Fruition met her there.

152. And when she was led thus to the high seat I have already described, the eagle, who had previously spoken to me, said: "Now see through the Countenance, and become the veritable bride of the great Bridegroom, and behold yourself in this state!" And in that very instant I saw myself[113] received in union by the One who sat there in the abyss upon the circling disk, and there I became one with him in the certainty of unity. Then the eagle said, when I was received: "Now behold, all-powerful one, whom I previously called the loved one, that you did not know all you should become, and what your highest way was, and what the great kingdom was that you as bride should receive from your Bridegroom. When previously you fell down before the Countenance, you, like an ordinary soul, confessed it as frightening. When you stood up and contemplated it, you saw yourself perfect,[114] together with us, a veritable bride, sealed with love. You, all-powerful one, have received most profoundly that *hidden word* which Job understood, in the text beginning: *Porro dictum est*" (Job 4:12).

172. In that abyss I saw myself swallowed up. Then I received the certainty of being received, in this form, in my Beloved, and my Beloved also in me.

VISION 13

THE SIX-WINGED COUNTENANCE

N the Sunday before Pentecost, before dawn, I was raised up in spirit to God, who made Love known to me; until that hour, she had ever been hidden from me. There I saw and heard how the songs of praise resounded, which come from the silent love humility conceals; humility imagines, and says, and swears that it does not love, and that it gives honor and right to neither God nor man in love or service of veritable virtue. There I saw and heard how the songs of praise resounded and adorned the Love of all loves. 13. In this hour was revealed to me *a new heaven* (Apoc. 21:1), which never appeared to me before, and the Allelujah song of the Seraphim.[115] 15. And one Seraph cried with a loud voice and said: "See here the new secret heaven, which is closed to all those who never were God's mother with perfect motherhood, who never wandered with him in Egypt or on all the ways, who never presented him where the sword of prophecy pierced their soul (cf. Luke 2:35), who never reared that Child to manhood and who, at the end, were not at his grave: for them it shall remain eternally hidden!"[116]

24. After the song and after this voice, the new heaven was opened. There revealed itself that Countenance of God with which he will satisfy all the saints and all men for the full length of his eternity. The Countenance had six wings (cf. Isa. 6.2; Apoc. 4:8); they were all closed outwardly, but within they were ceaselessly in flying motion.

31. Then all the locks of the wings came open outwardly, and I saw where and in what directions they were flying. The two highest flew in the height in which God enjoys the highest power of love. The two middlemost flew in the amplitude of Love's perfect modes of action. The two lowest flew in the fathomless depth in which he swallows up all beings. All the wings were straight (cf. Ezech. 1:23) and smooth on the Countenance; the seals that, outside the wings, closed themselves about the Countenance are the veritable attributes of the mighty Godhead, in the perfection of which no one can himself participate unless he wishes to live God and Man.

45. After that I saw a great throng of Seraphim, who all sang: "Allelujah! Amen!"

46. They brought a great number of adorned spirits with them, each Seraph bringing the one that was his; they were all adorned with loftiest fidelity to godly reason, with powerful love. They bore in their hands the open seal of love, that is, full fidelity of love to all things; and they bore this name on their foreheads. They are the glorious hosts to which the Seraphim render service, because they have conquered in love so that they are conquered (cf. Gen. 32:24–31) as the invincible power of growing Love.[117]

57. Then the Seraphim received them and with the seals in their hands unlocked the two middlemost wings of the Countenance. And they advanced therein and possessed the amplitude and adorned it with their new coming, for this amplitude had been left unknown in exalted love. And they also rejoiced there with that mysterious song which, in love, in a mysterious way, has always cried out *with a loud voice* (Mark 13:37).

66. The Seraph who belonged to me and who had brought me there lifted me up, and instantly I saw in the eyes of the Countenance a seat. Upon it sat Love, richly arrayed, in the form of a queen.[118] The crown that rested on her head was adorned with the high works of the humble, who pay homage to veritable Love and suppose it true that they are not serving and loving Love; this their veracity continually swears, for they know themselves to be nothing, and they know Love alone to be all. For this reason their sad, outgoing song of praise reverberates through the amplitude that was never flown through. And this praise gave adornment and joy with a new song, which no one shall ever understand except those who, through their humility, had hidden all love.

82. From Love's eyes proceeded swords full of fiery flames. From her mouth proceeded lightning and thunder. Her countenance was transparent, so that through it one could see all the wonderful works Love has ever done and can do. I must pass over this, for concerning what I saw there, one might write more than David's Psalter contains.[119] So I hold my peace now and, I think, forever. She had opened her arms and held embraced in them all the services that anyone has ever done through her. Her right side was full of perfect kisses without farewell.[120] Her body was wholly full of ever-welling marvels; and in the amplitude under her feet she had the seven gifts (cf. Isa. 11:2; Apoc. 1:4).[121] And opposite her she had a seat standing.

97. The Seraph who had lifted me up placed me upon it and said to me: "Behold, this is Love, whom you see in the midst of the Countenance of God's Nature; she has never yet been shown here to a created being.[122] Although Mary knew veritable Love and the seven gifts in the work of perfect virtues, she never experienced heavenly revelations before her Assumption. For she was full of silent reasoning and of divine Love, and was confirmed by association with her Son and by his behavior, through which, enough to the full, the inmost and the highest heaven was made known to her."

109. Then he said: "Behold, all these attributes of Love are better known to you than to me. For you, mother of Love, have looked upon these three hidden states,[123] which you see in the Countenance of Love. We see it in the service with which we serve you, in wonder; but you see it, and you will see it, in clear reason and understanding, as a human being. Now contemplate and possess from henceforward this whole kingdom, which you see that Love possesses here; then contemplate these three adorned states—the ornaments you here see adorning Love—and the high song of praise that gives so much bliss. In all these three, contemplate and find yourself, but nevertheless possess yourself here wholly and adorned with the totality of the virtues with which you see Love adorned."

124. When I considered this, I realized it was so. And then I asked the Seraph to open for me the two uppermost and the two lowermost seals of the wings that were on the Countenance; and he did so. When he had opened the two highest seals, these spirits came out who had been wholly annihilated in humility and could nevermore believe they would be able by any service to attain Love's affection; so they considered themselves at every hour to be most unblessed in love. But the beauty they brought with them was more inexpressible than anything anyone ever read of or saw in our times. It was these beings who had crowned Love and adorned her countenance. Their song sounded with so sweet a voice that praise flowed upward with new veins of song, and the flames were so fanned with new enkindlement that they might have caused an eternally new conflagration. All the highest height was heightened by them in so many ways, and through them the amplitude became so wonderfully wide and beautiful, surpassing all those who had already come forth from the middlemost seals.

147. And in the abyss of Love resounded both a new noise, which set everything in motion, and an amazing and unheard-of song

of praise; and a new rushing flood surged upward with new storm to fill the new arrivals, who there took fire. These spirits with their adornments came with noble tidings before Love and before me in that winged Countenance. And they were placed there then, each by his Seraph. And at the same instant they were all adorned with the very form that Love possessed where she was sitting adorned—and that she had given to me.

159. Now when the two lowest seals of the wings of the Countenance were opened there came out a small number, but with many more wonderful deeds than all others had had. These were they who, in the liberty of love between them and their Beloved, had cast off humility and had placed knowledge between them and their God, how he is constituted in his power where reason is concerned, and in his kingdom, his goodness, his sweetness, and his whole Being, in which he himself holds sway. They had learned to know these attributes through the seven gifts, of which I have just related that Love had them under her feet. But when they served because of the gifts, they had the humility of Mary and of those who came forth from the highest seal and disavowed their love out of humility; but they realized they were so near the truth of Love and so high above themselves that they knew nothing else of themselves except that they were annihilated in Love.

179. The seven gifts are seven signs of love, but the eighth is the Divine Touch,[124] giving fruition, which does away with everything that pertains to reason, so that the loved one becomes one with the Beloved. But because they had the seven gifts and made progress toward a knowledge of the eighth, and Love demanded this of them, they called continually for fruition and did not believe in the love of their Beloved; it rather appeared to them that they alone were loving and that Love did not help them. Unfaith[125] made them so deep that they wholly engulfed Love and dared to fight her with sweet and bitter. That which Love gives turns bitter and is consumed and devoured. That which Love holds back is enriched by great strength to follow Love's demand that they be always great like her, so that all God's artifice may not separate them from Love.

195. These now came forth adorned like Love as to all their attire and ornaments. I know the number of these persons, which is very small,[126] and I know all those who belong to it, the ones in heaven and the ones on earth.

198. And they who are full-grown with all three of these attri-

butes, and will be from among those who are already conformed to God—only twenty-nine of them are now in heaven, and only fifty-six live here; eleven are now born in the cradle, and six run playing in the streets; five will yet be born, and outside of these no one among all beings will be full-grown. Their sum is one hundred and seven.[127] In two of these attributes, the middlemost and the lowest together, are three thousand and eight full-grown; in the lowest and the highest, four thousand and eighty-three; and in the middlemost amplitude alone, six thousand two hundred and eighty-four.

211. And the surge of the flood, of which I spoke a short time ago, came with a great stormy rush and swallowed up equally all the rest.

214. And I spoke with a loud, fiery voice: "You Seraphim, whose function it is to minister to our wonder, stand firm and watch over our glory! We all shall become one; and one, all!"[128]

128. And Mary, who was the highest of the twenty-nine, said to me: "Behold, everything is fulfilled![129] Penetrate all these attributes and fully taste Love. For you cherished Love with humility; you adorned and led Love with loyal reason; and, with this lofty fidelity and this entire power, you vanquished Love and made Love one. Through this, and on account of your lofty power, is this secret heaven thus made known to you. Love, as you see her here, is thus adorned and praised with this song. For the denial of Love with humility is the highest voice of Love. The work of the highest fidelity of reason is the clearest and most euphonious voice of Love. But the noise of the highest unfaith is the most delightful voice of Love; in this she can no longer keep herself at a distance and depart. These you have possessed from the beginning, since you first received the Godhead, these three states; and since then, Love has been always so adorned by you in this all-embracing Countenance of the eternal Godhead as no man has ever adorned her except those of the smallest number, among whom I complete the twenty-nine.

241. "See, if you wish to have ampler fruition, as I have, you must leave your sweet body here. But for the sake of those whom you have chosen to become full-grown with you in this, but who are not yet full-grown, and above all for the sake of those whom you love most, you will yet defer it. And as soon as you wish, we call you back; but now after you return to yourself, the world will scarcely let you live; and then, a short time after the fortieth day,[130] you will again resume your body, which you keep so nobly for Love."

252. And that Countenance disclosed itself wholly with everything that was; and Love sat there adorned. In that Countenance I knew and beheld all things, and in it I saw height, amplitude, and depth. Then fruition overcame me as before, and I sank into the fathomless depth[131] and came out of the spirit in that hour, of which one can never speak at all.

VISION 14

NEW POWER TO LIVE CHRIST

was and am continually in great desire and in the madness of love, so that I thought and was well aware that I could not live any longer with such great inquietude as I was in then and continually am, unless God gave me some new strength. And then he did so, thanks be to him! 7. The throne signified a new state of power, with which he wished to make me richer in his powerful richness than I was before. I was then rich in many powers of virtue, above what is now ordinary. But the new power he then gave me, which I did not possess previously, was the strength of his own Being, to be God with my sufferings according to his example and in union with him, as he was for me when he lived for me as Man. That was the strength to endure, as long as the fruition of Love was denied me: really to endure the arrows Love shot at me.[132]

21. The throne was the loftiness of the life of union to which I was chosen. The clarity of its appearance was purity from many kinds of pollution into which aliens fall whom God has not chosen to be such as—for this I thank him—he chose me to be. Alas! When I think of what God wills with me, and what he has done for me in preference to others, it is a wonder how I remain alive, unless because of the great Love who can do all things. But it is certainly a great marvel to me when I think that God prefers me to all creatures I ever saw; so I wonder much more about the men who live and to whom he gives so much less than to me—that they let me live so long, and that they offer me protection or respect or favor, and that they do not afflict me with ever-new torments. Also on this account, that God

promised me so much suffering for the sake of likeness to himself that I, in preference to all men and more than all men, should suffer this in order to content him and to live as a perfect human being.

43. That one could see all things through the clarity of the throne was possible because its being was the very Being of God, and also because I found and knew all the works, which I had from him, or those that were commanded me by him, in the Being of his own will, in which he commanded me this through the high power of love. But nowhere else did I ever find it, and I did not dispense with his will in any of my works.

52. That I saw through all things in the throne means all my works in God, and my will, freely and proudly in him, with all the madness of love by which I was overwhelmed in his regard in such great horror as I continually was from Love and still continually am.

57. And because I loved you so greatly, and neither could nor can forget you in any hour; and because I felt this death and your nonfulfillment in Love so closely with you, in stormy desire of God—that I was closer to God than you, pained me the more. And it was yet more painful to me because you were a child and on the human level, and because I was previously so powerful in Love, and then Love had thus left me in the lurch, as it is clear to me that she did, since the new throne is shown me, clear and rightly adorned as is befitting for the great Lover, who is the Creator of love and whose Being and Essence are one.

71. In the midst of the new throne stood a seat, resembling the highest omnipotence and the place where all are taken under protection. Upon it sat the Creator of our love, the Master of justice, who passes judgment on Love in her adherents with final sentence.

77. The Countenance, which he had at that moment, was invisible and inaccessible to the sight for all creatures who never lived human and divine love in one single Being, and who could not grasp or cherish the notion of attaining union with the Divinity, so as to have been flowed through by the whole Godhead, and to have become totally one, flowing back through the Godhead itself.[133]

85. In the form of the Countenance that was there, I had never seen him before that moment, although I had already seen him at an earlier time in the same Transfiguration in which Saint Peter and those who were with him on Thabor beheld it. I had desired to see this a very long time before it happened to me. I had heard it said that Saint Peter, from the time he saw it, never laughed again; I would

gladly have taken this upon me, so as to be miserable and to content him in dread and longing, and not to prefer to die but always to suffer in misery.

95. When this befell me, I received a power so great that I could endure with equanimity everything that came to me before—joy or grief, laughter or weeping, in disgrace and in trouble—in all manners without sorrow; and all kinds of graces and of powers that are still higher than grace. These I received ever since then, without exalting myself because of them; there were all kinds of powerful miracles and works; and there were persons I delivered from sins, persons I delivered from despair, or persons who rose from spiritual death through the power that God desired in me—this happened to the four.

110. I am continuing this too long, because you are glad to hear in what that happiness consisted which was so beautiful, or so beyond human nature, and so conformed to the Humanity of God; but since that day I have remained unwavering in all things. I did as God did, who delivered back all his works to his Father, from whom he had them;[134] but what I have from him, I received from the Transfiguration and from other visions in other forms of his Countenance, about which I wrote you recently; and from many others, about which I have written you nothing. I am sorry, nevertheless, because I desire to do your will. And since you wish to know all that concerns me, I am very sorry that you do not know everything you wish to know.

125. Once in a single night and day I saw three times that unbearably beautiful Countenance of our Love, who is all, and each time the Countenance had a different form, corresponding to the different gifts that he bestowed on me each time. Each time then and always I received new gifts, which made known to me how far I had then advanced, and to what stages of development I had been raised.

133. So was it with other revelations in great number, with *the spirit of prophecy* (Apoc. 19:10), and with the vision of the things—heaven, earth, purgatory, and hell: with the understanding of various reasons that pertain to these four things; and with the understanding of Love, how he is our Love in himself, and outside himself he is Love in us; and that Love at one time slays and at another time heals, and why Love chooses the lowlier ones and rejects the greater ones. I pass over, besides, other kinds of understanding.

145. Once I lay for three days and the same number of nights in entrancement of spirit at the Countenance of our Beloved; and this has often lasted for that length of time; and also for the same length

of time entirely out of the spirit, lost here to myself and to all persons, in fruition of him: to know how in fruition he embraces himself. To be out of the spirit and to be in him—this surpasses all that one can have from him and all that he himself can accomplish; and then one is not less than he himself is. With the exception of being out of the spirit, all the other revelations were nothing in comparison with the Countenance of our Beloved, which I perceived on the new throne (cf. Ps. 9:5). For each revelation I had seen partly according to what I was myself, and partly according to my having been chosen; but now I saw this and was associated also with my choir, to which I was chosen in order that I might taste Man and God in one knowledge, what no man could do unless he were as God, and wholly such as he was who is our Love.

166. He who sat on the new throne (cf. Ps. 9:5), which was I myself, had the imposing appearance of the fearful, wonderful Countenance, and there spoke to me a Voice of loud thunder (cf. Apoc. 6:1), with a noise like stormdrifts, which would silence everything so that it alone could be heard.

172. The Voice said to me: "O strongest of all warriors! You have conquered everything and opened the closed totality,[135] which never was opened by creatures who did not know, with painfully won and distressed Love, how I am God and Man! O heroine, since you are so heroic, and since you never yield, you are called the greatest heroine! It is right, therefore, that you should know me perfectly."

POEMS IN COUPLETS

POEMS IN COUPLETS

1 THE NATURE OF LOVE

God be with you! From my greeting
May you draw some small profit;
Then because of your request to me,
And that you may find pleasure in it,
5 I answer you with pleasure,
In simple terms, not at great length,
Concerning what you told me to treat of.[1]
For it occurs to me as to a child
That repeats what it has heard said,
10 Before it has known or experienced it.
Love's nature is to me unknown,
For her being and her depths
Are hidden from me.
With regard to my views on this subject
15 I can just as well keep silent
As carry something to an unknown place.[2]
May Love herself make you experience
How with love one loves in Love.
May her nature make you understand in fiery longing
20 How one sees with longing in longing.
May God make you strive in your deficiencies
And understand in your victories;
May God make you live in despair,[3]
With all the service you can render,
25 And after that be victorious in hope
And fail not in the nature of Love.
I did not speak thus because I wished
To pray for you or to win your good will,
But because you requested it as a greeting,
30 And for this reason I had to speak to you thus.
How Love acts according to her nature,
How Love takes and gives—
She does so in procedures of all kinds,
By which she adorns her being.
35 In Love's being everything is comprised;

Victory, deficiency, hope, and despair.
But these things are entirely excluded
Which men hear of and see,
And all they can know and understand:
40 It is nonvictory; it is nonfulfillment.

He who wishes to serve Love according to Love's deserts
Must in all be affable.
Through Love, all suffering must be pleasing to him;
He must resign himself to all things,
45 Not only easy but hard,
Exactly as if he were her serf.
He must not be afraid of any need,
Anguish or pain, loss or death;
What he possesses, he must take his chance on;
50 What he loves, he must subsist on.
And when he most gladly accepts
To be affable in love,
And close at hand to feel and experience Love
In lofty understanding of her nature,
55 He so far falls down into nothing
That what he then sees and hears
And understands in the nature of Love
Seems to him remote and unreachable.
The nature of Love so stormily demands the loved one's nature
60 And makes the loved one endure such great unrest
That longing swallows up all Love's gifts,
And she must continually press this mode of action.

Victory lessens the mind's strength,
And brings on many modes of behavior.
65 For when a man has repose, he quietly keeps silence;
He would not remain inactive were his role unpleasant.
He who conquers repose will often be
Among the lords of true Love.
So he has come in show to court,
70 And he fancies he will dwell in the circle
Of those consoled and gifted by Love;
But there he shall be long without sustenance!

Victory also elevates the mind
In very many proud winnings.
75 Because he obtains what he strives for,
I think joy comes over him;
For he who stands ready to serve grows sad
When his winnings are unreachable.
But jousts and noble deeds
80 He often performs, as well becomes
Those who with proud mind
Imagine they can conquer veritable Love;
Just as valiant knights never fail
In their great-heartedness[4] to perform
85 Noble deeds with their lance:
By this we understand the power of their great-heartedness,
And that they win by their deed
The favor of Love.
So likewise does the noble mind
90 In which nature experiences longing:
And there is no joy in Love so high
And no suffering so painful
That its great-heartedness will draw back:[5]
It wishes to conquer as its right.

95 Nonvictory is a nobler deed,
Which is rooted in strong longing.
For he who knows what is lacking in him
Is the one who postpones anything.
If only he knows where the place is
100 Where his being would be free;
Then he will spare no pain:
He will proceed with longing in the storm,
Be it against God or with him:
That is the mode of action of lavish love.
105 This I say not in order to praise it,
But because I point out the way to Love,
Maiden; also, not that I instruct you,
But that I praise the liberty of Love.
But in Love as it ought to be,
110 There never was anything that we begin against God.
All I say here about the mighty power

That Love has in her possession,
I know less, you know better.
You have checkmated me, and I am defeated.

115 Of hope I can say nothing;
You will possess it in its being at closer range.
Therefore I am much too timorous about it
And speak to you of it much too reluctantly,
For you know it at closer range from custom.
120 He who with longing loves in hope,
Gives and takes with profit;
He understands many a noble purpose:
How one shall take and give
And apply himself to veritable Love,
125 Which is all? And he understands
Where his profit is at hand for him:
He gives to all who have need of his goods;
He consoles the sorrowful;
He counsels those who know little;
130 He reaches many a high act of daring;
He assaults pleasure;
And he understands the high dignity
That, with lavish love,
One can gain through works inspired by hope.
135 What use was there in my speaking of hope?
Hope is not afraid of any trouble;
With noble hope we conquer all
That is, and was, and shall be.

Despair means greater storms,
140 Which rouse unsatisfying modes of action.
Despair makes us serve evil as much as good;
It seems to be bad luck in great success.
He who lives in despair
Takes and gives in vain.
145 If he speaks, it seems to him that no one listens.
In despair he traverses the gamut—
The repose and the anguish of Love's storm.
Hence he has unsatisfying modes of action;
To him who lives and suffers in despair

150 Everything seems to be without completion.
Whatever service he renders, he fears
That what he wants will never happen to him.
What he experiences seems to him nothing.
Thus shaken by the storm, he newly begins to serve;
155 His service seems to him too slight in work;
That always holds him strong in Love.
What he is given seems to him too little;
That always holds him in storminess.
It is despair that always detains him
160 From exerting himself with the greatest strength.
All this is indeed a beautiful work;
It is unconquerable and extremely strong;
It gives all that one should give;
It experiences all that one should experience;
165 It has all that one should have;
It wills all that God ever willed
In poverty, in wealth, in lowliness, in exaltation,
In despair, and in great sufferings.
The soul that in all things thus works and exerts itself
170 And in trouble neither gives way nor withdraws
Conquers all that God shall be in it
Eternally in the kingdom of heaven.

If I wished to say what happens
In such a soul through noble longing,
175 It would be presumption on my part.
For I am not so free
That I have renounced anything of myself,
As one in longing will do.
He who would conquer anything in longing
180 Must forsake himself in all things
And renounce honor and repose.
One who bears the weight of heavy burdens
And must travel far—
Of this I am certain—
185 Will be late in reaching journey's end,
If he does not renounce all for All's sake
And leave off attending to many things,
So as to jubilate over them in turn,

Or trying to deal with alien concerns,
190 Or taking small griefs to heart,
Or giving up spiritual liberty for the sake of honor,
Or doing injudicious work.
For these are marks of failure
And not of the conquest of Love.
195 Veritable longing is the deepest desire,
Which breaks many a heart.
Desire always longs so boundlessly
That I avoid drawing a comparison,
Since all comparisons are too small
200 For such longing as I mean.
The very being of desire is longing;
In whatever situation desire finds itself,
Tasting and learning do not suffice it.
Who can hold out when desire thus oppresses him?
205 If he had desired everything that Love
Can accomplish above all thought,
Still he would remain unsatisfied.
Thus in longing one can conquer
Both disquiet and torture without pity,
210 Yet continually be in great unrest.
What I have said about longing
Is little in comparison with what it contains.

That I discussed Love previously
Gives me too little consolation;
215 I included so many powers
That I praised affable Love
To the full, according to her dignity,
And the wonderful labor
That she gives to the one who loves,
220 In whom she recognizes herself.
She makes him desire the unreachable
And live on the unattainable;
She makes him shun the great good within reach;
She makes him fear sweet service;
225 She makes his liberty stand on trial;
From being a lord, she makes him a servant;
She makes his serfhood free;

She makes him poor, however rich he is;
She deprives him of power over all things,
230 By which he moved the power of Love.
In the nature of sublime Love
We can learn to know wonder.
Love makes us overtake all that escapes;
She makes us conquer what we fear;
235 She has power on earth and in heaven;
She makes the loving soul so daring
That it fears neither effort nor grief,
If it is not ready for all her service,
Whether in ill fortune or in good.
240 This is all that makes lavish Love successful.
Why in good fortune, why in ill?
Why in gain, why in loss?
For this reason in good: that man shall receive
What comes to him from Love by right and according to worthiness.
245 For this reason in ill: that man can fully
Acquire no right of Love;
Thus must he examine himself in all things,
If he is to conquer veritable Love.
For this reason in gain: He who conquers Love,
250 Learns what is hers without compensation.
For this reason in loss: All that can be
Adjudged to men for Love's sake—sadness,
Shame, pain, bitterness, and sorrow—
All this the lover has chosen
255 For Love or for true profit.
In this choice he spares neither heart nor mind;
So he receives bitter as gladly as sweet,
On condition that he may content Love.
In good, Love shows satisfaction;
260 In ill, that we lack something of hers;
In gain, she shows that her winnings
Continually give riches and love;
In loss, she shows that her power
Has brought heaven down to earth;
265 That profit came from loss,[6]
And grace from sin.

The lover who wishes to understand Love
Will gladly undergo pain;
He will adorn himself with Love's nature
270 And purify the ways by despair.
Deficiency examines the depths of Love;
Victory makes her wealth known.
Nonvictory rouses keen efforts;
Hope makes the lover fly to Love's sublimity.
275 By longing shall we have fruition of Love
And perfectly taste and experience
Her glory and her splendor,
Our gladness and our bliss,
Our joy and our delight
280 In the eternal new time.

Since we can win
The nature of Love by these means,
It follows that he who wastes an hour is a fool,
If he does not give himself to the adventure
285 That confronts him; for by doing so he can learn
How he can secure these means
And command them to his advantage,
As if they were his hired servants.
Thus he has joy with love in all,
290 As the loving soul shall have fruition in the Beloved.
If to receive love from Love is his wish,
As long as he is in his right mind,
He gives himself up wholly to Love.
Thus to win love from Love is in his power.
295 God gives Love to all who strive after love.
I am one who knows nothing of her,
Nor do I expect to know before my death;
May he who prescribed Love have mercy on my ignorance!

2 THE STRONGEST OF ALL THINGS

Four masters discussed before a king[7]
What the strongest thing is
That can be found in the world.

Then each of them expressed my opinion—
5 Although I was not there then—
And each one spoke the truth according to his heart.
The first said that wine
Is rightly to be considered the strongest;
It is medicinal and relieves the afflicted,
10 And has many other virtues
That make it effective in numerous ways.
The second said: "A king,
On account of his extensive power."
I omit reasons too long to tell you.
15 The third said: "The works of woman
Conquer every kind of strength."
The fourth said: "The truth
Is the strongest of all strength."
These are four great forces,
20 For him who understands and carefully reweighs them.
Wine is sorrow (on account of baseness),
And penance, and labor.
Yes, sorrow—because, in every respect,
Man falls short of great love, which demands
25 That he be always in hope and in fear,
In the inebriation of this wine.[8]
The master who praised this power
Praised it because it achieves great works.
The second strong being is the king:
30 He despises all things
Except what belongs to veritable Love,
And he wants no other consolation.
This is the hallmark of the spiritually poor,
And therefore I lament from my heart
35 That I could never be one of them,
For Love never showed me favor.
He who is *poor in spirit*[a] is a king,
And all things he easily conquers:
To possess, to will, and to desire;
40 Honor, repose, enjoyment, and rich fare.
Things of this sort the poor do not want,

a. Matt. 5:3.

But only what Love commands.
Thus he is poor, for he does not have
Anything at all to which his pleasure cleaves.
45 He is a king, for he holds in his power
And refuses all that is not brought him by Love.
The third is woman, who is the strongest.
The reason, which the third master ventured to explain,
Is that she is truly able
50 To conquer the king and all men.
This woman is humility,[9]
And she so keeps herself in lowliness
That she never exalts herself.
Even if she could practice all the virtues
55 That all men living could practice,
It would give her no repose.
Nothing touches her depths.
True humility did not understand
All that Love could accomplish,
60 For to humility it seemed not to give perfect fulfillment.[10]
Woman indeed is rightly the strongest:
She made the Lord a slave;[b]
Although he was the noblest in heaven,
Her deep humility made him so submissive
65 That he fell from his sublimity
Into this unfathomable chasm.
For her humility was so great
That she summoned the King to come to her.
She was the strongest, that is undeniable.
70 Anyone then who wishes to live in the valley
Of humility must conquer
All the power of great Love.
You have too little desire of opprobrium:[11]
That hinders you here particularly.
75 The fourth is truth: It conquers all
That was, and is, and shall be.[12]
Its power is to live for Love;
Its exercises and its gifts
Rule the achievement of the four forces

---

b. Cf. Phil. 2:7.

80 And make all live according to truth's counsel.
It deprives of their strength wine,
And the king, who is ordinarily the strongest,
And woman, who is yet stronger;
And causes them to yield to truth itself.
85 When the soul loves perfectly
And truly understands all these powers,
It loves eternally as it should—
And as I gladly loved and willed to love.
He who loves neither fears nor passes judgment
90 As to whether Love hates him or loves him.[13]
He who loves does not feel he lacks anything,
Whether gain or loss befalls him.
Love knows no distinctions;
She is free in every way;[14]
95 She knows no measure in her functions;[15]
Therefore she cannot heed the purely reasonable truth.
She is so noble and so valiant,
Both in omitting and in doing,
That she considers neither loss nor gain,
100 If only she returns into herself.

3 THE TOTAL GIFT TO LOVE

May God be God to all who love him,
And who acknowledge him alone as worthy of love.
It is they who begin with words, with works,
And with the law of Holy Church,
5 And moreover range farther in the counsel of Love:
After despair in darkness, high confidence.
Alas, how unheard-of are the ways of Love,
Before Love wins victories with love!
He who wishes to win victories in love
10 Must adorn himself in every way
And, in accordance with Love's deserts, renounce the whole of himself,
And with her condemn or bless
Both himself and what he hates and loves.
All the right he has he so gives over to Love

15 That he wishes nothing, and Love does not need
To refuse him anything she gives him.
For to him who loves, all alien repose
Is both pain and a heavy burden.
Desire cuts, as it were, an abyss in him;
20 So Love must fill it completely.
Alas, how entirely must anyone forsake himself
When he wholly gives himself up to Love,
And how steadfast he must be to her in miserable pains!
Her words and her works make that obvious.
25 This the Mother of Love truly showed:[16]
In her could man first learn to know it.
Although others before her strove for Love,
Men could best understand it through her.
She observed the law and family traditions,
30 But paid no heed to rewards, threats, praise, or laments.
So she left all for the sake of her unique Beloved.
Justly then did Love exalt her,
When Love made her the Mother of Love.
Why did not some wise man think of this?
35 To speak of her is too great for me.
For I never fulfilled what Love commanded:
And she fulfilled Love's highest counsel
And ranged onward with confidence in Love.
Through this she mounted into the highest land,[17]
40 Where she found Love in fruition to the full.
Thus my baseness makes me keep silence about her,
And bow before her high stature.
Although her tree bore many fruits
Whereof one might also speak—
45 Lords, ladies, and maidens,
Who through love of highest fidelity
Were submissive, to the death,
In all that Love commanded—
Concerning one (I pass over all the others)
50 I wish to write something
By which we may learn to recognize
Great marks of spiritual love,
And also find a great example
In what union she gave herself to Love.

55 This was Mary Magdalen,
Who was one in unity with Love.
Yes, Origen says of Mary:[18]
He who can confess the love of spiritual Love,
And they who lead the life of Mary to the end
60 And give themselves up wholly in love;
And they who can point him out with delight,
And say: "He said these things to me! I saw him!"[a]
They shall live very miserably—
But, as far as they are concerned, wisely.
65 When they meet persons in pain or in repose,
In enlightenment, or difficulty, or oppression,
In order that they may content Love,
They should rejoice over all of them alike.
When anyone thus gives himself in all things to Love,
70 What Love has not said to him,
God reveals to him in flight,
In a beautiful vision of good to come,[19]
And speaks to him hidden words,[b]
Which he learns to know but which were never audible
75 To an alien heart that denies something to Love
And never fixes its gaze on Love at any time.
For souls that are high-minded and sincere in love
Read their judgments in Love's countenance,
And they are always vigilant in love.
80 The wonder of unity is approaching them;
Yes, wonder for us who do not know Love,
But justice for them who give all to Love.
For the most beautiful life I know,
Although I know I am indeed unprepared for it,
85 Would be the one in which we let God freely act
In taking or in giving, in storm or in peace,
Were it in loving, or were it in hating:
In which all events would be rated just alike;
If God willed to come, or if he willed to go,
90 We should understand it all in love,
And see that he himself is Love,

a. John 20:18.
b. Job 4:12.

And accept no emotional pleasure in it.
For it is best to receive God with God,
And to keep and understand him most intimately.
95 If anyone is searching by himself for God,
I fancy God must remain out of his reach;
For no one can content him
So long as he bears the image of the earthly man.[c]
If we feel something, we call it the divine touch,
100 And we lose reason, and wish to lean on this feeling,
And fancy we are one with what we love.
Thus we upset the game before we win it.
But he who rather wears the earthly man as a garment
Considers what is owed to reason,
105 Which is his rule of life[20] and teaches him the works
By which he can turn from himself to Love,
And how he can keep Love,
And how with Love he repays Love.
If we thus encounter God with love,
110 And by love can know so much of him
That the earthly man attempts nothing more by himself,
As he thus finds God one Love with him,
His soul is engulfed in one will,
Which, in the highest noise, gives the deepest stillness.
115 Job said he had received hidden words.[d]
Other souls too have been granted them since.
Rightly is this hidden from those who welcome
And for pleasure's sake—alien consolations.
They who wish to adapt God to themselves,
120 And seek contentment in everything,
And neglect their rule of life,
And seek to be touched without work,
Shall not see God or understand concerning him
As Love[21] and Job understood,
125 And as do those who spurn all for God's sake
And condemn or bless everything with him,
No matter who is concerned; for them God's work
Supersedes all satisfaction of their pleasure.

---

c. 1 Cor. 15:49.
d. Job 4:12.

To him who loves, there seems no use in anything
130 That he can dare for Love's sake.
About Love's unlimited mode of action
I must keep silence because of my baseness,
Until I learn to know her better.
If Love gives anyone oppressive woe,
135 It will be the thing that most clings to him.
But Love will sooner cure him
If he gives her free rein,[22]
And is submissive to her besides,
And traverses the ways according to Love's counsel:
140 Let that be his richest confidence,
And let him remain of one mind with her.
I say: "O noble Love, do now
Your high will with me in all things:
Whether death or life, let all be the debt I owe you!"

4 IMAGE OF THE TRINITY

I pray God, who is the Master of all virtues,
That he make you conformed to Love,
And protect you by his holy power,
And nourish you with his sweet Love.
5 I pray the Holy Trinity,
Through its grace and for the sake of its goodness,
As it has honored you with its image,[23]
That through your being you become so fully instructed
That with reason you may understand
10 What God has done through you,
And what he would purpose in all;
And the design through which he has inwardly revealed himself to you,
That you might pay attention to it and understand it
With perfect service of Love.
15 If you live with reason in truth,
You enlighten all your labor;
So your will is pleased to live well
And to give all service to the full,
And so it is fervent and strong

20 And fears neither pain nor work;
And then your memory becomes valiant,
And in it shall reign glory,
And likewise confidence with fidelity,
That it may contemplate its God to the full.
25 He who has confidence in his God
Loves counsel and loves commandment;
All pain is pleasant to him;
For he gladly won perfection
Whereby he contented God,
30 And whereby he touched the Trinity,
Which dwells in us as an ornament, and so beautifully adorns
That kingdom of heaven, that high throne,[24]
Which everyone has in his nature.
With all this, each creature had the means
35 To give satisfaction, if he would but learn
With what burning love
God gave these three faculties;
And yet men lived by them so basely,
Just as those who do not understand
40 Veritable Love, now live by them.
What good did it do for me to speak of Love?
Love, for you, is something too high.
For you are young, and have no knowledge
Of how he who loves contents Love.
45 Make haste therefore to virtue
With all you can accomplish,
Omitting what it is fitting to omit,
And shunning all that disturbs Love,
And doing all that honors Love in any way.
50 And seek in everything what Love teaches,
And pay back what you owe to Love,
And you are wholly patient to the death.
You shall not only endure
Adversity without complaint,
55 But you must not know that it is to your advantage,
But say continually: "I lack the virtue
By which I should conquer Love.
How long shall I thus fail Love?
And shall I never content Love?"

60 No other thing shall sadden you;
You must not know that you possess virtue:
For the honor of Love it brings all satisfaction,
Like the instruments of good works.[25]
Your reason will enlighten and strengthen this.
65 You shall not only be generous,
But as one who neither possessed nor wished to possess.
Look upon all things as thorns,[a]
And do not turn to see or hear
Whatever has to do with alien things,
70 Or indeed what concerns various creatures
In which you might take pleasure;
But always feed at the noble manger
That Love may never find you with a grievance
Against her and against her counsels.
75 All the wrong that men can do you possesses grace,
Through Love's command, through Love's counsel.
So resemble the sublime nature of Love,
Who is so sweet that at every hour
She engulfs in love what men do to her,
80 Be it pleasure or pain, be it evil or good.
Love is alive to all love;
She can know nothing else but love.
If anyone does all for Love's honor,
His service promptly attains good success,
85 And his will always has new ardor.
Therefore I pray you that you be the one
Who for Love's sake always makes keen efforts
To please her; gladly suffer
For Love's sake: all you can
90 Do without, do without in your youth.
Offer up totally to love
Your heart without reluctance.
Thus let your will live in ardor,
And see to it that you content Love.
95 And continually, whatever you do,
Remain always in one mind;[b]

---

a. Cf. Gen. 3:18.
b. Cf. Acts 1:14.

So shall your memory become valiant,
And read its judgments in God,
And contemplate God with fidelity.
100 By this everything that could distress
Your being shall flee from you.
Do all that can content Love,
And all that enables you to succeed in virtues;
And ever abide by virtuousness.
105 Thus keep the image of the Trinity well-ordered within you,
And love God sweetly.

5 SUFFERING IN LOVE

In all things may God be your consolation,
And make known to you the taste of Love—
By which you can suffer everything—
And may he acquaint you with veritable virtue.[26]
5 Love—himself—is best honored
By sufferings from which many a person gladly flees.
For anyone who at the moment has no consolation
Presumes his life is leading nowhere;
And anyone who has repose according to his pleasure
10 Presumes that he fully matches perfection.
Thus the crowd are now deceived,
And fancy they are perfect: that is untrue.
If they considered with reason
What would happen to them if they were perfect,
15 And gave themselves to Love in suffering,
They would shudder that they live.
If you wish to approach sublime Love
And learn her ways perfectly,
You must always, with burning eagerness,
20 Seek new sufferings for Love's sake.
You must let Love—himself—act;
He will repay all pain with love.
If you let your sufferings be a burden to you,
You do not love him, that is evident.
25 If you wish to make a scene and display your suffering,
You have completely forgotten our Love,

Who conquers all, and will conquer
Anyone who wishes to belong wholly to her.
And if you wish to turn with me to Love,
30 See in what suffering I have borne
What you were unready to suffer.
Come, desire to suffer in order to ascend,
So that we together in one knowledge
May have fruition of our Love.
35 Now let us both so adorn ourselves
That Love herself may lead us
Into the blessedness that has been prepared
In which Love shall be eternally.[a]

6 ALONE WITH GOD

I pray God that he may direct your understanding
In his veritable Love,
And that he may enlighten you with himself,
And lead you by his deeper truth.[27]
5 For from me you shall much lack this,
Although I also wished to speak for your profit.
Those who are with you help you little;
Thus it is left for you to live alone with God:
With him you will fare the best.
10 If you wish to live free and valiant,
And to make progress in him at all times,
Turn all your ardor upon him,
And consider and learn in all knowledge
The storms of veritable Love.
15 Whether men do you evil or good,
Keep your equanimity in everything;
Remain undivided in all concerns.
Thus you will learn to know and taste Love.
What I said to you you must better understand—
20 That veritable Love and poor judgment
Cannot well harmonize,

a. John 14:2.

For Love pursues an honorable fief:
Veritable truth, sure fidelity,
Joy, gladness, and sweet grief.
25 Suffer sadness gladly,
And know that it is Love's mode of action;
And help with fidelity all those
Whom you know you can assist somewhat toward Love.
In fidelity and in noble service,
30 Console those with whom you are most friendly,
And those who in fidelity keep fidelity to you.
I recommend you to true Love,
And I pray to noble fidelity[28]
That she may contemplate your being
35 With the eyes of love,
And enable you to know all her being.

God be with you at all times.[29]
And cause all your delight to be in him,
Without any alien cares:
40 May he give you Love as a pledge of this.
It grieves me that you can know so little
How he manifests himself in his Love:
I should be very glad to see
That through me something might befall you sooner;
45 I would very gladly suffer to this end,
And make it evident by my actions.
I pray God that he give you
Success in this, and that he enlighten
Your mind according to his nobleness;
50 And may he cause you to desire
The sublimity of his Nature,[30]
And to feed upon his noble Nature,
Which can nourish your being
55 And protect it to the profit of us both.[31]
O my love! fix all your thought
On the Love of God who created you.[32]
Commend all your being to Love;
So shall you heal all torments
60 And pains, and you shall fear nothing,
And shall not flee from adversity in anything.

You should trust to Love,
To love and to hate as her law requires.
65 Be at peace with all things:
This sign marks your accord with Love's mode of action.
That you are so easily grieved
Robs you of many a beautiful gift.
If you wish to trust yourself to God,
70 And keep yourself in charity,
Nothing shall remain out of your reach,
And then you will truly conquer your Beloved.

7 TO WILL WITH HIM

I recommend your understanding to God,
That he may give you love therein,
And teach you to live his will
And rightly to give truth to the Truth,
5 And to live in fidelity without dissembling;
And that he may mercifully look down on your life.
Now see to it that you make haste to virtue
With all that you can accomplish,
And serve all those who love,
10 In order that they may help you know the ways
That belong to sublime Love—
They whom God had chosen with work:
He did the will of his Father
And the Holy Spirit's thoughts,[a] which were united to that will.
15 A will thus united was all Love's work.
Will with him, and become united and strong.
And give up all your thought in love
To the sweet God who created you,[33]
Who has helped you by this,
20 That you are living among those
Who bear God high love—
And mention is made of it to you in writings.
And you know the highest virtue,
Which you can readily learn,

a. Cf. 1 Cor. 2:11.

25 And you must be glad of the life in common
Through which you now have guidance toward Love.
Men strike the iron while it is hot.[34]
Therefore must you make haste at once,
While you have your youth
30 And can acquire virtue.
But if you become slothful and remiss,
And fail to carry into effect
What I wish and have imposed,
You would still wander from your aim;
35 All your friends would forsake you;
You would live under great disadvantage.
But this is not to be feared.
Our God who called you into being
Must help you and succor you
40 In whatever can oppress you.
Let nothing be oppressive for you;
Thus you will cure all by Love.
Be humble and patient,
With the fidelity that you owe to God,
45 And willingly desire to be always
Miserable and friendless;
For the honor of Love, trust yourself to God,
And free him from misery.
If you do anything less, you will be ashamed of it.
50 May God grant you conformity to what his majesty requires.

8 FULL GROWTH

He who holds back anything in his heart
Cannot attain to the full growth of love.
One must dare to fight all love with love
If Love is to be contented.
5 But no one can effect this
With all the service of Holy Church:
He needs to give himself up completely in Love,
And live far from all joys,
And seek support in no emotional pleasure,
10 And continually search for what is never to be had—

Being glad not to spare
Deeds of love, or storm, or disquiet,
For the sake of Love's dignity.
The Book of Wisdom says this:
15 *Glorious fruit* shall he know[a]
Who suffers much for the sake of glorifying Love.

May God give you success in love,[35]
And may he elevate your lofty mind
In his nobleness,
20 And may he cause you to desire
All the truth of his Nature
And make you live in his noble Love,
Which can nourish your love
And protect it, to the profit of both of us.
25 I would gladly see you ready for this growth.
That you hinder it makes me sad;
It is hard for me that you delay somewhat;
About this I am often angry with you.

9 NO FROG, NO ELDERBERRIES

May God be your consolation in veritable Love
And make sublime Love known to you
And the truth that you owe to him,
And may he direct toward himself all your ardor.
5 If you wish to begin this work of Love,
You should begin with that work
The Son of God began with,
When he came to us to live as a Man.[a]
As he lived, you should live,
10 And renounce all joy for his sake.
As he renounced his joys, whoever wishes[b]
To live in true Love must renounce his joys.
I beg you to renounce

a. Wisd. 3:15.
a. Heb. 10:5–7.
b. Heb. 12:12.

Yourself, and to live for Love
15 In misery and adversity.
I do not wish that mischance—what happens to you,
Through God, in Love—should cause you grief.
For all pain, through Love, is of value,
If one suffers much for Love's sake,
20 On condition that one shows measure in no way—[36]
As do those who seem in displeasure because of love,
And complain and make an exhibition of themselves:
That is pain devoid of value,
And no one derives profit from it.
25 For displays of nonacceptance
Sadden and hinder Love in every way.
But you have little need of this.
I wish you were wise and valiant
To engage in a combat against God.
30 For this combat takes away the sweet taste
That Love gives to the loved one,
So that one lives never an instant in peace.
Give to God likewise your intellect, united to him,
Pure in veritable Love,
35 In order to live in such sweet understanding
That you welcome no concerns
But only God or nothing.
For he who has something of the taste of God,
If he is touched from within
40 In right feeling of his single love,
Becomes readier to welcome concerns:
But all things turn bitter in his estimation;
Neither he himself, nor saints, nor men on earth
Are any longer the object of his wish.
45 All things whatever are pain to him,
Except to be for Love's sake in the service of Love,
Continually to die and for Love's sake wither away,
Or to rejoice in the feeling of love.
In this you must extol God;
50 And do not allow yourself expertise in other things.
Although I say *Deo gratias*[c] for this,

c. 1 Cor. 15:57.

I never knew to whom it was
That Love gave joy and a free way:
Contending with Love I have suffered defeat.
55 But it is right that I silence my complaint
Of having from her night by day:[d]
I have made but scant efforts
Whereby I might live free for Love's sake.
But although I have no fish,
60 I do not want any frog;
Or any elderberries either,
Instead of a bunch of grapes:
Although I have no love,
I do not want anything else,[37]
65 Whether Love is gracious to me or hostile.

10 NOT FEELING BUT LOVE

He who strives after particular points of knowledge[38]
Lacks something important in veritable Love.
All such knowledge we often demand prematurely;
And this is not enough.
5 For it seems a yearning of the will,
And not a guidance of the Spirit;
For were it a guidance of the Spirit,
God would very speedily accomplish it.
And there is too much childishness in love,
10 When one wants many particular things,
And prefers to be in delight.
This is a failure in loftiness of life.
Not for feeling's sake must we learn to serve,
But only to love with love in Love.
15 If anyone did not fear hell,
And did not serve for the hope of heaven,
And if for hell's sake and for heaven's sake
He were equally glad and equally daring,
And if he loved without rest,
20 And desired above measure,

d. Job 5:14.

And above reason, and above thought,
That were great profit in love.
As he received, he would give:[a]
And what Love demanded, he would experience.
25 The soul, when knowledge is given it,
Knows that it lives in Love;
And when it feels misery,
It can learn to know Love's mode of action.
Love will then order and command
30 All that the soul can accomplish:
If then it lives so as to content Love,
That is truly Love's wish.
We must apply ourselves with heart and mind,
And follow with fidelity and with love.
35 Although we know nothing about Love,
Here any knowledge would be a loss.
Love has put in chains our heart and powers
And all our mind and will;
And the man in us must undergo
40 As many sufferings as this life holds:
With the miserable, he must suffer need;
With the slain, death;
With beggars, he suffers bodily torment;
And with lovers, pain of soul.
45 He who wishes to stand at Love's service for Love's sake
Must undergo pressure from many sides.
The proximity of the nature of Love
Deprives the soul of its rest:
The more Love comes, the more she steals;
50 The more she discloses, the more she keeps secret.
He who with love shall remain faithful to Love
Must enter still living into death,[39]
Lest he remain without something in Love
That he could win by labor.
55 Love's nature, which conquers all powers,
Gives and takes both death and life;
Love's nature is then powerful in its activity,
Fearing nothing, ever valiant;

a. Cf. Matt. 10:8.

In it is all the power of God.
60 Love's being is in her commandments;
Where love is with Love in love,
The abyss is unfathomable;[40]
There all those who let themselves sink in her
Must be drowned in her;
65 And to those who attend her in her nature
She gives an unquiet life.
Love springs out of her own nature
And causes hearts, in Love, to be in constant striving;
They who follow the power of Love, which draws them,
70 Must profess the nobility in which she holds them.
Nobody who has loved Love with love
Could explain to others,
Or write, or bring to their understanding,
All the wonders he finds in Love's sublimity.
75 Desires of love, moreover, cannot
By all these explanations be quieted.
Desire strives in all things for more than it possesses:
Love does not allow it to have any rest:
Even if all the suffering were massed together
80 That ever was, or is, or shall be,
It could not conquer so much
As desire of veritable Love can.
Desire snatches at suffering above measure
And at work that Love will grant it;
85 So it is allotted perturbation and turbulent unrest.
Love does not allow it to be at rest;
It undergoes pressure from noble unfaith,
Which is stronger and higher than fidelity:[41]
Fidelity, which one can record by reason,
90 And express with the mind,
Often lets desire be satisfied—
What unfaith can never put up with;
Fidelity must often be absent
So that unfaith can conquer;
95 Noble unfaith cannot rest
So long as it does not conquer to the hilt;
It wishes to conquer all that Love is:
For that reason it cannot remain out of her reach.

Consequently the soul feels much bitterness,
100 Which Love could heal in a short time;
This the soul bears as if it came from unfaith,
When it well knows it comes from fidelity.
Through desires of unquiet love
The soul can win no repose,
105 And through desires of strong love
It loses repose and inner quiet.
So it drowns in sublime Love,
And so it finds its unattainable desire nearby;
For anyone in misery cannot find contentment
110 Unless desire can be fulfilled;
For desire comes from such a lofty nature,
It cannot be at rest in any small thing.
Love flees, and desire follows hard after,
And never finds a resting place.
115 It cannot conquer sublimity;
What Love herself is must remain out of its reach.
Could the soul know the Nature
Wherein it is loved by God with love,
It would languish in longing
120 And flow away completely in delight.
That would really be immoderate good fortune!
Whoever loves must suffer many griefs:
Suppose someone ready for fidelity's service,
Who wishes to receive fidelity from fidelity,
125 And wishes to live in lofty fidelity,
And to take and give in its service
According to its right, and is free, strong, and valiant
Always to do fidelity's dearest will;
If for all that he spares honor or rest,
130 He is the friend who left us in the lurch!

11 THREE SUBTLE POINTS

God be with you, and grant you
To love all that we shall love,
And to hate what is to be hated,
And to be conformed to all truth!

5 Serve the truth where you can,
And do not spare yourself for any virtue,
Or for the sake of rest or honor.
Therefore suffer gladly many vicissitudes:
Truth has to pay no honors;
10 It is always intrepid in itself.
Keep your nobility forever,
And do not spare any labor;
Be kind to those who need you;
Comfort the sorrowful;
15 Serve Love at all times,
And fix all your ardor on her.
Through her you shall bow before all storms;
Through her you shall silence credit to yourself,
When you speak too readily;
When you would very gladly sleep, keep vigil;
20 When you would gladly be silent, speak;
And no one will be the loser.[42]

In all your mode of action, keep to just measure
In your doing and your omitting.
25 The debt that you owe to God
Pay gladly at all times,
Both in hating and in loving;
Do your utmost to learn what this means.
In what comes into your mind,
30 Pay heed to your loss or gain by it,
Whether it is your own will or something spiritual;
In this lies the greatest subtlety of all.
People preconceive themselves to be led by the Spirit,
When it is chiefly their own will.
35 Again, something that ruins them
They think is consolation and comes from God.

These are three subtle points,
Which, of all the principles we put in practice,
Perfect man the most.
40 The wisdom they contain
Has not been learned or understood;
For people accept nothing,

And do not want pain for the honor of Love:
They are now so often inconstant.

45 Do not be angry that I speak thus;
Fidelity causes me to speak, not your shortcomings.
You know in part how you should arrange your life
In order to renounce carelessness.
God be with you at all times,
50 And cause you to find all your delight in him!

12 DAUGHTER OF THE FATHER

In God, because he is our Love,
As far as I know love,
It would be grief to me were it other
Than he alone whom we love and strive after:
5 With such love as he is,
Dear heart, I greet you,
And with what I am, wholly and entirely.
You know well, although I make it known to you,
Love wishes to act on what is hers in the soul,
10 And to know what the soul is to her; then she lives free.
She always wishes to hear
And to give herself to rejoicing[43] and sadness;
Love cannot be without either;
She is always mingling both in a wonderful way;
15 So strongly active is Love's nature
That she cannot rest one instant
Without involving her loved one in sweet love,
Or in a storm of the understanding.
God has dealt with us in a wonderful way
20 In that he has charged himself with us through love.
Since we are made for this,
To know with love how Love tastes,
Apply yourself with veritable virtue
To sweet Love as much as you can,
25 And give yourself to all good modes of action,
With sweet intent and with full peace.
Wait in the chains of veritable Love,

And strive to understand the voice
With which Love herself speaks.
30 See that you do not fail her in any way:
If Love is sweet to you, or if she is cruel to you,
Be always ready for her will.
    This is how I ever behaved;[44] and as I understand,
I also stand written: *Audi filia.*[a]
35 Be you the daughter, and give ear to the Father;
Be entirely ready for his service.
First you shall contemplate God's work
And supply the wants of all those
Who are in need of you, just as he did,
40 In will, in works, and in thought.
In the second place he commands to incline the ear,
So that one may hear Love's voice:
To be obedient outwardly and inwardly,
And to know nothing but Love's will.[45]
45 When we are thus obedient to Love,
We shall by this means forget everything—
The people of aliens and of familiars,
Of the honored and of the loved—
And forget all creatures
50 In order to think of the sweetness of Love's nature.
He commands the daughter to forget her father's house,
Because he wants a total fruition of her;
And he wills that all who are hers be entirely forgotten—
Those who have possessed heaven
55 (Angels and saints), and here on earth, men:
Although one may have the wish to remember them,
One must by his help forget them all,
And know only the unity of Love.
If you will thus come to nought for his sake,
60 *The King shall desire your beauty.*[b]
For in his Nature no beauty
Is satisfying except his pure Nature.
When the soul can think of nothing else
But experiencing his kiss and being immersed in him,

---

a. Ps. 44:11.
b. Ps. 44:12.

65 That is a life conformed to God and to his pleasure.
If one thus gives up his whole self to Love alone,
God desires his beauty and adorns him with it,
According to his pleasure, according to Love's mode of action.
People say: "So-and-so leads a life conformed to God!"
70 But if to anyone this kind of godliness never comes,
The King does not desire his beauty.
If by his mercy it comes to you even slightly,
You will then see that the King desires you.
It seems to me I am afraid of this,
75 That he remains unstriven for, and unknown,
And unloved by those who are his;
That he cannot with his Nature
Have fruition of what he had predestined in love.
O forsake everything else, and demand that All,
80 And see what wonders he shall then work!
That most awesome wonder that ever was,
The most costly beauty that the King desires,
Of which he with his whole Nature
Wishes to have fruition in one permanence—
85 And that beauty will meet with one Beauty,[46]
And they will greet with one single greeting.
And that kiss will be with one single mouth,[c]
And that fathoming will be of one single abyss,[47]
And with a single gaze will be the vision of all
90 That is, and was, and shall be;
And that all are wise with one wisdom,
And with one will of a single thought,
And with one dominion all equally powerful,[48]
In one form, in one likeness,
95 And in one experience, in one power of all—
Whoever attains to oneness shall yet have knowledge of this.
Alas, it is unknown to me who that is!
May God and his lovers have mercy on him!
I know the expedient of the service of Love,
100 But when it comes to the exercise of it,

c. Cf. Song 1:1.

How anyone deals with the Beloved with love,
My knowledge of that is quickly stated.
So I fare as the blind man is wont to do,
And let the beginning be my ending.
105 When the lover sets out to live love with the loved one,
He should make fair beginnings:
But how it must end, he is not one who knows,
And he is unprepared for the experience of love.
Now although the King does not desire us—
110 That is woe and grief to us—
We shall incline our ears gladly
And, as one of his children, hear
And see, and consider, and understand
What he wills and has done for our sake.
115 And we shall forget alien things,
And all the particular joys
Of friends on earth or in heaven,
And we shall praise Love for all suffering,
And hope for good success,
120 Which may yet give us Love to the full.
If only, for Love's sake, we could renounce
Alien consolations and compensations,
And if only we could adorn ourselves in a beautiful vision,[49]
In noble will and in noble deed!
125 If we loved with love all that Love loves,
And if her glory were known to us,
She would communicate herself in it
In one fruition and in one knowledge.
In this may we be helped by Jesus Christ,[50]
130 Who himself has revealed
All the delight and all the suffering of Love,
And has made them clear with his radiance;
He must make Love known to us,
And shed his radiance on all our concerns
135 And on our heart and our mind,
And place in them his unitive Love,
Which may make known to us how we should
Live in all perfection.
Now encompass yourself completely with truth,

And make haste, that you never sadden us.
The time is short,[d] and there is much to do;
Be generous to Love and valiant.

13 THE PARADOXES OF LOVE

What is sweetest in Love is her tempestuousness;[51]
Her deepest abyss is her most beautiful form;
To lose one's way in her is to touch her close at hand;
To die of hunger for her is to feed and taste;
5 Her despair is assurance;
Her sorest wounding is all curing;[a]
To waste away for her sake is to be in repose;
Her hiding is finding at all hours;
To languish for her sake is to be in good health;
10 Her concealment reveals what can be known of her;
Her retentions are her gifts;
Wordlessness is her most beautiful utterance;
Imprisonment by her is total release;
Her sorest blow is her sweetest consolation;
15 Her ruthless robbery is great profit;
Her withdrawal is approach;
Her deepest silence is her sublime song;
Her greatest wrath is her dearest thanks;
Her greatest threat is pure fidelity;
20 Her sadness is the alleviation of all pain.

We can say yet more about Love:
Her wealth is her lack of everything;
Her truest fidelity brings about our fall;
Her highest being drowns us in the depths;
25 Her great wealth bestows pauperism;
Her largesse proves to be our bankruptcy;
Her tender care enlarges our wounds;
Association with her brings death over and over;
Her table is hunger; her knowledge is error;

d. 1 Cor. 7:29.
a. Job 5:18.

30 Seduction is the custom of her school;
Encounters with her are cruel storms;
Rest in her is in the unreachable;
Her revelation is the total hiding of herself;
Her gifts, besides, are thieveries;
35 Her promises are all seductions;
Her adornments are all undressing;
Her truth is all deception;
To many her assurance appears to lie—
This is the witness that can be truly borne
40 At any moment by me and many others
To whom Love has often shown
Wonders by which we were mocked,
Imagining we possessed what she kept back for herself.
After she first played these tricks on me,
45 And I considered all her methods,
I went to work in a wholly different way:
By her threats and her promises
I was no longer deceived.

I will belong to her, whatever she may be,
50 Gracious or merciless; to me it is all one!

14 ALLEGORY OF LOVE'S GROWTH

In the high name of Love,
Who must make her being known to you,
I send you her kindest greeting
And beg her that she may show you all
5 Her being to its depths,
Which we never could fathom.
Oh how deep is the abyss of Love,
Which no one could know!
All that man knows is of little use
10 As long as something must be lacking in it.
What is lacking to us comes from what we suffer
Because we stride forward so slowly,
And live with poor consolation,
And give so little in the storm of Love.

15 Our minds and our powers,
Which should walk the ways
Upward to sublime Love, stand fettered,
Without peace and without grace.
The ways that anyone walks in Love
20 Cannot be known by persons
Who maintain moderation in their works
And invigorate themselves on pleasures,
And live in sorrow over loss and joy over success,
By their earthly-mindedness in pride.
25 But the perfect man, who would know
That powerful being of Love,
Should with a humble heart[a]
Judge sweetness and pain the same,
And receive as meriting equal glory,
30 In one will and in one memory,
Sweet and bitter with like pleasure,
And all pain without sadness:
For Love can very well repay
Those who painfully follow her paths.
35 Provided anyone sinks low enough in humility—
Lower by far than the thought of all men
Who are born into the world—[b]
Greatness of love will come by this means.
If you were willing to fall thus and to bow in all things,
40 You would obtain perfect Love.[52]
For that brought God down into Mary,
And he would yet acknowledge the same in one
Who could hold himself so humble in love:
He could not refuse his sublimity to him,
45 But such a one would receive him and carry him for as long
As a child grows within its mother.

Faithful fear is the first month;[53]
Fear attends to all works and urges on
To the holy law and the commandments of truth.

---

a. Cf. Matt. 11:29.
b. Num. 12:3.

50 Hence fear motivates monastic profession in God:
You know well that he who makes monastic profession
Must promise to be of one mind
With the community where he is,
To be conformed to all obedience.
55 Since fear then is the first month,
The soul has thus recalled the obligation
To all obedience, the perfect service
Of Love where it can know it,
In death, in life, and in all things;
60 Thus the soul receives as Mary received,
And in all this obedient service still deeper humility:
That is, *Ecce ancilla domini.*[c]
Thus the first month is accomplished;
The soul has received with faithful fear.
65 The second month is joyful suffering
For the sake of perfection, and keen efforts
By which one can learn perfection.
Therefore do not spare even coming to blows;
Where you can, go hunting for suffering;
70 There truth blindfolds the eyes of knowledge.
If you endure this without guilt on your part,
You carry love to the highest degree;
For by patience one learns to know
How one can exercise greater love;
75 For patience most causes to grow and dilate
That bosom in which Love is received.
The third month raises the number,
As the soul thus can carry all,
And it knows that it carries Love;
80 This is the exercise that we have for it:
Always ardent and unconquerable,
And in this we can control ourselves
According to Scripture, which also teaches us:
Sobrie pie juste vivamus in hoc seculo.[d]
85 The fourth month is that state of sweetness

---

c. Luke 1:38. *Behold the handmaid of the Lord.*
d. Titus 2:12. *We should live soberly and justly and godly in this world.*

Amid which so noble a creature
As Love is shall grow up,
And her multitudinous members everywhere:
In that place where the soul carries Love,
90 And wherever Love has members,[54]
The soul shall watch over them with that same sweetness
And feed them with ardent works of mercy.
The fifth month in secret brings to effect
The most sweet burden that the soul has received—
95 To apply itself in secret to this sweet Love—
And the severe pain that Love brings about,
Which is felt by the soul that thus carries Love
And has received Love with humility.
The sixth month is confidence,
100 From which the soul receives all wealth
And consolation that that Child, with fruit, shall come
Full-grown and powerful, and shall give all benefits;
Thus to trust in Love with full reliance
And to long for the high day
105 When this noble Child will be born
And to the full, in full, fully loved.
The seventh month is justice;
This frustrates all work.
Justice condemns or commends
110 Each being according to its time,
And receives and gives according to Love's pleasure
And above the understanding of all minds.
The effects of justice are above nature
And make the soul certain and pure;
115 And no suffering better assures the soul
That it is in the truth of love
Than do those sufferings contrary to nature
In which it finds a sweet taste without bitterness:
This means to be glad in adversity,
120 This means to have joy in opprobrium,
And to love those who harm you.
That certainly is the noblest deed of love.
A friend with friends, *joyful with the joyful*,[e]

---

e. Rom. 12:15.

That is the custom of Love at all times.
125 But this is contrary to nature, beyond man's power,
And the highest part of justice,
By which the soul carries God most properly speaking,
And inwardly possesses him growing to the full.
The eighth month is the wisdom of Love,
130 And knowledge of her being in all ways:
As much as Love can love,
Wisdom wholly engulfs from within.
The ninth month is as if wisdom engulfs
All that it loves in love.
135 Then Love's moment of power comes
And continually assaults wisdom.
As man with all that man is
Contents Love and is conformed to Love,
So in the ninth month is born
140 The Child that lowliness had chosen.
Then humility has its wish
By which it satisfies itself.
Between these two is brought to term that Child
Which has lain in that great place:
145 In the depths of lowliness, in the heights of love,
Where with all, in every way,
The soul lives for God with all power,
In new love, day and night.
So its whole life becomes divinized;[55]
150 For he has said in Scripture,
So that he cannot fail in it:
He shall measure to us with the same measure
With which we measure to him.[f]
To them who in this manner, filled with love,
155 In will and in work above thought,
Content Love according to her whole will,
He shall then, if he wills, measure with the same measure;
So must he give them that loftiness,
According to their will, as they themselves give,
160 If he really will live wholly in union with them;

f. Luke 6:38.

Otherwise the compensation would be falsehood,
If he did not measure the same measure.

Now is born full-grown this Child
Who was chosen by humility,
165 And is full-grown in sublime Love,
And carried to term nine months.[56]
And each month has four weeks,
And each calls for preparation and adornment
Before the great high day,
170 So that Love can be born perfect.
The first week is power; the second, knowledge;
The third, will; and steadfast affection
Perfects those four weeks
And fills up the month completely.
175 Each week is of seven days;
The days are the seven gifts;
The soul must have these gifts if it is to complete
The nine months to their full time.
Wisdom teaches what we do;
180 Understanding testifies to the works as good;
With counsel we understand how to content Love;
With fortitude we carry out her wish;
With knowledge we shall follow the Beloved;
With piety we shall give great gifts;
185 With holy fear[g] we shall watch over
All who work, and nourish them with fidelity.

15 WERE I BUT LOVE

I greet what I love
With my heart's blood.
My senses wither
In the madness of Love.

5 O kindest sweet Love,
Grow up fully in me according to your being;

g. Isa. 11:2–3.

So may my senses
Recover from death.

O most beloved Lord!
10 Were you really for me what you are
In yourself, I should
Have a little time of rest.

O sweetest Repose,
Had you everything that is your due,
15 My burdens would be lightened
That now weigh on me so heavily.[57]

O very sweet nature,
Is your heart satisfied?
I cannot hold out a single moment;
20 I must belong wholly to Love.

O dearly loved maiden,
That I say so many things to you
Comes to me from fresh fidelity,
Under the deeper touch of Love.

25 Oh had we what we loved,[58]
We should both be so rich
That few could be found
Anywhere like us.[59]

Oh! I am inflamed in mind, hoping for success
30 In the blessing of belonging fully to Love.
Oh! to be wise in violence, that is success—
Yes, to be free in the violence of Love.

I long, I keep vigil, I taste
The things that seem to me sweet;
35 I know, intellectually, that relief
For my adversity is found in Love.

I suffer, I strive after the height,
I suckle with my blood;

I greet the Sweetness that can
40 Alleviate my madness of Love.

I tremble, I cling, I give,
I live on high expectation
That my pain, noble in itself,
Shall receive everything in the pain of my Beloved.

45 Beloved, if I love a beloved,
Be you, Love, my Beloved;
You gave yourself as Love for your loved one's sake,
And thus you, Love, uplifted me, your loved one, with you!

O Love, were I but love,
50 And could I but love you, Love, with love!
O Love, for love's sake, grant that I,
Having become love, may know Love wholly as Love!

16 LOVE'S SEVEN NAMES

Love has seven names,
Which, as you know, are appropriate to her:
Chain, light, live coal, and fire—
These four names designate the awe Love inspires.
5 The other three names are great and strong—
Forever insufficient, but resonant of eternity:[60]
They are dew, living spring, and hell.
If I mention these names to you,
It is because they are found in Scripture:
10 In order to say enough of their nature,
And what they bear witness to and show forth.
That I am not deceiving you,
And that Love does behave as I say
Is known by everyone who lives, wholly for Love,
15 This life full of wonders
I have already told you about.
Love is truly a chain,[a] because she binds

---

a. Col. 3:14.

And grasps everything in her power.
Her chains, when learned of, are fully welcome,
20 As anyone who has experienced them well knows.
For Love, midway, withdraws our consolation[61]
But comforts us again in our worst griefs.
Her chains encircle me within so tightly
That I think I shall die of pain;
25 But her chains conjoin all things
In a single fruition and a single delight.
This is the chain that binds all in union
So that each knows the other through and through
In the anguish or the repose or the madness of Love,
30 And eats his flesh and drinks his blood:
The heart of each devours the other's heart,
One soul assaults the other and invades it completely,
As he who is Love itself showed us
When he gave us himself to eat,[b]
35 Disconcerting all the thoughts of man.[c]
By this he made known to us
That love's most intimate union
Is through eating, tasting, and seeing interiorly.
He eats us; we think we eat him,
40 And we do eat him, of this we can be certain.[62]
But because he remains so undevoured,
And so untouched, and so undesired,
Each of us remains uneaten by him
And separated so far from each other.
45 But let him who is held captive by these chains
Not cease to eat his fill,
If he wishes to know and taste beyond his dreams
The Godhead and the Manhood!
The chains of Love explain these words:
50 *I to my Beloved, and my Beloved to me!*[d]
Light is a name of Love that reveals[63]
What most offends the Beloved,
And what is most in accord with Love,

b. Cf. John 6:52.
c. Cf. John 6:41, 66.
d. Song 2:16.

Or what things Love principally condemns.
55 In this light we can learn
How we shall love the God-Man
In his Godhead and in his Manhood:
This is an infinitely rich fief.
Live coal is another name for Love. Judge with me
60 What it symbolizes in Scripture.[e]
The live coal is a wonderful present
That God gives interiorly to the soul,
It consists in all the soul receives or is deprived of
In conciliation, in threats, in punishment,
65 In consolation, joy, and work,
And in all the contradictory behavior I spoke of.
This live coal is a swift messenger
That serves Love admirably;
Its mission is never broken off
70 And is indispensable to Love.
This live coal inflames him who was cold;
It makes the proud man timid;
It bids the horseman go afoot;
It fills the vassal with pride;
75 It places the pauper in a kingdom[f]
Where he is second to none.
And all these contraries—falling, getting up again,
Taking, giving, receiving—
This name, the coal, sets afire and extinguishes
80 By the madness of Love. Now apply your mind
To this question, and judge
The unheard-of wonders the live coal works
Until it comes back again to the fire
In which it wholly damns,
85 Burns to death, engulfs, and consumes
Man's desire and God's refusal.[64]
Fire[g] is a name of Love by which she burns to death
Good fortune, success, and adversity:
All manners of being are the same to fire.

---

e. Isa. 6:6.
f. Cf. Matt. 5:3.
g. Matt. 3:11, Luke 12:49, Acts 2:3, Heb. 12:29.

90 Anyone whom this fire has thus touched
Finds nothing too wide, and nothing too narrow.
But once this Fire gains control,
It is all the same to him what it devours:
Someone we love or someone we hate, refusal or desire,
95 Winnings or forfeits, convenience or hindrance,
Gain or loss, honor or shame,
Consolation at being with God in heaven
Or in the torture of hell:
This Fire makes no distinction.
100 It burns to death everything it ever touches:[65]
Damnation or blessing no longer matters,[66]
This I can confess.
Dew is a name under which Love works:
When that Fire has burned up all in its violence,
105 The dew falls, imparting moisture everywhere
Like a strong wind[h] of unheard-of sweetness.
It calls forth the kiss of noble natures
And gives them constancy in the midst of changes.
Love's zeal engulfs her gifts to such an extent
110 That the dew's gentle action must always be present.
Then are appeased all the storms
That previously arose in the soul;
Calm reigns at last,
When the loved one receives from her Beloved
115 The kisses that truly pertain to love.
When he takes possession of the loved soul in every way,
Love drinks in these kisses and tastes them to the end.
As soon as Love thus touches the soul,
She eats its flesh and drinks its blood.[i]
120 Love that thus dissolves the loved soul
Sweetly leads them both
To the indivisible kiss—
That same kiss which fully unites
The Three Persons in one sole Being.[67]
125 Thus the noble dew appeases the conflagration
That had been raging in the land of Love.

---

h. Dan. 3:49–50.
i. Cf. John 6:54.

Living spring,[68] her sixth name,
Is truly appropriate to Love after that of dew.
This flowing forth and this reflux
130 Of one into the other, and this growth in God,
Surpass the mind and understanding,
The intelligence and capacity
Of human creatures.
But still we have it in our nature:
135 The hidden ways[j] where Love makes us walk
And where she lets us receive, amid blows, that sweet kiss—
Here it is that we receive that sweet living life,
So that Life shall give life in our life.[69]
This name is living spring because this spring nourishes
140 And preserves in man a living soul:
The spring gushes forth, living itself, from life
And, from this life, brings new life to our life.
The living spring flows at all times,
In long-standing virtues and in new ardor.
145 As the river pours forth its waves
And receives them back again into itself,
So Love engulfs all her gifts.
This is why Love is named spring and life.
Hell is the seventh name
150 Of this Love wherein I suffer.
For there is nothing Love does not engulf and damn,
And no one who falls into her
And whom she seizes comes out again,
Because no grace exists there.
155 As Hell turns everything to ruin,
In Love nothing else is acquired
But disquiet and torture without pity;
Forever to be in unrest,
Forever assault and new persecution;
160 To be wholly devoured and engulfed
In her unfathomable essence,
To founder unceasingly in heat and cold,
In the deep, insurmountable darkness of Love.
This outdoes the torments of hell.

---

j. Job 3:23.

165 He who knows Love and her comings and goings
Has experienced and can understand
Why it is truly appropriate
That Hell should be the highest name of Love.[70]

Now judge how these names contain
170 All the essence and the modes of true Love.
No heart is so wise that its thoughts
Can reveal the thousandth part
Of the chain of Love, though it were to leave
The other six names aside.
175 By the chain we are assured of this,
That there is no separation from Love,
Either by miracle or by power.[k]
Such is the might of the gift of wisdom.
The human heart by itself cannot bear it,
180 But by this very chain it suffers the chains of Love.
By light we learn the customs of Love
And know her well under all its forms:
Why we must love and attain knowledge
Of the Humanity like the Divinity.
185 By the live coal, Love sets the two aflame;[71]
By the fire, she burns them in the Unity,
Just as in the fire of the salamander
The phoenix burns to ashes and metamorphoses itself.[72]
By the dew the conflagration is appeased,
190 And balm is poured out, a unitive strong wind.
The bliss and the madness of Love
Then cast them into the abysmal Flood,
Unfathomable, ever living,
Which with life receives, in the Unity of the Trinity,
195 God and man in one single love:
Such is the Trinity above all thought.
The seventh name, just and sublime,
Calls Love hell,
As she is indeed according to her nature.
200 For she ruins the soul and the mind
To such a degree that they never recover;

---

k. Cf. Rom. 8:38–39.

They who love no longer have virtues to do anything
But wander in the storms of Love,
Body and soul, heart and thought—
205 Lovers lost in this hell.
If anyone wishes to face this, he must be on his guard,
Since for Love nothing succeeds
But the constant acceptance of caresses and blows.
The offering of veritable Love must be sought
210 In the depths of the heart possessed of fidelity.
If we act thus, we must conquer.
Though we are far off, we shall reach knowledge.

NOTES

ABBREVIATIONS

Bernard *SC*	Bernard of Clairvaux, *Sermones super Cantica.*
CCSL	*Corpus Christianorum Series Latina* (Turnhout, 1954–).
DS	*Dictionnaire de spiritualité* (Paris, 1932–).
MG	*Patrologiae cursus completus, Series Graeca.* Ed. J. Migne.
ML	*Patrologiae cursus completus, Series Latina.* Ed. J. Migne.
OB	*Sancti Bernardi Opera.* Ed. J. Leclercq, C. F. Talbot, H. M. Rochais (Rome, 1957–).
OGE	*Ons geestelijk erf* (Antwerp, 1927–).
SC	*Sources chrétiennes,* ed. H. de Lubac and J. Daniélou (Paris, 1942–).
Spaapen	Bernard Spaapen, S. J., "Hadewijch en het vijfde Visioen." The five sections of this article, published in OGE, will be identified by date (1970–1972) and page numbers.
TNTL	*Tijdschrift voor Nederlandse taal- en letterkunde.* (Leiden, 1885–).
VBS	*Hadewijch: Brieven.* Trans. [into modern Dutch] F. Van Bladel, S. J., and B. Spaapen, S. J. (Tielt: Lannoo, 1954.)
W	Ruusbroec, *Werken.* 4 vols. 2nd ed. (Tielt: Lannoo, 1944–1948.)
William *NDA*	William of St. Thierry, *De natura et dignitate amoris.*

NOTES

INTRODUCTION

1. Cf. Simone Roisin, *L'hagiographie Cistercienne dans le diocèse de Liège au xiiie siècle* (Brussels: Editions Universitaires, 1947).

2. Van Mierlo, *Hadewijch, een Bloemlezing* (Amsterdam: Elsevier, 1950), p. 14.

3. Stephanus Axters, O.P., *Geschiedenis van de vroomheid in den Nederlanden*, vol. 1 (Antwerp: De Sikkel, 1950), p. 344.

4. Léonce Reypens, S.J., "Een nieuw Hadewijch-handschrift," *OGE* 37 (1963): 345. Norbert de Paepe dates it 1510; cf. *Hadewijch: Strofische Gedichten* (Ghent-Louvain: E. Story-Scientia, 1978), p. 9, note 24.

5. *De Wetten van de Minne: met de tekst van Hadewijchs 45 Strofische Gedichten volgens HS. 385 II van het Ruusbroecgenootschap*, 2 vols. (Bonheiden: Zusters Benedictinessen Priorij Bethlehem, [1977]).

6. Van Mierlo, *Bloemlezing*, p. 17; Jean Baptiste Porion, O.Cart., "Hadewijch, mystique flamande et poétesse, 13e siècle," DS 7 (1968): 15. Porion in *Hadewijch d'Anvers: Ecrits mystiques des Beguines* (Paris: Seuil, 1954), pp. 40–41, said that the doubts cast on the authenticity of the "List" have not been proved.

7. Axters, *Geschiedenis*, vol. 1, p. 345.

8. Alcuin Mens, *Oorsprong en betekenis van de Nederlandse Begijnen- en Begarden- beweging* (Antwerp: Standaard, 1944), pp. 409–427.

9. Jacques de Vitry, *Secundus Sermo ad Virgines*, quoted by Ernest McDonnell, *The Beguines and Beghards in Medieval Culture: With special emphasis on the Belgian Scene* (New Brunswick, N.J.: Rutgers University Press, 1954), p. 433.

10. Jacques de Vitry, *Epistola prima;* see R. Röhricht, *Briefe des Jacobus de Vitriaco*, in *Zeitschrift für Kirchengeschichte* 14 (1894): 103.

11. For Van Mierlo's opinion, see *Brieven*, vol. 1, p. 214. Cf. Porion, Hadewijch, *Lettres spirituelles: Béatrice de Nazareth, Sept degrés d'amour, traduction du moyen-néerlandais* (Geneva: Martingay, 1972), p. 194, note 1.

12. Barnard Spaapen, S.J., "Hadewijch en het vijfde Visioen," OGE (1970): 391.

13. Gosuin of Bossut, *Vita Idae Nivellensis*, 32, in Chrysostom Henriquez, *Quinque prudentes virgines* (Antwerp, 1630), pp. 284–285.

14. *Letters* 2: P. 14; 16: P. 56; 24: P. 1. Stanzaic Poem 8:26.

15. *Vita Beatricis: de autobiographie van de Z. Beatrijs van Tienen O. Cist. (1200–1268)*, ed. L. Reypens, S. J. (Antwerp: Ruusbroecgenootschap, 1964), cf. 1.2.19, pp. 23–24; 1.3.21, p. 25; and 1.6.35, p. 33.

16. *Vita Idae Lewensis* 2.6.13, in *Acta Sanctorum*, October, vol. 13 (Paris, 1883), p. 112. Cf. Reypens, "Ida van Zoutleeuw of Ida van Gorsleeuw?", OGE 26 (1952): 329–334.

17. The school of love is mentioned in the following Stanzaic Poems: 2:66; 6:54; 7:61; 11:48; 14, in five stanzas; 16:99; 28:48–54; and also in Poem 13:30.

18. Theodor Weevers, *Poetry of the Netherlands in its European Context 1170–1931* (London, 1960), p. 35.

NOTES

19. On the question of the models used by Hadewijch, see H. Schottmann, "Die Natureingang in den Liedern Hadewijchs," *Beiträge zur Geschichte der deutschen Sprache und Literatur* 93 (1971): 213–227.

20. Cf. Porion, *Hadewijch d'Anvers*, pp. 118–119; Alan of Lille, *De planctu naturae, quaest.* 6 (ML 210: 455–456).

21. Cf. H. Rahner, S. J., "Dreifaltigkeit," *Lexikon für Theologie und Kirche*², 3, 553.

22. J. Daniélou, S.J., *Platonisme et théologie mystique: doctrine spirituelle de Saint Grégoire de Nysse*, new ed. (Paris: Aubier, 1953), pp. 292–295.

23. The text of this lengthy poem is printed under Hildebert of Lavardin (ML 171:1411); only the title, with cross reference, under Peter Abelard (ML 178: 1818).

24. *Sententiarum Libri Tres*, 1.2.3 (ML 83:546).

25. *The Antiquities of the Jews*, 11.3.2–6, in *The Life and Works of Flavius Josephus*, trans. William Whiston, 1737 (Philadelphia: Winston reprint, 1957), pp. 324–325; Peter Comestor, *Historia Scholastica, Esdras 3* (ML 198: 1481).

26. Axters, *Geschiedenis*, vol. 1, pp. 367–368. *Hadewijch: Strophische Gedichten*, ed. Van Mierlo (Antwerp: Standaard, 1942), vol. 2, p. 121.

27. Norbert De Paepe, *Hadewijch Strofische Gedichten. Een studie van de minne in het kader der 12ᵉ en 13ᵉ eeuwse mystiek en profane minnelyriek* (Ghent: Koninklijke Vlaamse Academie, 1967), p. 331.

28. Spaapen, "Een boek over de minne bij Hadewijch," *Streven* 21: 811–813. A similar view is expressed by P. Mommaers in his forthcoming article "Hadewijch" in the *Verfasserlexikon:* "We truly wonder, however, whether his [De Paepe's] interpretation does not lose sight of the objective, divine reality to which this term certainly also refers."

29. *De Trinitate*, 10.11–12.17–19 (ML 42:982–984).

30. William NDA, 2.3 (ML 184:382). Cf. Porion, *Hadewijch, Lettres*, p. 173, note 9; and Etienne Gilson, *The Mystical Theology of St. Bernard*, trans. A. Downes, 2nd ed. (New York: Sheed and Ward, 1955), pp. 203–204.

31. R. Vanneste, "Over de betekenis van enkele abstracta in de taal van Hadewijch," *Studia Germanica* 1 (1959): 84.

32. Cf. Bernard of Clairvaux, *De diversis sermo XLV*, 1; OB 6–1: 262: "Memory becomes powerless and weak, reason imprudent and darkened, and the will impure and unclean."

33. Cf. Letter 28: P. 80, 101; Letter 30; Vision 11: P. 70; Vision 12: P. 105, P. 140, P. 152; Poem 16:191–196.

34. Porion, *Hadewijch, Lettres*, pp. 24–25.

35. In *Brieven*, vol. 1, p. 136.

36. Porion, *Hadewijch, Lettres*, p. 25.

37. *Brieven*, vol. 1, pp. 265–276; cf. Van Mierlo, "Adelwip," *Verslagen en Mededeelingen der Koninklijke Vlaamsche Academie* (1933): 581–598; and "De Adelwip uittreksels," ibid. (1934): 537–555.

38. F. Gooday, "Eine bisher unbekannte Hadewijch-Übersetzung," *Zeitschrift für deutsches Altertum und deutsche Literatur* 102 (1973): 236–238.

39. Axters, *Geschiedenis*, vol. 2 (1953), pp. 138–149.

40. Lode Moereels, "Giovanni di Ruysbroeck, beato," *Bibliotheca Sanctorum*, vol. 6 (1965), p. 881.

41. Letter 17; Ruusbroec, *Dat Rijcke der ghelieven,* 5: W vol. 1, pp. 99–100, lines 33–17.

42. Poem 16:30–40; *Dat Rijcke,* W vol. 1, p. 52, lines 14–25.

43. Porion, "Hadewijch, mystique," DS 7:21. See also Axters, *Geschiedenis,* vol. 2, pp. 270–273.

44. Vision 1: P. 341 (lines 351–356); Ruusbroec, *Die gheestelike brulocht,* W vol. 1, p. 111, lines 15–18; pp. 121–122, lines 32–4.

45. Letter 17: P. 11, P. 66, and P. 74: *Brulocht,* W vol. 1, p. 174, lines 13–25; p. 239, lines 17–20; pp. 248–249, lines 23–19.

46. Letter 12: P. 174; *Brulocht,* W vol. 1, p. 224, lines 8–9.

47. *Letters* 6: P. 227; 19: P. 46; 22: P. 90; 28: P. 121; Vision 7: P. 14; *Brulocht,* W vol. 1, p. 240, lines 13–15.

48. Letter 22: P. 348; *Brulocht,* W vol. 1, pp. 246–247.

49. Vision 1: P. 185; *Brulocht,* W vol. 1, p. 141, lines 26–28.

50. Letter 20: P. 113: *Brulocht,* W vol. 1, p. 200, lines 28–30.

51. Poems in Stanzas 30:46; 19:15–16; 6:69–72; Ruusbroec, *Vanden XIJ Beghinen,* W vol. 4. p. 4. Stanzaic Poem 11:88–89; *Vanden XIJ Beghinen,* p. 5, lines 16–17.

52. Letter 20: P. 97; Ruusbroec, *Van seven trappen,* W vol. 3, p. 268.

53. Cf. Gilson, *The Mystical Theology,* pp. 70–73.

54. Ruusbroec, *The Spiritual Espousals,* trans. E. Colledge (New York: Harper, 1953), p. 180.

55. See Van Mierlo's lists in *Brieven,* vol. 1, p. 307, and in *Visionen,* vol. 2, p. 114.

56. Cf. Visions 2: P. 18, and 3: P. 8 and note.

57. Cf. Van Mierlo, "Hadewijch en Willem van St.-Thierry," OGE 3 (1929): 45–59; Axters, *Geschiedenis,* vol. 1, p. 375; and P. Verdeyen, "De invloed van Willem van Saint-Thierry op Hadewijch en Ruusbroec," OGE 51 (1977): 3–19.

58. Cf. Marie Schalij, "Richard van St. Victor en Hadewijchs 10e Brief," TNTL 62 (1943): 219–228.

59. *Beatrijs van Nazareth. Van seuen manieren van heileger minnen,* ed. H. Vekeman and J. Tersteeg (Zutphen: Thieme, [1970]).

60. Porion, *Hadewijch, Lettres,* p. 217.

61. Jef Janssens, "Hadewijch en de riddercultur van haar tijd," *Ons geestelijk Leven* 54 (1977): 156–157.

62. Jannsens, *ibid.*, p. 163.

63. Tornada is the Provençal term for a concluding stanza that is shorter than the rest and repeats some of the rhymes of the stanza immediately preceding it.

64. Bosch, "Vale milies: De structuur van Hadewijch's bundel 'Strofische Gedichten,' " TNTL 90 (1974): 173–175.

65. Ibid., pp. 161–182.

66. De Paepe, *Hadewijch* (1967), p. 224, p. 215.

67. H. Schottmann, "Autor und Hörer in den 'Strophischen Gedichten' Hadewijchs," *Zeitschrift für deutsches Altertum und deutsche Literatur* 75 (1973): 34–35.

68. G. Kazemier, "Hadewijch en de minne in haar Strofische Gedich-

ten," TNTL 87 (1971): 255–257. J. Reynaert, "Het doodsmotief bij Hadewijch," *Studia Germanica Gandensis* 17 (1976): 8, does not speak explicitly of imprisonment or execution.

69. T. Brandsma, O. Carm., "Wanneer schreef Hadewych hare Visioenen?", *Studia Catholica* 2 (1926): 240–247.

70. McDonnell, *The Beguines,* p. 491.

71. Cf. Spaapen (1970) 11; Vekeman, "Hadewijch," p. 360.

72. *Benjamin Major,* 5.12 (ML 196: 180–182).

73. Gunnar Qvarnström, *Poetry and numbers: on the structural use of symbolic numbers* (Lund: Gleerup, 1966), pp. 24–25.

74. *Visioenen,* vol. 2 (1925), p. 52; and *Hadewijch: een Bloemlezing,* p. 16. See De Paepe, *Hadewijch* (1967), pp. 149–151. Cf. Spaapen (1970): 36–37; and (1972): 198–199.

75. Vekeman, "Angelus sane nuntius. Een interpretatie van het visioenenboek van Hadewijch," OGE 50 (1976): 259.

76. Ruusbroec, *Brulocht,* W vol. 1, pp. 163–164, trans. Colledge, *The Spiritual Espousals,* p. 107.

77. Vekeman, "Angelus," p. 240.

78. Spaapen (1970): 9.

79. *Visioenen,* vol. 1, p. 79; cf. P. Mommaers, "Het VIIe en VIIIe Visioen van Hadewijch: affectie in de mystieke beleving," OGE 49 (1975): 110.

80. Cf. Bosch, "Vale milies," pp. 177–179; Huisman, J., *Neue Wege zur dichterischen und musikalischen Technik Walthers von der Vogelweide. Mit einem Exkurs über die symmetrische Zahlenkomposition im Mittelalter* (Utrecht: Kemink, 1950), pp. 53–65. See Bernard of Clairvaux, *In Assumptione Beatae Mariae Sermo 2,* 9; OB 5:238; and *In Nativitate Beatae Mariae Sermo,* 9 and 11; ibid., pp. 281 and 283.

81. Porion, private letter, quoted by Spaapen (1972): 132, note 43.

82. *Enarrationes in Ps. 49,* 9 (CCSL 38: 583–584). It must be noted that strong expressions against the Jews are frequent in Christian writing of the past. They would be contrary to contemporary norms as stated for instance in the *Declaration on the Relation of the Church to Non-Christian Religions* of Vatican II.

83. Of the fourteen verses of Ps. 107, verses 1–5 are practically identical with Ps. 56:8-12; and verses 8–14 are practically identical with Ps. 59, verses 8–14. In Augustine's *Ennarationes,* for Ps. 107 the reader is referred to the appropriate verses of Ps. 56 and Ps. 59. For Ps. 107:2, see Enarrationes in Ps. 56, 15 (CCSL 39: 705).

84. Augustine is tenth, Paul fourteenth ("List," p. 180 and p. 185).

85. See for instance Letter 28: P. 30.

86. *Enarrationes in Ps. 56,* 17 (CCSL 39: 706–707).

87. *Enarrationes in Ps. 59,* 8 (CCSL 39: 759–760).

88. Rhymed Letter 8 is very short, and seven lines are closely similar to Rhymed Letter 6:47–53.

89. Cf. M. Brauns, S.J., "Hadewych en haar school," *Streven* N.R. 6 (1952): 10, and 15–16.

90. *Hadewijch: Mengeldichten,* ed. Van Mierlo (Antwerp: Standaard, 1952), pp. vi–vii.

NOTES

91. Cf. Axters, "Hadewijch en de scholastiek," *Leuvense Bijdragen* (1942): 107–108.

92. Origen, *Selecta in Genesim* (MG 12: 124C). Augustine, *Sermo CXCII, In Natali Domini*, 2 (ML 38: 1012); and *Sancta Virginitas*, 5 (ML 40: 399). Bede, *In Lucae evangelium expositio*, 4.11.28 (CCSL 120: 237).

93. Guerric, *De annuntiatione Domini Sermo 2*, 4–5 (ML 185: 122D–124A).

94. Poem 1:8–9, 11–13, 111–114, and 296–297.

95. *Epistola ad Fratres de Monte Dei*, P. 263 (SC 223: 354). *Expositio super Cantica Canticorum*, P. 95 and 132 (SC 82: 220–222 and 282–284).

96. Cf. Vision 1: P. 163. Van Mierlo indicates the main divisions of Letter 28 as follows: Introduction, 1–9. Part 1, the contemplation of God, 10–120. Part 2, Contemplation of God and the soul united with God: with the Father, 121–195; with the Son, 196–241; and with the Holy Spirit, 242–270.

97. Brauns, "Hadewych," pp. 9–10.

98. Van Mierlo, in *Hadewijch: een Bloemlezing*, p. 41.

99. Caesarius of Heisterbach, *Dialogus Miraculorum: Distinctio duodecima de praemio mortuorum*, 1–22, ed. J. Strange (Cologne: Heberle, 1851; Gregg reprint 1966), vol. 2, pp. 315–332; Gosuin of Bossut, *Vita Idae Nivellensis*, 13–14, pp. 232–237.

100. *Hadewijch: een Bloemlezing*, p. 41.

101. "List," p. 188.

102. Brauns, "Hadewych," p. 11.

103. Vatican Council II: Dogmatic Constitution on the Church, *Lumen Gentium*, in *Acta Apostolicae Sedis* 57 (1965): 66–67.

104. Cf. *L'Osservatore Romano Weekly edition in English* N. 12. 573 (March 19, 1979): 12–13.

LETTERS

1. See Introduction p. 10 and p. 16.

2. The translation "in imitation of the Son" seems called for by the word *ieghenwordeghen*, used here by Hadewijch with the implication of "in conformity with the Son." The basic idea of her use of this word and its cognates, that of the "presence" of the Son to the Father, will recur a number of times in Letter 28 (see P. 12, etc.). As regards the soul's relation to God, this "presence" carries the sense of conformity. (Cf. Van Mierlo, *Brieven*, vol. 1, p. 312, col. 2; and VBS, p. 17.)

3. Cf. Poem 12:129–139.

4. See Bernard of Clairvaux, *De consideratione, Praef.*; OB 3:394: "I will instruct you therefore not as a master, but as a mother: in fact as a lover."

5. Hadewijch now speaks of the Trinity as Truth (the Son), Goodness (the Holy Spirit), and Totality (the Father).

6. The Father is seen here not only as the Source without source of the Trinity but also as the whole Divine Nature in which, before the procession of the Persons, all works and attributes of the Three Persons lie hidden. VBS, p. 17. See Introduction, p. 7.

7. The phraseology of this Letter now and then suggests Letter 28.

8. J. Reynaert, "Het licht in de beeldspraak van Hadewijch," OGE 48 (1974): 30, says of this: "Emanating from God, the light—which is Love—reaches no terminus in the loving soul but is as it were horizontally prolonged in the relation of a man to the world surrounding him." Hadewijch says also in Letter 30: P. 114: "At all hours one wills the will of Love . . . and exercises all the virtues . . . and enlightens all creatures according to what they are." Cf. Letter 12: P. 204, and Vision 10: P. 29, "Sinners . . . are enlightened by the knowledge of your union."

9. Hadewijch frequently mentions the Angels and their choirs but, unlike most medieval writers, she rarely refers to the devil.

10. Theme of self-knowledge. See Introduction p. 16.

11. Hadewijch often refers to the importance of grace. Cf. Letter 10: P. 1.

12. See Introduction p. 7, Hadewijch's dynamic approach to spirituality.

13. "The hidden word" is actually mentioned by Eliphaz. The *locus classicus* for the mystical application of this text is Gregory the Great, *Moralia*, 5.28.50 (ML 75:705–706). Spaapen (1970): 127, note 34, lists occurrences of the word "hidden" in Hadewijch.

14. "Proud" (*fier*) in the good sense; see Letter 6: P. 191, note.

15. Reference to our ideal existence in God. See below, note 22.

16. Hadewijch is making the same statement as Gregory of Nyssa, who says in *The Life of Moses*, Prologue, P. 7, p. 31: "Certainly whoever pursues true virtue participates in nothing other than God, because he is himself absolute virtue." Cf. Spaapen (1971): 143.

17. The repeated command "Reform yourself!" explains Hadewijch's emphasis on the errors of reason. Some special difficulty made this instruction necessary. From many other passages in her works we know how highly she prized the faculty of reason as bestowed on us by God to enable us to walk securely in his paths. On the image of the Trinity in the soul, see Introduction pp. 9–10.

18. Cf. Bernard *SC 61*, 3.7–8; OB 2:153.

19. Bernard of Clairvaux, *De gratia et libero arbitrio*, 5.15; OB 3:177, teaches that in ecstasy man's lost liberty is momentarily restored; here Hadewijch points out an attitude radically opposed to ecstasy. For the whole question of the meaning Hadewijch attaches to liberty, see below, note 34.

20. Cf. Virgil, *Eclogae*, 10.69: "Love conquers all things."

21. See Introduction, p. 12.

22. Our ideal life in God. See Introduction, "exemplarism," p. 6.

23. The preceding lines are a clear reference to the latter part of Vision 1.

24. Bernard *SC 85*, 3.8; OB 2: 312: "Where there is love, there is no labor."

25. "Of both" means of the Humanity and Divinity in Christ.

26. Evidently a reference to Vision 13: P. 66.

27. "To read one's judgments in God's countenance" is a formula derived by William of Saint Thierry from Ps. 16:2, *Let my judgment come forth from thy countenance.* See William *NDA*, 8.23 (ML 184:394BC): "Knowing all

her judgments from his face, she finds it sweet to gaze upon that face constantly, and to read therein, as if in the book of life, the laws by which she should live." Hadewijch often returns to this idea; in her poetry she usually speaks of "the countenance of Love."

28. Supreme Truth, according to Spaapen (1970): 120, note 22, is to be understood here in the Johannine sense, as the divine Reality that in the Father lies open to the Son, and the Father reveals in the Son. The mystically graced soul is taken up with the Son in this Reality.

29. Cf. Poem 16:100, on "fire" as a name of love: "It burns up everything it ever touches."

30. Hadewijch uses the noun *fierheit* with the meaning of pride in the good sense nine times, and far more frequently the corresponding adjective *fier*. It is particularly interesting that Beatrice of Nazareth uses the same term (*naturalis et nobilis illa superbia*), *Vita Beatricis*, 2.10.222, p. 87. In this passage Beatrice also mentions "the contrary pride," *ex contrarie radice superbie;* this indicates that the source behind both authors is Jerome's *Commentarius in Isaiam.* Regarding Isa. 61:6, *You shall eat the wealth of the Gentiles, and in their glory you shall take pride,* he says (ML 24:601D–602A): "Not with that pride which is evil, which God resists so that he may give grace to the humble [cf. James 4:6]; but with that pride which appertains to power and glory"; and again, *Glossa ordinaria,* on Isa. 60:15 (ML 113:1304A): "*Because there was none that passed through thee, I will make thee to be an everlasting cause of pride, a joy unto generation and generation*—a pride that is sometimes good and sometimes bad." Good pride is not unknown to the classic authors (cf. Horace, *Carminum Liber*, 3.30.14), but the Church Fathers except for Jerome speak of pride only as a vice. See Porion, *Hadewijch, Lettres,* pp. 30–33.

31. See Introduction, p. 16. For this theme cf. *Letters* 22: P. 90; 28: P. 121; and Vision 7: P. 14.

32. On the theme of dying to the world as an aspect of the life of love, J. Reynaert, "Het doodsmotief," pp. 11–12, quotes apposite passages from Augustine, Gregory the Great, William of Saint Thierry, Bernard of Clairvaux, and the anonymous *De charitate.*

33. Allusion to the Sacred Heart's love as the fulfillment of the greatest commandment; cf. Letter 15: P. 16, and Letter 24: P. 64.

34. The term *liberty* in Hadewijch differs from the modern sense, especially in that it is rather metaphysical than psychological. Her thought here can be understood from Bernard of Clairvaux's *De gratia et libero arbitrio.* Man, Bernard says, created to God's image and likeness, could not, by the fall, lose the image (chiefly in free will), but he did lose the likeness (capacity to do the good and capacity to possess and enjoy the good). In other words, man lost liberty from sin and liberty from misery, and these two liberties he must recover. See E. Gilson, *The Mystical Theology*, pp. 46–52.

35. Cf. Stanzaic Poem 9:21.

36. The mystical Divine Touch. L. Reypens, "Ruusbroec-Studien, I. Het mystieke 'gherinen,'" OGE 12 (1938): 158, traces the use of the word in this sense to Hugh of Saint Victor who, in the *Soliloquium de arrha animae* (ML 176:970C) says of the soul's Bridegroom: "He comes that he may touch thee, not that he may be seen by thee." Reypens lists many instances in the

NOTES

Poems in Stanzas; cf. Stanzaic Poem 7:24. The Touch is also mentioned in *Visions* 4: P. 50 and 11: P. 98. The striking passage in Vision 13: P. 179 ascribes it to the Holy Spirit; elsewhere, Hadewijch refers it to Love.

37. The Platonic axiom: "Only like knows like."

38. Cf. Stanzaic Poems 38:53; 39:99; and 40:22, 66.

39. This concept of paradoxical "noble unfaith" (*ontrouwe*) recurs in Vision 13: P. 179, and in Poem 10:87–102. Porion, *Hadewijch d'Anvers,* p. 119, thinks she may well have borrowed it from Alan of Lille, *De planctu, quaest.* 6 (ML 210:456A): "And it is faith not to have had faith."

40. Cf. Poem 11:18–22.

41. The subtitle we have given this poem (John 15:5) seems appropriate, the text being mentioned as illustrative of Letter 9 by both Van Mierlo, *Brieven,* vol. 1, p. 79, and VBS, p. 24.

42. "Who God is and what God is." Cf. William of Saint Thierry, *Meditativae orationes,* 3.1 (ML 180:241C): "For [Moses] would perhaps have looked upon the Lord face to face, if he had wished to look upon God not as who he is, but as what he is." The theme was taken over by Ruusbroec, *Vanden XIJ Beghinen,* W 4:21–22. "Behold me, who and what I am!" Cf. *Visions* 2: P. 18, and 3: P. 8, for "What and who is Love."

43. Theme of the Sacred Heart. See Letter 24: P. 64 and 70.

44. See Introduction, p. 17. After the first three or four lines of preliminaries, this letter (except for lines 19–50, which are Hadewijch's own), is a free adaptation of thoughts in Richard of Saint Victor's *Explicatio in Cantica Canticorum,* 6 (ML 196:422B–423C). Richard's text is reprinted by Van Mierlo in *Brieven,* vol. 2, pp. 39–40.

45. Nearly all the repetitions of the word *grace* in this Letter come from Hadewijch's source; but elsewhere in Letters and Visions she stresses the importance of grace.

46. "To be Love"; this theme occurs likewise in Visions 2, P. 8, and 3, P. 8. See also Beatrice, *Van seuen manieren,* p. 41.

47. "His Lovcress" is the Virgin Mary. Bernard of Clairvaux, *In laudibus virginis matris, Homilia 1,* 5; OB 4:17–18, says that it was chiefly because of Mary's humility that the Holy Spirit came upon her and she conceived Christ. Mary's humility is one of Hadewijch's major themes; cf. Stanzaic Poem 29; Poems 2:47–72, and 14:35–44; and Vision 13: P. 159 and P. 218 (where Hadewijch hears Mary praise humility).

48. This is the only humility formula in Letter 12.

49. The theme of eternal progress even in the life of heaven, as found in Gregory of Nyssa, is alluded to in this passage; see also a little further on in P. 40, and the comments of Spaapen (1971): 151–152. Cf. Introduction p. 7.

50. *Regiratio.*

51. Stressing the opposites *love* and *hate,* Hadewijch is referring in a roundabout way to the theme of loving and hating with God. This theme originates in the *Visions,* most if not all of which occurred before the *Letters* were written. See Vision 5: P. 12 and note.

52. For reason as our rule, see also Letter 18: P. 154; Vision 12: P. 98; and Poem 3: 104–106.

NOTES

53. Principal statement of Hadewijch's theme that we must conquer God so that God may conquer us, on the model of Jacob's wrestling with the Angel. (The rhyme more or less hidden in lines 184–185: *Want iacob bleef ten stride cranc, Ende ye sider ane die een side manc,* is found again in the return of the theme in Stanzaic Poem 28:41–43: *Si maect den staerken cranc, . . ., Si maect den rechten manc.*) This theme of wrestling with God like Jacob is set forth by Guerric of Igny, *In nativitate sancti Joannis Baptistae Sermo 2,* 1–2 (ML 185-1:167–168). The idea expressed by Hadewijch of becoming or being Jacob is found in Richard of Saint Victor, *Benjamin Major,* 1.2 (ML 196:65D).

54. Idea that they who love are a source of light, already met with in Letter 1: P. 33; see Vision 10:29.

55. *We should live soberly and justly and godly in this world.*

56. *My Beloved to me, and I to him.*

57. Self-knowledge by self-examination.

58. Here, as in Letter 6: P. 324, Hadewijch implies that the Sacred Heart's love is the perfect fulfillment of the greatest commandment.

59. Bernard *SC 15,* 3.6: OB 1:86.

60. This paragraph, warning against idleness and emphasizing good works, shows how far Hadewijch is from teaching quietism.

61. See Introduction, p. 11.

62. The Father as the Principle of the Trinity (see Introduction p. 7.) With reference to the present passage, Axters, "Hadewijch als voorloopster van de zalige Jan van Ruusbroec," in *Dr. L. Reypens-Album* (Antwerp, 1964), pp. 67–68, quotes Augustine, *De Trinitate,* 4.20.28: ". . . Showing that the principle of the whole Divinity, or more correctly speaking, of the whole Deity, is the Father." Ruusbroec also quotes this passage of Augustine in *Van den gheestelijken tabernakel,* 5.64: W 2:151, lines 5–7.

63. Idea of darkness of the Divine Unity, as surpassing all knowledge.

64. The Father as the Principle of the Trinity. That the Father "engulfs" the Son in himself means the return into the Godhead.

65. "Those in hell" may mean persons still living, who by their sins merit damnation.

66. Van Mierlo, *Brieven,* vol. 1, p. 143, explains that as long as man is fully united to love, he is Godlike (conformed to God); and the will, work, and power of such a man are simple in his simplicity, as the Three Persons are one in the Divine Being.

67. This kiss is a token of Hadewijch's union with the Son, VBS, p. 288, note 48.

68. Hadewijch insists that the life of the virtues is the only way to attain to the fruition of Love.

69. See Introduction, p. 16.

70. Allusion to our ideal life in God.

71. "Bless" is here translated "commend." For the theme see Letter 22: P. 108.

72. This beautiful image of love as the crown of the soul recurs in Letter 30: P. 214, and seems implied in Vision 13:195 where we hear of the souls "adorned like Love as to all their attire and ornaments."

73. Cf. William of Saint Thierry, *De contemplando* 11 (SC 61:98), "Thou

dost love thyself in us." The editor, J. Hourlier, p. 99, note 2, traces this statement back to Scotus Erigena's translation of Dionysius, *De Devisione naturae,* 1.76 (ML 122:522BC).

74. Hadewijch's borrowing from William NDA, 8.21–23 (ML 184:393–395), begins with P. 80 and ends just before P. 130. The two texts are printed in parallel columns in *Brieven,* vol. 2, pp. 22–25.

75. This carefully balanced statement on false liberty is important for our understanding of Hadewijch.

76. Reason as our rule.

77. The reference to John's resting on Christ's breast implies the theme of the Sacred Heart.

78. Song 2:16.

79. Good pride.

80. Exemplarism.

81. Hadewijch has altered the second half of this verse from Jeremiah.

82. Spaapen (1971): 134 thinks this last sentence is based on William of Saint Thierry, for instance, *Epistola,* P. 258 (SC 223:348–350): "To be unable to will anything except what God wills—this is to be already what God is."

83. J. Reynaert, "Het licht" (see pp. 31–39), maintains that in lines 62–72, mystical love and reason are set forth under the symbols of sun and moon.

84. See Introduction, p. 17.

85. A Fonck, "Mystique (Théologie)," *Dictionnaire de Théologie Catholique,* vol. 10–2 (Paris, 1929): 2612–13, thinks Hadewijch's mysticism, especially as expressed in Letter 20, is related to the theory of the "mystical circle" of love in Pseudo Dionysius, *De divinis nominibus,* 4.14 (MG 3:712–713); cf. G. Horn, "Amour et extase d'après Denys l'Aréopagite," *Revue d'ascétique et de mystique* 6 (1925): 283–286. (Other scholars do not urge any direct influence.)

86. From this sentence it is inferred that the Twelve Hours fall into three groups of four, corresponding respectively to the seeking mind, desiring heart, and loving soul.

87. For this text, cf. Letter 22: P. 362.

88. Theme of loving without measure. See Bernard of Clairvaux, *De diligendo Deo* 1.1; OB 3:119: "The reason for loving God, is God; the measure is, to love without measure." Also found in a letter to Augustine, *Epistola CIX* (ML 33:419), from Severus of Mileve in Numidia: "No measure in loving God is imposed on us, since the very measure in this is to love without measure."

89. Cf. Stanzaic Poem 13:61.

90. The word *mastership* connotes that the command "Love ye Love" is the first principle taught by Love in her school. Cf. Axters, "Hadewijch en de Scholastiek," p. 99.

91. Cf. Ruusbroec, *Brulocht,* W 1:200: "Here man is possessed by love, so that he is able to forget himself and God, and know of nothing else but love." Probably Hadewijch's meaning is best understood by comparing her other passages on love, especially where she refers to the primacy of love in Scripture. When she writes on *Audi filia, Hearken, O daughter* (Ps. 44:11–12) in Poem 12:45–65, she establishes a harmonious relation between God's scriptural command to the soul and the concept of pure love.

92. Vanneste, "Over de betekenis," p. 60, points out that Hadewijch's

thought here corresponds to that of Bernard of Clairvaux in *De praecepto et dispensatione*, 20.60: OB 3:293: "He who loves God is present to God in proportion as he loves him. For insofar as he loves God less, he is certainly absent from him."

93. The source of Letter 22 is a stanza of the hymn *Alpha et Omega, magne Deus*, ascribed both to Hildebert of Lavardin, Bishop of Tours (ML 171:1411), and to Peter Abelard (ML 178:1818). See Introduction p. 7 and p. 17. The text of the stanza is as follows:

Super cuncta, subter cuncta;
Extra cuncta, intra cuncta.
Extra cuncta, nec exclusus;
Intra cuncta, nec inclusus;
Super cuncta, nec elatus;
Subter cuncta, nec substratus.

The theme of these verses occurs in several of the Fathers, for instance, in Gregory the Great, *Moralia*, 2.12.20 (ML 75:565). The passage closest in wording to *Alpha et Omega* is found in Isidore, *Sententiarum Libri Tres*, 1.2.3 (ML 83:541), particularly in the words: *Immensitas divinae magnitudinis ita est, ut intelligamus eum intra omnia, sed non inclusum; extra omnia, sed non exclusum.*

94. Vanneste, "Over de betekenis," p. 24, note 1, points out that this word *heeft* in Hadewijch's text may be either "exalts" (accepted by Van Mierlo), or "has," and that "has" gives a richer sense, corresponding to Augustine, *De Trinitate*, 6.4.6 (ML 42:927): "For the human soul, to be is not to be strong, or prudent, or just, or temperate; it can be a soul and have none of these virtues. But for God, to be is to be strong, or just, or wise, and anything else you may mention of that simple multiplicity or multiplex simplicity whereby his substance is signified." Cf. E. Gilson, *The Christian Philosophy of Saint Augustine*, trans. L. Lynch (London: Gollancz, 1961), p. 353, note 6.

95. The Divine Essence is thought of as obscure, and the procession of the Persons as radiant (cf. Porion, *Hadewijch, Lettres*, p. 171, note 5).

96. For the theme of "condemn or bless," see Vision 5: P. 12.

97. The preexistence of creatures in God.

98. Axters, "Hadewijch en de Scholastiek," p. 105, explains the four ways as mystical union with God.

99. Is this an echo of Augustine, *Ennarationes in Ps. 101*, 10 (CCSL 40:1445): "Eternity is the very substance of God"? Quoted by Gilson, *The Christian Philosophy*, p. 22 and p. 258, note 46.

100. Theme of the created Trinity in the soul. Cf. William *NDA*, 2.3 (ML 184:382). For Vanneste's explanation of this passage of Hadewijch, see Introduction, p. 9. Her longest development of the theme is in Poem 4:15–24.

101. Theme of the Eucharist; see also P. 285.

102. Theme of the kiss. See Letter 24: P. 38.

103. This is the first instance of "despair" (*onthope*) used in the paradoxical sense of a virtue. It is closely related to paradoxical "unfaith"; see above, Letter 8, P. 27 and note 39. Schottmann, "Autor," p. 29, points to a few phrases used by Richard of Saint Victor to describe the fourth degree of charity in his *De quatuor gradibus violentae caritatis*, ed. G. Dumeige, *Ives: Epître à Séverin sur la charité, Richard de Saint-Victor: les quatre degrés de la violente char-*

ité (Paris: Vrin, 1955). Richard singles out the notes of despair and of a contradictory state of hating and loving at one and the same time (15–16, pp. 141–143).

104. Theme of the Sacred Heart; see Letter 24: P. 64 and 72.

105. Into the Father, seen as unity of Nature; cf. VBS, p. 289, note 76.

106. Exemplarism; in the Son all creatures exist ideally.

107. On the choirs of Angels, see below, Vision 1: P. 24, note.

108. These three words not in the text are required by the argument.

109. "Right" as attribute of the Father before the procession of the Persons. (VBS, p. 289, note 77).

110. This text is applied to Love in Letter 20: P. 38.

111. Van Mierlo, *Brieven,* vol. 1, p. 85, explains that the justice of the Father and the jubilation of the Spirit are deep and dark, as in the Unity.

112. The extraordinary vividness of the imagery in this and the following paragraph suggests that Hadewijch may be speaking of one of the visions she did not write out.

113. No later than the second century the four living creatures in Ezechiel and the Apocalypse began to be taken as symbols of the four Evangelists. The first writer known to have made this application is Irenaeus in *Adversus haereses* 3.11.8 (MG 7:885–890), where he assigns the lion to John and the eagle to Mark. Since Jerome's *Commentarius in evangelium secundum Matthaeum, Prologus* (ML 26:19), the custom familiar to us of assigning the lion to Mark and the eagle to John has predominated.

114. Theme of the eagle as symbolizing the contemplative soul. Cf. Gregory the Great, *Moralia,* 31.47.94 (ML 76:625CD).

115. Found in Tertullian, *Liber de anima,* 8.4 (CCSL 2:794); Ambrose, *Hexaemeron,* 5.18.60 (ML 14:246B), and *In Psalmum CXVIII,* 19.13 (ML 15:1549C); and Isidore, *Etymologiae,* 12.7.11 (ML 82: 460B).

116. *Sancti Benedicti Regula Monachorum,* ed. P. Schmitz, 2nd ed. (Maredsous, 1955), 4:88–89, p. 58.

117. Ibid., 71:16–18, p. 138.

118. Here and in P. 72 Hadewijch passes immediately from the Sacred Heart to the heart of man; she makes the same association in Letter 30: P. 123. Cf. Letters 9: P. 41; 18: P. 174; 22: P. 183 and 201; and 28: P. 149.

119. Theme of the necessity of living the life of the virtues.

120. See Introduction p. 4.

121. Definition of the Beloved's kiss.

122. A numerical study by J. Reynaert, "Attributieproblemen in verband met de *Brieven* van Hadewijch," OGE (1975): 225–247, supports the old claim of Marie Van Der Zeyde, in *Hadewijch. Een studie over de mens en de schrijfster* (Groningen: 1934), p. 126, that Hadewijch could not be the author of Letter 28, which differs so greatly from her other works. Vekeman, however, in "Hadewijch, een interpretatie van de Brieven," pp. 349–361, has just pointed out unmistakable similarities between Letter 28 and Letter 1, arguing that since information lacking in Letter 1 is found in Letter 28, the latter must have been written previous to Letter 1, and thus incidentally upholding the authenticity of Letter 28.

123. Vekeman, in the article of 1974 just mentioned, p. 353, suggests that

this passage is perhaps a parallel of William *NDA,* 11.32 (ML 184:400B): "In the height recognize power; in the depth, wisdom; in the breadth, charity; and in the length, eternity or truth. And this is the cross of Christ."

124. The Father as the Source without source of the Godhead (VBS, p. 290, note 89).

125. This sentence recalls Vision 6: P. 76: "Wonder seized me because of all the riches I had seen in him."

126. Clarification of the Trinity formulas of the preceding paragraph.

127. Another paragraph on the Trinity.

128. Compare this sentence, and the allusion to God's nobility a few lines above, with Letter 6: P. 350: "Love shall manifest herself and reveal her noble power and rich omnipotence on earth and in heaven."

129. The "throne of thrones" (Biblical style) means God's throne.

130. Theme of God, Christ, as the soul's friend. The repetition four times of the term *friendship* is remarkable. This theme occurs in Letters 11: P. 10; 12: P. 53; and 14: P. 3; and in Vision 5: P. 12.

131. Idea of the darkness of the Divine Essence, as surpassing all knowledge.

132. "One person" means Hadewijch herself.

133. Theme of the Sacred Heart.

134. Theme of love without measure; God's measureless love answers that of the soul. See below, P. 214.

135. Inebriation in the mystical sense—the *sobria ebrietas* of Ambrose's liturgical hymn sung on Monday at Lauds, *Splendor paternae gloriae.* The image is borrowed from the writings of Philo Judaeus, see for instance his *Vita Mosis,* 1.34.187. Cf. Gregory of Nyssa, *The Life of Moses,* p. 178, note 198.

136. The theme of mystical play; see 2 Kings 6:5 and 21, and particularly Prov. 8:30, speaking of wisdom: *I was with him forming all things: and was delighted every day, playing before him at all times; playing in the world.* Cf. G. Petitdemange, "Jeu," DS 8:1159–62.

137. Vekeman, "Hadewijch. Een interpretatie van de Brieven," p. 359. points out the correspondence between "no one blames her," and the *Nihil ibi agunt conturbationes hominum,* "here the disturbance of men effects nothing" (cf. Ps. 30:21) in William of Saint Thierry's presentation of spiritual inebriation in his *Expositio super cantica canticorum,* 117 (SC 82: 254).

138. The opposites *silence* and *noise,* in the spiritual sense, occur several times in Hadewijch. See for instance Stanzaic Poem 25:30.

139. Here VBS, p. 259, and Porion, *Hadewijch: Lettres,* p. 209, expand "Both" to "Both these souls," referring to P. 196 and P. 207 of the text.

140. Vanneste, "Over de betekenis," p. 74, quotes P. 262 as corresponding to Bernard of Clairvaux, *De gratia,* 5.15; OB 3:177 (the recovery in ecstasy of man's lost liberties).

141. For the persecution of Ida of Nivelles, see Introduction pp. 4–5.

142. Cf. Vision 5: P. 68. This may refer to either charismatic or mystical graces.

143. Spaapen (1971): 147 says that Hadewijch has had, and wishes to have, no other fulfillment of her longing for God except that it remain unsatisfied—the theme of Gregory of Nyssa, cf. *The Life of Moses,* P. 235, p. 115.

144. The source and meaning of these expressions are unknown.

145. Van Mierlo, in *Brieven*, vol. 1, p. 241, thinks this means that Hadewijch assisted others in a miraculous way, and that they harmed her by making this known. Three references can be found to Hadewijch's wonderful deeds or miracles, all of them obscure (*Visions* 1: P. 364; 11: P. 98; and 14: P. 95). Cf. Vekeman, "Hadewijch, een interpretatie van de Brieven," pp. 346–347.

146. M. Brauns, "Hadewych," pp. 12–13, finds this passage significant as showing that in the feminine qualities of her mind and heart, Hadewijch was transformed by the Divine Touch.

147. Exemplarism.

148. See Introduction, p. 17. Van Mierlo discusses Letter 30 in "Hadewijch: une mystique flamande du treizième siècle," *Revue d'ascétique et de mystique*," 5 (1924): 288–289.

149. On the importance of the theme of the death of Christ in Hadewijch's mysticism, see J. Reynaert, "Het doodsmotief," p. 8 and especially note 9. Cf. Letter 6: P. 272–290 and P. 361; Stanzaic Poem 13:61; and *Visions* 12 P. 112 and 3: P. 8.

150. Parallel passage to Letter 1: P. 33.

151. "Power" is referred to the Father.

152. Theme of the Sacred Heart.

153. Both VBS, p. 275, and Porion, *Hadewijch, Lettres*, p. 222, translate "is" here as "lives."

154. The lightning and thunder are a powerful nature-image of the gift of grace from God's infinite light in the Trinity, and then the merciless demand of the Unity that the soul enter into oneness. Cf. Spaapen (1970): 125.

155. The meaning appears to be: "It becomes all that Love is."

156. Beginning of the true mystical life, when the soul passes from multiplicity of gifts into oneness with the Giver.

157. Theme of the soul as mother of Christ. See Introduction p. 33.

158. This spiritual hunger is an expression of the theme of eternal progress for which Hadewijch is indebted to Gregory of Nyssa. Gregory usually employs the figure of thirst. "Thirst" is used by Hadewijch only once (Stanzaic Poem 40:39), but "hunger" in this sense she introduces quite frequently.

159. The phrase *liberty of love* occurs in *Visions* 1: P. 138, and 13: P. 159; and in Poem 1: 108.

POEMS IN STANZAS

1. On the interpretation of Stanzaic Poem 1, see Introduction, p. 21.

2. The Latin refrain is drawn from the Latin Sequences of the Church, as is shown by J. Bosch, "Vale Milies," pp. 173–175, where he quotes apposite Latin phrases from *Analecta Hymnica Medii Aevi*, ed. G. Dreves and C. Blume (Leipzig: Reisland, 1886–1922).

3. In the *Poems in stanzas*, Hadewijch often follows the troubadours by beginning with a nature picture that, thanks to her consummate art, enhances her spiritual message. Cf. H. Schottmann, "Die Natureingang in den

Liedern Hadewijchs," *Beiträge zur Geschichte der deutschen Sprache und Literatur*, 93 (1971): 213–227.

4. This is a theme of courtly love; cf. J. Reynaert, "Het doodsmotief," pp. 12–13.

5. Axters, *Geschiedenis*, vol. 1, p. 374, states that Maria Schalij—in "Richard van St. Victor en Hadewijchs 10de Brief," TNTL 42 (1943): 219–228, and "S. Bernardus' De Diligendo Deo de grondslag voor het 41stc Limburgse Sermoen," ibid. pp. 256–269—discovered in Letter 10 the schema of Bernard of Clairvaux's *De diligendo Deo*, viz. his four degrees of love. Compare Stanzaic Poems 1, and 12:19–20.

6. Jerome seems to have been the first to use this phrase; cf. *Epistola LXXXII*, 11 (ML 22:742); Richard of Saint Victor, *Explicatio in Cantica*, 28 (ML 196:488C). Hadewijch repeats it in Stanzaic Poem 45:23.

7. Theme of the Eucharist.

8. For the school theme, see Introduction p. 5. The fullest development of the school of love occurs in Stanzaic Poem 14; see also 6:54; 7:61; 11:48; 16:99; 28:48–54; and Poem 13:30.

9. Cf. Stanzaic Poems 36:114 and 40:13.

10. Theme of hunger for God (for Love): see Letter 31: P. 1. Hadewijch's fullest development is found in Stanzaic Poem 33.

11. Schottmann, "Autor and Hörer," p. 27, remarks that the tornada, as often, changes from "I" to "we"; Hadewijch is addressing her young Beguines as a group.

12. Lines 16–17 are the same as Poem 16:20–21.

13. The series of antitheses referring to Love, which begin each of the four remaining stanzas of the poem, will develop what is meant by these "hours."

14. Lines 43–44 refer to Love's modes of action.

15. Lines 35–36 describe the effect on the soul of the sun of Love.

16. Schottmann, "Autor und Hörer," p. 31, points out that in this stanza Hadewijch addresses her complaints to Love not in her own behalf, but in behalf of her young Beguines.

17. Renewal is one of the principal motifs of Hadewijch's writings; cf. Spaapen, "Le Mouvement des 'Frères du libre esprit' et les mystiques flamandes du xiiie siècle," *Revue d'ascétique et de mystique* 42 (1966): 435–436. Stressed especially in Stanzaic Poems 1 and 33, it is most explicitly set forth in Stanzaic Poem 7. By way of the renewal of plant life in springtime, Hadewijch arrives at the renewal of the mind by Love, playing on three antitheses—old versus new, old versus young, and old-and-young. Age combined with youth is a literary theme; Boethius's Philosophy is a woman "of undiminished strength yet of extreme old age," *De consolatione philosophiae* 1, *prosa* 1 (CCSL 94:2); and Martianus Capella's Grammar is "an old woman indeed but of great charm," *Martianus Capella and the Seven Liberal Arts*, vol. 2, *The Marriage of Philology and Mercury*, trans. W. Stahl and R. Johnson (New York: Columbia University Press, 1977), p. 64. Of course Hadewijch is thinking not of many or few years, but of mature experience and youthful ardor.

18. This is the first mention in the *Poems in Stanzas* of the mystical Divine Touch, which will recur many times.

NOTES

19. The term used here by Hadewijch, *orewoet,* denotes a state of intense longing for God. The translation "madness of love" suggests itself because *orewoet* is considered to be the equivalent of *insania amoris,* employed by William of Saint Thierry, cf. *NDA* 3.2 (ML 184:383–384); *insania cordis* occurs in Adam of Saint Victor, *Sequentia de sancto Vincentio,* line 62 (ML 196:1478). Not used in the *Letters, orewoet* is the theme of Stanzaic Poem 28 and occurs in eight other Stanzaic Poems. It is found in Vision 14: P. 1 and 52, and the state to which it applies is sometimes described without the use of the term, as for instance in Vision 1: P. 1. *Orewoet* is the theme of Poem 15, and is mentioned in Poem 16:29 and 191. The word *orewoet* is used also by Beatrice, in *Van seuen manieren,* fifth manner, p. 44.

20. Spaapen (1971): 154, note 58, and p. 155, identifies this with Phil. 3:11, the text continually cited by Gregory of Nyssa for his theme of eternal progress. Hadewijch does not use this text anywhere else.

21. This stanza, together with the first five lines of stanza 5, is one of the places where Hadewijch insists that only by the life of the virtues can anyone attain to "becoming Love."

22. Analogies between Stanzaic Poem 9 and Vision 12 are pointed out by H. van Cranenburgh, "Hadewijch's twaalfde visioen en negende strophisch gedicht: Een proeve van tekstverklaring," OGE 36 (1961): 361–384.

23. "Sweet exile" occurs in Letter 6: P. 350.

24. Allusion to Matt. 22:11.

25. An allusion to Gen. 1 and John 1 is pointed out by J. Alaerts, *De wetten,* p. 54.

26. Man has the liberty to reject God. Cf. C. Kerstens, "De wazige spiegel van Hadewijch: het onuitsprekelijke diets gemaakt in beelden," OGE 47 (1973): 372.

27. Reference to the degrees of love; see Stanzaic Poem 1, note 5.

28. See Letter 6, note 27.

29. The Scripture reference is proposed by J. Bosch, "De plaats van Maria in Hadewych's 29e lied," in *Taal- en Letterkundig gastenboek voor Prof. Dr. G.A. van Es* (Groningen, 1975), pp. 171–175.

30. Gregory the Great, *Homilia in Evangelium 30,* 1 (ML 76:122OC); see also Stanzaic Poem 27:71.

31. This personification of Love as vanquishing God and having thereby brought Christ to death is not original with Hadewijch. It is found in twelfth-century writers with whose thought she was familiar; cf. Guerric of Igny, *In nativitate s. Joannis Baptistae Sermo 2,* 3 (ML 185:168–169); and Hugh of Saint Victor, *De laude charitatis* (ML 176:974BD).

32. Cf. Augustine, *Sagittaveris tu cor nostrum caritate tua,* in *Confessiones* 9.2.3. (ML 32:764) See also Vision 14: P. 7. With the troubadours, the arrows of love are a commonplace, probably taken from Ovid.

33. Theme of Love conquering us, so that we may conquer Love. Courtly poetry likewise affirms that we can overcome love only by submitting to love's laws. Porion, *Hadewijch d'Anvers,* p. 92, note 3, cites the theme in Hendrik van Veldeke.

34. The phrase *the law of love,* which Hadewijch uses repeatedly, is infrequent before Thomas Aquinas and Bonaventure. Yves Congar, in "Var-

iations sur le thème 'Loi-Grâce'," *Revue Thomiste* (1971): 425, cites it in Augustine, for example in *Epistola 167,* 6.19 (ML 33:740): "Therefore the law of liberty is the law of charity."

35. Allusion to Jacob's combat with God, Gen. 32:22–32.

36. *Amabar,* "I was loved"; *Utinam,* "Would that."

37. "To taste death" is a Scriptural phrase (Matt. 16:28, etc.). Cf. Stanzaic Poem 24:12.

38. Theme of the mystical game of love; cf. Stanzaic Poems 39:32; 40:49; 42:62; 44:22. See H. Rahner, S.J., *Man at Play: or Did you ever practise eutrapelia?,* trans. B. Battershaw and E. Quinn (London: Burns & Oates, 1965), pp. 54–55. Rahner finds its explanation in the teachings "cultivated in the secret cells of the mystics . . . that God's election by grace is a game."

39. Schottmann, "Autor und Hörer," p. 27, note 12, points out that this line and line 96 imply that Hadewijch is addressing her young Beguines (contrasted with "aliens"); and that in lines 83–87 she is proposing her own lot and aspirations as an example for others.

40. Theme of paradoxical "despair"; cf. Letter 22: P. 169.

41. The idea of the Godhead is associated by Hadewijch with the image of the sun; cf. Stanzaic Poem 19:46. See Reynaert, "Het licht," p. 19.

42. Alaerts, *De wetten,* p. 92, designates stanzas 2–4 as pure self-surrender.

43. Theme that Love must conquer us, so that we may conquer Love.

44. Reynaert, "Het doodsmotief," pp. 16–17, points out that this sentiment belongs to the poets of courtly love.

45. For Love's rich teaching, see Stanzaic Poems 20:76 and 27:7; for Love's noble teaching, 36–73.

46. Cf. Stanzaic Poems 36:93 and 39:5.

47. This picture of the scorpion can be found in Gregory the Great, *Homiliae in Ezechielem 1,* 9.21 (ML 76:879CD), and in Richard of Saint Victor, *In Apocalypsim,* 3.6 (ML 196:783D).

48. Prior to the Council of Trent, as Porion notes (*Hadewijch d'Anvers,* p. 96), the opposition between nature and grace was not regarded as incompatible with a high esteem for the nature of the soul. See Bernard *SC 83,* 1.1; OB 2:299: "All it [the soul] has to do is remain true to the nobility of its nature in honesty of life." See also William *NDA,* 1.2 (ML 184:381A): "Love, as has been said, was placed naturally in the human soul by the Author of nature."

49. Personification of disloyalty.

50. Tanis Guest remarks (*Some aspects of Hadewijch's poetic form in the 'Strofische Gedichten'* [The Hague: Nijhoff, 1975), p. 63] that this poem "is one of the very few" where Hadewijch "indulges in verbal pyrotechnics for their own sake" as she does here with crossed-pair grammatical rhymes.

51. Cf. Vision 1: P. 288.

52. The "hidden ways" of suffering cause sweetness; cf. Van Mierlo, *Strophische Gedichten,* vol. 1, p. 159.

53. Richard of Saint Victor in *Benjamin Major* 5:12 (ML 196:180–182) speaks of the Queen of Sheba's ecstasy. Hadewijch goes on to stress her total gift.

54. This stanza in particular displays Hadewijch's power in wielding the opposites and paradoxes of which she and her contemporaries were so fond.

55. The beginning of stanza 5 alludes to Jacob's wrestling with God; we saw the two rhyming words of line 41 and line 43 in Letter 12: P. 174.

56. The theme of humility heralds Mary. She is shown as the highest of all the human beings in salvation history, because of her share in the Incarnation.

57. "Mountain" here means God, and "valley" means Mary; "palace" refers to the Divinity. Cf. W. Breuer, "Das mystische Präsenzerlebnis des Frommen: Zu Hadewijch, Strophisches Gedicht Nr. 29," in *Studien zur deutschen Literatur und Sprache des Mittelalters: Festschrift für Hugo Moser zum 65. Geburtstag,* ed. W. Besch (Berlin: E. Schmidt, 1974), p. 178.

58. Viz., the Savior.

59. Job is mentioned because he prophesied the living Redeemer. Cf. Stanzaic Poem 16;16–62.

60. That is, they held to self-will.

61. Her humility was much deeper.

62. Personification of Fidelity.

63. Pride in the good sense; cf. Stanzaic Poem 32:51.

64. This is Hadewijch's fullest development of the theme of mystical hunger.

65. Cf. Stanzaic Poems 21:7 and 39:5.

66. Cf. Stanzaic Poem 35:33 (see Job 23:8–9).

67. Cf. Stanzaic Poems 3:41 and 40:13.

68. Cf. William of Saint Thierry, *Epistola,* P. 250 (SC 223:344): "She rejoices and jubilates in the memory of the abundance of God's sweetness."

69. The fabled swan song, often referred to in the classics, is mentioned by Jerome, *Epistola LII,* 3: *Select Letters* (Loeb Library), pp. 194–195. It is also found in the *De bestiis* of Pseudo-Hugh of Saint Victor 2.53 (ML 177:510), a work known to Hadewijch, but the passage differs greatly from Hadewijch's poem.

70. The mystical Divine Touch. Cf. Stanzaic Poem 39:10.

71. Cf. Stanzaic Poems 21:7; 36:93.

72. Theme of the game of love; cf. Stanzaic Poems 40:49 and 44:20.

73. In the law of the tournament, fencing under the shield was forbidden. Cf. R. Demeyer, "De ballade van de untrouwe god," *Innerlijk leven* 30 (1976): 221 and note 46.

74. Cf. Stanzaic Poems 3:41 and 36:114.

75. The Jacob theme.

76. Theme that Love conquers us so that we may conquer Love.

77. Cf. Vision 4:P. 9.

78. Dom (later Abbot) Truijen was the first to discover that the Latin phrases used here by Hadewijch are from a Latin sequence beginning: *Mariae praeconio;* cf. "De Mariavereering van Hadewijch," *Tijdschrift voor geestelijk leven* 2 (1946): 239. J. Bosch has gone over the subject ("Vale millies," p. 172, note 16) and supplies the reference for this sequence, *Analecta Hymnica Medii Aevi,* 54:392. The translation of these phrases is as follows: "True love"; "The

cry of the heart"; "Praise and honor"; "Fragrance drew me"; "My remedy"; "Queen"; "Sweet refreshment"; "Sacrament"; "To the Redeemer"; and "Whence to die."

VISIONS

1. Cf. Introduction, pp. 24–25.
2. Hadewijch is describing the state of *orewoet.*
3. This desire for union with God is the main theme of Vision 1; cf. P. 15, 246, 265, and 364.
4. On the angelic choir of Thrones, see Gregory the Great, *Homilia in Evangelium 34,* 10 (ML 76:1252A). Here he refers to Ps. 9:5: *Thou hast sat on the throne, who judgest justice.* He believes that the Thrones are too exalted to be sent on missions to men; but nevertheless a Throne may himself send a lower Angel on such a mission, and the Angel thus sent might be called a Throne because he had been sent by a Throne (ibid., 14, col. 1055C). See also Bernard of Clairvaux, *De consideratione,* 5.4.8; OB 3:473.
5. This concept of self-knowledge—the strength of the soul and the passing beauty of the flesh—differs entirely from that familiar to Bernard of Clairvaux and the tradition preceding him. It seems to be, like so much else in Vision 1, a strongly scriptural image; cf. James 1:11.
6. Van Mierlo, *Visioenen,* vol. 1, p. 14, states that "the reason of the great God" means Christ. (We have noted that in speaking of the created Trinity in the soul Hadewijch uses the term "reason" as corresponding to the Son.) The general idea here would be reason enlightened by faith.
7. A reference to Hadewijch's young Beguines.
8. Cf. P. 134, the third branch.
9. These and all the other colors mentioned in Vision 1 are found in the Apocalypse.
10. This may imply that Hadewijch had made a vow of chastity at an early age, see Van Mierlo, *Visioenen,* Vol. 1, p. 16.
11. Cf. Vision 4: P. 44.
12. Again a reference to Hadewijch's young Beguines.
13. See J. Reynaert, "Doodsmotief," p. 8, note 10.
14. Theme of the soul's motherhood of God; for the use of the term *Love,* cf. Poem 14:163–170.
15. Love is *carried* in the active service of love, and *felt* in passive prayer, contemplation; see Spaapen (1970): 40–41.
16. Cf. Letter 12: P. 1, and Vision 3: P. 8.
17. This sentence strongly affirms both the emphasis Hadewijch's spirituality lays on the virtues and the supremacy of love. See Van Cranenburgh, "Hadewijchs twaalfde visioen," p. 379, and Spaapen (1970): 41–44.
18. "God's high will" is that with which he wills nothing other than himself. Cf. Stanzaic Poem 41:53–54.
19. Viz., the Virtue in which all virtues are one, in which all virtues find their source, to which they all refer. His virtue is his holiness, his perfect essentiality; see Spaapen (1970): 123. Cf. Letter 1: P. 25; Letter 3: P. 2.

20. The two lovers are, on the one hand, the Three Persons of the Trinity who enter into their Unity, and on the other hand the graced soul that is taken up into this essential union of the Three Persons; Van Mierlo, *Visioenen*, vol. 1, p. 124. For a similar concept, see Poem 16:185.

21. The title of *mistress* was perhaps used because Hadewijch was already a Beguine mistress, as is implied by several statements in the last part of the Vision. Spaapen, however ([1970] 126), believes the Angel uses this title because Hadewijch now knows by experience the ways that lead to the knowledge of God; she is proficient in the spiritual life and qualified to instruct others.

22. The phrases with the words *secret* or *hidden* used in Vision 1 from this point onward belong to the mystical life Hadewijch is now entering. They recur in *Visions* 8, 12, and 13, as well as elsewhere in her works.

23. "The hidden counsel" is *Verbum absconditum*, Job 2:14. The *locus classicus* for its mystical application is Gregory the Great, *Moralia*, 5.28.50 (ML 75:705–706).

24. At this point in the vision, Hadewijch passes from the life of virtues to the life of love. This passing from one life to the other occurs also in *Visions* 6, 12, and 14.

25. "Dark" implying the incomprehensibility of the Divine Essence.

26. For topaz, amethyst, and sardonyx, cf. Pseudo-Hugh of Saint Victor, *De bestiis*, 3:58 (ML 175:115).

27. The theme of falling down and standing up occurs also in Vision 12: P. 152.

28. Apparently her ideal existence in God is referred to. Cf. Letter 19: P. 37.

29. *Sancti Benedicti Regula* 58:13–14, p. 120: "Skilled in winning souls."

30. "Totality" signifies the Divinity and Humanity in one.

31. See P. 364 of this vision, and Stanzaic Poem 24:61–62.

32. The strong emphasis in this and the following paragraph on the gifts of the Holy Spirit is echoed in Vision 13, P. 159 and 179, and in Poem 14:175–186.

33. This passage is singled out by Spaapen ([1970]: 396, note 127), as the high point of the vision, since Christ tells Hadewijch the "hidden truth" that his essential love for the Father consisted in fulfilling as Man, in weakness, the will of the Father.

34. That this passage implies the theme of the suffering Servant of Yahweh is perceptively brought out by W. Corsmit, "De Heilige Schrift bij zuster Hadewijch," *Ons geestelijch leven* 40 (1963): 160.

35. It was suggested by Van Mierlo, *Visioenen*, Vol. 1, p. 33, that this could mean that Hadewijch had been preached to in order to draw her away from the life of love. Vekeman's anthology, *Van minne spreken . . . Nederlandse mystieke teksten uit de 13^e^ eeuw* (Nijmegen: Dekker & Van Vogt, 1976), p. 43, note 21, advocates this interpretation as a criticism of spiritual leaders who keep the mystic from the true dimensions of her calling.

36. The leaf signifies a degree of love, namely the knowledge of Christ's will; the rose signifies a second degree of love—the feeling of Christ's love, and sometimes in fruition, Van Mierlo, *Visioenen*, vol. 1, p. 4.

37. See Thomas of Cantimpre, *Vita Lutgardis* 1.2.40 in *Acta Sanctorum*, June, vol. 4 (Paris, 1867), p. 203.

38. See Vision 3.

39. Theme of reading one's judgments in God's Countenance.

40. Cf. Letter 12: P. 1, and Vision 1: P. 138.

41. J. Reynaert, "Doodsmotief," p. 8, note 9, compares this with Vision 12: P. 112, "and that she died with him."

42. Cf. Letter 9, "God . . . who he is . . . and what he is." The general meaning of Vision 3, according to Van Mierlo (*Visioenen*, vol. 1, p. 40), is that the soul must live the whole God-Man; when it lives his Humanity, it lives "what Love is"; and when it thus comes to his Divinity, it possesses Love in the sense of "who Love is."

43. Hadewijch was surely familiar with Wisd. 5:17, which completes the thought of the Epistle (or as we now say "Reading") by stating that the just *shall receive a kingdom of glory . . . at the hand of the Lord.*

44. This passage implies the Ptolemaic system with its series of concentric spheres, mentioned by Hadewijch with some variants. First, that of the earth; then that of the planets (here the moon, sun, and "stars"). Hadewijch's "paradise" is understood by Van Mierlo to mean the firmament and the fixed stars. The "throne" is the *primum mobile* or the crystalline heaven. He holds (*Visioenen*, vol. 1, pp. 46–47) that the expression "the dwellers in paradise" apparently means Angels, perhaps the Angels who watched over the stars. Cf. Stanzaic Poem 40:54–60, where Hadewijch speaks of the firmament, the planets, the signs (of the Zodiac), and astronomical calculations.

45. Cf. Vision 1: P. 112.

46. Theme of the mystical Divine Touch.

47. Even the briefest dialogue between Hadewijch and the Lord is extremely rare.

48. Spaapen ([1972]: 177, note 173) points out that here Hadewijch is acknowledging a fault, namely that she doubted whether her heaven and God's heaven could ever become alike. God had to free her from her lowness so that she could realize this; cf. P. 72.

49. "Her to whom one heaven pertained" means the ideal Hadewijch—in her image in God.

50. This means the Divinity of Christ and the conformity of the ideal Hadewijch to it.

51. At this point the Angel identifies himself with the Beloved, that is, with Christ, the Angel of the great counsel—the title used in the Introit of the third Mass of Christmas, *et vocabitur nomen ejus magni consilii Angelus* (Isa. 9:6, Vulgate, *Admirabilis consiliarius*)—and spoke to Hadewijch in her ideal being. From this point onward, "you" means the ideal Hadewijch and "she," "her," the real Hadewijch.

52. "In me," viz., my secret.

53. First work, the practice of all the virtues, in consolation.

54. Second work, the practice of many greater virtues, in suffering and misery.

55. Third work, discouragement and uncertainty that she can ever attain to perfection and conformity with Christ.

56. "This maiden" is the ideal Hadewijch.

57. For paradoxical "despair," cf. Letter 22: P. 169.

58. Fourth work, painful experience of absence of the Beloved (which will bring her to perfection).

59. According to the lengthy analysis in Spaapen (1972): 125, this vision is made up of two phases, the first of which (P. 1) is an imaginative vision of the three highest heavens. The same paragraph also indicates the character of the second phase, which will be an intellectual vision of the Three Divine Persons. After the interruption of the theme of the four souls, the intellectual vision begins with P. 59.

60. On the four living creatures as symbolizing the four Evangelists, see Letter 22; P. 376.

61. John's words signify the singular loftiness of the intellectual vision that will follow. "The things which I saw as man" should be taken as referring to two specific texts: Apoc. 4:2–6, which speaks of the One sitting on the throne, surrounded by the twenty-four elders and the four living creatures; and Apoc. 5:6, where the Trinity and circumincession are to be understood by the Lamb with seven horns (which symbolize the Father) and seven eyes (which symbolize the Holy Spirit).

62. Cf. P. 52. The two pairs of opposites, "to love and hate with God," and "to condemn and bless with God," are, as Van Mierlo remarks (*Visioenen*, vol. 2, p. 59) "ordinary concrete locutions (*pars pro toto*) to express total union with God's will. In God all extremes—hating and loving, condemning and blessing—meet. The soul also must strive for this unity."

63. That God should proclaim himself to Hadewijch as Trinity is extraordinary. The three angelic choirs (contemplated by her in the initial imaginative phase of the vision) are now explained as revealing in image what God is in his Being. The Thrones point to the Son; the Cherubim to the Holy Spirit; and the Seraphim to the Father, the Father being here understood not as Person but as the Source of the Trinity. See Spaapen (1972): 145–146 and note 82.

64. Cf. Letter 29: P. 14.

65. Axters thinks January 6 was probably Hadewijch's birthday (*Geschiedenis*, vol. 1, p. 352).

66. Here in P. 1 and also in P. 92 occurs the theme of the perfect will; cf. Visions 1: P. 60 and 12: P. 140.

67. Bernard *SC 31*, 2.5; OB 1: 222 speaks of this type of angelic action. Cf. Vekeman, "Angelus," p. 24.

68. Axters, "Hadewijch en de Scholastiek," pp. 101–102, quotes this passage as depending directly on Augustine, *De diversis quaestionibus LXXXIII*, 46 (ML 40:29–31).

69. See Vision 5: P. 12.

70. The half an hour of Apoc. 8:1 is taken by the mystics to symbolize the brevity of ecstasy; see also Vision 10: P. 70. Cf. Bernard of Clairvaux, *De gradibus humilitatis*, 7.21; OB 3:33, and comment by Gilson, *The Mystical Theology*, p. 104, note 147.

71. P. Mommaers, "Het VI[e] Visioen van Hadewijch," OGE 49 (1975): 14, in analyzing the structure of this Vision, points out the whole of P. 92

as the "lesson" (cf. Introduction, p. 24–25). We notice at once the command she receives from Christ that she must never more "condemn or bless" anyone except as he wishes.

72. This statement suggests the theme of paradoxical unfaith; cf. Letter 8: P. 27, last sentence, and Vision 13: P. 159, "[they] disavowed their love out of humility."

73. Theme "to be God with God."

74. There may be an allusion here to Exod. 3:2–4, where God speaks out of the burning bush.

75. A paragraph series begins here that explains the five ways: the fifth way, P. 33; the fourth, P. 51; the third, P. 61; the second, P. 68; and the first, P. 75–79.

76. The thought is: "I have sent you this hour for your imitation of me, and you must pass it on to those who are yours, for their imitation of me" (see Spaapen (1970):36).

77. Van Mierlo (*Visioenen,* vol. 1, p. 81 and p. 89) holds that in the last part of this paragraph Hadewijch's practice of love is clearly approved and defended in the eyes of her young Beguines by Christ himself, in order to incite them to remain faithful to her, and that Christ addresses her as a spiritual leader and confirms her in that capacity.

78. This dialogue with the Champion is unexpected, for Hadewijch did not speak to any of her guides in the previous visions.

79. Hadewijch does not reveal the Champion's identity. Considering that he is well informed concerning four ways of attaining God, two possibilities suggest themselves. If Hadewijch supposed the prominent twelfth-century figure Abelard to be the author of the poem *Alpha et Omega, magne Deus,* from which she derived the four paradoxes that constitute Letter 22, the Champion might be he. Even if of recent years Abelard is less unfavorably appraised, his disciples are known to have defended the thesis that "Christ, as man, is nothing." Cf. E. Portalié, "Abélard, Pierre," *Dictionnaire de Théologie Catholique,* vol. 1 (Paris, 1930): 47. On the other hand, the Champion might be Richard of Saint Victor. In his short but notable work *De quatuor gradibus violentae caritatis,* Richard says that the fourth degree of charity consists in the configuration of the soul to Christ; but his masterpieces on mysticism—*Benjamin Minor* and *Benjamin Major*—follow a speculative method in which Christology hardly plays a part.

80. Perhaps the lively character of Hadewijch's encounter with Reason in this vision explains a similar tone in those *Stanzaic Poems* where reason is personified with dialogue—25, 30, and 43.

81. The Song of Songs begins: *Let him kiss me with the kiss of his mouth.* The "perfect kiss" would seem to imply unity through being conformed to God, unity of likeness. The same term appears in *Visions* 12: P. 112, and 13: P. 82.

82. V. Truijen, "De Mariavereering," p. 240, points out that in the *Roman Breviary* Ps. 44 is the first psalm of the Second Nocturn for this feast.

83. Discretion here should be compared with Hildegard's vision in *Liber Vitae Meritorum* 2.14.22, *Responsum Discretionis; Analecta Sanctae Hildegardis opera,* ed. J. Pitra (Montecassino: 1882, Gregg Reprint: 1966), p. 69. Hil-

degard's personified virtue of Discretion, in her rebuke to the personified vice of Excess, speaks as follows: "All things, indeed, which are in God's plan, have a mutual correspondence. For raindrops shine in the light of the moon, and the moon has her light from the fire of the sun; and all things are subject to things greater than themselves, and do not exceed their own measure.... But I walk in the course of the moon and in the course of the sun, and I consider God's plan, and with these beings I increase in moral beauty, and I count them fully in charity. For I am a princess in the King's palace, and I search the depths of all his secrets."

84. Boethius, *De consolatione*, 1, *Prosa* 2 (CCSL 94:4): *Agnoscisne me?*

85. The meaning is of course, reason enlightened by faith. Reason as a queen is found in William of Saint Thierry, *De natura corporis et animae*, 2.3 (ML 180:711).

86. Viz., in their ideal life in God.

87. Since Hadewijch is adorned with the gold robe of virtues, Reason has no further complaint against her.

88. Theme of spiritual inebriation. Cf. Richard of Saint Victor, *Benjamin Major*, 5.5 (ML 174BC).

89. Theme that they who love are a source of light in the intellectual sense. Cf. Letter 1: P. 33.

90. Beatrice of Nazareth, in her Christmas vision (A.D. 1216), also saw David playing the harp; cf. *Vita Beatricis*, 1.11.55; p. 46.

91. Theme of the soul as mother of Christ.

92. The symbolism of the phoenix is explained in P. 49.

93. The old-young antithesis, weaving in and out through this entire paragraph, mounts to an unexpected climax in the affirmation of eternal progress.

94. See Vision 13: P. 82. Probably a vague reminiscence of John 21:25.

95. The emphasis here on love in Saint Augustine certainly connects Hadewijch's conception of love with his. Van Mierlo affirms the connection but does not cite this proof (Cf. "Hadewijch une mystique," p. 277).

96. Cf. Introduction, p. 6.

97. Theme of eternal progress.

98. This may refer to the purity of Hadewijch's love, or to the part of each person that God reserves for himself. Cf. Porion, "La onzième vision de Hadewijch," *Nova et Vetera* 19 (1949): 47, note 2.

99. Van Mierlo regards this statement as *fierheit* (good pride), expressing the wish to love God as perfectly as possible (*Visioenen*, vol. 1, p. 116).

100. "These souls" refers to Hadewijch's young Beguines; see Spaapen (1970): 38 and note 53.

101. This seems to mean the fruition of God to which she has a right.

102. Good pride.

103. Viz., Person.

104. By using the word *repose* in five different senses in the account of this vision, Hadewijch comes to this strong climax.

105. For a robe embroidered with symbols, see for instance Boethius, *De consolatione* 1, *prosa* 1 (CCSL 94:2), π and Θ embroidered to symbolize *praxis* and *theoria;* Chrétien de Troyes, *Erec et Enide,* 6738ff., embroidered represen-

tations of Geometry, Arithmetic, Music, and Astronomy, in reference to Macrobius; and Alan of Lille, *Anticlaudianus* (ML 210:494A), embroidered representations of famous friendships.

106. In Vision 9: P. 25 we saw the cosmic elements in the description of Discernment; something similar suggests itself here, in setting heaven, hell, and purgatory each in its place.

107. Cf. Augustine, *De civitate Dei,* 14.13.1 (ML 41:421): "This seems to be paradoxical, that loftiness should tend downwards and lowliness upwards."

108. Theme of reason our rule.

109. Here Hadewijch brings together the two themes of loving and hating, blessing and condemning. See Poem 3:12–13.

110. This passage is important as showing Hadewijch's participation in all Christ's mysteries, starting with the Annunciation and ending with the Ascension to the right hand of the Father.

111. J. Reynaert, "Doodsmotief," p. 8, note 9, compares this with Vision 3: P. 8, "until the death that will make you alive."

112. *Sancti Benedicti Regula,* 4: "The instruments of good works." The phrase is quoted by William, *NDA,* 14.3 (ML 184:405A).

113. Van Cranenburgh, "Hadewijchs twaalfde visioen," p. 363, calls attention to the fact that in this vision Hadewijch does not see herself as the Bride until the very end, P. 152. He points out that in five earlier Visions she saw herself identified with some other reality, and never at the beginning, but later on; thus, as a kingdom, Vision 4: P. 72; as the fifth way, Vision 8: P. 33; she sees her reason, the faculty of her own soul, as a queen, Vision 9: P. 40; her free conscience as a city, and her blessed soul as the bride in the city, Vision 10: P. 29; and she sees herself as an eagle, Vision 11: P. 49.

114. The same theme of "falling down" and "standing" occurs in Vision 1: P. 246 and 265.

115. Beatrice of Nazareth, in one of her visions (*Vita Beatricis,* 2,19.173–174; pp. 114–117) was rapt "into the heavenly regions" in the choir of the Seraphim. The Latin translator of her *Vita* endeavors to show that this was the "third heaven" of Saint Paul, 2 Cor. 12:2.

116. Theme of the soul as mother of Christ.

117. The Jacob theme.

118. The personification of love as a queen, found in the Fathers, for instance in Zeno of Verona, *Tractatus,* 1.2 (ML 11:272B), occurs in Richard of Saint Victor, *Adnotationes mysticae in Ps. 44* (ML 196:321–322).

119. Cf. Vision 11: P. 37.

120. Cf. Vision 9: P. 1.

121. The emphasis in Vision 13, from this point onward, on the gifts of the Holy Spirit, is one of the parallels between it and Vision 1. Cf. Vision 1: P. 325 and note.

122. To justify Hadewijch's extraordinary privilege of thus seeing Love, Van Cranenburgh ("De teksten van Hadewijch over het delen in Maria's goddelijk moederschap," OGE 33 [1959]: 384 and note 8) calls attention to the *Breviary* Antiphon in the Common of Confessor Bishops, "No one was found

like him in keeping the law of the Most High," pointing out that every soul is graced by God in a way personal to it.

123. The speech of the Seraph in this passage corresponds to that of John in Vision 5: P. 1, where John says that Hadewijch is granted a vision of God that he is not granted. The three "states," and the three pairs of wings of the Countenance, symbolize the Trinity.

124. This is the only passage where Hadewijch ascribes the mystical Divine Touch to the Holy Spirit.

125. Paradoxical noble "unfaith" (*ontrouwe*). Vekeman ("Angelus," p. 246 and p. 248) calls this the most audacious statement anywhere in Hadewijch's *Visions.* This concept of "unfaith" occurs also in Letter 8: P. 27 and in Poem 10:87–102.

126. On the subject of the numbers that follow, see Introduction, p. 28.

127. See Introduction, pp. 29–31.

128. Here Van Mierlo (*Visioenen,* vol. 1, p. 151) sees an allusion to 1 Cor. 15:28.

129. Reminiscent of the *Benedictus* Antiphon in the *Breviary* for December 23, *Ecce completa sunt,* "Behold, all things are accomplished!"

130. Allusion to the Ascension.

131. The abyss of God's Being; cf. Vanneste, "Over de betekenis," p. 40.

132. Cf. Stanzaic Poem 13:65.

133. *Regiratio.*

134. Cf. William of Saint Thierry, *NDA* 12.35 (ML 184:402A): "In order that the work which the Father had done through him, but which had failed, he might deliver back to the Father repaired and renewed."

135. "Totality" signifies the Divinity and Humanity in one.

POEMS IN COUPLETS

1. The structural outline of this long poem is as follows: 1–40, exordium; 41–62, unconditional service of Love; 63–94, victory; 95–114, nonvictory; 115–138, hope; 139–172, despair; 173–212, longing; 213–266, effects of Love and their explanation; 267–280, summary; 281–298, conclusion.

2. The first sixteen lines of the exordium contain several modesty formulas, as taught by rhetoric. Cf. E. Curtius, *European Literature and the Latin Middle Ages,* trans. W. Trask (New York: Pantheon, 1953), pp. 83ff.

3. Paradoxical despair; see lines 139–172.

4. Pride in the good sense.

5. Notice the same form of words here as in Letter 6: P. 191.

6. Cf. Liturgy of Holy Saturday (Easter Vigil), the *Exsultet* (*O felix culpa*).

7. See Introduction, pp. 7 and 33. This poem is based on a legend found in the pseudohistorical apocryphal book of 3 Esdras 3:1–5:6. In the legend, three bodyguards of King Darius hold a discussion in the King's presence as to which is greatest—wine, the king, woman, or truth. Flavius Josephus related this legend in *The Antiquities of the Jews,* 11.3.2–7. It later

found a place in Jerome's Vulgate, for he included the book of 3 Esdras. We would suppose that Hadewijch drew it from the Vulgate as more accessible to her than Josephus. She evidently did not use Peter Comestor, who inverts the order of the first two subjects in his *Historia Scholastica, Ezdras* 3 (ML 198:1481), based on Josephus. Hadewijch finds in each of the four subjects an entrance point for an instruction on love. She presents the whole legend in the form of the *disputatio* of the medieval schools, cf. Axters, "Hadewijch en de Scholastiek," pp. 107–108. The exercise of the *disputatio* consisted of a *quaestio*, a *disputatio*, and a *determinatio*. In this Poem the *quaestio* is proposed in the first three lines, and the next ninety-seven lines constitute the *disputatio*—the arguments of the disputants. Hadewijch has turned the bodyguards into university "masters." Her poem lacks only the *determinatio*, which in actual practice was often given on a later date than the *disputatio* itself.

8. Theme of spiritual inebriation. In the state here described, inebriation means the fluctuation between hope and fear inherent in spiritual progress. Cf. Letter 28: P. 196.

9. Hadewijch refers to Mary.

10. Probably the *How shall this be done?* of Luke 1:34.

11. *Sancti Benedicti Regula* 58: 16–17: "Whether he is zealous . . . for opprobrium."

12. Perhaps Hadewijch is playing with Cicero's famous dictum, "Truth, through which things that are, and were before, and shall be, are said to be unchanged" (*De inventione rhetorica* 2.53.162).

13. Theme of hating and loving.

14. The soul in ecstasy recovers its lost liberties. See Letter 4: P. 84 and note 19.

15. Theme of loving without measure.

16. The "Mother of Love" is Mary; this title, *mater caritatis*, is given her in Bernard *SC 29*, 4.8; OB 1:208. Especially in view of the fact that the number of the said Sermon is 29, it would seem that in line 33 below, Hadewijch is definitely alluding to it, for Bernard says: "That she [Mary] might become the Mother of Love, whose Father is God who is Love." See also J. Bohnen, "Minne en moederschap bij Hadewijch" [dated 1951], in *Uit de School van Michels. Opstellen aangeboten aan Prof. Dr. L. C. Michels bij zijn afscheid als hoogleraar te Nijmegen op 30 mai 1958* (Nijmegen, 1958), pp. 9–10.

17. Reference to the Assumption.

18. Hadewijch may be alluding to the *Homilia de Maria Magdalena* long attributed to Origen.

19. Cf. Poem 12:123.

20. Theme of reason our rule.

21. Probably "Love" means Christ.

22. Literal translation: "If he lays the bridle on her neck." Van Mierlo sees in this line the image of "the steed of Love" in Letter 19:18, *Mengeldichten*, p. 19.

23. Theme of the image of the Trinity in the soul.

24. "Throne" appears to mean the soul as the throne of the Godhead (Van Mierlo, *Visioenen*, vol. 1, p. 28).

NOTES

25. *Sancti Benedicti Regula* 4. At the end of this chapter Benedict says the Lord will reward us for the instruments of good works.

26. Cf. Letter 30, necessity of work and suffering. In lines 21–24, Hadewijch identifies Love with Christ.

27. This passage is the *salutatio* of the first of two letters.

28. Fidelity personified.

29. Here begins the *salutatio* of the second letter.

30. Line numbers are thrown off here by a repetition of two lines in the MSS.

31. This and the seven preceding lines greatly resemble Poem 8: 17–24.

32. Cf. Poem 7:17–18.

33. Cf. Poem 6:57–58.

34. Maxim 262 of Publius Syrus.

35. This line and the following seven lines correspond to Poem 6:47–56.

36. See Letter 20: P. 64.

37. Verses 59–60, 61–62, and 63–64 must in each case be read together as a single verse. (This is shown from the rhymes in the original.) The total number of verses therefore is not sixty-five but sixty-two.

38. Van Mierlo finds the poetic form of this poem rather careless and judges it a first draft (*Mengeldichten*, p. 45).

39. Reynaert, "Het Doodsmotief," p. 9, note 4.

40. Vanneste ("Over de betekenis," p. 39) takes this as the divine abysses attainable by men, and compares Stanzaic Poem 21:26–27.

41. Paradoxical noble unfaith, as in Letter 8: P. 27 and in Vision 13: P. 179ff.

42. Axters, *Geschiedenis*, vol. 1, p. 338, points out that lines 18–21 are a rhymed version of two sentences in Letter 8: P. 47.

43. See Introduction, p. 5. Ps. 44:11–12 reads: *Hearken, O daughter, and see, and incline your ear; and forget your people and your father's house. And the King shall greatly desire your beauty.*

44. Hadewijch sometimes proposes her own example; for instance in Letters 11, *passim;* 17: P. 26; 26: P. 11.

45. Here Hadewijch avails herself of Ps. 44 to reinforce the theme of the perfect will.

46. This verse may be a reminiscence of Job 5:24, which is used by William of Saint Thierry in *Expositio*, P. 17 (SC 82:90), *Epistola*, P. 174 (SC 223:284), and *Meditativae Orationes*, 10.4 (ML 180:236A).

47. Anacoluthon here and in 1. 96.

48. Lines 91–93 refer to the Trinity.

49. Cf. Poem 3:72.

50. These concluding lines may be compared to the opening of Letter 1, Van Mierlo, *Hadewijch: een Bloemlezing*, p. 266.

51. Porion (*Hadewijch: Lettres*, pp. 118–119) points out that this almost certainly depends on Alan of Lille, *De planctu, quaest.* 6 (ML 210:455–456).

52. Poem 14 is Hadewijch's fullest development of the theme of the soul as mother of Christ. See Introduction, pp. 33–34.

53. This Poem, divided into months that correspond to stages in the de-

velopment of the mystical life, may be compared to the twelve stages called hours in Letter 20.

54. The members of Christ.

55. Lines 146–149 are climactic, forming a close-wrought summary of the entire process of "becoming God."

56. This closing section of the Poem is an application of the main theme to the four weeks (the month) and the seven days (the week). The four weeks correspond to living the Trinity (power, the Father; knowledge, the Son; and will and affection, the Holy Spirit). The seven days correspond to the seven gifts.

57. Porion (*Hadewijch d'Anvers*, p. 122) views the first four stanzas as referring to God, and the next three to "a friend of Hadewijch."

58. Since the rhyme indicates that the MS. reading *hebben* should probably be *minden*, it seems advisable to translate "loved."

59. The rhyme scheme shows that the Poem is divided at the end of this stanza into two main parts.

60. Probably we should understand that dew is brief and hell is long.

61. Lines 20–21 are the same as Stanzaic Poem 5:16–17.

62. Theme of the Eucharist.

63. Both here and in lines 181–184, Hadewijch thinks of light under the intellectual aspect. Cf. Reynaert, "Het licht," p. 22.

64. Porion translates this line (86): "Man's desire and God's refusal" (*Hadewijch d'Anvers*, p. 125). He also notes (p. 129, note 2), that Ruusbroec borrows phrases from this passage in his *Tabernakel*, W 2:233, lines 10–13.

65. Cf. Letter 6: P. 172, "Love is that burning fire which devours everything."

66. Perhaps Hadewijch means that in this degree of love the soul is so conformed to God that, without any need for reflection, it condemns and blesses with him.

67. The mystical concept of the kiss of the Trinity can be found both in William of Saint Thierry—for instance, *Epistola*, P. 283 (SC 223:354)—and in Bernard—*SC 8*, 1.2: OB 1:37.

68. The term *living spring* implies "living water," according to John 4:10 and Jer. 2:13. The closest Latin equivalent seems to be *fons vivus*, found in the celebrated tenth-century hymn of uncertain authorship, *Veni Creator*.

69. In *Een spieghel der eeuwigher salicheit*, W 3:211ff., Ruusbroec takes over the theme of the living life that is hidden within us.

70. William of Saint Thierry, *Meditativae orationes* 3.4 (ML 180:212AC), speaks of the love and longing for God that torment his soul and then exclaims: "I beseech you, Lord, is this my hell?" Cf. P. Verdeyen, "La théologie mystique de Guillaume de Saint-Thierry," OGE 51 (1977): 347. And Alan of Lille (*De planctu, quaest.* 6 [ML 210:455B]) describes love as "an agreeable hell, a sad paradise."

71. "The two" in line 185 (as well as "them" in line 192) refers to the soul and the Divine Lover. A comparison may be made with Vision 1: P. 163: The virtue "engulfs the two lovers in one and casts them into the abyss," corresponding to Poem 16: 185–186 and 192–193.

72. Mixed symbolism.

SELECTED BIBLIOGRAPHY

TEXTS

Van Mierlo, Jozef, S.J. *Hadewijch: Visioenen.* 2 vols. Louvain: Vlaamsch Boekenhalle, 1924–25.

———*Hadewijch: Strophische Gedichten.* 2 vols. Antwerp: Standaard, 1942.

———*Hadewijch: Brieven.* 2 vols. Antwerp: Standaard, 1947.

———*Hadewijch: Mengeldichten.* Antwerp: Standaard, 1952.

Alaerts, Joseph, S.J. *De Wetten van de Minne: met de tekst van Hadewijchs 45 Strofische Gedichten volgens HS. 385 II van het Ruusbroecgenootschap.* 2 vols. Bonheiden: Zusters Benedictinessen Priorij Bethlehem, [1977].

STUDIES

Bosch, J. "Vale milies: De structuur van Hadewijch's bundel 'Strofische Gedichten'." TNTL 90 (1974): 161–182.

———"De plaats van Maria in Hadewijch's 29e lied." In *Taal-en Letterkundig gastenboek voor Prof. G.A. van Es.* Groningen, 1975.

Corsmit, Ward. "De Heilige Schrift bij zuster Hadewijch." *Ons geestelijch leven* 40 (1963): 151–160.

Kerstens, Sr. Christilla, O.S.U. "De wazige spiegel van Hadewijch. Het onuitsprekelijke Diets gemaakt in beelden." OGE 47 (1973): 347–385.

Mommaers, Paul, S.J. "Het VIIe en VIIIe Visioen van Hadewijch: affectie in de mystieke beleving." OGE 49 (1975): 105–131.

Porion, Jean-Baptiste, O. Cart. "Hadewijch, mystique flamande et poétesse, 13e siècle." DS 7:13–23.

Reynaert, J. "Het doodsmotief bij Hadewijch." *Studia Germanica Gandensis* 17 (1976): 5–18.

———"Het licht in de beeldspraak van Hadewijch." OGE 48 (1974): 3–45.

Schottmann, Hans. "Autor und Hörer in der 'Strophischen Gedichten' Hadewijchs." *Zeitschrift für deutsches Altertum und deutschen Literatur* 102 (1973): 20–37.

Spaapen, B., S.J. "Hadewijch en het vijfde visioen." OGE 44–46 (1970–1972).

———"Een boek over de minne bij Hadewijch." *Streven* 21 (1968): 811–813.

SELECTED BIBLIOGRAPHY

Van Mierlo, J. "Hadewijch, une mystique flamande du 13e siècle." *Revue d'ascétique et de mystique* 5 (1924): 269–289, 380–404.

Vanneste, R. "Over de betekenis van enkele abstracta in de taal van Hadewijch." *Studia Germanica* 1 (1959): 9–95.

Vekeman, Herman. "Hadewijch, een interpretatie van de Br. I, II, XXVIII, XXIX als dokumenten over de strijd rond de wezensmystiek." TNTL 90 (1974): 337–366.

———"Angelus sane nuntius. Een interpretatie van het visioenenboek van Hadewijch." OGE 50 (1976): 225–259.

ENGLISH BIBLIOGRAPHY ON HADEWIJCH

Axters, Stephanus, O.P. *The spirituality of the old Low Countries.* Trans. Donald Attwater. London: Blackfriars, 1954, pp. 9–40; 84–85.

Colledge, E., trans. *Medieval Netherlands Religious Literature.* Leiden: Sythoff, 1965, pp. 31–67, *Hadewijch of Antwerp: Letters* [1–20].

Gooday, Frances. "Mechtild of Magdeburg and Hadewijch of Antwerp: A Comparison." OGE 48 (1974): 305–362.

Guest, Tanis M. *Some aspects of Hadewijch's poetic form in the "Strofische Gedichten."* The Hague: Nijhoff, 1975.

Hart, Mother Columba, OSB. "Hadewijch of Brabant." *American Benedictine Review* 13 (1962): 1–24. Includes translation of 9 letters.

Paepe, Norbert De. "Hadewijch, B1." *New Catholic Encyclopedia.* New York, 1967. Vol. 6, p. 886.

Vandenbroucke, François, OSB. "New milieux, new problems from the twelfth to the sixteenth century." In *A history of Christian Spirituality,* vol. 2: *The Spirituality of the Middle Ages.* Trans. The Benedictines of Holme Eden Abbey, Carlisle. New York: Desclée, 1968, pp. 361–364.

Weevers, Theodor. *Poetry of the Netherlands in European Context, 1170–1930.* London: University of London, Athlone Press, 1960, pp. 26–44; 212–217.

Brief references are found in the following works: Bolle, Kees W. *The Freedom of Man in Myth.* Nashville: Vanderbilt University Press, 1968, p. 124; Déchanet, Jean Marie, OSB. *William of St. Thierry: The Man and his Work.* Trans. Richard Strachen. Cistercian Studies 10. Spencer, Mass.: Cistercian Publications, 1972, p. 161 reference to Hadewijch (in masculine gender); McDonnell, Ernest. *The Beguines and Beghards in medieval culture: With special emphasis on the Belgian scene.* New Brunswick, N.J.: Rutgers University Press, 1954. Many passing references, no basic discussion; Monchanin, Jules. *In Quest of the Absolute.* Ed. and trans. J. G. Weber. Cistercian Studies 51. Kalamazoo: Cistercian Publications, 1977, p. 130.

NOTE. If the reader explores any of the items in this bibliography, he should bear in mind the exceptional complexity of Hadewijch studies and the fact that many new interpretations have been advanced in the 1970s. May we be permitted to note in Dr. Gooday's article an inaccurate statement: "Hadewijch only mentions God's mother twice" (p. 317). Dr. Guest has published the only book in English on Hadewijch, in which she aims to present a modern viewpoint in accordance with her own ideas. Since in her study of the Poems in Stanzas *she ignores Hadewijch's other works and fails to take into account the findings of scholars other than De Paepe (whose views she partly modifies), the book is one-sided and incomplete. At the same time, as Vekeman points out in his review (in* Nieuwe Taalgids *69 [1976]: 546–549), it is well planned and well written and offers not a little valuable information about troubadour poetry and Hadewijch's extraordinary poetic power. He commends it as introducing Hadewijch to English readers and specially praises the last four pages of Chapter 9 (pp. 244–248).*

INDEX TO FOREWORD PREFACE, INTRODUCTION AND NOTES

INDEX

INDEX

INDEX

INDEX

INDEX

INDEX

INDEX

INDEX TO TEXTS

INDEX

INDEX

INDEX

INDEX

INDEX

INDEX

INDEX

INDEX